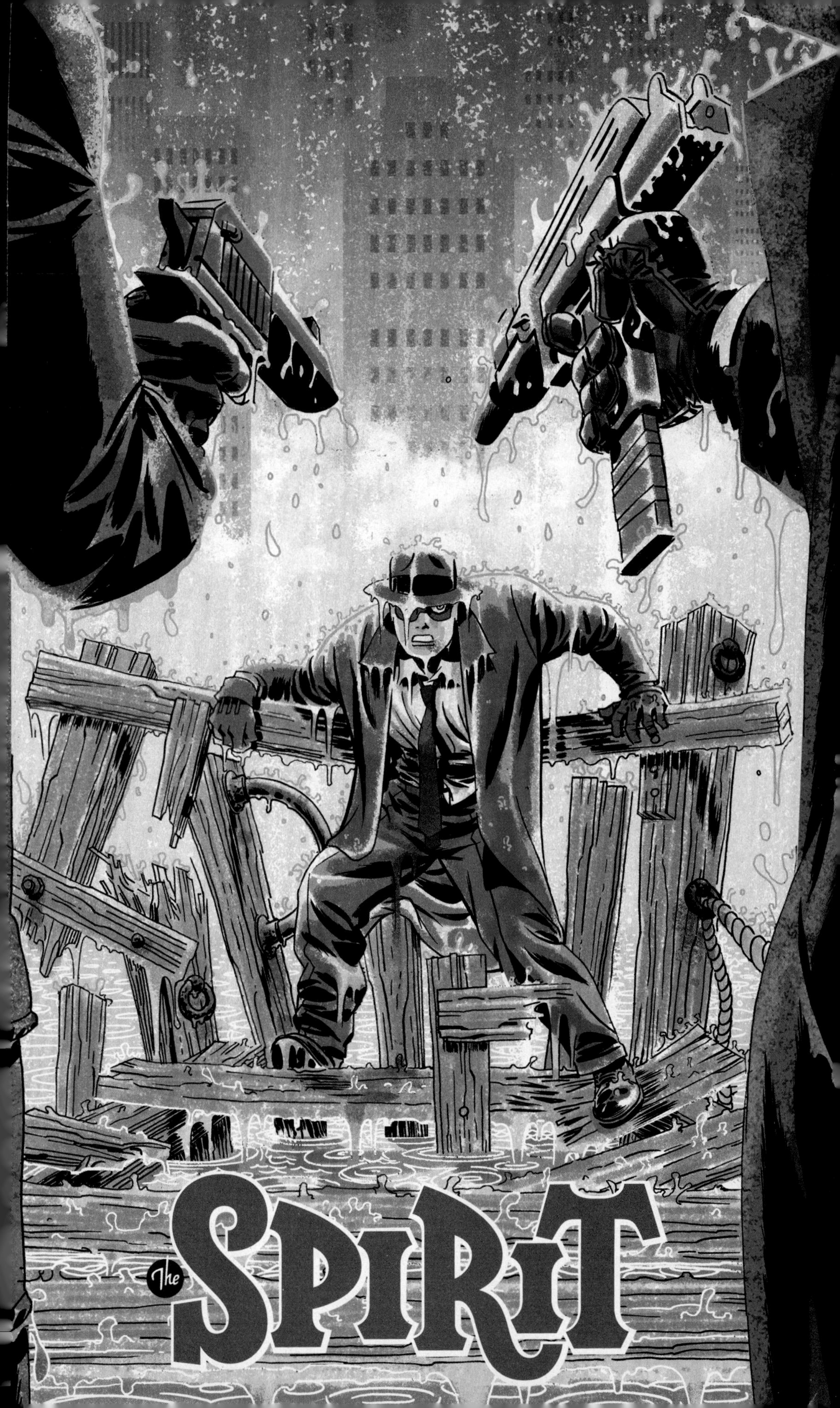
The SPIRIT

# THE SPIRIT
## Story and Art by Darwyn Cooke
### Inks and Finishes by J. Bone
### Colors by Dave Stewart
### Letters by Jared K. Fletcher

# BATMAN/THE SPIRIT
## Storytellers Jeph Loeb
## and Darwyn Cooke
### Inks by J. Bone
### Colors by Dave Stewart
### Letters by Jared K. Fletcher

Original series covers and Collected Edition cover by Darwyn Cooke

The Spirit created by Will Eisner
The Batman created by Bob Kane

Special thanks to Denis Kitchen

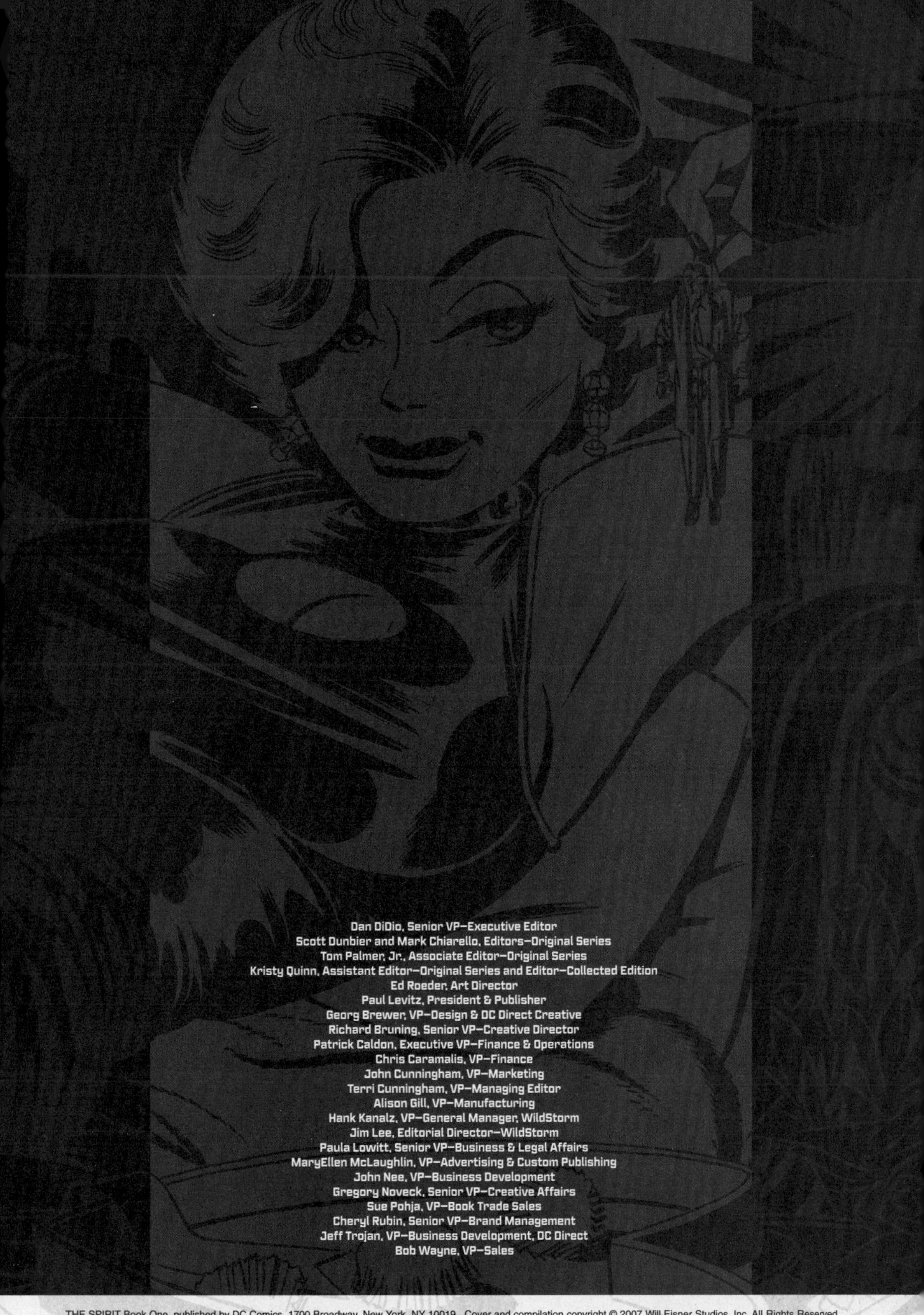

Dan DiDio, Senior VP—Executive Editor
Scott Dunbier and Mark Chiarello, Editors—Original Series
Tom Palmer, Jr., Associate Editor—Original Series
Kristy Quinn, Assistant Editor—Original Series and Editor—Collected Edition
Ed Roeder, Art Director
Paul Levitz, President & Publisher
Georg Brewer, VP—Design & DC Direct Creative
Richard Bruning, Senior VP—Creative Director
Patrick Caldon, Executive VP—Finance & Operations
Chris Caramalis, VP—Finance
John Cunningham, VP—Marketing
Terri Cunningham, VP—Managing Editor
Alison Gill, VP—Manufacturing
Hank Kanalz, VP—General Manager, WildStorm
Jim Lee, Editorial Director—WildStorm
Paula Lowitt, Senior VP—Business & Legal Affairs
MaryEllen McLaughlin, VP—Advertising & Custom Publishing
John Nee, VP—Business Development
Gregory Noveck, Senior VP—Creative Affairs
Sue Pohja, VP—Book Trade Sales
Cheryl Rubin, Senior VP—Brand Management
Jeff Trojan, VP—Business Development, DC Direct
Bob Wayne, VP—Sales



HC ISBN: 1-4012-1461-4 HC ISBN-13: 978-1-4012-1461-6
SC ISBN: 1-4012-1618-8 SC ISBN-13: 978-1-4012-1618-4

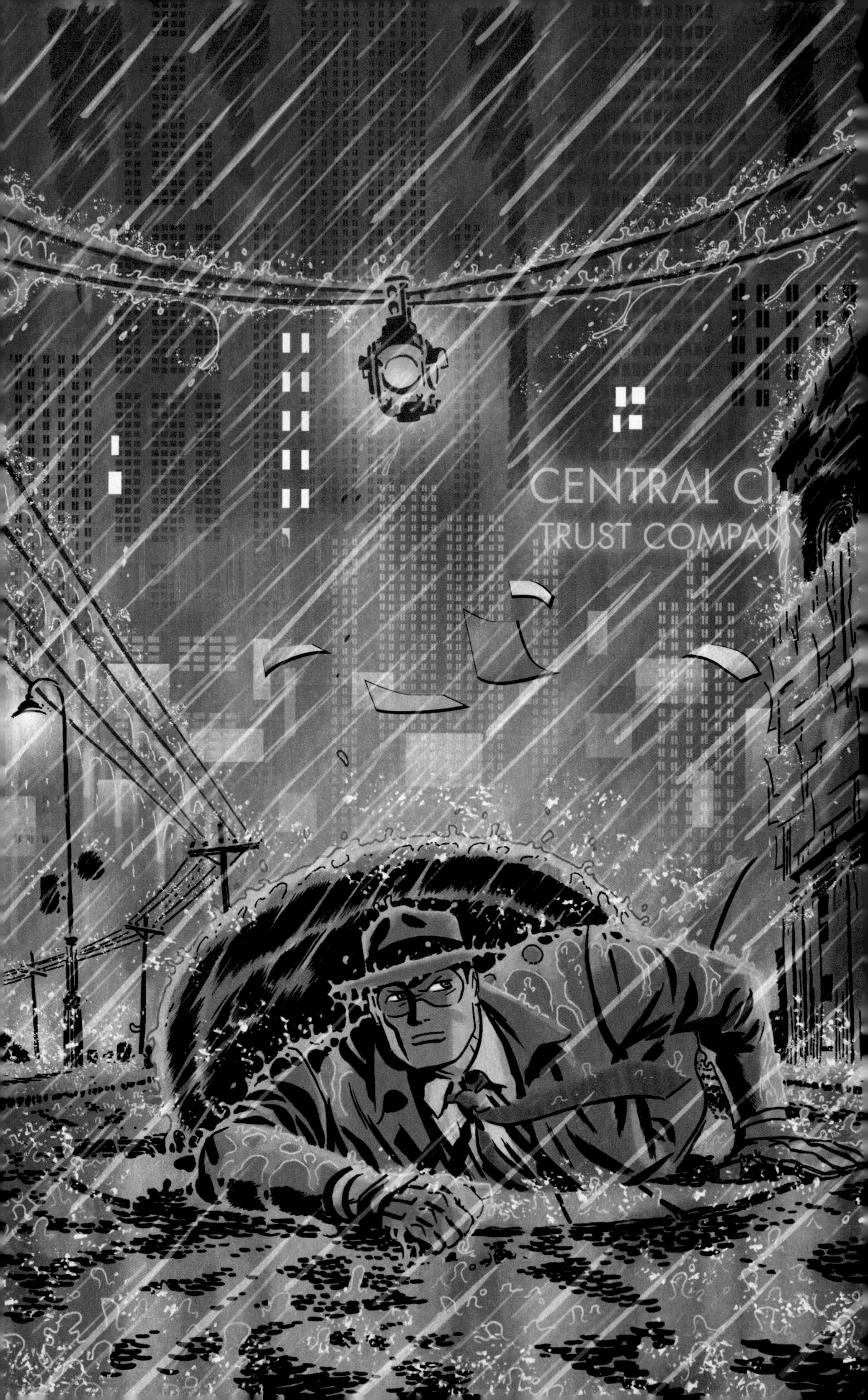
CENTRAL CI
TRUST COMPAN

# 1

ACTION • Mystery • ADVENTURE

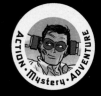

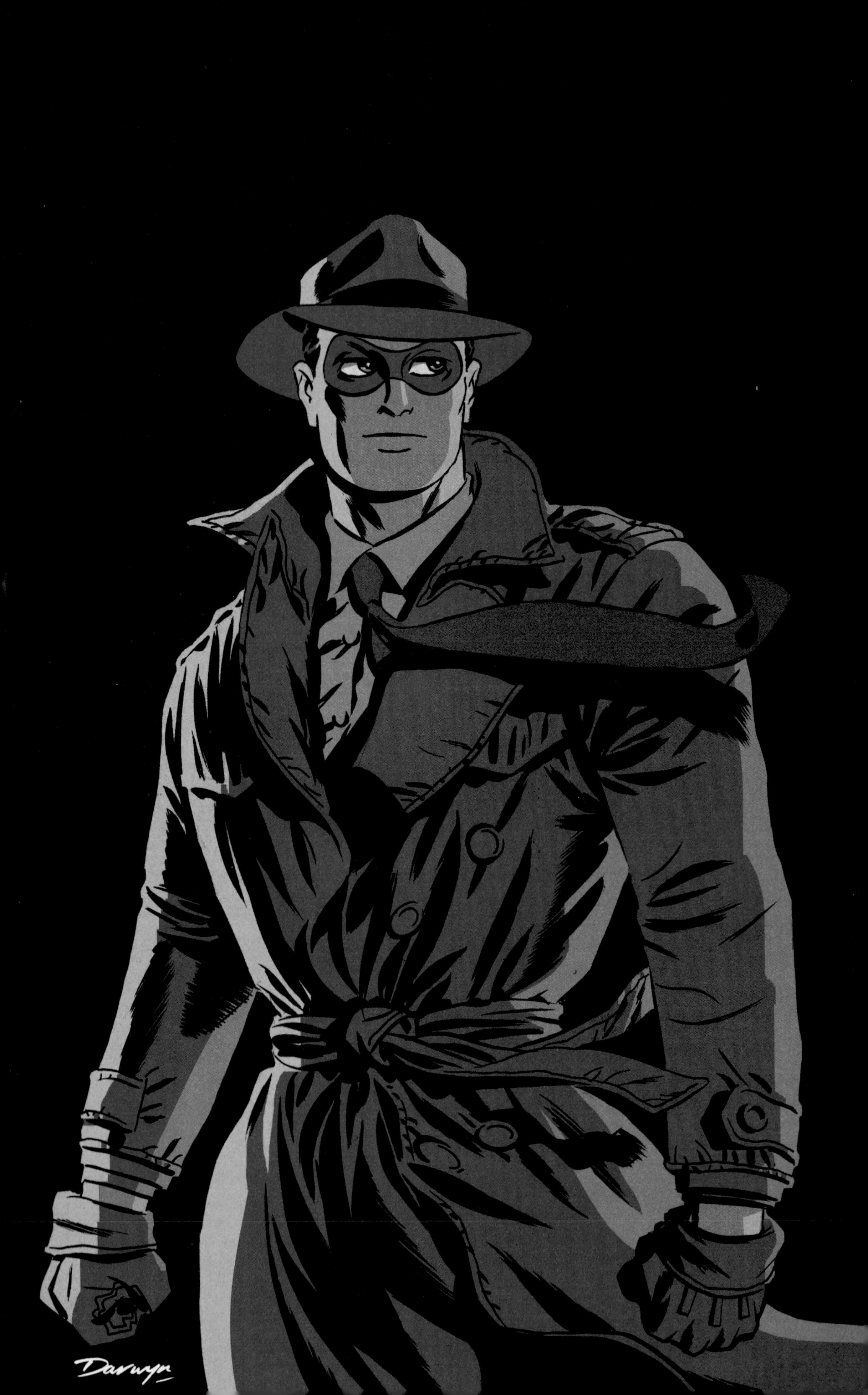
Darwyn

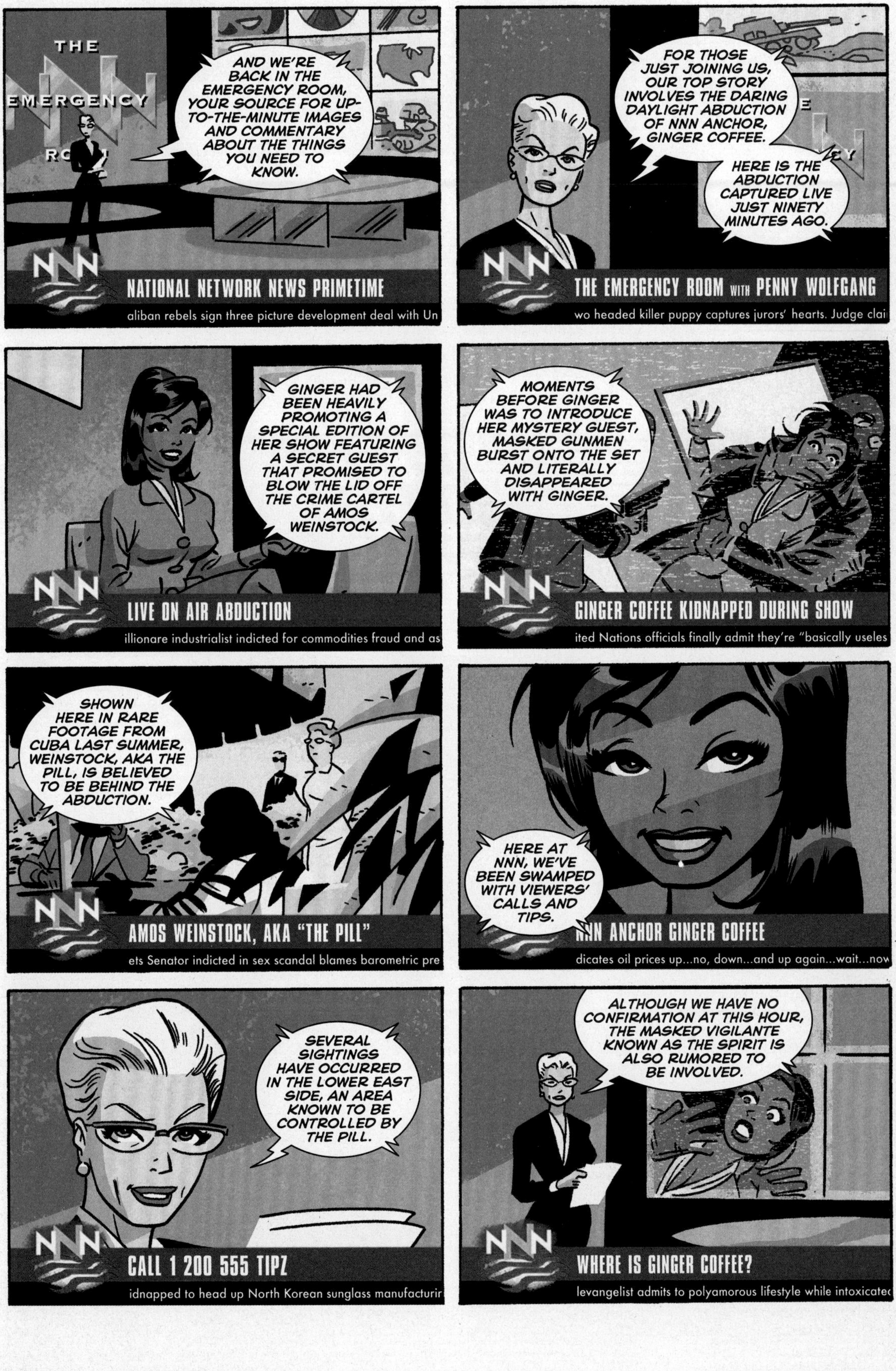
THE NNN EMERGENCY ROOM
AND WE'RE BACK IN THE EMERGENCY ROOM, YOUR SOURCE FOR UP-TO-THE-MINUTE IMAGES AND COMMENTARY ABOUT THE THINGS YOU NEED TO KNOW.
NNN
NATIONAL NETWORK NEWS PRIMETIME
aliban rebels sign three picture development deal with Un
FOR THOSE JUST JOINING US, OUR TOP STORY INVOLVES THE DARING DAYLIGHT ABDUCTION OF NNN ANCHOR, GINGER COFFEE.
HERE IS THE ABDUCTION CAPTURED LIVE JUST NINETY MINUTES AGO.
NNN
THE EMERGENCY ROOM WITH PENNY WOLFGANG
wo headed killer puppy captures jurors' hearts. Judge clai
GINGER HAD BEEN HEAVILY PROMOTING A SPECIAL EDITION OF HER SHOW FEATURING A SECRET GUEST THAT PROMISED TO BLOW THE LID OFF THE CRIME CARTEL OF AMOS WEINSTOCK.
NNN
LIVE ON AIR ABDUCTION
illionare industrialist indicted for commodities fraud and as
MOMENTS BEFORE GINGER WAS TO INTRODUCE HER MYSTERY GUEST, MASKED GUNMEN BURST ONTO THE SET AND LITERALLY DISAPPEARED WITH GINGER.
NNN
GINGER COFFEE KIDNAPPED DURING SHOW
ited Nations officials finally admit they're "basically useles
SHOWN HERE IN RARE FOOTAGE FROM CUBA LAST SUMMER, WEINSTOCK, AKA THE PILL, IS BELIEVED TO BE BEHIND THE ABDUCTION.
NNN
AMOS WEINSTOCK, AKA "THE PILL"
ets Senator indicted in sex scandal blames barometric pre
HERE AT NNN, WE'VE BEEN SWAMPED WITH VIEWERS' CALLS AND TIPS.
NNN ANCHOR GINGER COFFEE
dicates oil prices up...no, down...and up again...wait...now
SEVERAL SIGHTINGS HAVE OCCURRED IN THE LOWER EAST SIDE, AN AREA KNOWN TO BE CONTROLLED BY THE PILL.
NNN
CALL 1 200 555 TIPZ
idnapped to head up North Korean sunglass manufacturir
ALTHOUGH WE HAVE NO CONFIRMATION AT THIS HOUR, THE MASKED VIGILANTE KNOWN AS THE SPIRIT IS ALSO RUMORED TO BE INVOLVED.
NNN
WHERE IS GINGER COFFEE?
levangelist admits to polyamorous lifestyle while intoxicatec

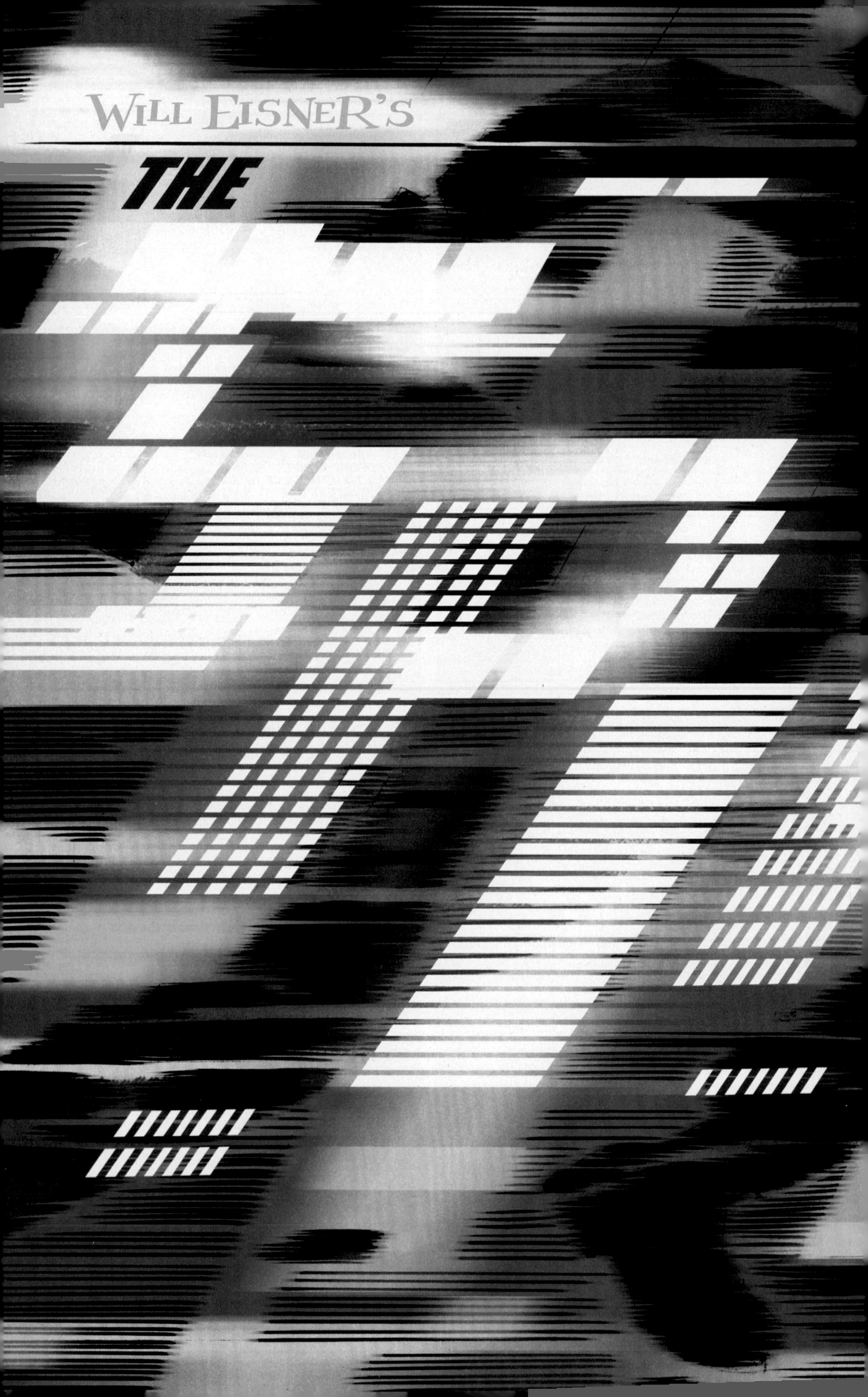
WILL EISNER'S
THE

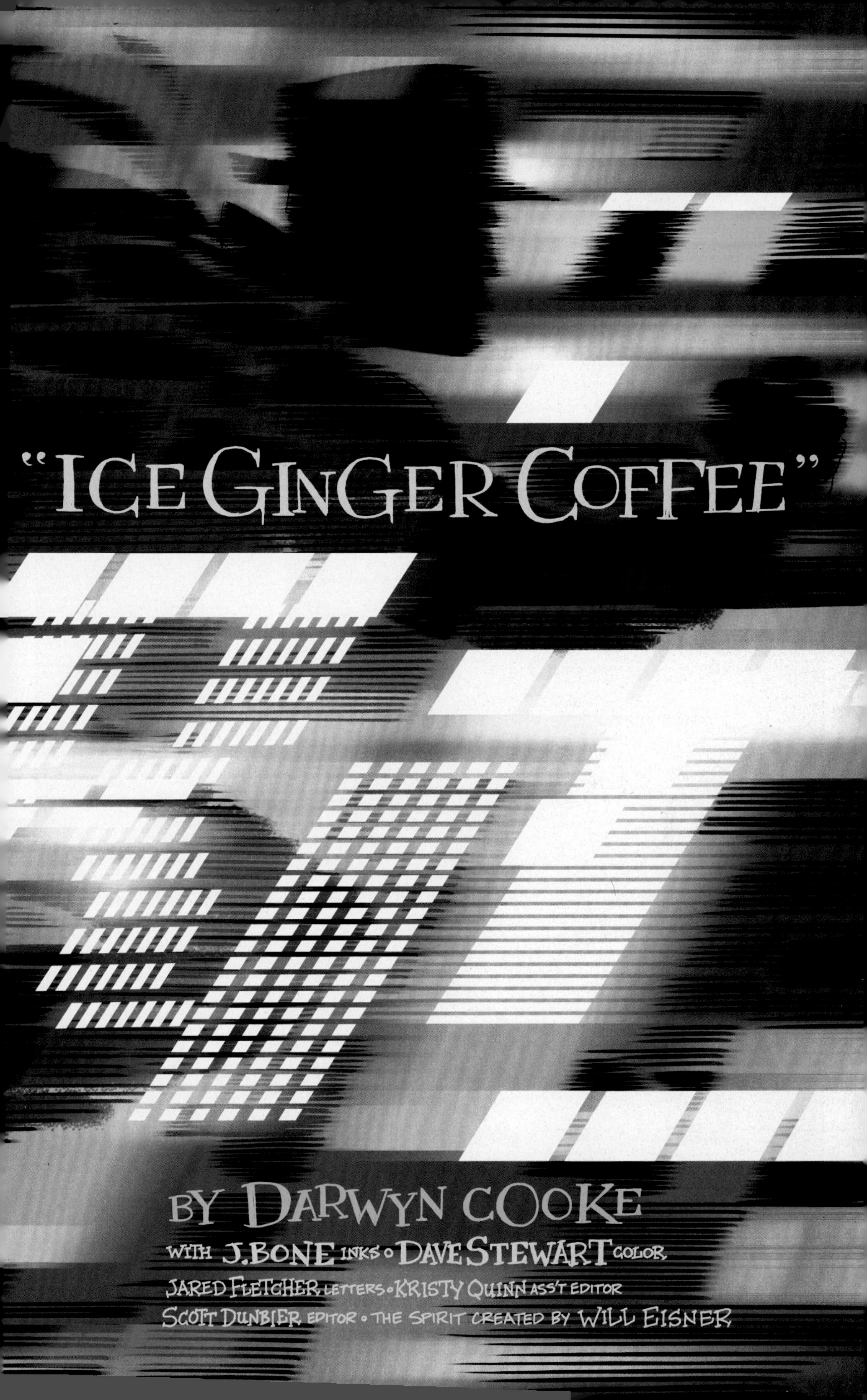
"ICE GINGER COFFEE"
BY DARWYN COOKE
WITH J.BONE INKS • DAVE STEWART COLOR
JARED FLETCHER LETTERS • KRISTY QUINN ASS'T EDITOR
SCOTT DUNBIER EDITOR • THE SPIRIT CREATED BY WILL EISNER

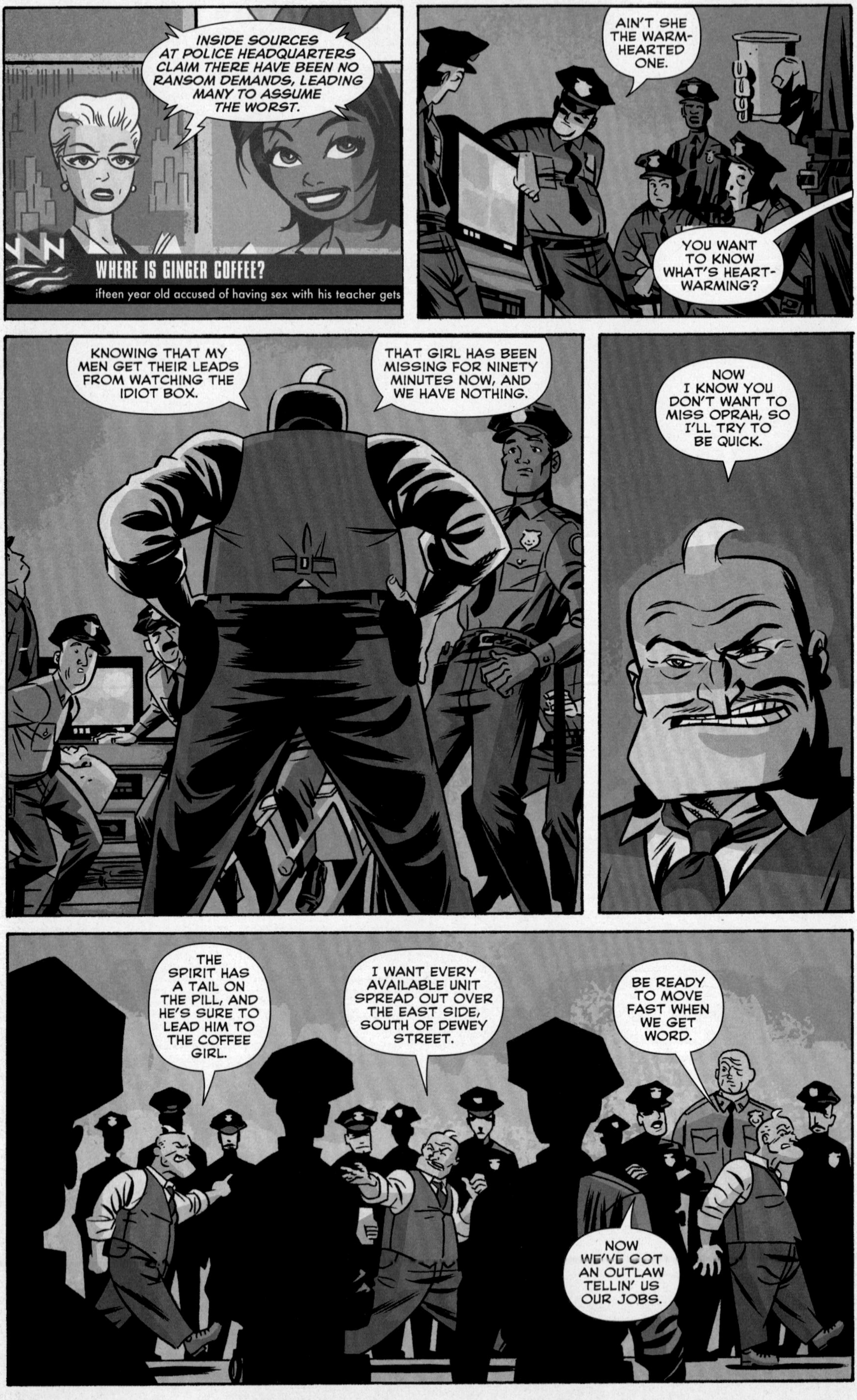
INSIDE SOURCES AT POLICE HEADQUARTERS CLAIM THERE HAVE BEEN NO RANSOM DEMANDS, LEADING MANY TO ASSUME THE WORST.
WHERE IS GINGER COFFEE?
ifteen year old accused of having sex with his teacher gets
AIN'T SHE THE WARM-HEARTED ONE.
YOU WANT TO KNOW WHAT'S HEART-WARMING?
KNOWING THAT MY MEN GET THEIR LEADS FROM WATCHING THE IDIOT BOX.
THAT GIRL HAS BEEN MISSING FOR NINETY MINUTES NOW, AND WE HAVE NOTHING.
NOW I KNOW YOU DON'T WANT TO MISS OPRAH, SO I'LL TRY TO BE QUICK.
THE SPIRIT HAS A TAIL ON THE PILL, AND HE'S SURE TO LEAD HIM TO THE COFFEE GIRL.
I WANT EVERY AVAILABLE UNIT SPREAD OUT OVER THE EAST SIDE, SOUTH OF DEWEY STREET.
BE READY TO MOVE FAST WHEN WE GET WORD.
NOW WE'VE GOT AN OUTLAW TELLIN' US OUR JOBS.

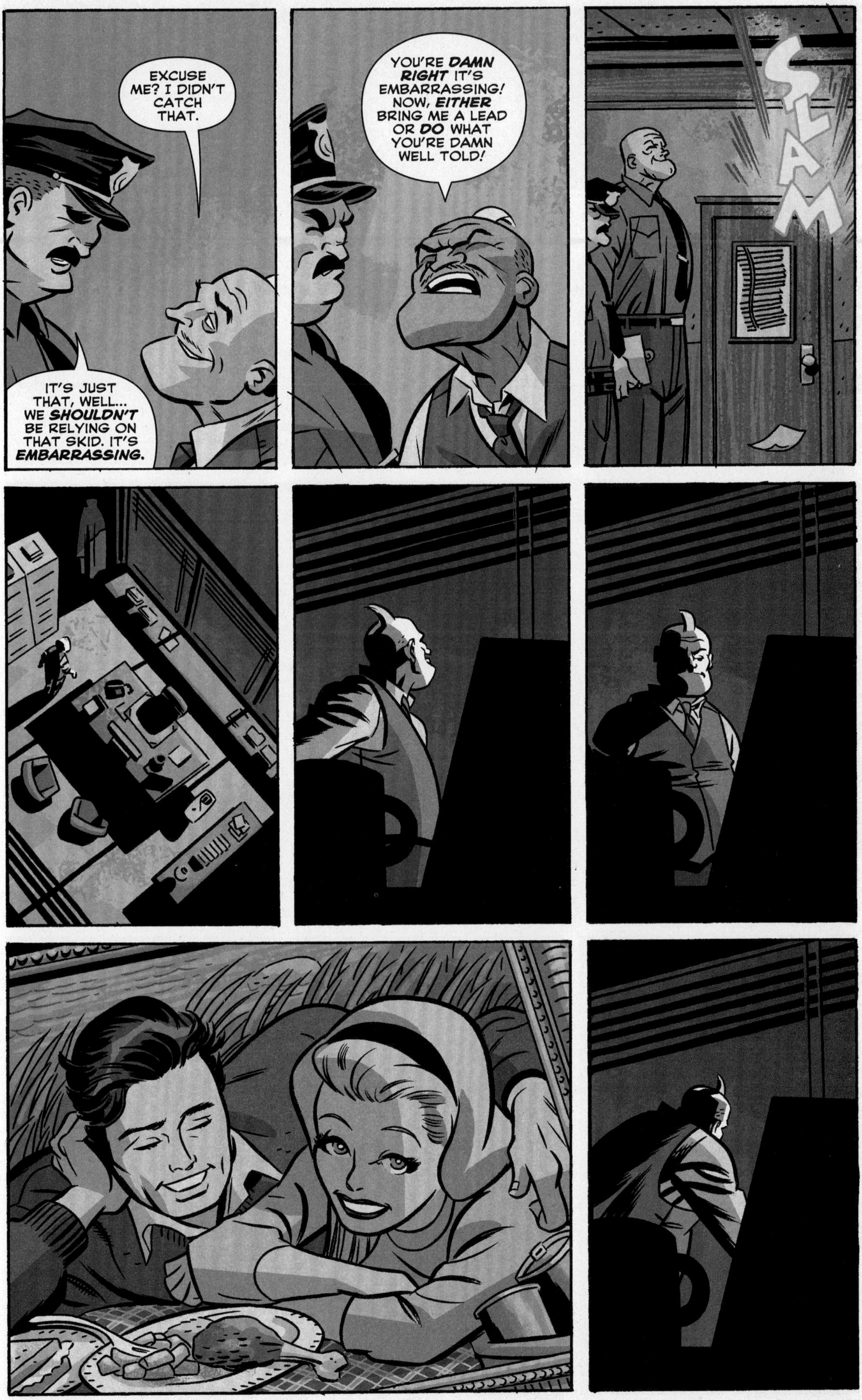
EXCUSE ME? I DIDN'T CATCH THAT.
IT'S JUST THAT, WELL... WE SHOULDN'T BE RELYING ON THAT SKID. IT'S EMBARRASSING.
YOU'RE DAMN RIGHT IT'S EMBARRASSING! NOW, EITHER BRING ME A LEAD OR DO WHAT YOU'RE DAMN WELL TOLD!
SLAM

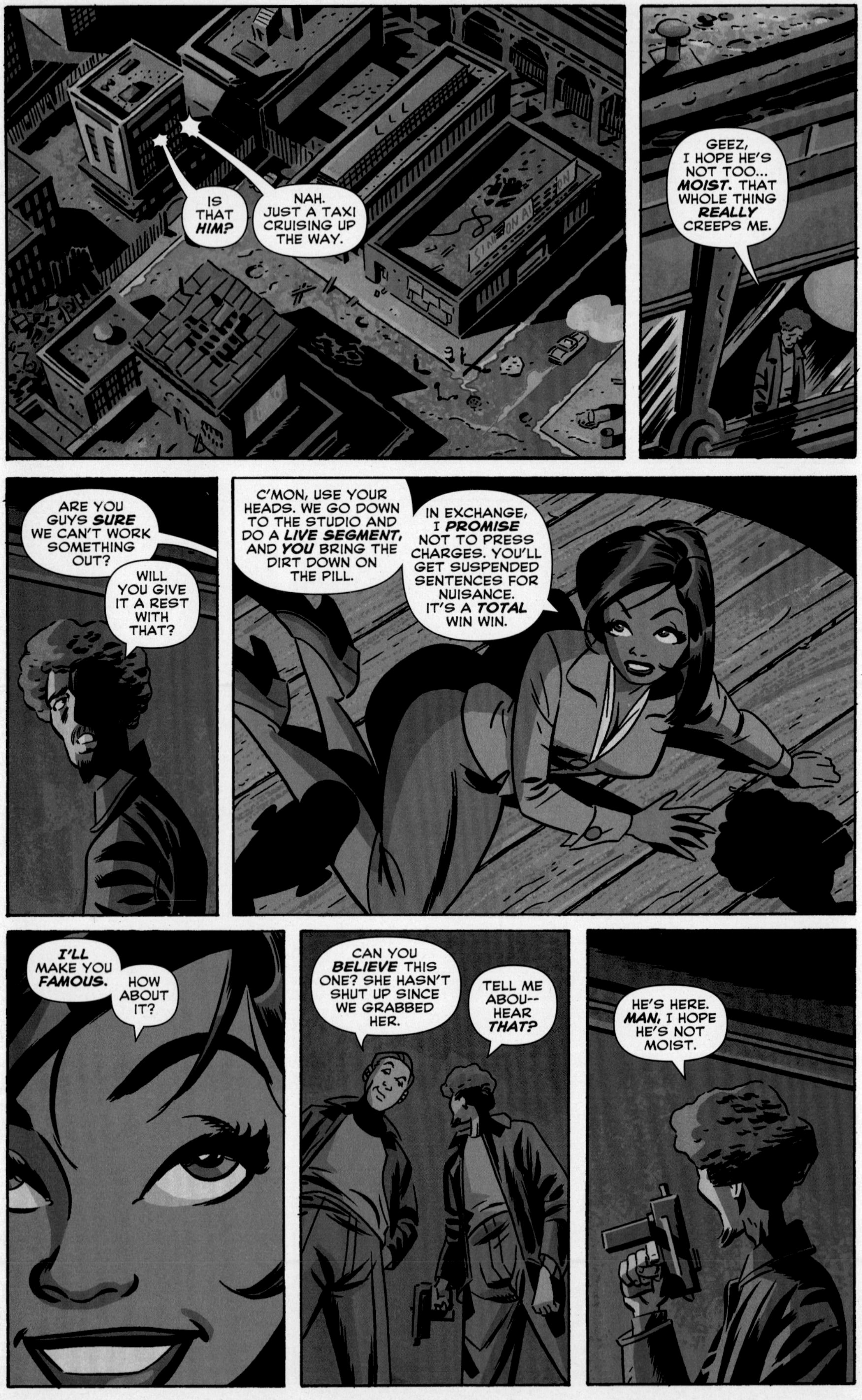
IS THAT *HIM?*
NAH. JUST A TAXI CRUISING UP THE WAY.
GEEZ, I HOPE HE'S NOT TOO... *MOIST.* THAT WHOLE THING *REALLY* CREEPS ME.
ARE YOU GUYS *SURE* WE CAN'T WORK SOMETHING OUT?
WILL YOU GIVE IT A REST WITH THAT?
C'MON, USE YOUR HEADS. WE GO DOWN TO THE STUDIO AND DO A *LIVE SEGMENT,* AND *YOU* BRING THE DIRT DOWN ON THE PILL.
IN EXCHANGE, I *PROMISE* NOT TO PRESS CHARGES. YOU'LL GET SUSPENDED SENTENCES FOR NUISANCE. IT'S A *TOTAL* WIN WIN.
*I'LL* MAKE YOU *FAMOUS.*
HOW ABOUT IT?
CAN YOU *BELIEVE* THIS ONE? SHE HASN'T SHUT UP SINCE WE GRABBED HER.
TELL ME ABOU-- HEAR *THAT?*
HE'S HERE. *MAN,* I HOPE HE'S NOT MOIST.

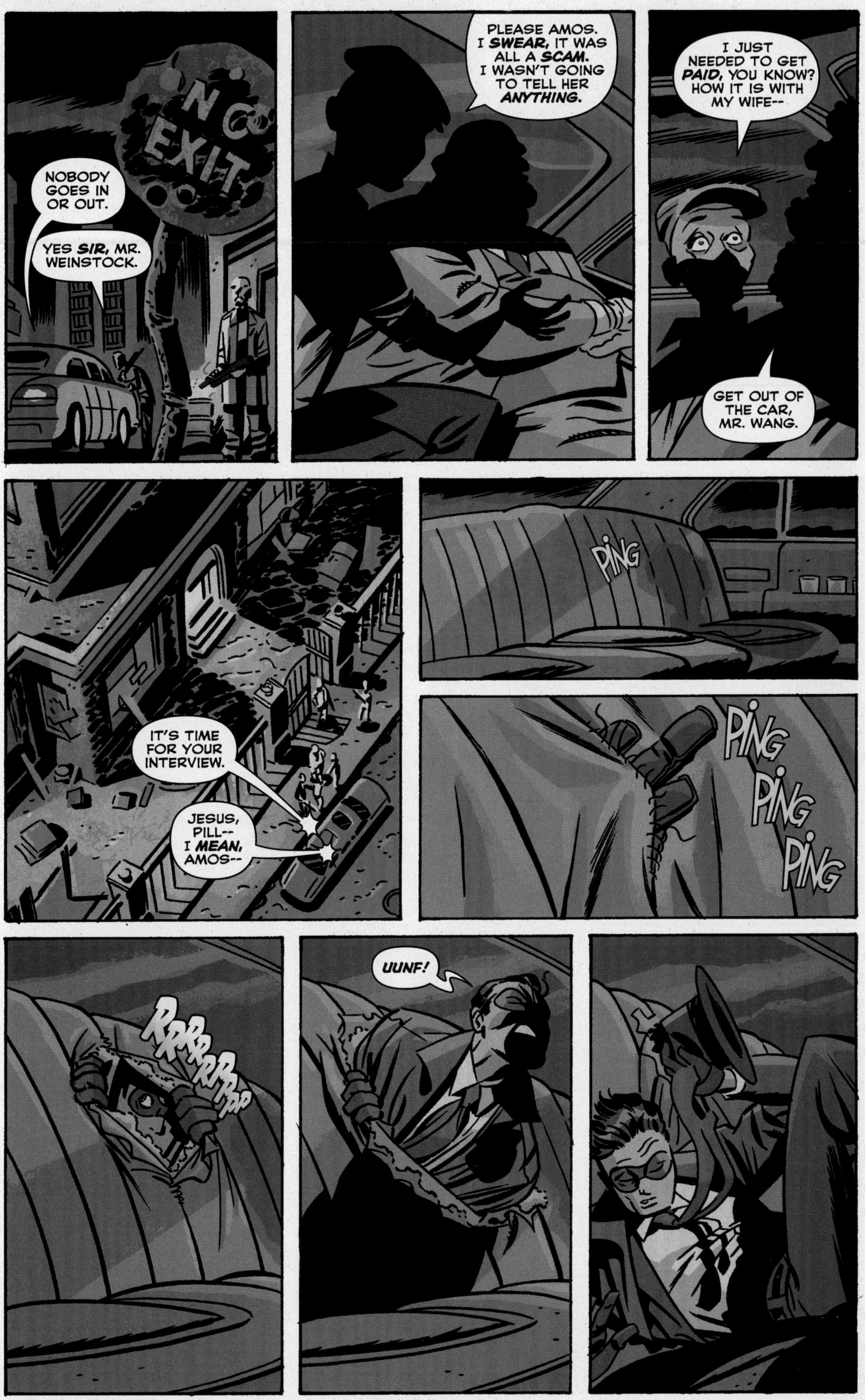

NO EXIT
NOBODY GOES IN OR OUT.
YES SIR, MR. WEINSTOCK.
PLEASE AMOS. I SWEAR, IT WAS ALL A SCAM. I WASN'T GOING TO TELL HER ANYTHING.
I JUST NEEDED TO GET PAID, YOU KNOW? HOW IT IS WITH MY WIFE--
GET OUT OF THE CAR, MR. WANG.
IT'S TIME FOR YOUR INTERVIEW.
JESUS, PILL-- I MEAN, AMOS--
PING
PING PING PING
RRRRRRRRRPPP
UUNF!

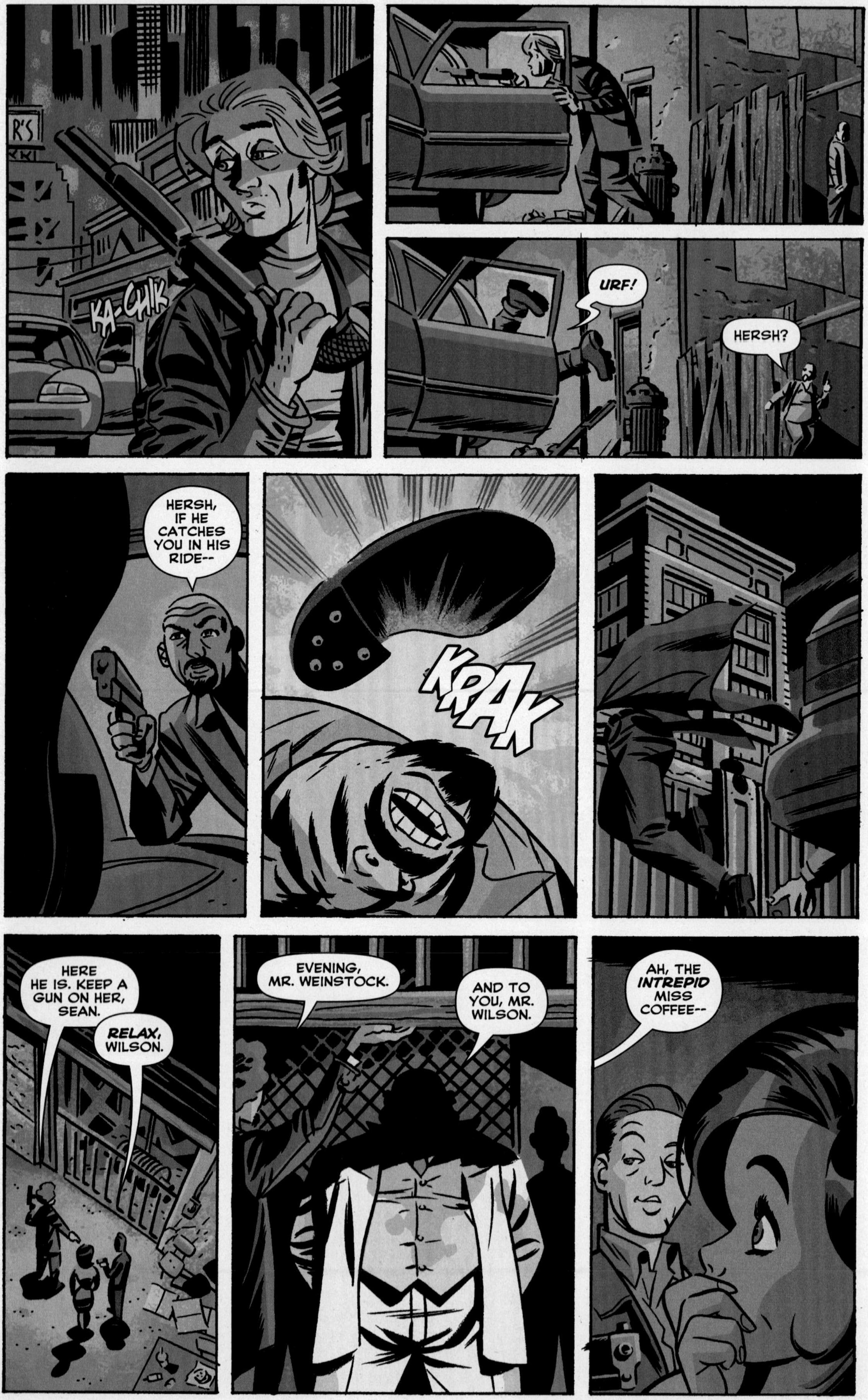
R'S
KA-CHIK
URF!
HERSH?
HERSH, IF HE CATCHES YOU IN HIS RIDE--
KRAK
HERE HE IS. KEEP A GUN ON HER, SEAN.
RELAX, WILSON.
EVENING, MR. WEINSTOCK.
AND TO YOU, MR. WILSON.
AH, THE INTREPID MISS COFFEE--

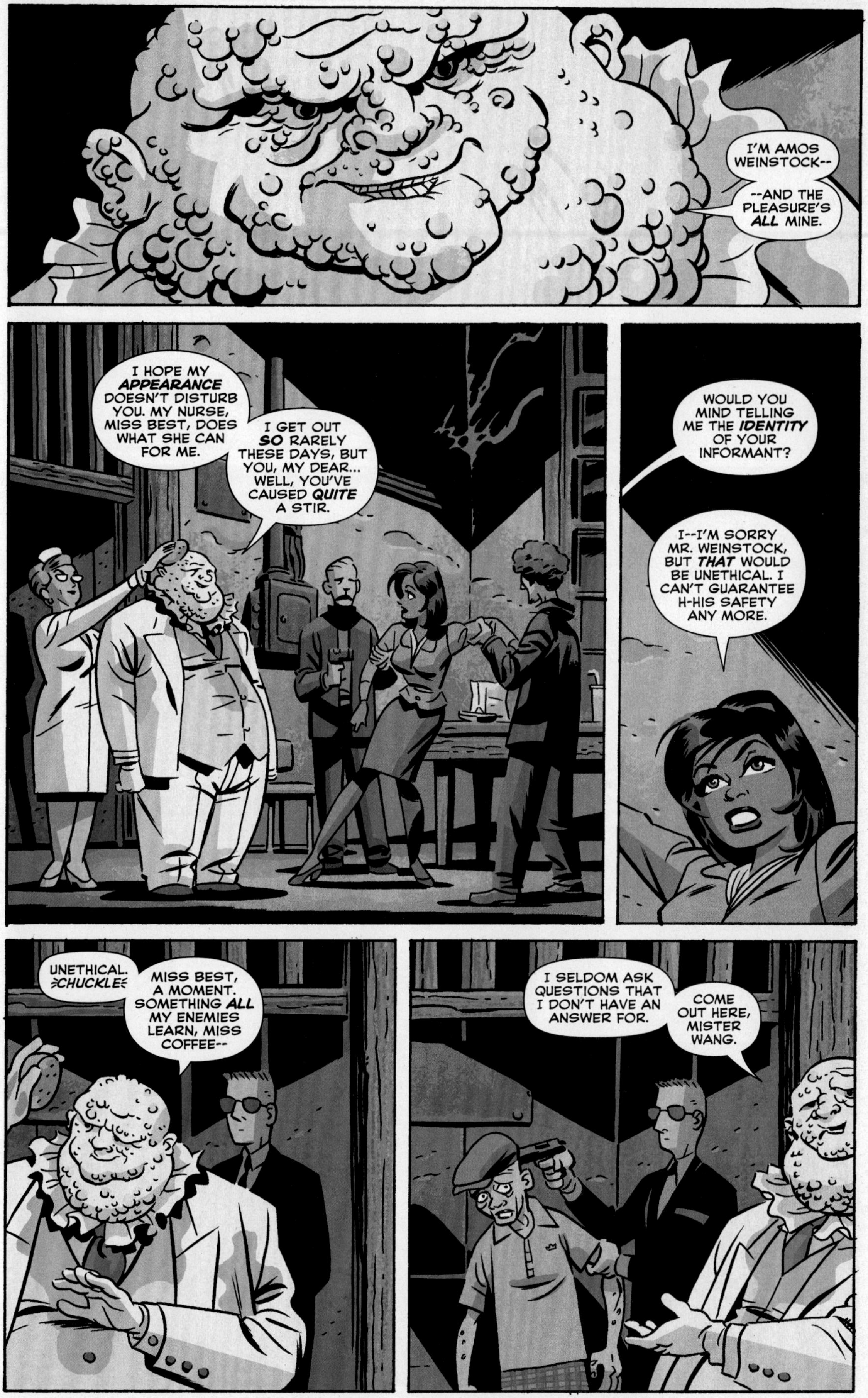
I'M AMOS WEINSTOCK--
--AND THE PLEASURE'S ALL MINE.
I HOPE MY APPEARANCE DOESN'T DISTURB YOU. MY NURSE, MISS BEST, DOES WHAT SHE CAN FOR ME.
I GET OUT SO RARELY THESE DAYS, BUT YOU, MY DEAR... WELL, YOU'VE CAUSED QUITE A STIR.
WOULD YOU MIND TELLING ME THE IDENTITY OF YOUR INFORMANT?
I--I'M SORRY MR. WEINSTOCK, BUT THAT WOULD BE UNETHICAL. I CAN'T GUARANTEE H-HIS SAFETY ANY MORE.
UNETHICAL. CHUCKLE
MISS BEST, A MOMENT. SOMETHING ALL MY ENEMIES LEARN, MISS COFFEE--
I SELDOM ASK QUESTIONS THAT I DON'T HAVE AN ANSWER FOR.
COME OUT HERE, MISTER WANG.

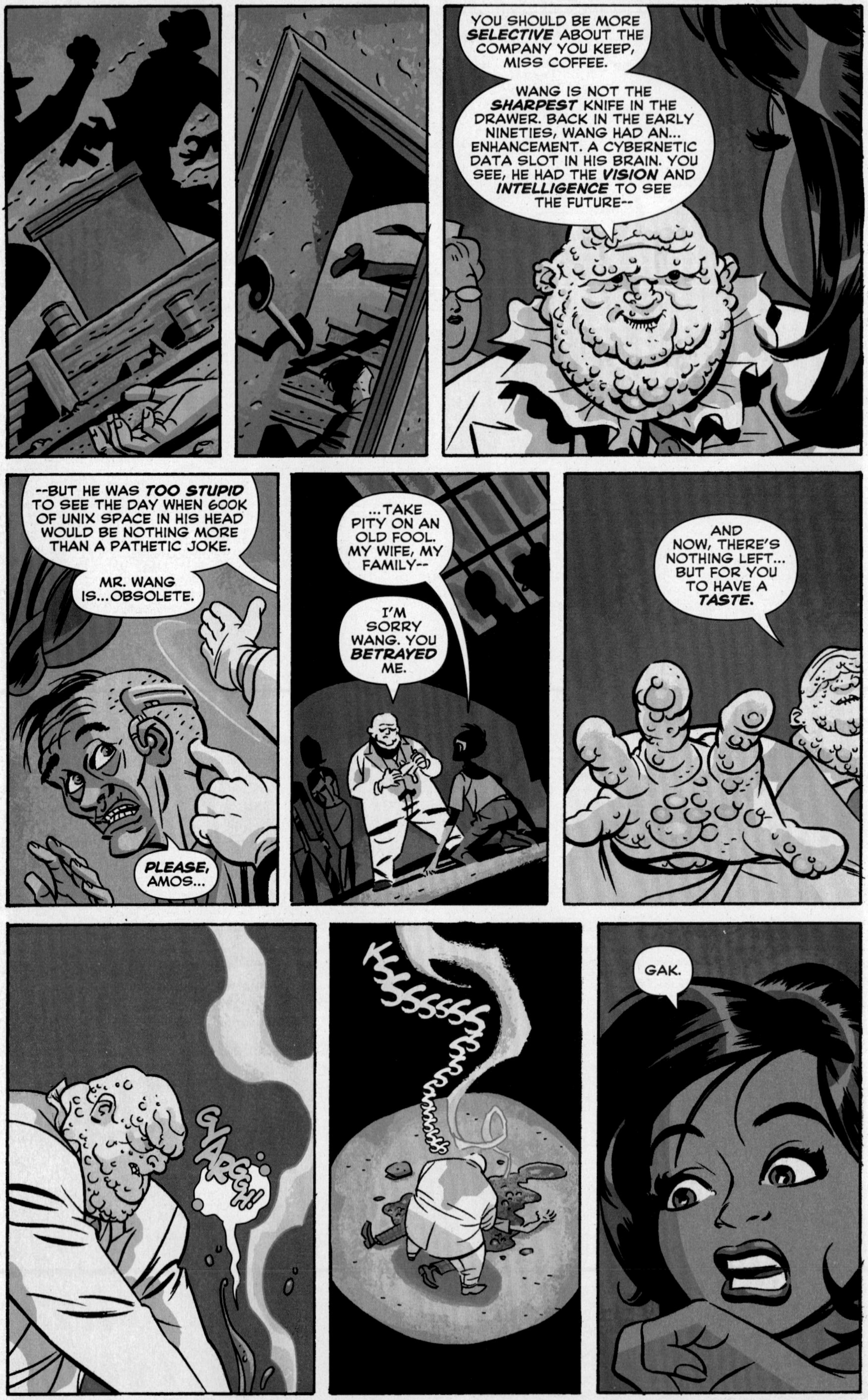
YOU SHOULD BE MORE SELECTIVE ABOUT THE COMPANY YOU KEEP, MISS COFFEE.
WANG IS NOT THE SHARPEST KNIFE IN THE DRAWER. BACK IN THE EARLY NINETIES, WANG HAD AN... ENHANCEMENT. A CYBERNETIC DATA SLOT IN HIS BRAIN. YOU SEE, HE HAD THE VISION AND INTELLIGENCE TO SEE THE FUTURE--
--BUT HE WAS TOO STUPID TO SEE THE DAY WHEN 600K OF UNIX SPACE IN HIS HEAD WOULD BE NOTHING MORE THAN A PATHETIC JOKE.
MR. WANG IS...OBSOLETE.
PLEASE, AMOS...
...TAKE PITY ON AN OLD FOOL. MY WIFE, MY FAMILY--
I'M SORRY WANG. YOU BETRAYED ME.
AND NOW, THERE'S NOTHING LEFT... BUT FOR YOU TO HAVE A TASTE.
GLARGH!
KSSSSSSSSSSSSSSSSSSS
GAK.

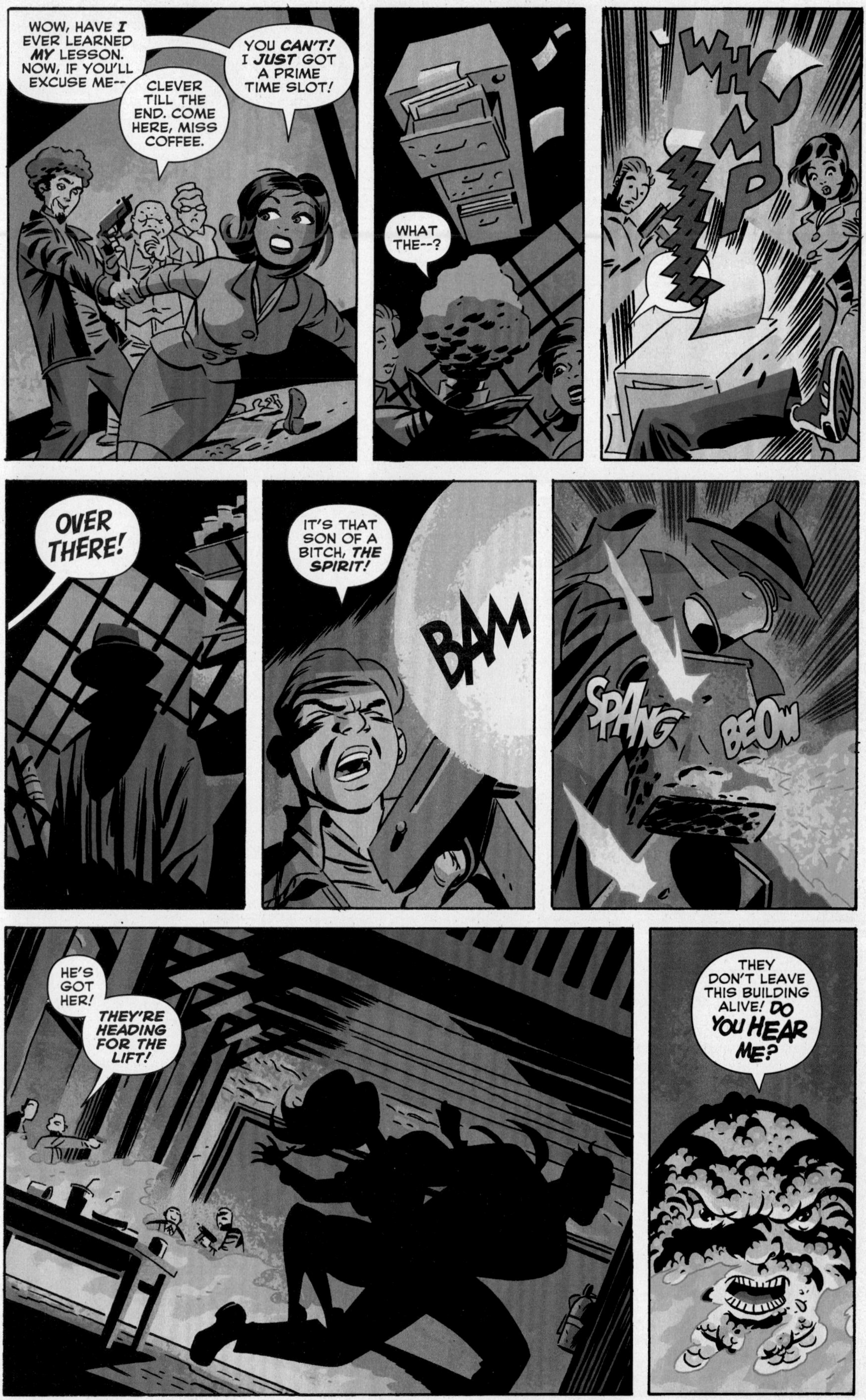
WOW, HAVE I EVER LEARNED MY LESSON. NOW, IF YOU'LL EXCUSE ME--
YOU CAN'T! I JUST GOT A PRIME TIME SLOT!
CLEVER TILL THE END. COME HERE, MISS COFFEE.
WHAT THE--?
WHAMP
OVER THERE!
IT'S THAT SON OF A BITCH, THE SPIRIT!
BAM
SPANG
BEOW
HE'S GOT HER!
THEY'RE HEADING FOR THE LIFT!
THEY DON'T LEAVE THIS BUILDING ALIVE! DO YOU HEAR ME?

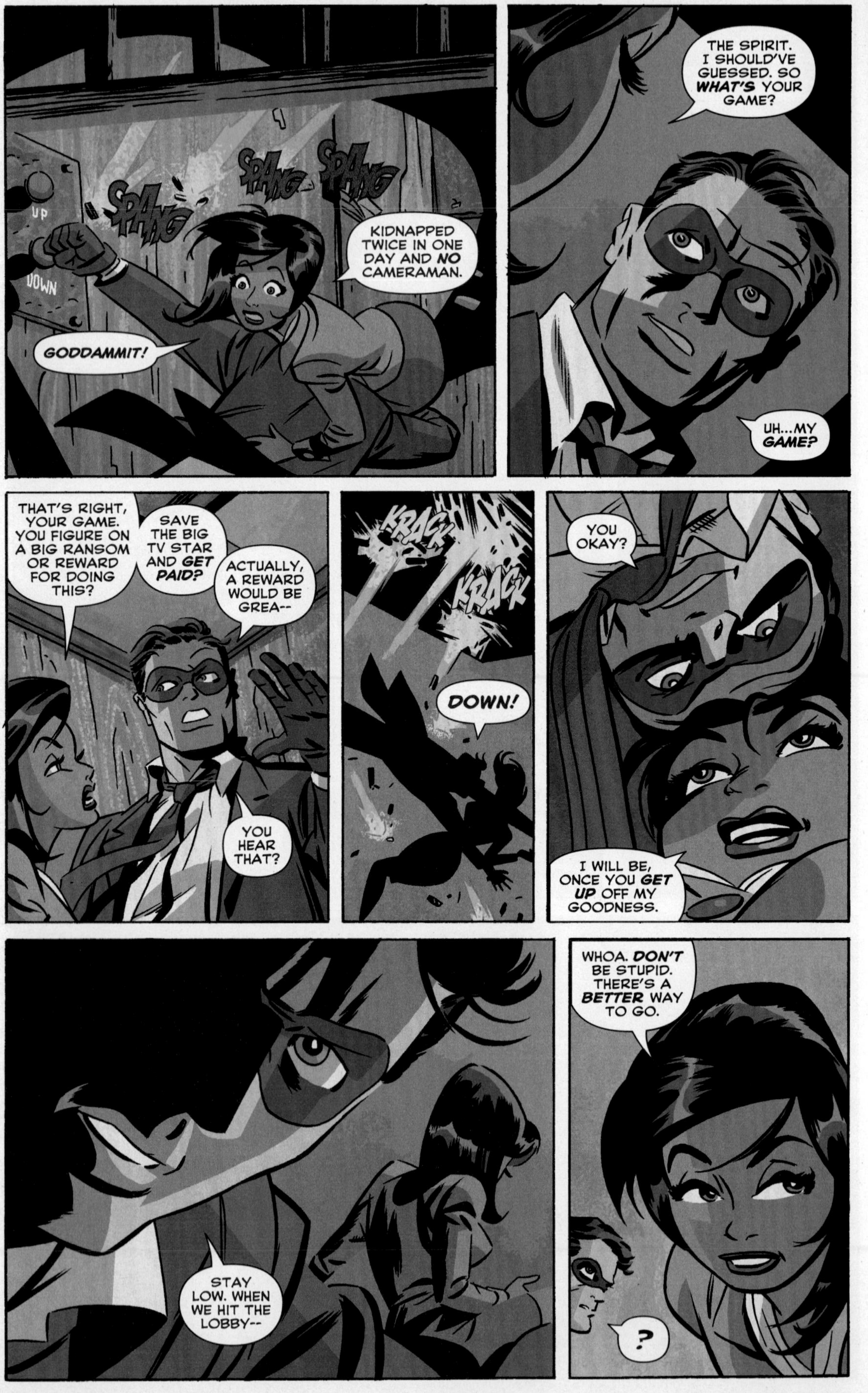
SPANG
SPANG
SPANG
UP
DOWN
KIDNAPPED TWICE IN ONE DAY AND NO CAMERAMAN.
GODDAMMIT!
THE SPIRIT. I SHOULD'VE GUESSED. SO WHAT'S YOUR GAME?
UH...MY GAME?
THAT'S RIGHT, YOUR GAME. YOU FIGURE ON A BIG RANSOM OR REWARD FOR DOING THIS?
SAVE THE BIG TV STAR AND GET PAID?
ACTUALLY, A REWARD WOULD BE GREA--
YOU HEAR THAT?
KRACK
KRACK
DOWN!
YOU OKAY?
I WILL BE, ONCE YOU GET UP OFF MY GOODNESS.
STAY LOW. WHEN WE HIT THE LOBBY--
WHOA. DON'T BE STUPID. THERE'S A BETTER WAY TO GO.
?

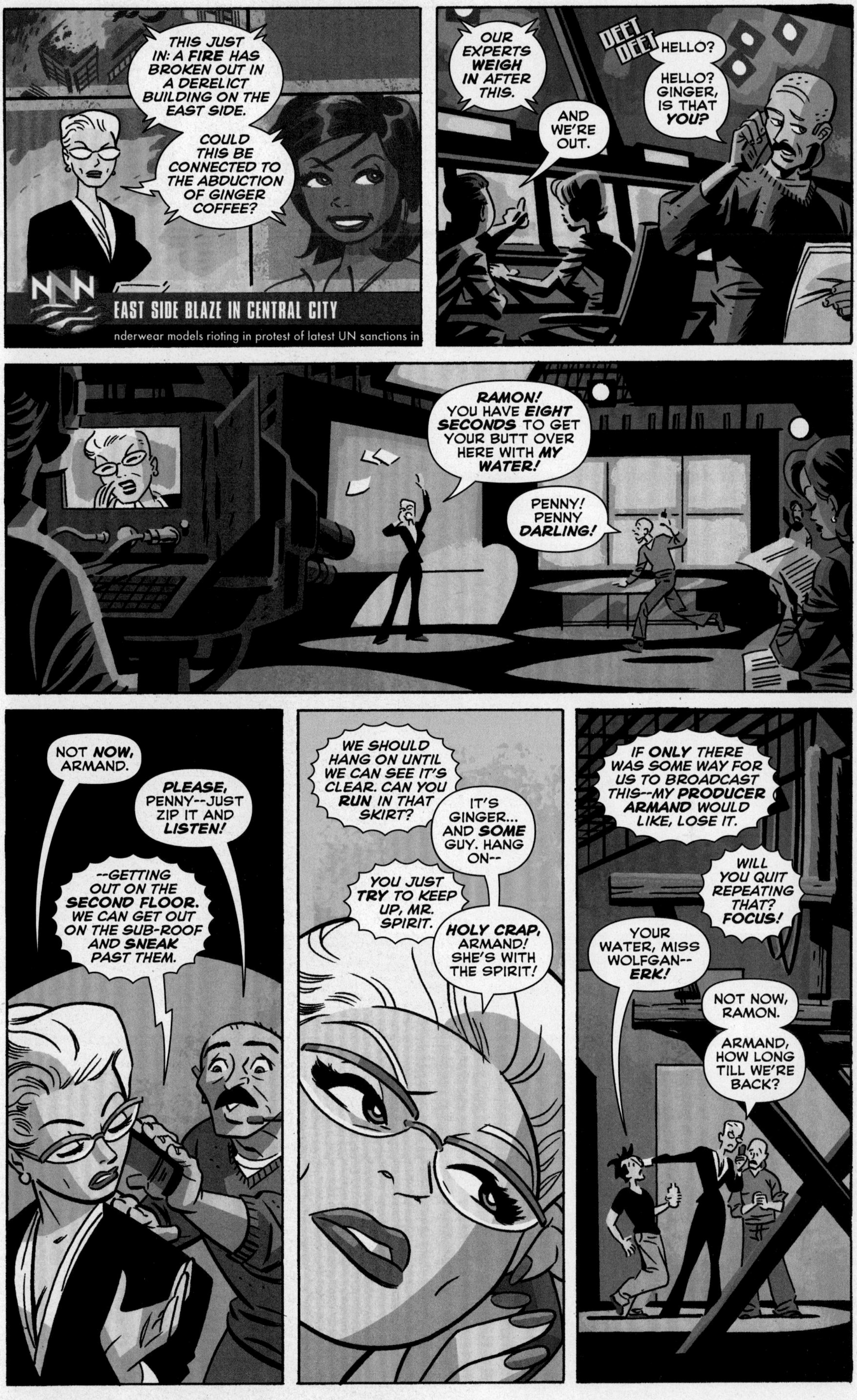
THIS JUST IN: A FIRE HAS BROKEN OUT IN A DERELICT BUILDING ON THE EAST SIDE.
COULD THIS BE CONNECTED TO THE ABDUCTION OF GINGER COFFEE?
NNN
EAST SIDE BLAZE IN CENTRAL CITY
nderwear models rioting in protest of latest UN sanctions in
OUR EXPERTS WEIGH IN AFTER THIS.
DEET DEET
HELLO?
HELLO? GINGER, IS THAT YOU?
AND WE'RE OUT.
RAMON! YOU HAVE EIGHT SECONDS TO GET YOUR BUTT OVER HERE WITH MY WATER!
PENNY! PENNY DARLING!
NOT NOW, ARMAND.
PLEASE, PENNY--JUST ZIP IT AND LISTEN!
--GETTING OUT ON THE SECOND FLOOR. WE CAN GET OUT ON THE SUB-ROOF AND SNEAK PAST THEM.
WE SHOULD HANG ON UNTIL WE CAN SEE IT'S CLEAR. CAN YOU RUN IN THAT SKIRT?
IT'S GINGER... AND SOME GUY. HANG ON--
YOU JUST TRY TO KEEP UP, MR. SPIRIT.
HOLY CRAP, ARMAND! SHE'S WITH THE SPIRIT!
IF ONLY THERE WAS SOME WAY FOR US TO BROADCAST THIS--MY PRODUCER ARMAND WOULD LIKE, LOSE IT.
WILL YOU QUIT REPEATING THAT? FOCUS!
YOUR WATER, MISS WOLFGAN-- ERK!
NOT NOW, RAMON.
ARMAND, HOW LONG TILL WE'RE BACK?

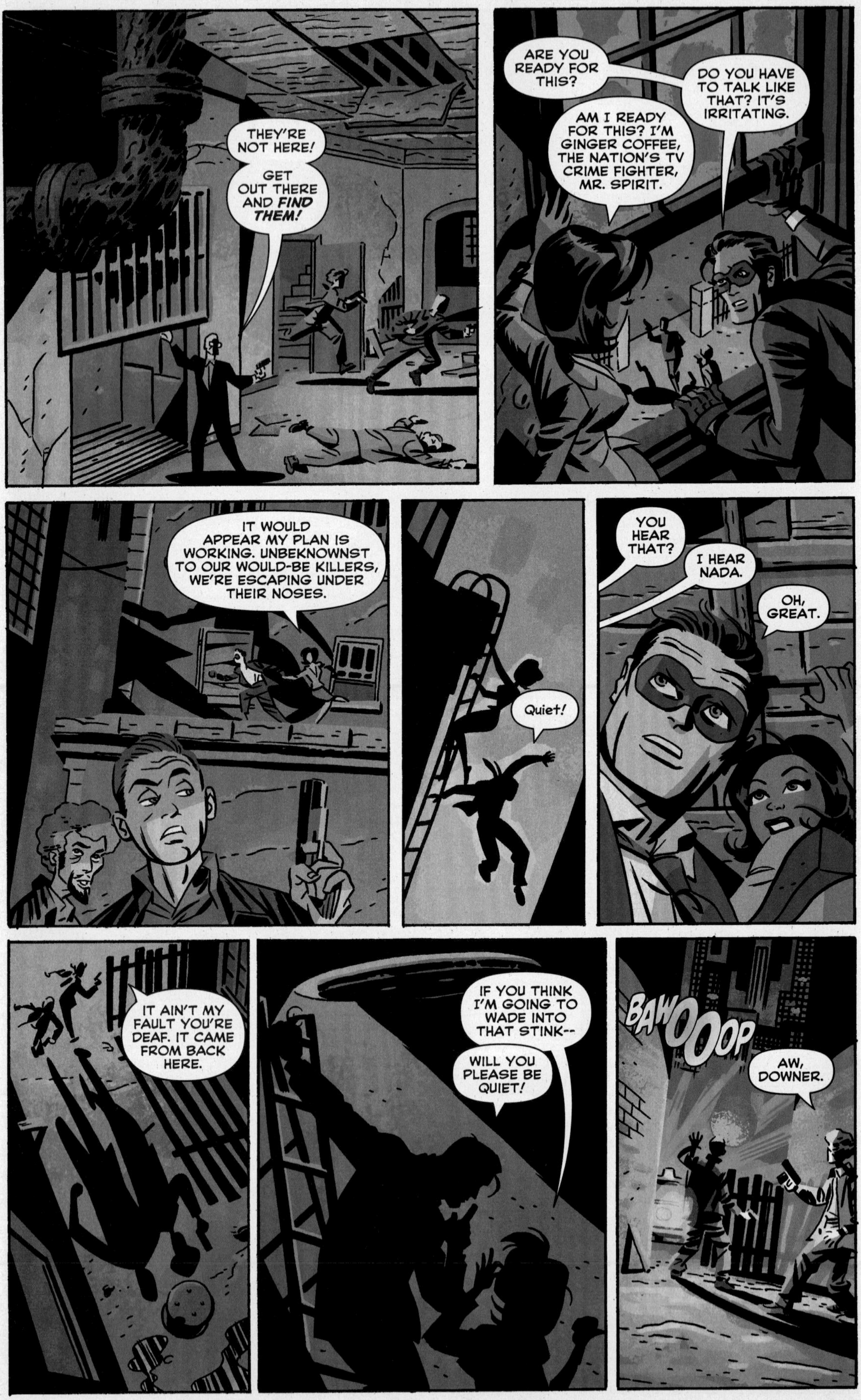
THEY'RE NOT HERE!
GET OUT THERE AND FIND THEM!
ARE YOU READY FOR THIS?
AM I READY FOR THIS? I'M GINGER COFFEE, THE NATION'S TV CRIME FIGHTER, MR. SPIRIT.
DO YOU HAVE TO TALK LIKE THAT? IT'S IRRITATING.
IT WOULD APPEAR MY PLAN IS WORKING. UNBEKNOWNST TO OUR WOULD-BE KILLERS, WE'RE ESCAPING UNDER THEIR NOSES.
Quiet!
YOU HEAR THAT?
I HEAR NADA.
OH, GREAT.
IT AIN'T MY FAULT YOU'RE DEAF. IT CAME FROM BACK HERE.
IF YOU THINK I'M GOING TO WADE INTO THAT STINK--
WILL YOU PLEASE BE QUIET!
BAWOOOP
AW, DOWNER.

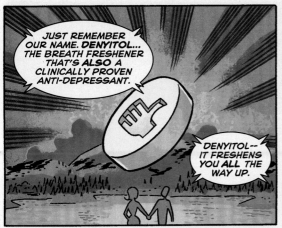

JUST REMEMBER OUR NAME. DENYITOL... THE BREATH FRESHENER THAT'S *ALSO* A CLINICALLY PROVEN ANTI-DEPRESSANT.

DENYITOL-- IT FRESHENS YOU ALL THE WAY UP.

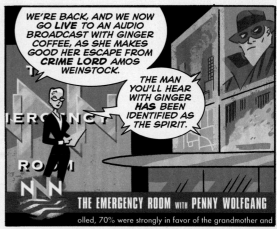

WE'RE BACK, AND WE NOW GO *LIVE* TO AN AUDIO BROADCAST WITH GINGER COFFEE, AS SHE MAKES GOOD HER ESCAPE FROM *CRIME LORD AMOS WEINSTOCK.*

THE MAN YOU'LL HEAR WITH GINGER *HAS* BEEN IDENTIFIED AS THE SPIRIT.

THE EMERGENCY ROOM with PENNY WOLFGANG

olled, 70% were strongly in favor of the grandmother and

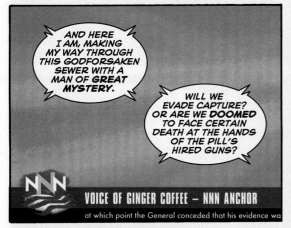

AND HERE I AM, MAKING MY WAY THROUGH THIS GODFORSAKEN SEWER WITH A MAN OF *GREAT MYSTERY.*

WILL WE *EVADE* CAPTURE? OR ARE WE *DOOMED* TO FACE CERTAIN DEATH AT THE HANDS OF THE PILL'S HIRED GUNS?

VOICE OF GINGER COFFEE — NNN ANCHOR

at which point the General conceded that his evidence wa

SERIOUSLY, IS THERE SOMETHING *WRONG* WITH YOU? WHY DO YOU KEEP *GIBBERING* IN THAT NEWSPEAK?

YOU'D BEST SAVE YOUR BREATH, 'CAUSE IT'S A *LONG HAUL* OUT OF THE WEST SIDE.

VOICE OF "THE SPIRIT" – VIGILANTE

and it had become clear that the actions taken were impro

THEY'RE HEADING EAST, THROUGH THE SEWERS. GET SOME MEN DOWN THERE NOW.

I WANT EVERYTHING WE'VE GOT AT THE FIRE SCENE. WE WORK *OUT* FROM THERE.

KLINK, YOU AND MURDOCH ORGANIZE THE CORDON DETAIL AND RADIO IN WHEN ALL UNITS ARE IN PLACE.

YES SIR!

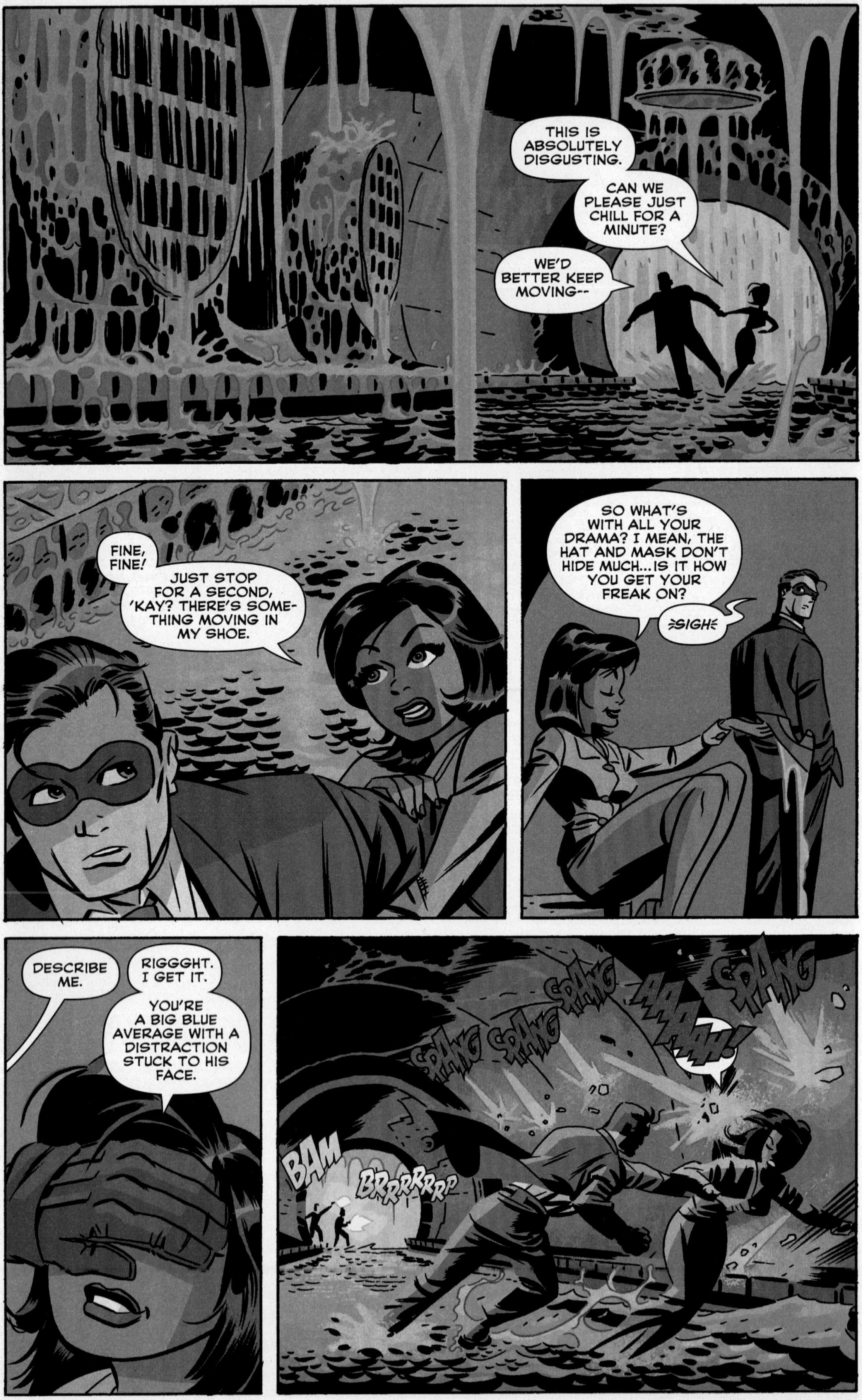
THIS IS ABSOLUTELY DISGUSTING.
CAN WE PLEASE JUST CHILL FOR A MINUTE?
WE'D BETTER KEEP MOVING--
FINE, FINE!
JUST STOP FOR A SECOND, 'KAY? THERE'S SOMETHING MOVING IN MY SHOE.
SO WHAT'S WITH ALL YOUR DRAMA? I MEAN, THE HAT AND MASK DON'T HIDE MUCH...IS IT HOW YOU GET YOUR FREAK ON?
SIGH
DESCRIBE ME.
RIGGGHT. I GET IT.
YOU'RE A BIG BLUE AVERAGE WITH A DISTRACTION STUCK TO HIS FACE.
SPANG
SPANG
SPANG
SPANG
AAAAAH!
SPANG
BAM
BRRRRRRP

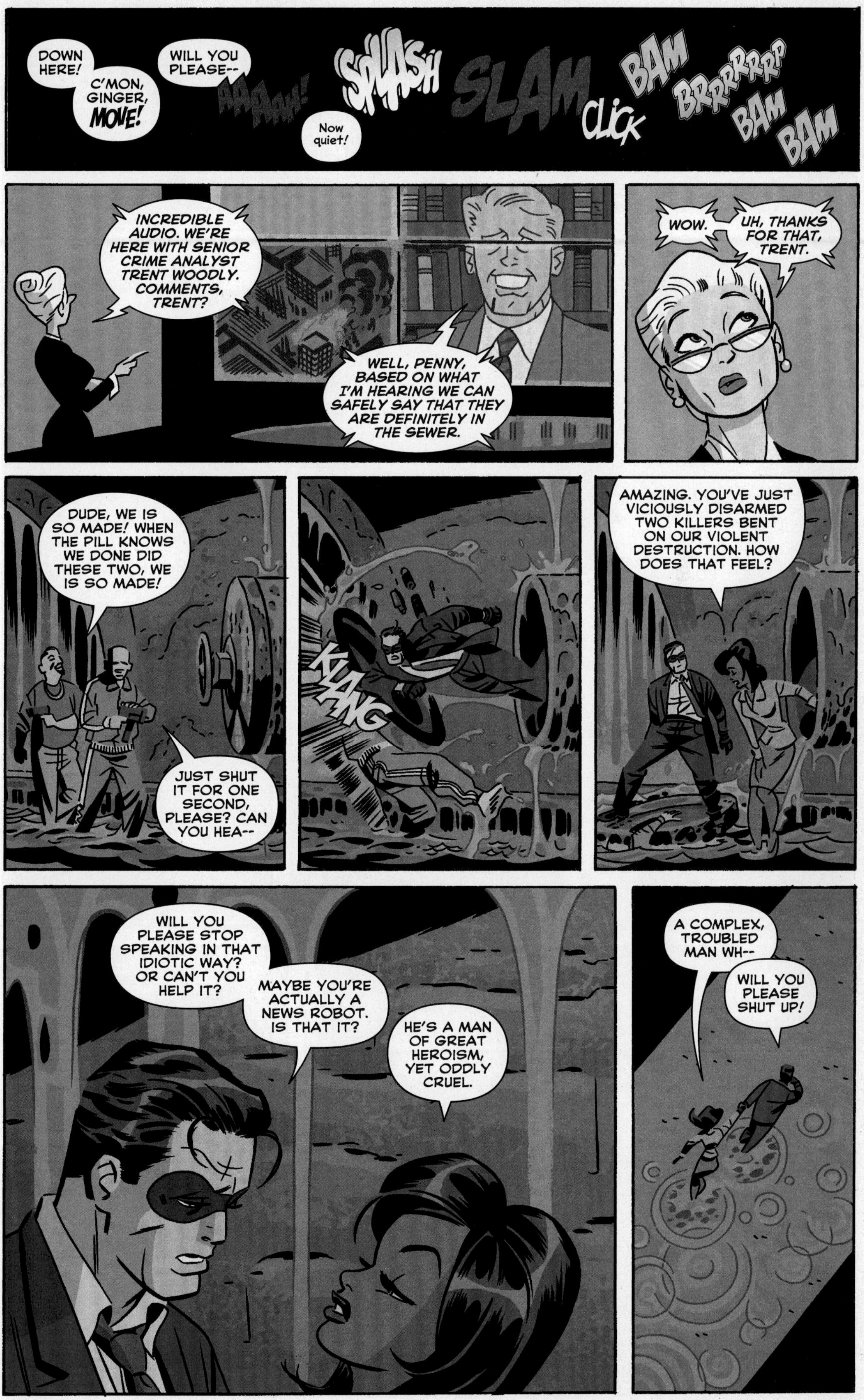
DOWN HERE!
C'MON, GINGER, MOVE!
WILL YOU PLEASE--
AAAAAAH!
SPLASH
Now quiet!
SLAM
CLICK
BAM
BRRRRRRP
BAM
BAM
INCREDIBLE AUDIO. WE'RE HERE WITH SENIOR CRIME ANALYST TRENT WOODLY. COMMENTS, TRENT?
WELL, PENNY, BASED ON WHAT I'M HEARING WE CAN SAFELY SAY THAT THEY ARE DEFINITELY IN THE SEWER.
WOW.
UH, THANKS FOR THAT, TRENT.
DUDE, WE IS SO MADE! WHEN THE PILL KNOWS WE DONE DID THESE TWO, WE IS SO MADE!
JUST SHUT IT FOR ONE SECOND, PLEASE? CAN YOU HEA--
KLANG
AMAZING. YOU'VE JUST VICIOUSLY DISARMED TWO KILLERS BENT ON OUR VIOLENT DESTRUCTION. HOW DOES THAT FEEL?
WILL YOU PLEASE STOP SPEAKING IN THAT IDIOTIC WAY? OR CAN'T YOU HELP IT?
MAYBE YOU'RE ACTUALLY A NEWS ROBOT. IS THAT IT?
HE'S A MAN OF GREAT HEROISM, YET ODDLY CRUEL.
A COMPLEX, TROUBLED MAN WH--
WILL YOU PLEASE SHUT UP!

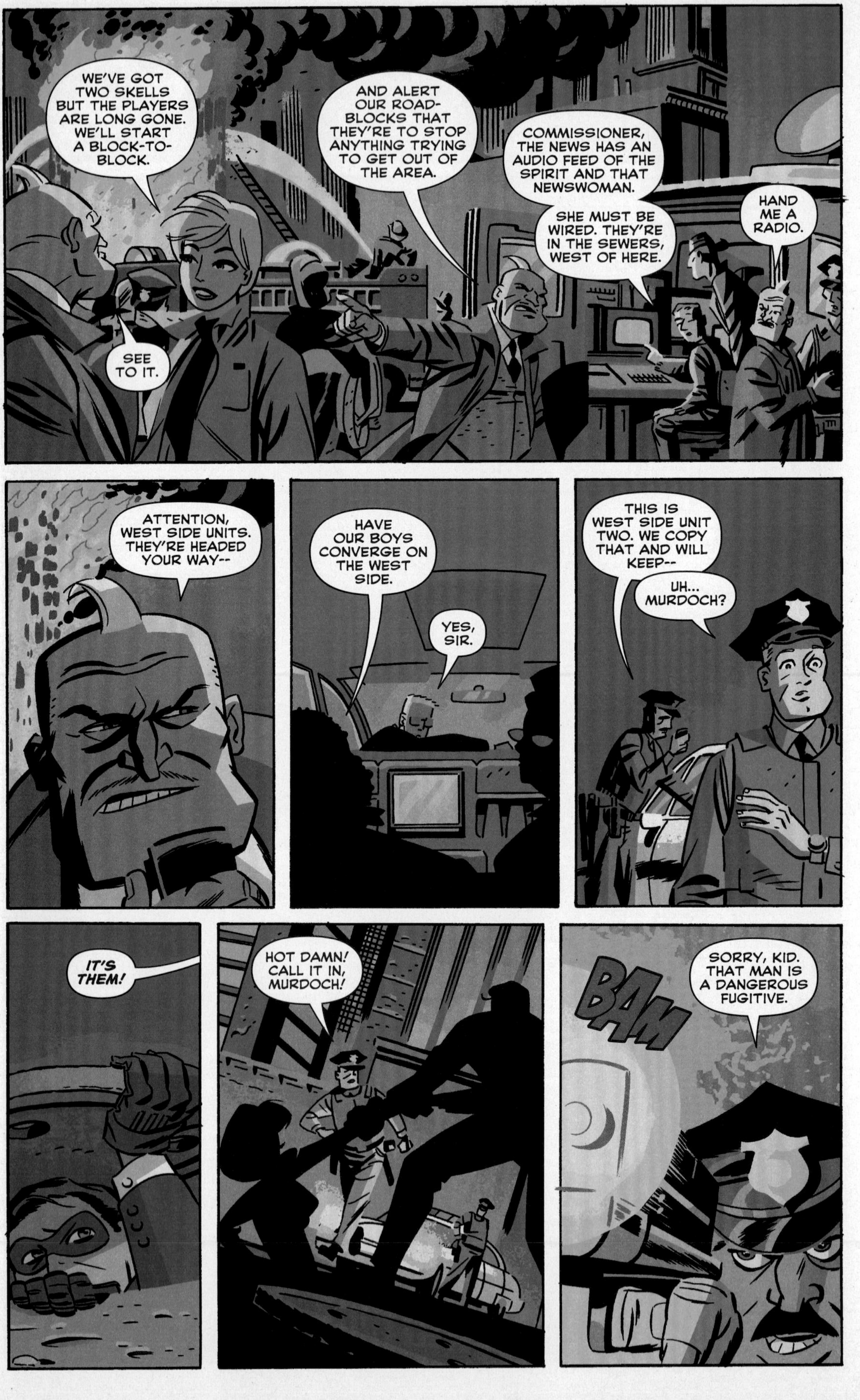
WE'VE GOT TWO SKELLS BUT THE PLAYERS ARE LONG GONE. WE'LL START A BLOCK-TO-BLOCK.
SEE TO IT.
AND ALERT OUR ROAD-BLOCKS THAT THEY'RE TO STOP ANYTHING TRYING TO GET OUT OF THE AREA.
COMMISSIONER, THE NEWS HAS AN AUDIO FEED OF THE SPIRIT AND THAT NEWSWOMAN.
SHE MUST BE WIRED. THEY'RE IN THE SEWERS, WEST OF HERE.
HAND ME A RADIO.
ATTENTION, WEST SIDE UNITS. THEY'RE HEADED YOUR WAY--
HAVE OUR BOYS CONVERGE ON THE WEST SIDE.
YES, SIR.
THIS IS WEST SIDE UNIT TWO. WE COPY THAT AND WILL KEEP--
UH... MURDOCH?
IT'S THEM!
HOT DAMN! CALL IT IN, MURDOCH!
BAM
SORRY, KID. THAT MAN IS A DANGEROUS FUGITIVE.

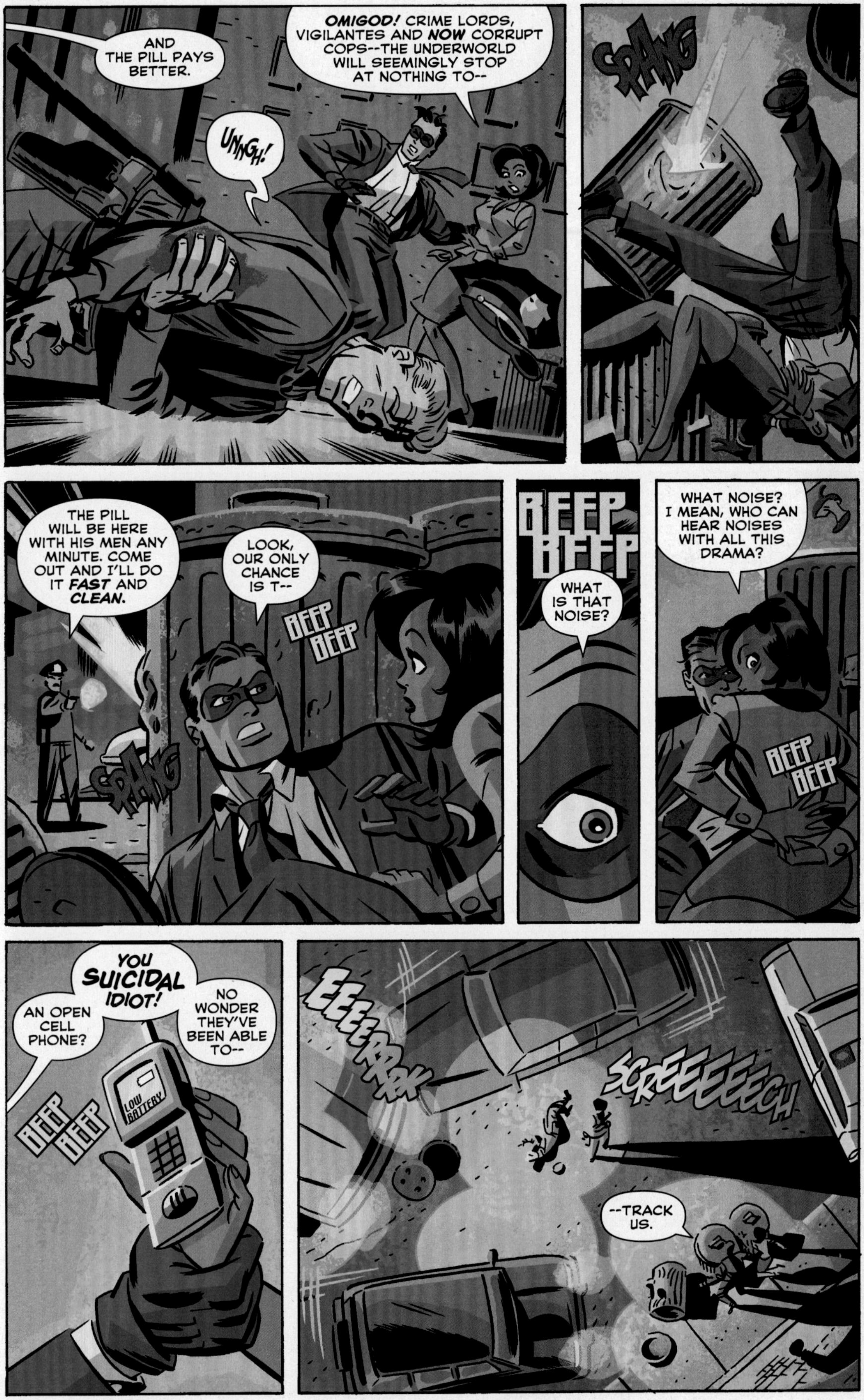
AND THE PILL PAYS BETTER.
OMIGOD! CRIME LORDS, VIGILANTES AND NOW CORRUPT COPS--THE UNDERWORLD WILL SEEMINGLY STOP AT NOTHING TO--
UNNGH!
SPANG
THE PILL WILL BE HERE WITH HIS MEN ANY MINUTE. COME OUT AND I'LL DO IT FAST AND CLEAN.
LOOK, OUR ONLY CHANCE IS T--
BEEP BEEP
SPANG
BEEP BEEP
WHAT IS THAT NOISE?
WHAT NOISE? I MEAN, WHO CAN HEAR NOISES WITH ALL THIS DRAMA?
BEEP BEEP
AN OPEN CELL PHONE?
YOU SUICIDAL IDIOT!
NO WONDER THEY'VE BEEN ABLE TO--
LOW BATTERY
BEEP BEEP
EEEERRRK
SCREEEEECH
--TRACK US.

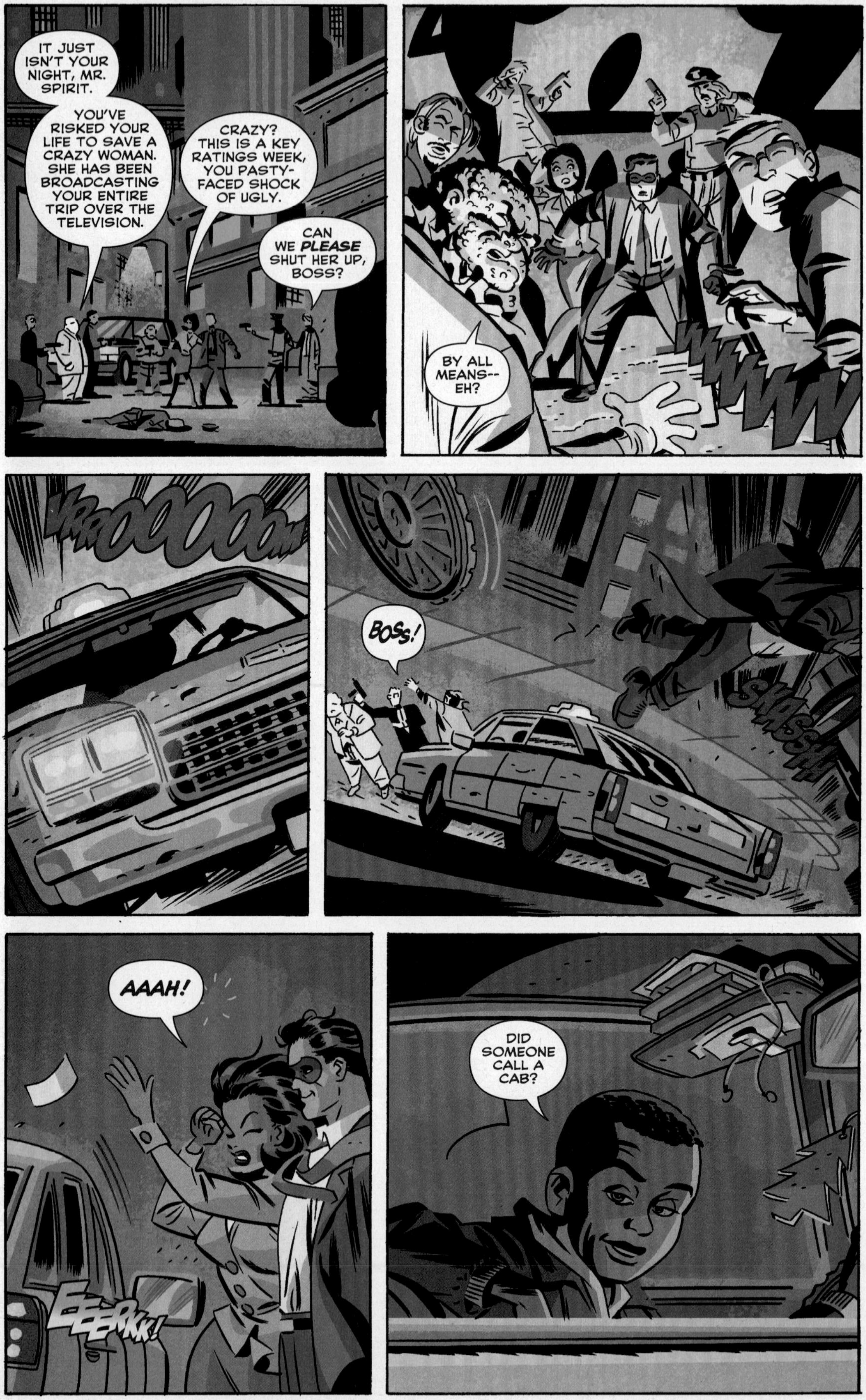
IT JUST ISN'T YOUR NIGHT, MR. SPIRIT.
YOU'VE RISKED YOUR LIFE TO SAVE A CRAZY WOMAN. SHE HAS BEEN BROADCASTING YOUR ENTIRE TRIP OVER THE TELEVISION.
CRAZY? THIS IS A KEY RATINGS WEEK, YOU PASTY-FACED SHOCK OF UGLY.
CAN WE *PLEASE* SHUT HER UP, BOSS?
BY ALL MEANS-- EH?
VRROOOOOOM
BOSS!
SKASSH
AAAH!
EEEERKK!
DID SOMEONE CALL A CAB?

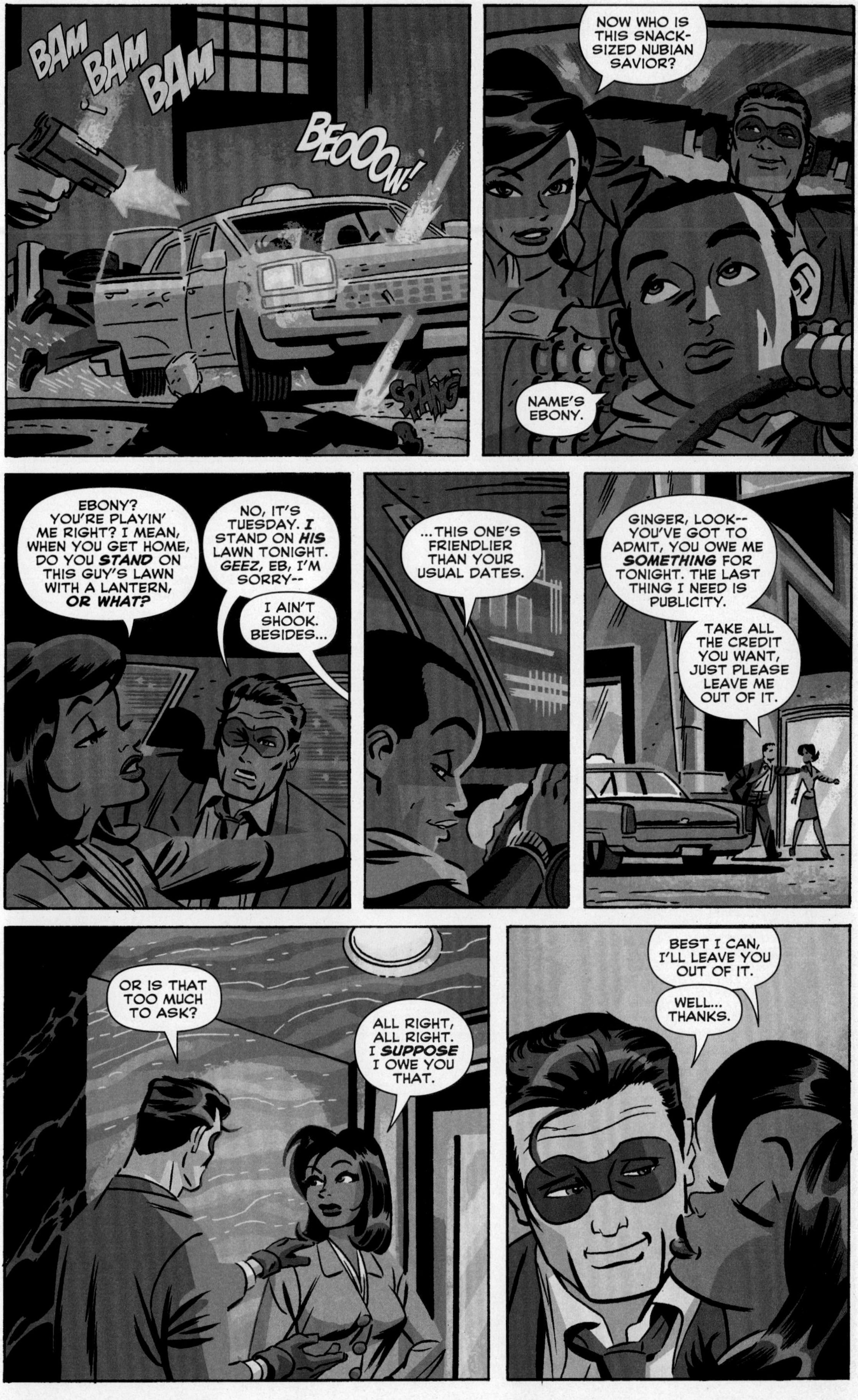
BAM BAM BAM
BEOOOW!
SPANG
NOW WHO IS THIS SNACK-SIZED NUBIAN SAVIOR?
NAME'S EBONY.
EBONY? YOU'RE PLAYIN' ME RIGHT? I MEAN, WHEN YOU GET HOME, DO YOU **STAND** ON THIS GUY'S LAWN WITH A LANTERN, **OR WHAT?**
NO, IT'S TUESDAY. **I** STAND ON **HIS** LAWN TONIGHT. **GEEZ,** EB, I'M SORRY--
I AIN'T SHOOK. BESIDES...
...THIS ONE'S FRIENDLIER THAN YOUR USUAL DATES.
GINGER, LOOK-- YOU'VE GOT TO ADMIT, YOU OWE ME **SOMETHING** FOR TONIGHT. THE LAST THING I NEED IS PUBLICITY.
TAKE ALL THE CREDIT YOU WANT, JUST PLEASE LEAVE ME OUT OF IT.
OR IS THAT TOO MUCH TO ASK?
ALL RIGHT, ALL RIGHT. I **SUPPOSE** I OWE YOU THAT.
BEST I CAN, I'LL LEAVE YOU OUT OF IT.
WELL... THANKS.

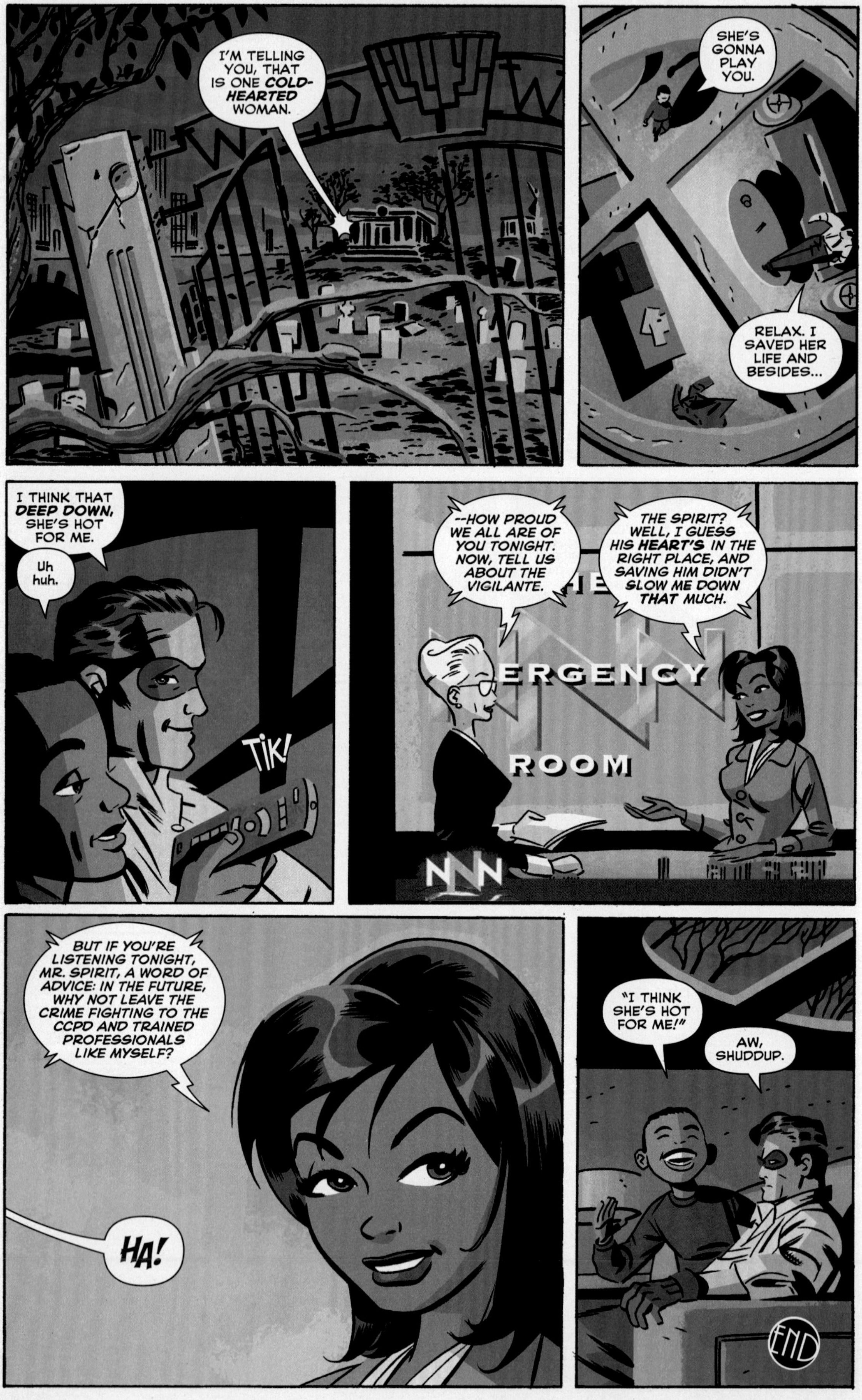
I'M TELLING YOU, THAT IS ONE COLD-HEARTED WOMAN.
SHE'S GONNA PLAY YOU.
RELAX. I SAVED HER LIFE AND BESIDES...
I THINK THAT DEEP DOWN, SHE'S HOT FOR ME.
Uh huh.
TIK!
--HOW PROUD WE ALL ARE OF YOU TONIGHT. NOW, TELL US ABOUT THE VIGILANTE.
THE SPIRIT? WELL, I GUESS HIS HEART'S IN THE RIGHT PLACE, AND SAVING HIM DIDN'T SLOW ME DOWN THAT MUCH.
ERGENCY
ROOM
NNN
BUT IF YOU'RE LISTENING TONIGHT, MR. SPIRIT, A WORD OF ADVICE: IN THE FUTURE, WHY NOT LEAVE THE CRIME FIGHTING TO THE CCPD AND TRAINED PROFESSIONALS LIKE MYSELF?
HA!
"I THINK SHE'S HOT FOR ME!"
AW, SHUDDUP.
END

2

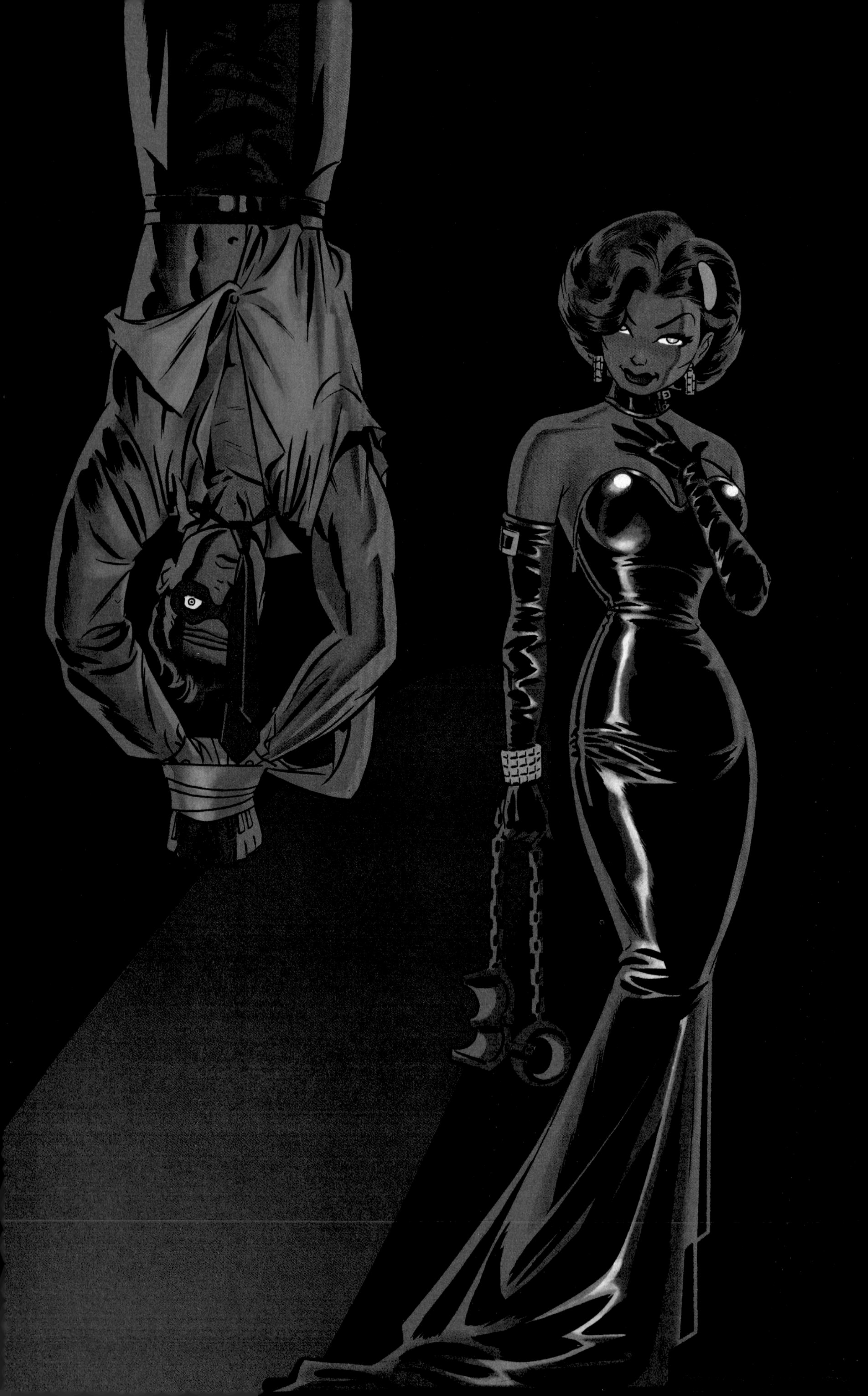

YOU SEE, MY DEAR, WE ARE BOTH IN A **MOST** DELICATE POSITION.

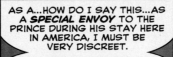

AS A...HOW DO I SAY THIS...AS A **SPECIAL ENVOY** TO THE PRINCE DURING HIS STAY HERE IN AMERICA, I MUST BE VERY DISCREET.

IT IS MY RESPONSIBILITY-- MY **HONOR**--TO ENSURE THAT THE PRINCE MEETS ONLY THE **FINEST** COMPANIONS WHILE HE IS HERE IN CENTRAL CITY.

IT IS RARE THAT A MAN CAN FIND WORK HE BOTH LOVES AND BELIEVES IN. I AM DOUBLY BLESSED.

YOU ARE CERTAINLY A STRIKING SPECIMEN, WITH A COLORING AND **VIGOR** THAT THE PRINCE WILL FIND **MOST** ALLURING.

ALL THAT REMAINS, IS A FINAL CHECK, YES?

I BELIEVE YOU YANKEES CALL IT "THE TEST DRIVE."

SLAP!

N-NOW, MADAM, THERE IS NO NEED TO GET VIOLENT. WE SUMMERED IN BANGKOK THIS YEAR AND THEY ARE FAR MORE...**SALES ORIENTED** THERE.

FORGIVE ME.

PERHAPS WE SHOULD MOVE ON TO THE BUSINESS, YES?

I HAVE BROUGHT THE INVITATIONS AND SECURITY LETTERS FOR THE ROYAL RECEPTION.

WITHOUT THESE, A POOR GIRL WOULD BE **VERY** HARD-PRESSED TO MEET HER PRINCE.

I MUST SAY MADAM, A WOMAN WHO CANNOT BE FORTHCOMING IN AN INTIMATE SENSE MUST AT LEAST BE GENEROUS IN A MATERIAL SENSE.

OR I COULD MAKE ALTERNATE ARRANGEMENTS. IT IS **MADAM P'GELL'S** CHOICE.

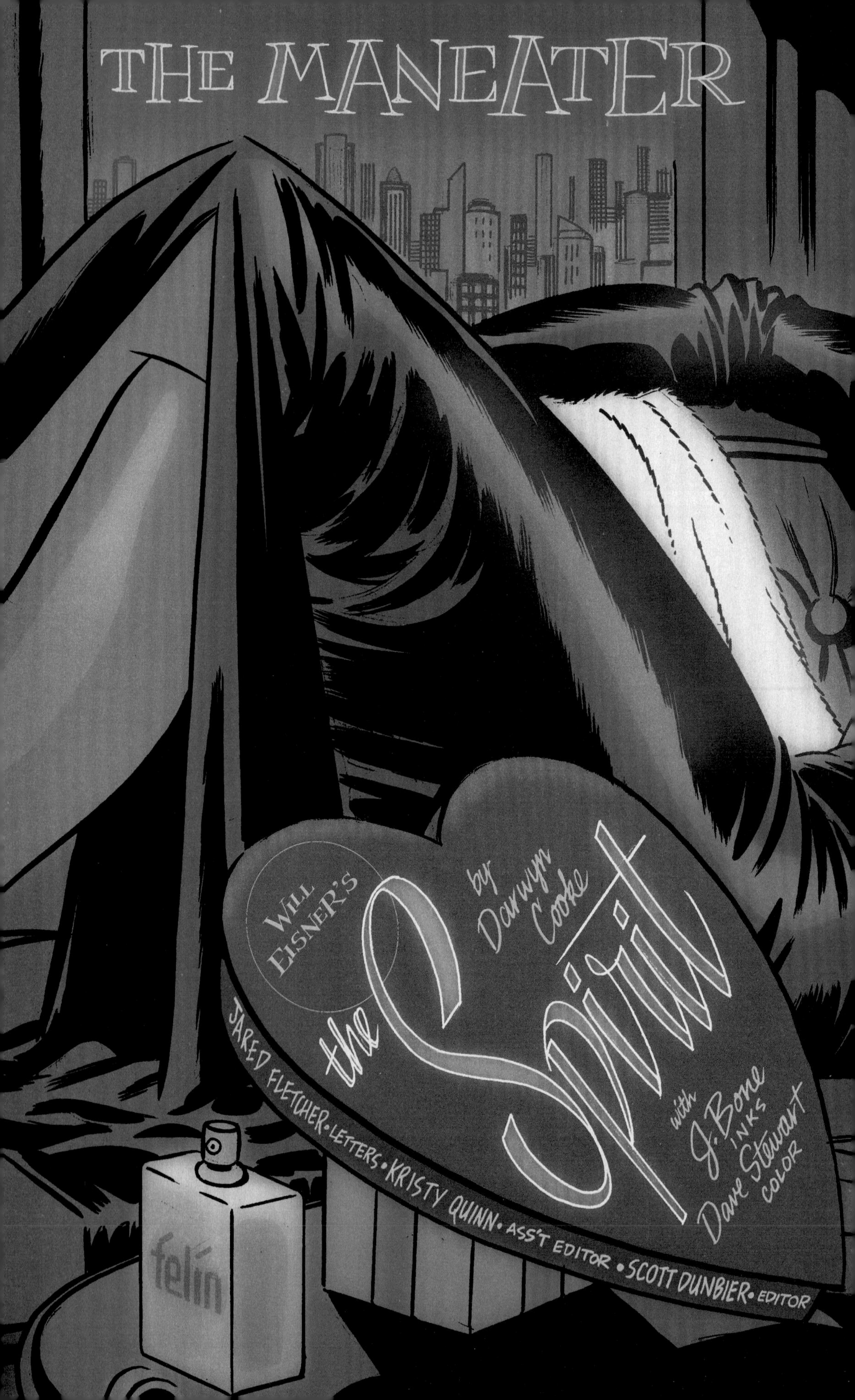
THE MANEATER
WILL EISNER'S
the Spirit
by Darwyn Cooke
with J. Bone INKS
Dave Stewart COLOR
JARED FLETCHER • LETTERS • KRISTY QUINN • ASS'T EDITOR • SCOTT DUNBIER • EDITOR
felin

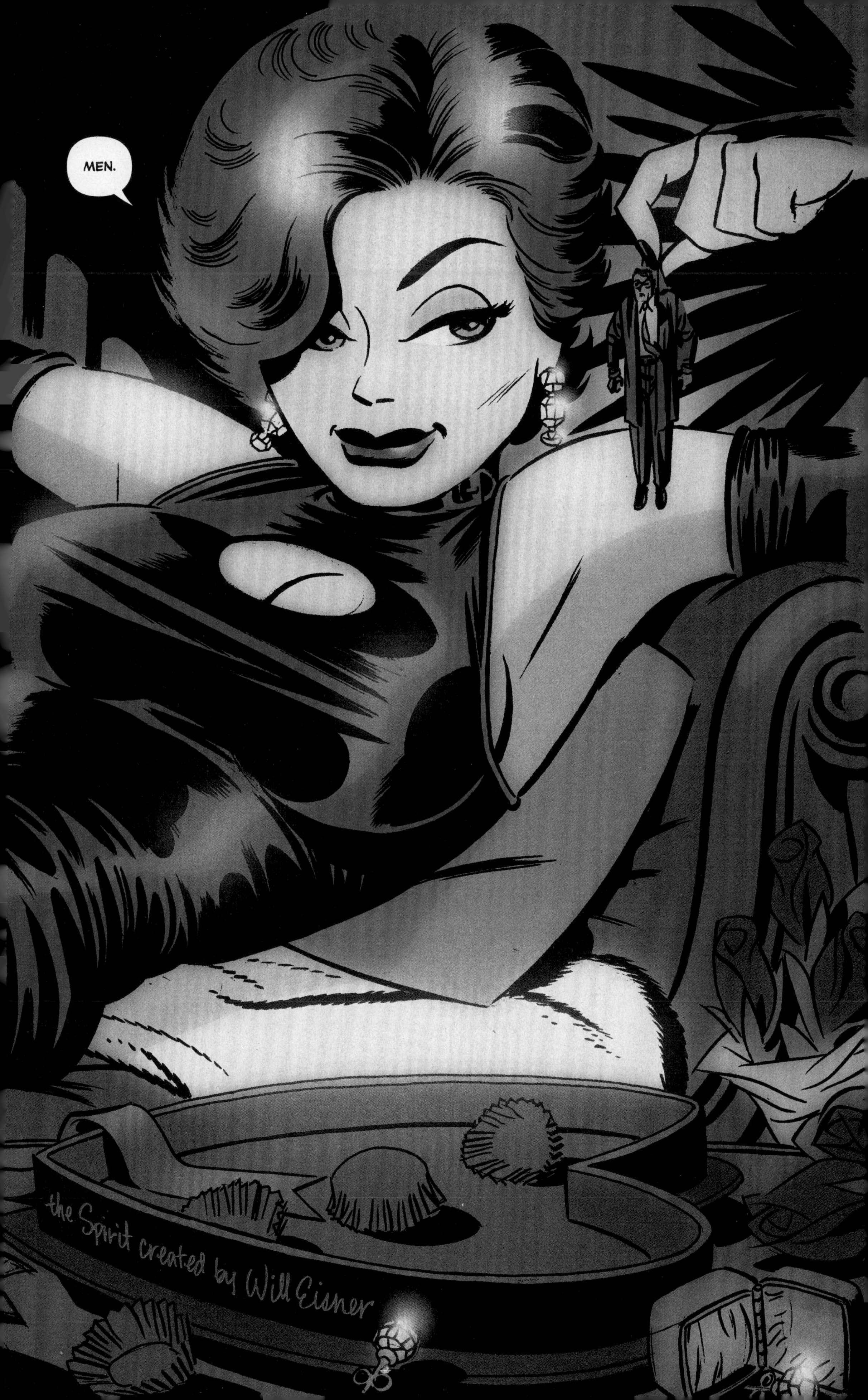
MEN.
the Spirit created by Will Eisner

MADAM P'GELL, I WOUL--

RELAX, HUSSEIN. HERE'S YOUR "PROCUREMENT" FEE.

OR ARE YOU STILL TOO OFFENDED TO DO BUSINESS?

I FEEL MY SENSE OF OFFENSE QUICKLY BOWING BEFORE MADAM'S SINCERITY.

*BY ALL MEANS*, HERE IS YOUR INVITATION.

WITH THAT I BID YOU GOOD EVENING, MADAM. UNLESS YOU HAVE SOME FURTHER USE FOR ME.

JUST BE THERE TO GIVE ME A PERSONAL INTRODUCTION TO THE PRINCE. THAT IS THE ONLY USE I HAVE FOR YOU.

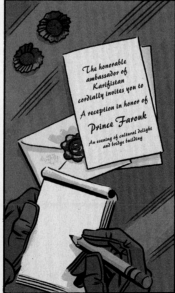

The honorable ambassador of Karifistan cordially invites you to A reception in honor of Prince Farouk

An evening of cultural delight and bridge building

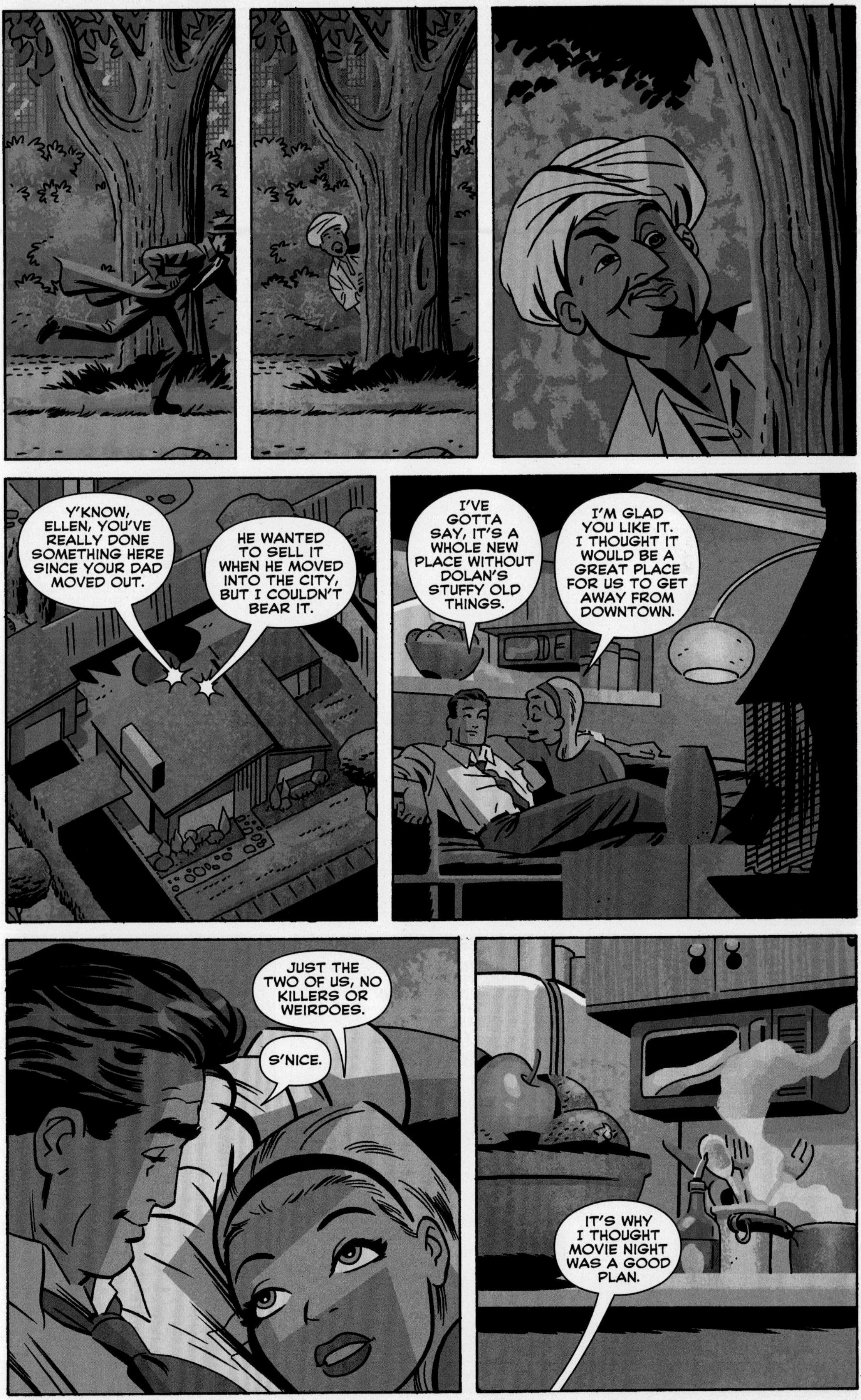
Y'KNOW, ELLEN, YOU'VE REALLY DONE SOMETHING HERE SINCE YOUR DAD MOVED OUT.
HE WANTED TO SELL IT WHEN HE MOVED INTO THE CITY, BUT I COULDN'T BEAR IT.
I'VE GOTTA SAY, IT'S A WHOLE NEW PLACE WITHOUT DOLAN'S STUFFY OLD THINGS.
I'M GLAD YOU LIKE IT. I THOUGHT IT WOULD BE A GREAT PLACE FOR US TO GET AWAY FROM DOWNTOWN.
JUST THE TWO OF US, NO KILLERS OR WEIRDOES.
S'NICE.
IT'S WHY I THOUGHT MOVIE NIGHT WAS A GOOD PLAN.

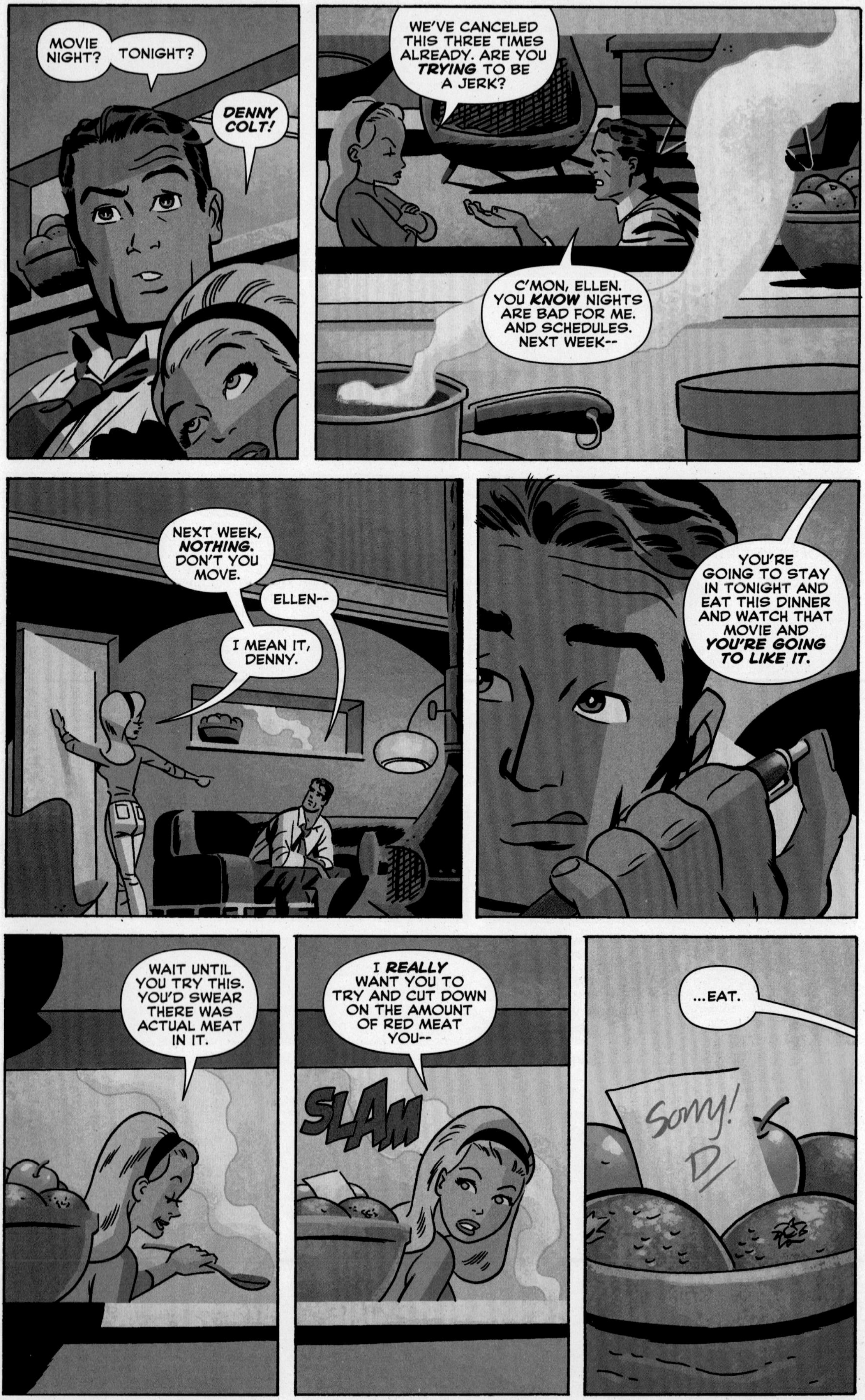
MOVIE NIGHT?
TONIGHT?
DENNY COLT!
WE'VE CANCELED THIS THREE TIMES ALREADY. ARE YOU TRYING TO BE A JERK?
C'MON, ELLEN. YOU KNOW NIGHTS ARE BAD FOR ME. AND SCHEDULES. NEXT WEEK--
NEXT WEEK, NOTHING. DON'T YOU MOVE.
ELLEN--
I MEAN IT, DENNY.
YOU'RE GOING TO STAY IN TONIGHT AND EAT THIS DINNER AND WATCH THAT MOVIE AND YOU'RE GOING TO LIKE IT.
WAIT UNTIL YOU TRY THIS. YOU'D SWEAR THERE WAS ACTUAL MEAT IN IT.
I REALLY WANT YOU TO TRY AND CUT DOWN ON THE AMOUNT OF RED MEAT YOU--
SLAM
...EAT.
Sorry! D

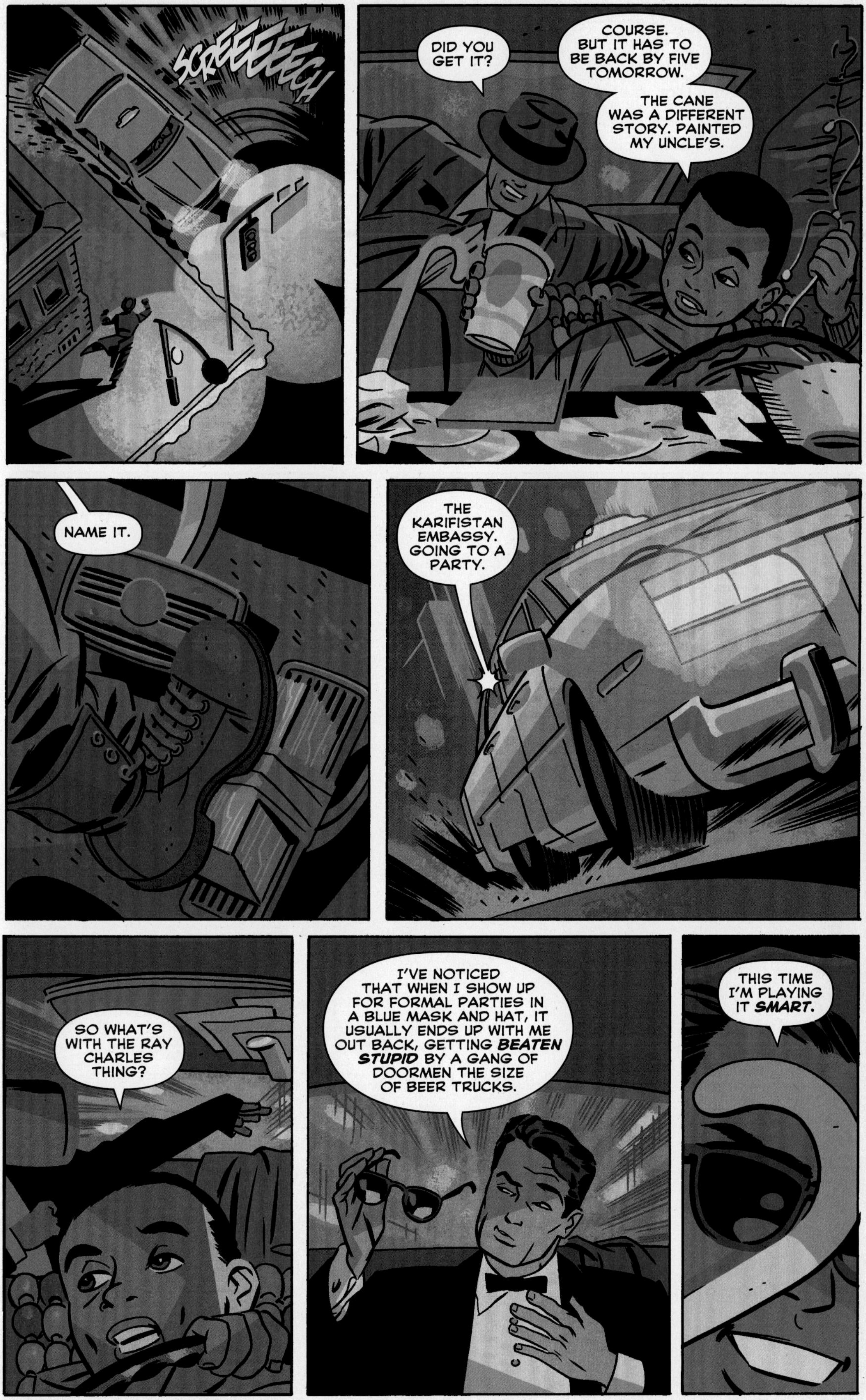
SCREEEEEECH
DID YOU GET IT?
COURSE. BUT IT HAS TO BE BACK BY FIVE TOMORROW.
THE CANE WAS A DIFFERENT STORY. PAINTED MY UNCLE'S.
NAME IT.
THE KARIFISTAN EMBASSY. GOING TO A PARTY.
SO WHAT'S WITH THE RAY CHARLES THING?
I'VE NOTICED THAT WHEN I SHOW UP FOR FORMAL PARTIES IN A BLUE MASK AND HAT, IT USUALLY ENDS UP WITH ME OUT BACK, GETTING BEATEN STUPID BY A GANG OF DOORMEN THE SIZE OF BEER TRUCKS.
THIS TIME I'M PLAYING IT SMART.

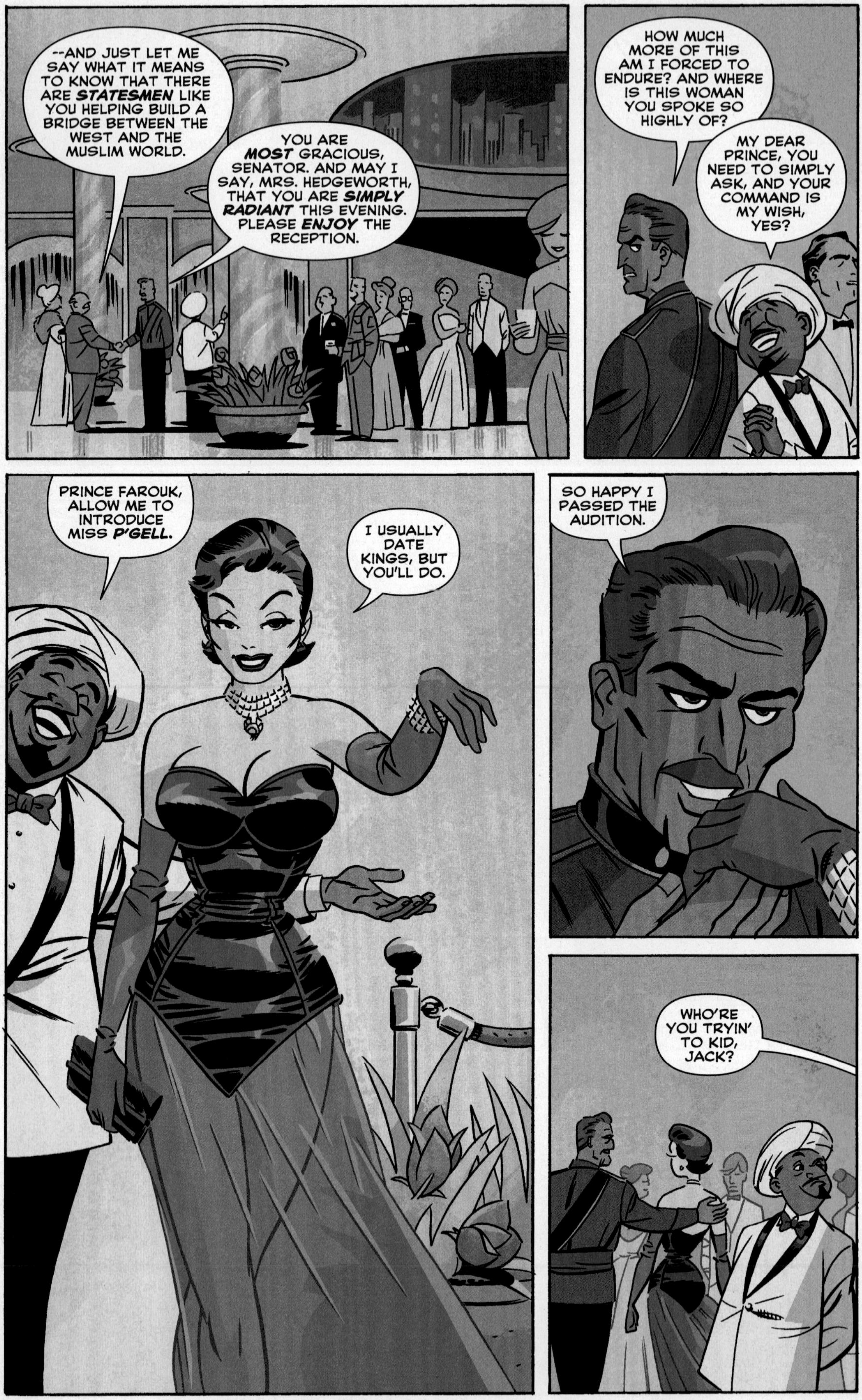
--AND JUST LET ME SAY WHAT IT MEANS TO KNOW THAT THERE ARE STATESMEN LIKE YOU HELPING BUILD A BRIDGE BETWEEN THE WEST AND THE MUSLIM WORLD.
YOU ARE MOST GRACIOUS, SENATOR. AND MAY I SAY, MRS. HEDGEWORTH, THAT YOU ARE SIMPLY RADIANT THIS EVENING. PLEASE ENJOY THE RECEPTION.
HOW MUCH MORE OF THIS AM I FORCED TO ENDURE? AND WHERE IS THIS WOMAN YOU SPOKE SO HIGHLY OF?
MY DEAR PRINCE, YOU NEED TO SIMPLY ASK, AND YOUR COMMAND IS MY WISH, YES?
PRINCE FAROUK, ALLOW ME TO INTRODUCE MISS P'GELL.
I USUALLY DATE KINGS, BUT YOU'LL DO.
SO HAPPY I PASSED THE AUDITION.
WHO'RE YOU TRYIN' TO KID, JACK?

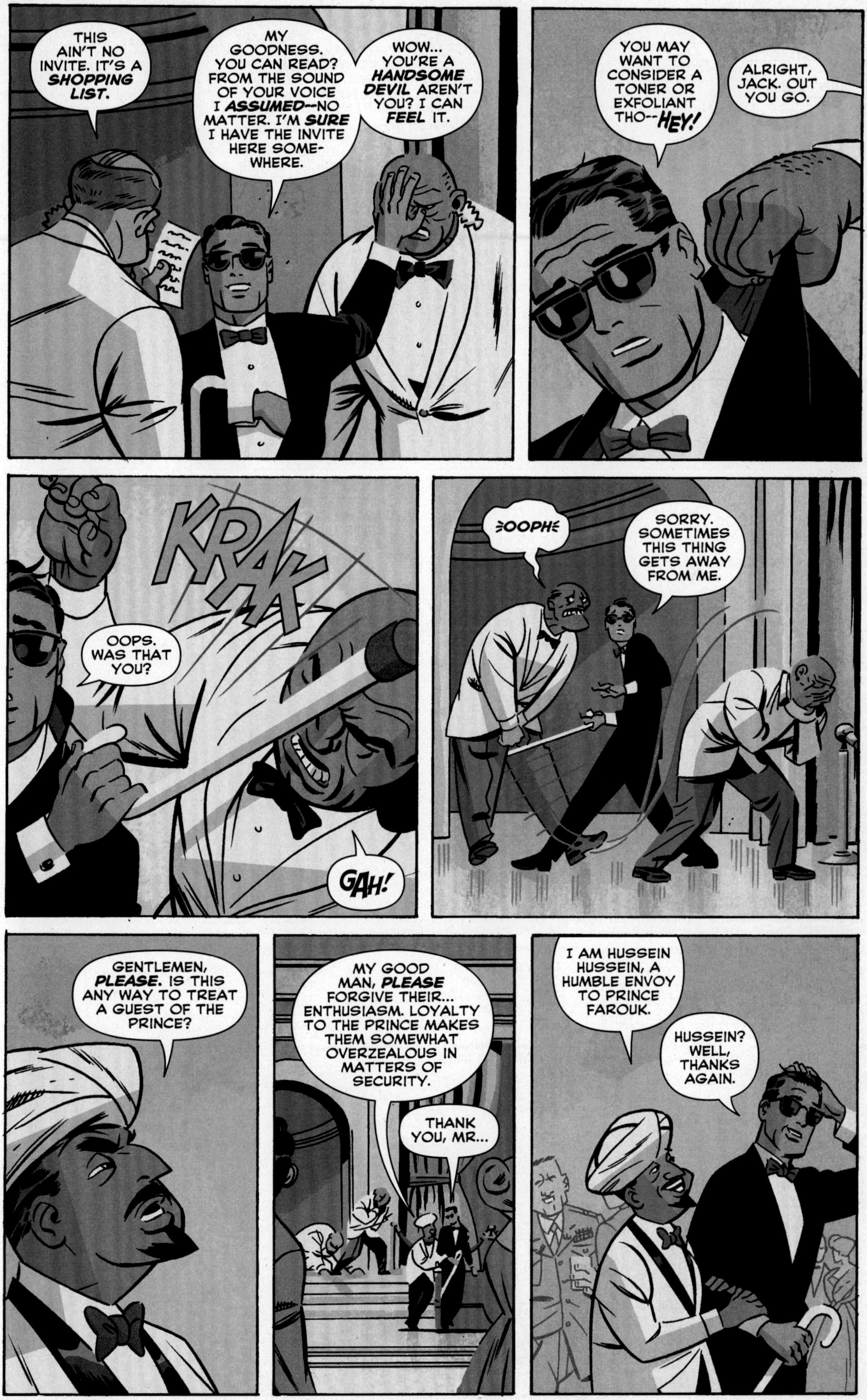
THIS AIN'T NO INVITE. IT'S A SHOPPING LIST.
MY GOODNESS. YOU CAN READ? FROM THE SOUND OF YOUR VOICE I ASSUMED--NO MATTER. I'M SURE I HAVE THE INVITE HERE SOMEWHERE.
WOW... YOU'RE A HANDSOME DEVIL AREN'T YOU? I CAN FEEL IT.
YOU MAY WANT TO CONSIDER A TONER OR EXFOLIANT THO--HEY!
ALRIGHT, JACK. OUT YOU GO.
KRAK
OOPS. WAS THAT YOU?
GAH!
OOPH
SORRY. SOMETIMES THIS THING GETS AWAY FROM ME.
GENTLEMEN, PLEASE. IS THIS ANY WAY TO TREAT A GUEST OF THE PRINCE?
MY GOOD MAN, PLEASE FORGIVE THEIR... ENTHUSIASM. LOYALTY TO THE PRINCE MAKES THEM SOMEWHAT OVERZEALOUS IN MATTERS OF SECURITY.
THANK YOU, MR...
I AM HUSSEIN HUSSEIN, A HUMBLE ENVOY TO PRINCE FAROUK.
HUSSEIN? WELL, THANKS AGAIN.

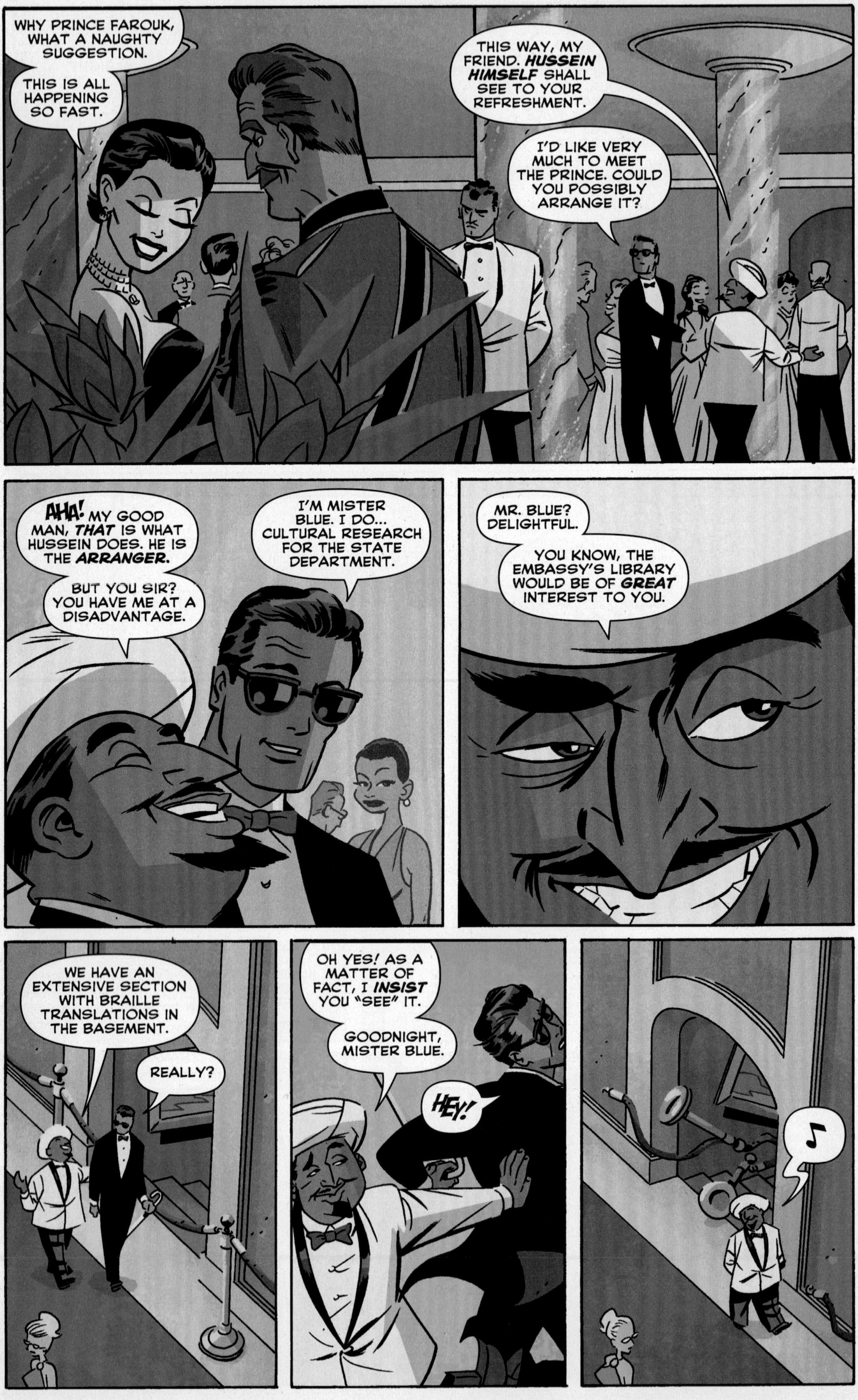
WHY PRINCE FAROUK, WHAT A NAUGHTY SUGGESTION.
THIS IS ALL HAPPENING SO FAST.
THIS WAY, MY FRIEND. **HUSSEIN HIMSELF** SHALL SEE TO YOUR REFRESHMENT.
I'D LIKE VERY MUCH TO MEET THE PRINCE. COULD YOU POSSIBLY ARRANGE IT?
AHA! MY GOOD MAN, **THAT** IS WHAT HUSSEIN DOES. HE IS THE **ARRANGER.**
BUT YOU SIR? YOU HAVE ME AT A DISADVANTAGE.
I'M MISTER BLUE. I DO... CULTURAL RESEARCH FOR THE STATE DEPARTMENT.
MR. BLUE? DELIGHTFUL.
YOU KNOW, THE EMBASSY'S LIBRARY WOULD BE OF **GREAT** INTEREST TO YOU.
WE HAVE AN EXTENSIVE SECTION WITH BRAILLE TRANSLATIONS IN THE BASEMENT.
REALLY?
OH YES! AS A MATTER OF FACT, I **INSIST** YOU "SEE" IT.
GOODNIGHT, MISTER BLUE.
HEY!
♪

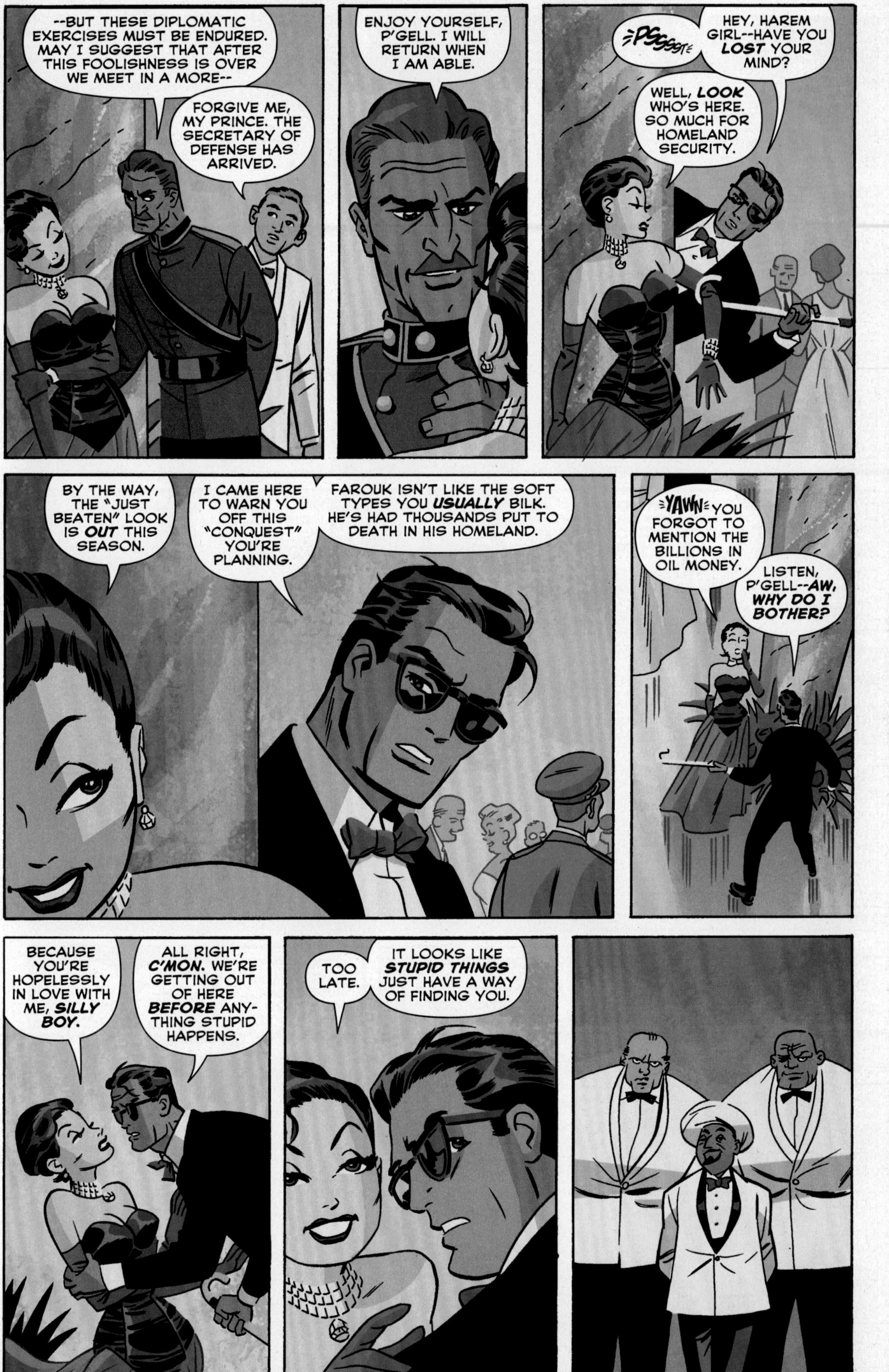
--BUT THESE DIPLOMATIC EXERCISES MUST BE ENDURED. MAY I SUGGEST THAT AFTER THIS FOOLISHNESS IS OVER WE MEET IN A MORE--
FORGIVE ME, MY PRINCE. THE SECRETARY OF DEFENSE HAS ARRIVED.
ENJOY YOURSELF, P'GELL. I WILL RETURN WHEN I AM ABLE.
PSSSSST
HEY, HAREM GIRL--HAVE YOU LOST YOUR MIND?
WELL, LOOK WHO'S HERE. SO MUCH FOR HOMELAND SECURITY.
BY THE WAY, THE "JUST BEATEN" LOOK IS OUT THIS SEASON.
I CAME HERE TO WARN YOU OFF THIS "CONQUEST" YOU'RE PLANNING.
FAROUK ISN'T LIKE THE SOFT TYPES YOU USUALLY BILK. HE'S HAD THOUSANDS PUT TO DEATH IN HIS HOMELAND.
YAWN YOU FORGOT TO MENTION THE BILLIONS IN OIL MONEY.
LISTEN, P'GELL--AW, WHY DO I BOTHER?
BECAUSE YOU'RE HOPELESSLY IN LOVE WITH ME, SILLY BOY.
ALL RIGHT, C'MON. WE'RE GETTING OUT OF HERE BEFORE ANY-THING STUPID HAPPENS.
TOO LATE.
IT LOOKS LIKE STUPID THINGS JUST HAVE A WAY OF FINDING YOU.

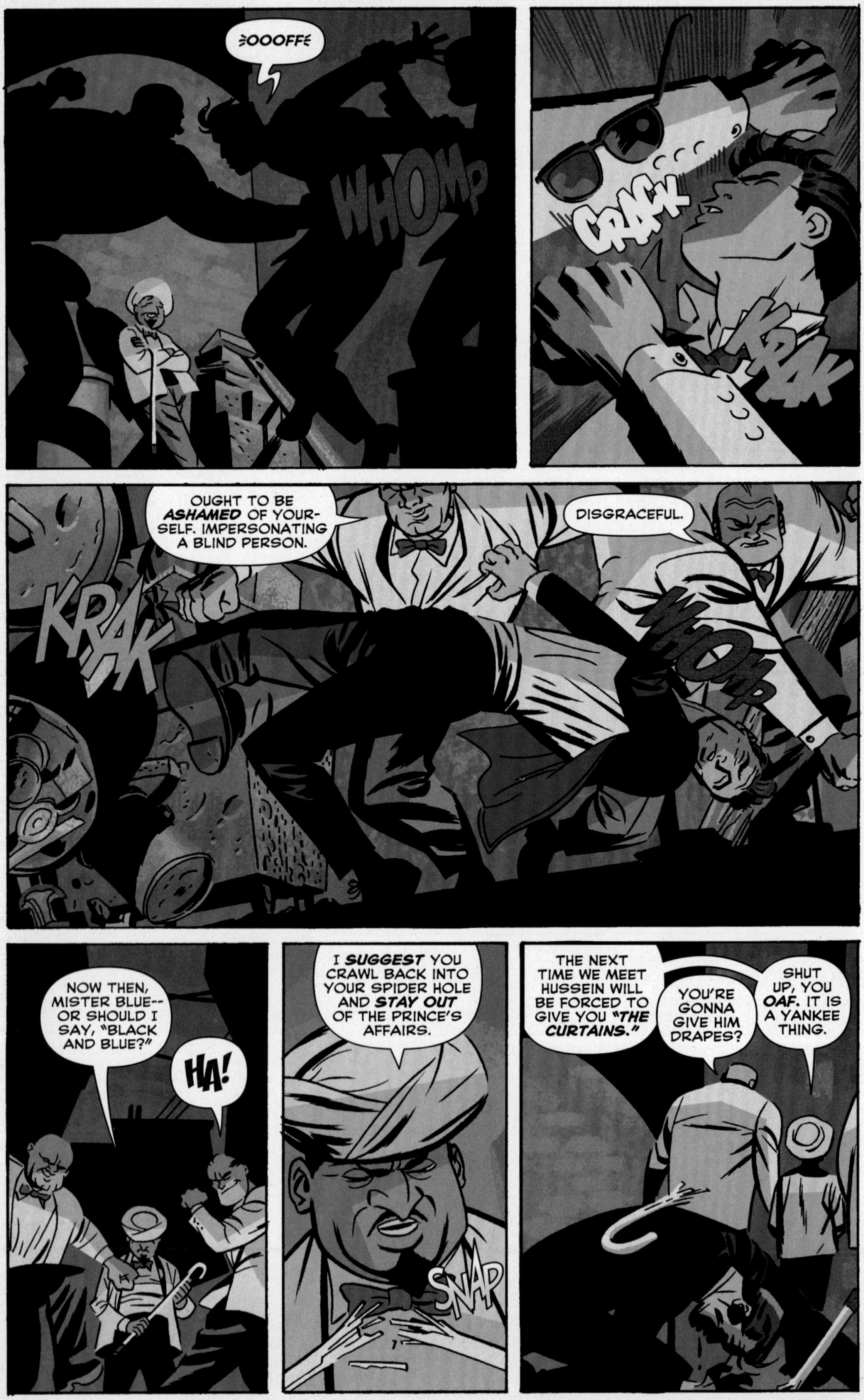
OOOFF
WHOMP
CRACK
KRAK
OUGHT TO BE ASHAMED OF YOURSELF. IMPERSONATING A BLIND PERSON.
DISGRACEFUL.
KRAK
WHOMP
NOW THEN, MISTER BLUE-- OR SHOULD I SAY, "BLACK AND BLUE?"
HA!
I SUGGEST YOU CRAWL BACK INTO YOUR SPIDER HOLE AND STAY OUT OF THE PRINCE'S AFFAIRS.
SNAP
THE NEXT TIME WE MEET HUSSEIN WILL BE FORCED TO GIVE YOU "THE CURTAINS."
YOU'RE GONNA GIVE HIM DRAPES?
SHUT UP, YOU OAF. IT IS A YANKEE THING.

YOU'RE IN *THE EMERGENCY ROOM,* WITH PENNY WOLFGANG.

TODAY, WE HAVE *LIVE COVERAGE* OF PRINCE FAROUK'S MARRIAGE TO THE CONTROVERSIAL SOCIALITE KNOWN AS P'GELL.

AFTER MEETING HERE IN CENTRAL CITY *JUST* TWO WEEKS AGO, THE COUPLE HAS BEEN *VIRTUALLY* INSEPARABLE.

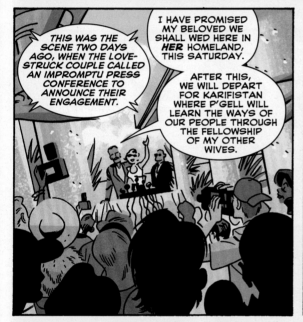

*THIS WAS THE SCENE TWO DAYS AGO, WHEN THE LOVE-STRUCK COUPLE CALLED AN IMPROMPTU PRESS CONFERENCE TO ANNOUNCE THEIR ENGAGEMENT.*

I HAVE PROMISED MY BELOVED WE SHALL WED HERE IN *HER* HOMELAND, THIS SATURDAY.

AFTER THIS, WE WILL DEPART FOR KARIFISTAN WHERE P'GELL WILL LEARN THE WAYS OF OUR PEOPLE THROUGH THE FELLOWSHIP OF MY OTHER WIVES.

*I SAT DOWN WITH THE LOVELY BRIDE-TO-BE YESTERDAY, HERE AT NNN.*

I'M CURIOUS, P'GELL. *WHY* WOULD YOU GIVE UP YOUR FREEDOM *AND* RELIGION TO JOIN THIS MAN'S HAREM OF WIVES?

HAVE YOU MET THE PRINCE?

HE'S A *VERY* POWERFUL AND MAGNETIC MAN. AS FOR HIS OTHER WIVES...

...LET'S JUST SAY I'M CONFIDENT THAT MY *LOVE* FOR THE PRINCE WILL DISTINGUISH ME.

I'M GETTING WORD THAT THE CEREMONY IS LETTING OUT. WE NOW GO *LIVE* TO THE EMBASSY.

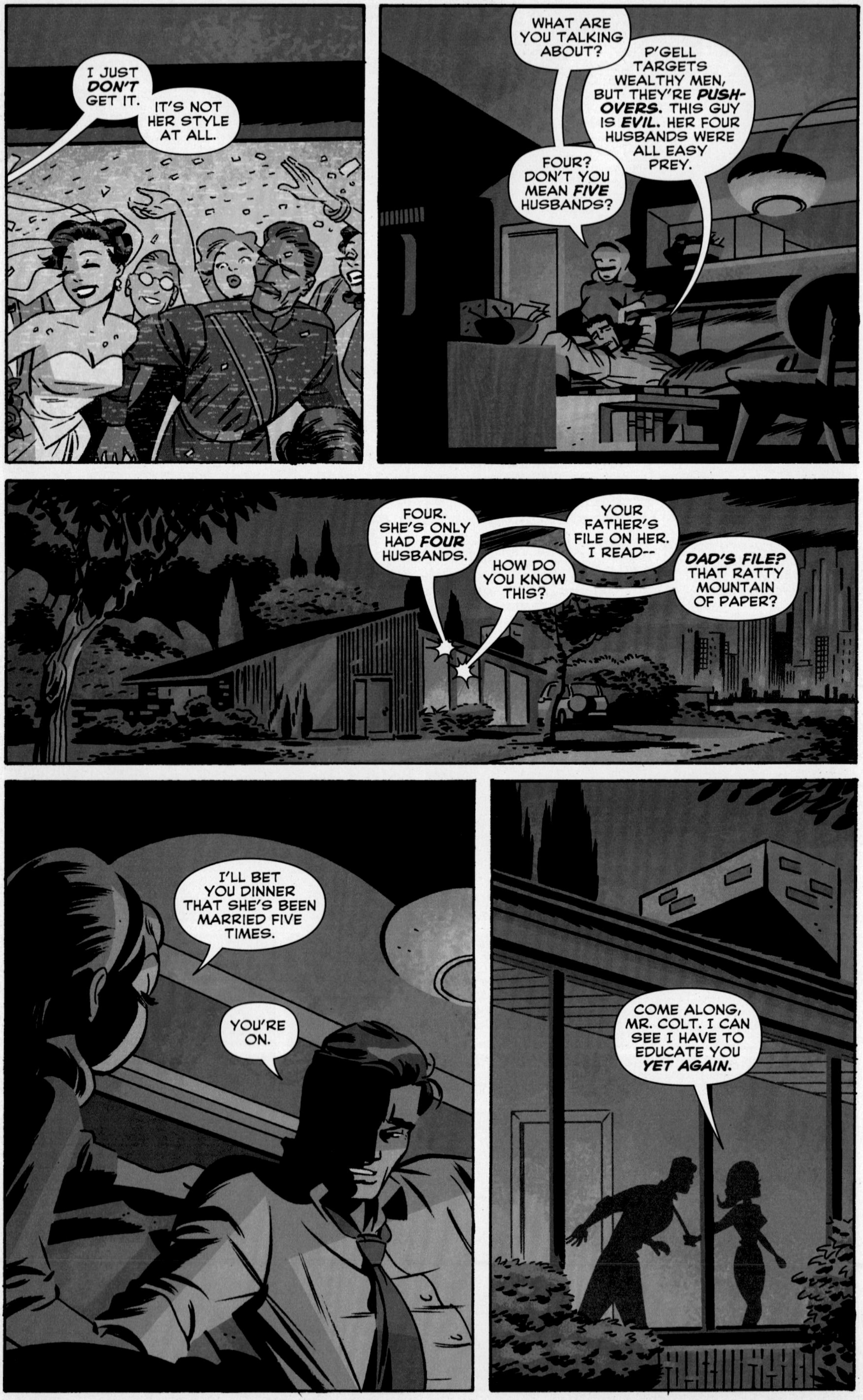

I JUST **DON'T** GET IT.
IT'S NOT HER STYLE AT ALL.
WHAT ARE YOU TALKING ABOUT?
P'GELL TARGETS WEALTHY MEN, BUT THEY'RE **PUSH-OVERS.** THIS GUY IS **EVIL.** HER FOUR HUSBANDS WERE ALL EASY PREY.
FOUR? DON'T YOU MEAN **FIVE** HUSBANDS?
FOUR. SHE'S ONLY HAD **FOUR** HUSBANDS.
YOUR FATHER'S FILE ON HER. I READ--
HOW DO YOU KNOW THIS?
**DAD'S FILE?** THAT RATTY MOUNTAIN OF PAPER?
I'LL BET YOU DINNER THAT SHE'S BEEN MARRIED FIVE TIMES.
YOU'RE ON.
COME ALONG, MR. COLT. I CAN SEE I HAVE TO EDUCATE YOU **YET AGAIN.**

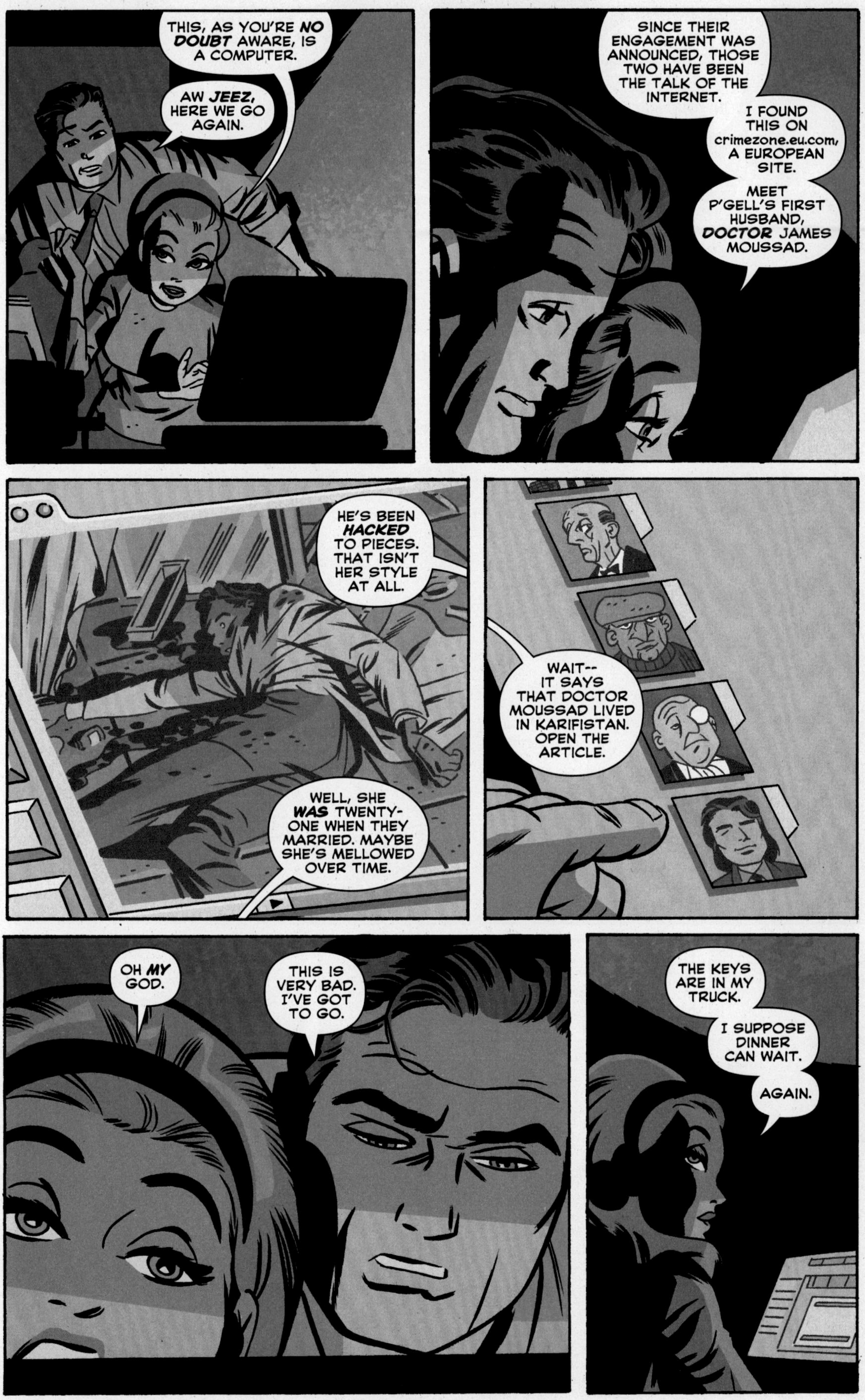
THIS, AS YOU'RE NO DOUBT AWARE, IS A COMPUTER.
AW JEEZ, HERE WE GO AGAIN.
SINCE THEIR ENGAGEMENT WAS ANNOUNCED, THOSE TWO HAVE BEEN THE TALK OF THE INTERNET.
I FOUND THIS ON crimezone.eu.com, A EUROPEAN SITE.
MEET P'GELL'S FIRST HUSBAND, DOCTOR JAMES MOUSSAD.
HE'S BEEN HACKED TO PIECES. THAT ISN'T HER STYLE AT ALL.
WELL, SHE WAS TWENTY-ONE WHEN THEY MARRIED. MAYBE SHE'S MELLOWED OVER TIME.
WAIT-- IT SAYS THAT DOCTOR MOUSSAD LIVED IN KARIFISTAN. OPEN THE ARTICLE.
OH MY GOD.
THIS IS VERY BAD. I'VE GOT TO GO.
THE KEYS ARE IN MY TRUCK.
I SUPPOSE DINNER CAN WAIT.
AGAIN.

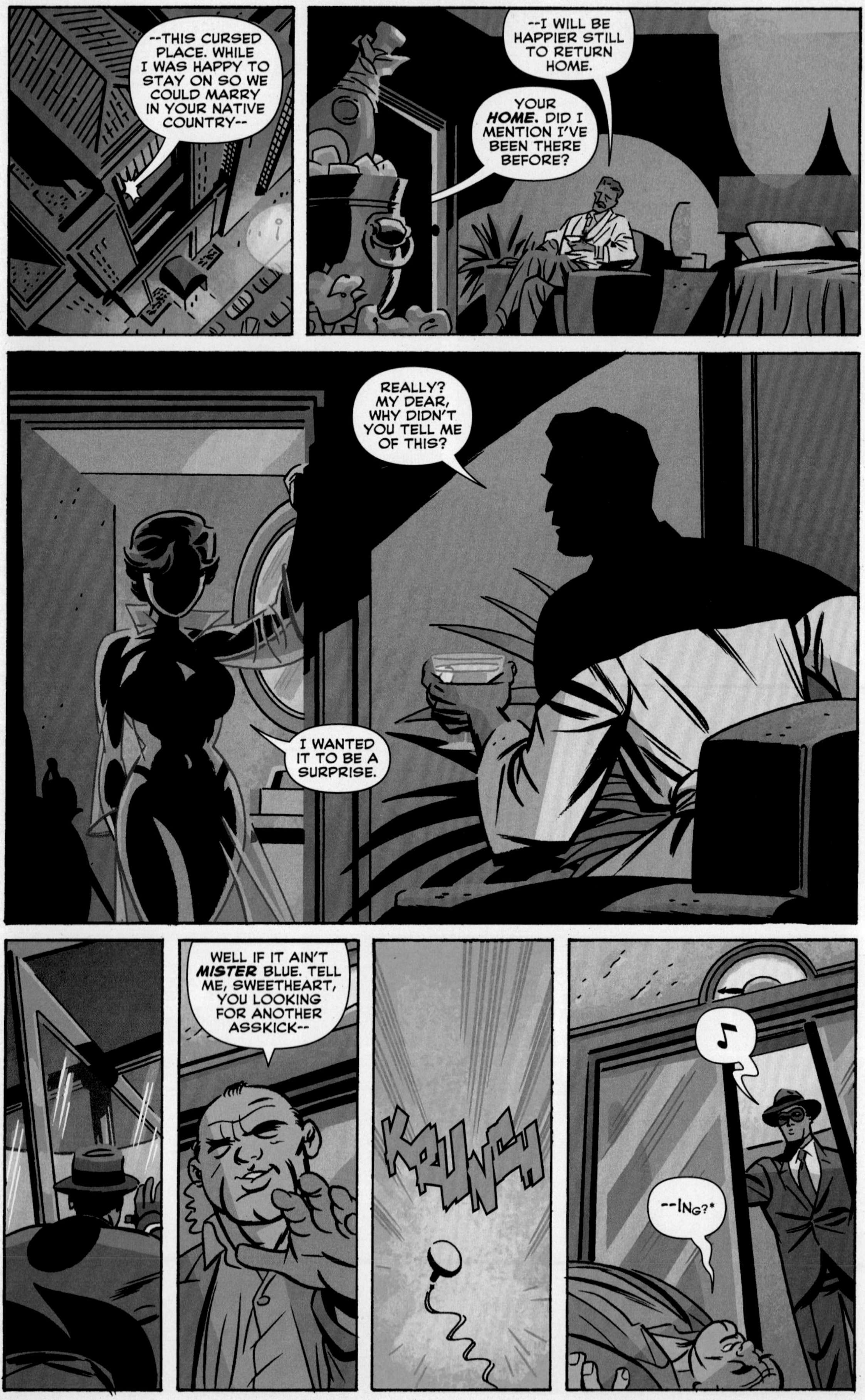
--THIS CURSED PLACE. WHILE I WAS HAPPY TO STAY ON SO WE COULD MARRY IN YOUR NATIVE COUNTRY--
--I WILL BE HAPPIER STILL TO RETURN HOME.
YOUR HOME. DID I MENTION I'VE BEEN THERE BEFORE?
REALLY? MY DEAR, WHY DIDN'T YOU TELL ME OF THIS?
I WANTED IT TO BE A SURPRISE.
WELL IF IT AIN'T MISTER BLUE. TELL ME, SWEETHEART, YOU LOOKING FOR ANOTHER ASSKICK--
KRUNCH
♪
--ING?*

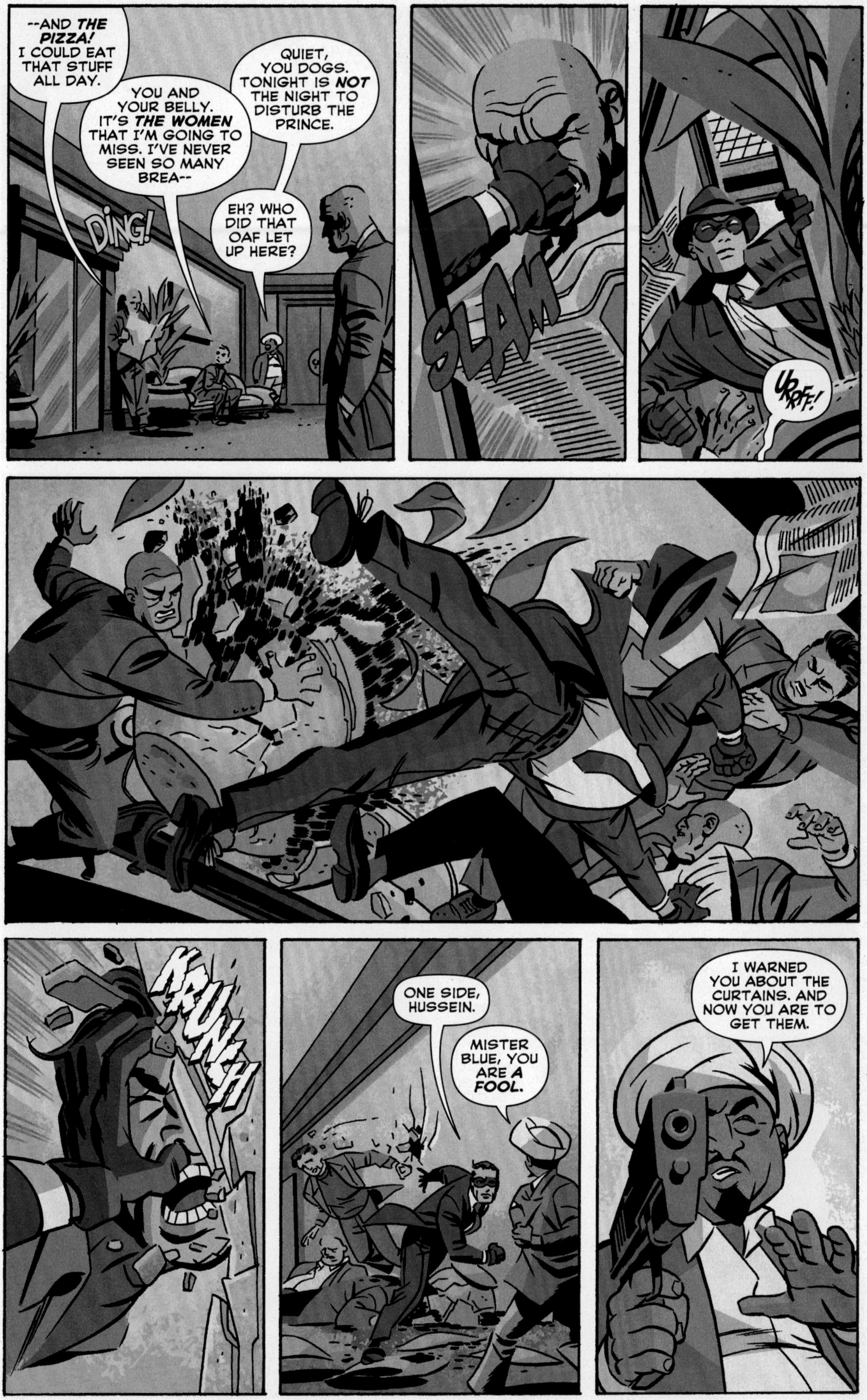
--AND THE PIZZA! I COULD EAT THAT STUFF ALL DAY.
YOU AND YOUR BELLY. IT'S THE WOMEN THAT I'M GOING TO MISS. I'VE NEVER SEEN SO MANY BREA--
DING!
QUIET, YOU DOGS. TONIGHT IS NOT THE NIGHT TO DISTURB THE PRINCE.
EH? WHO DID THAT OAF LET UP HERE?
SLAM
URRFF!
KRUNCH
ONE SIDE, HUSSEIN.
MISTER BLUE, YOU ARE A FOOL.
I WARNED YOU ABOUT THE CURTAINS. AND NOW YOU ARE TO GET THEM.

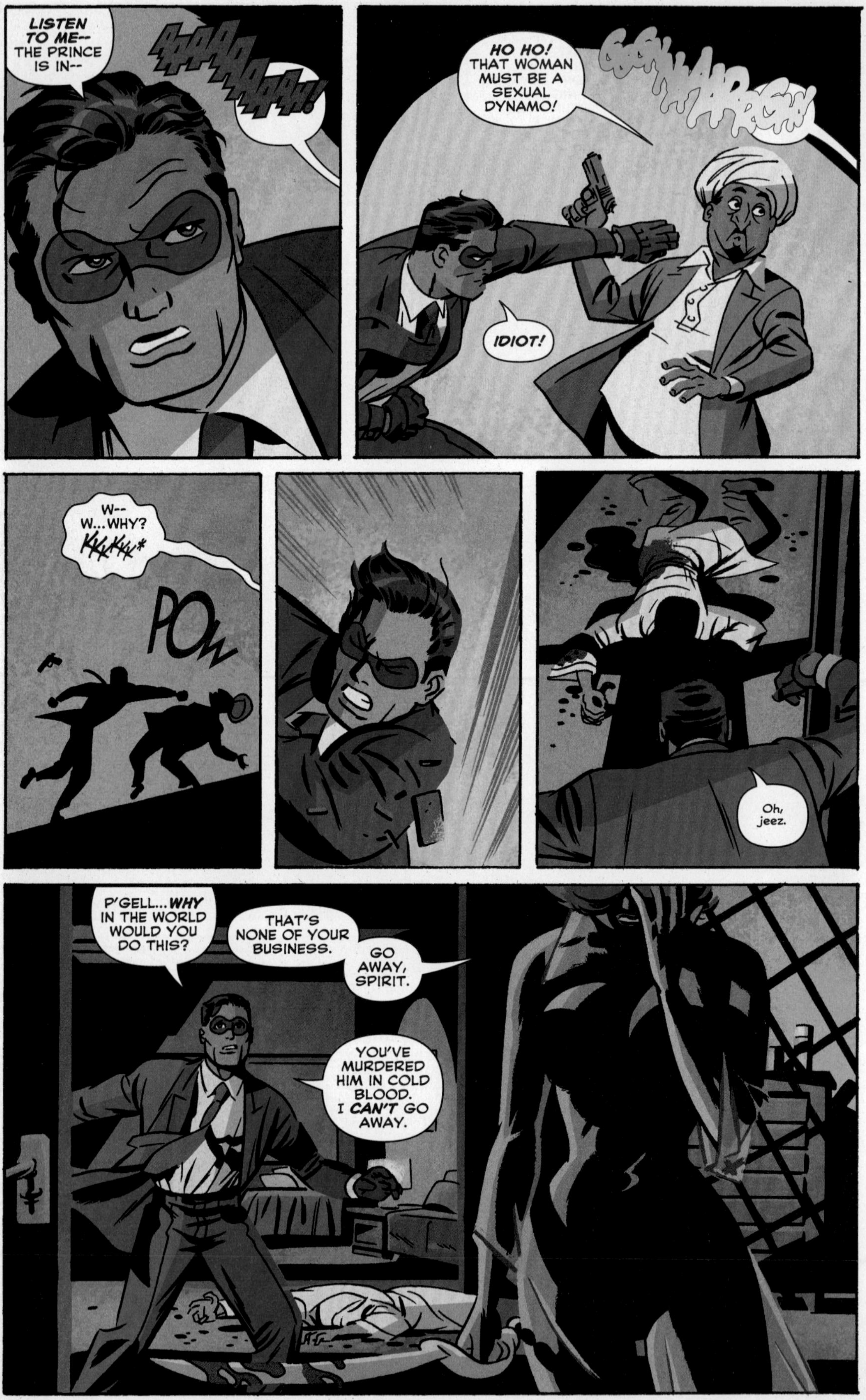
LISTEN TO ME-- THE PRINCE IS IN--
HO HO! THAT WOMAN MUST BE A SEXUAL DYNAMO!
IDIOT!
W-- W...WHY?
POW
Oh, jeez.
P'GELL...WHY IN THE WORLD WOULD YOU DO THIS?
THAT'S NONE OF YOUR BUSINESS.
GO AWAY, SPIRIT.
YOU'VE MURDERED HIM IN COLD BLOOD. I CAN'T GO AWAY.

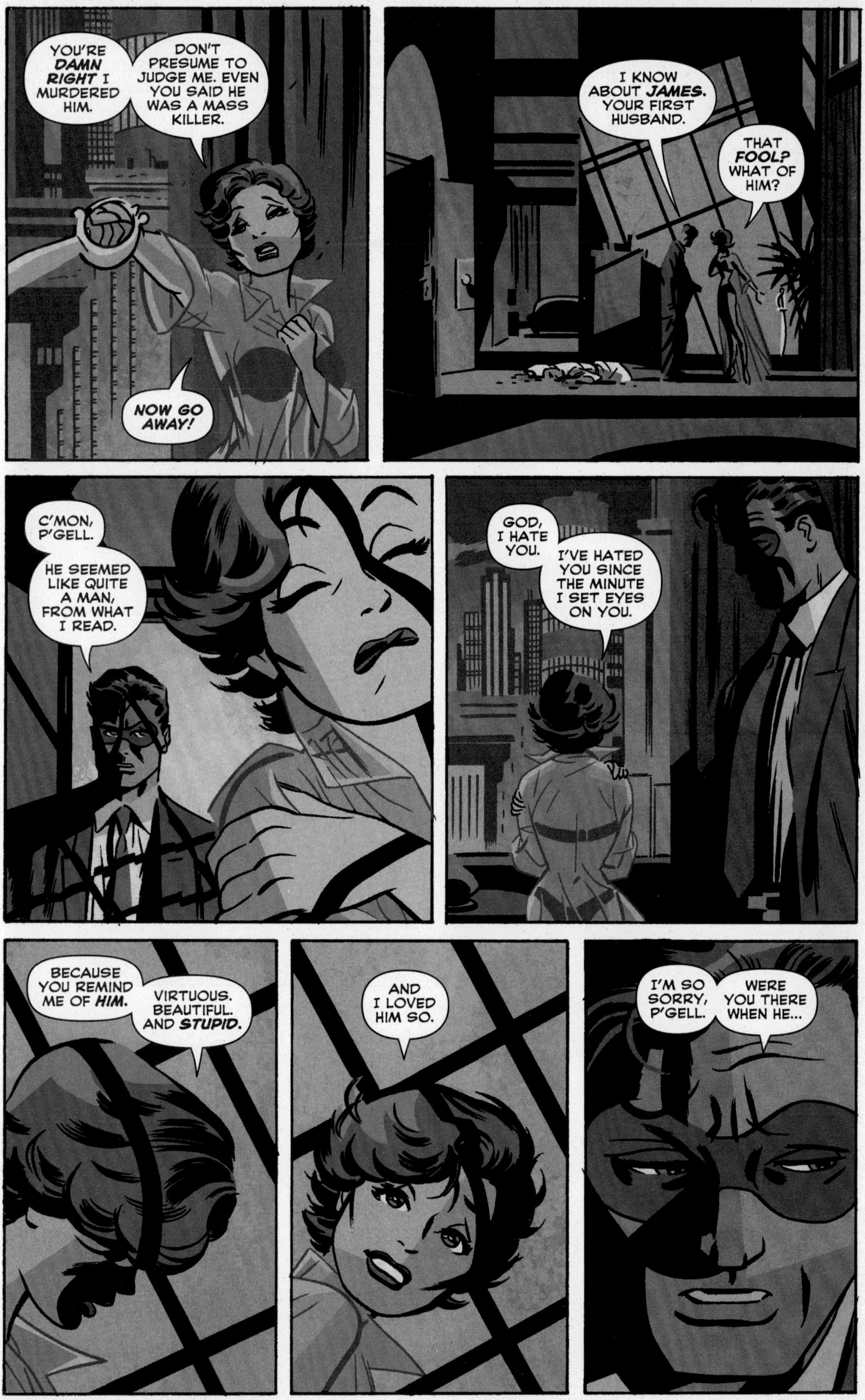
YOU'RE DAMN RIGHT I MURDERED HIM.
DON'T PRESUME TO JUDGE ME. EVEN YOU SAID HE WAS A MASS KILLER.
NOW GO AWAY!
I KNOW ABOUT JAMES. YOUR FIRST HUSBAND.
THAT FOOL? WHAT OF HIM?
C'MON, P'GELL.
HE SEEMED LIKE QUITE A MAN, FROM WHAT I READ.
GOD, I HATE YOU.
I'VE HATED YOU SINCE THE MINUTE I SET EYES ON YOU.
BECAUSE YOU REMIND ME OF HIM.
VIRTUOUS. BEAUTIFUL. AND STUPID.
AND I LOVED HIM SO.
I'M SO SORRY, P'GELL.
WERE YOU THERE WHEN HE...

DIED? NO. BUT I SENT HIM TO HIS DEATH.

I'd met James when I was hiking around the world. One of those idiotic trips you make when you're fresh out of school.

He was a doctor from a wealthy family, but he chose to run a small clinic in a dangerous region. You know how it is. Romance is more than a word when you're young. We loved and married and I became his partner there.

During our second year, an epidemic was sweeping through the villages in the hills. A frantic boy arrived and begged James to come back with him.

As always, James pulled his medicines together and set out with the boy in his truck. It was the last time I saw him.

The epidemic was staged. It was part of the Prince's "secular cleansing." When James arrived, he was met by the Prince and his murderous army.

Every man, woman and child... my James...all gone.

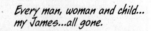

I had to flee for my life, but I knew that if I ever got the opportunity--

I'D WATCH THAT *PIG* DIE FOR WHAT HE DID TO ME.

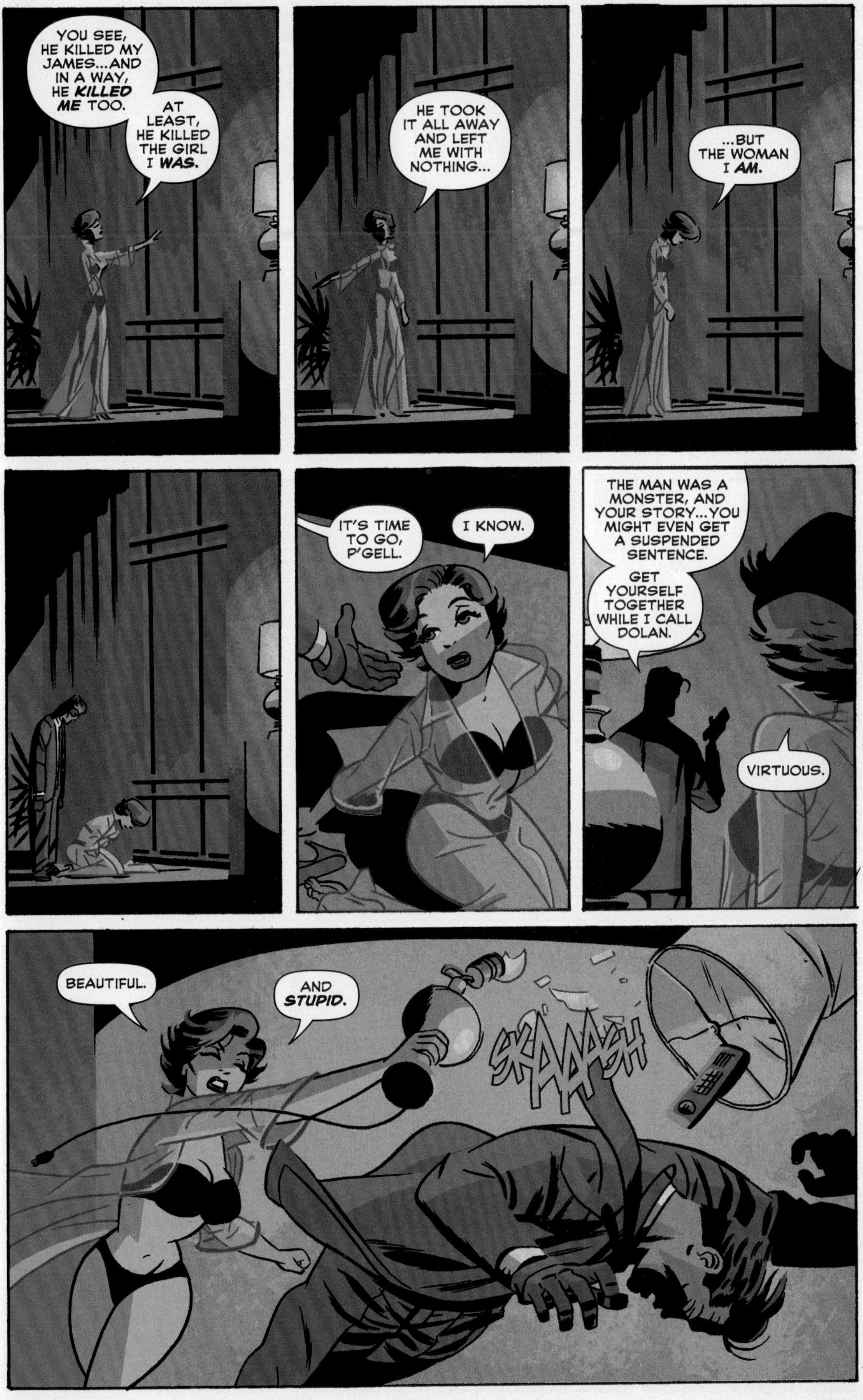
YOU SEE, HE KILLED MY JAMES...AND IN A WAY, HE KILLED ME TOO.
AT LEAST, HE KILLED THE GIRL I WAS.
HE TOOK IT ALL AWAY AND LEFT ME WITH NOTHING...
...BUT THE WOMAN I AM.
IT'S TIME TO GO, P'GELL.
I KNOW.
THE MAN WAS A MONSTER, AND YOUR STORY...YOU MIGHT EVEN GET A SUSPENDED SENTENCE.
GET YOURSELF TOGETHER WHILE I CALL DOLAN.
VIRTUOUS.
BEAUTIFUL.
AND STUPID.
SKAAASH

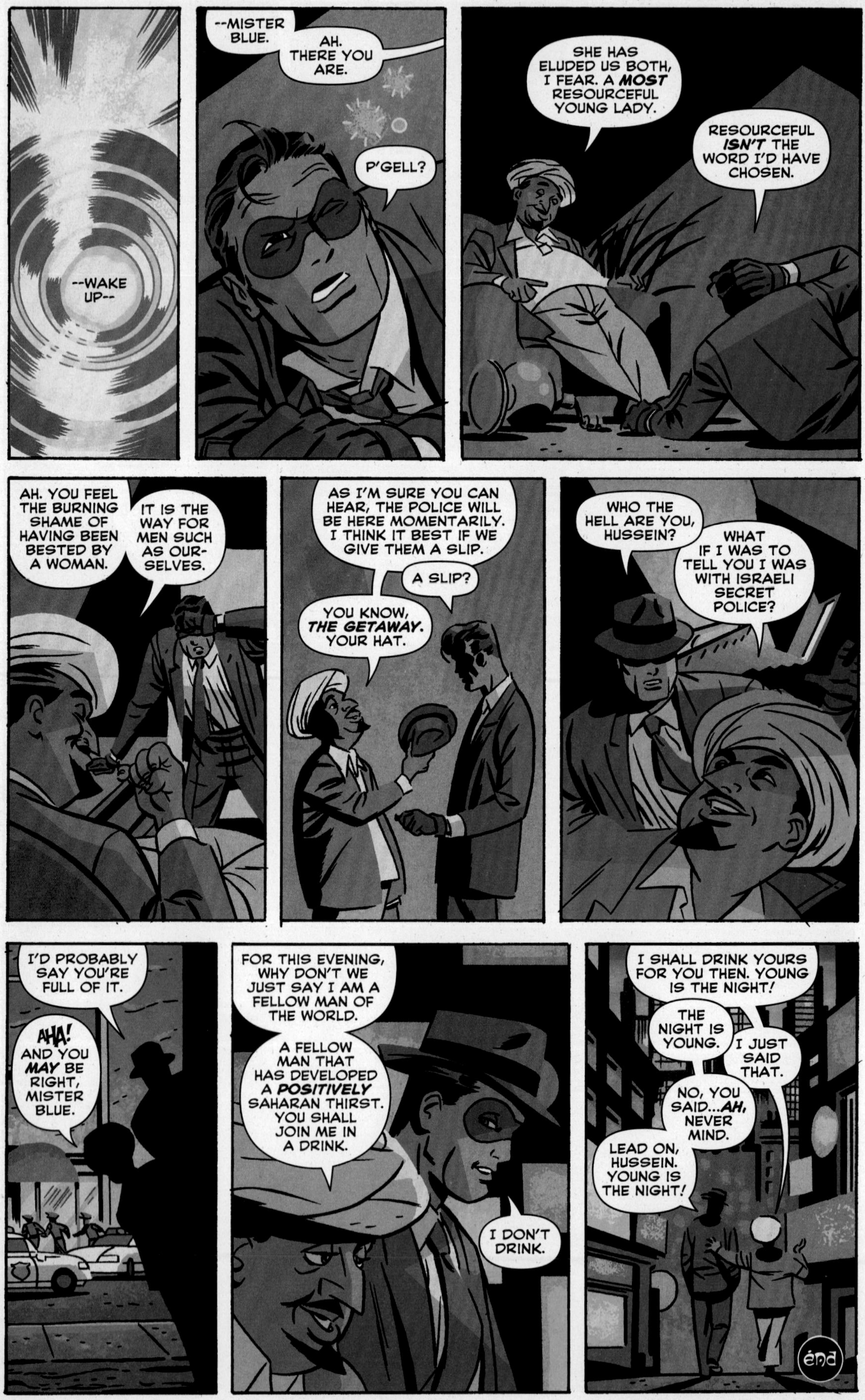
--WAKE UP--
--MISTER BLUE.
AH. THERE YOU ARE.
P'GELL?
SHE HAS ELUDED US BOTH, I FEAR. A MOST RESOURCEFUL YOUNG LADY.
RESOURCEFUL ISN'T THE WORD I'D HAVE CHOSEN.
AH. YOU FEEL THE BURNING SHAME OF HAVING BEEN BESTED BY A WOMAN.
IT IS THE WAY FOR MEN SUCH AS OURSELVES.
AS I'M SURE YOU CAN HEAR, THE POLICE WILL BE HERE MOMENTARILY. I THINK IT BEST IF WE GIVE THEM A SLIP.
A SLIP?
YOU KNOW, THE GETAWAY. YOUR HAT.
WHO THE HELL ARE YOU, HUSSEIN?
WHAT IF I WAS TO TELL YOU I WAS WITH ISRAELI SECRET POLICE?
I'D PROBABLY SAY YOU'RE FULL OF IT.
AHA! AND YOU MAY BE RIGHT, MISTER BLUE.
FOR THIS EVENING, WHY DON'T WE JUST SAY I AM A FELLOW MAN OF THE WORLD.
A FELLOW MAN THAT HAS DEVELOPED A POSITIVELY SAHARAN THIRST. YOU SHALL JOIN ME IN A DRINK.
I DON'T DRINK.
I SHALL DRINK YOURS FOR YOU THEN. YOUNG IS THE NIGHT!
THE NIGHT IS YOUNG.
I JUST SAID THAT.
NO, YOU SAID...AH, NEVER MIND.
LEAD ON, HUSSEIN. YOUNG IS THE NIGHT!
end

# 3

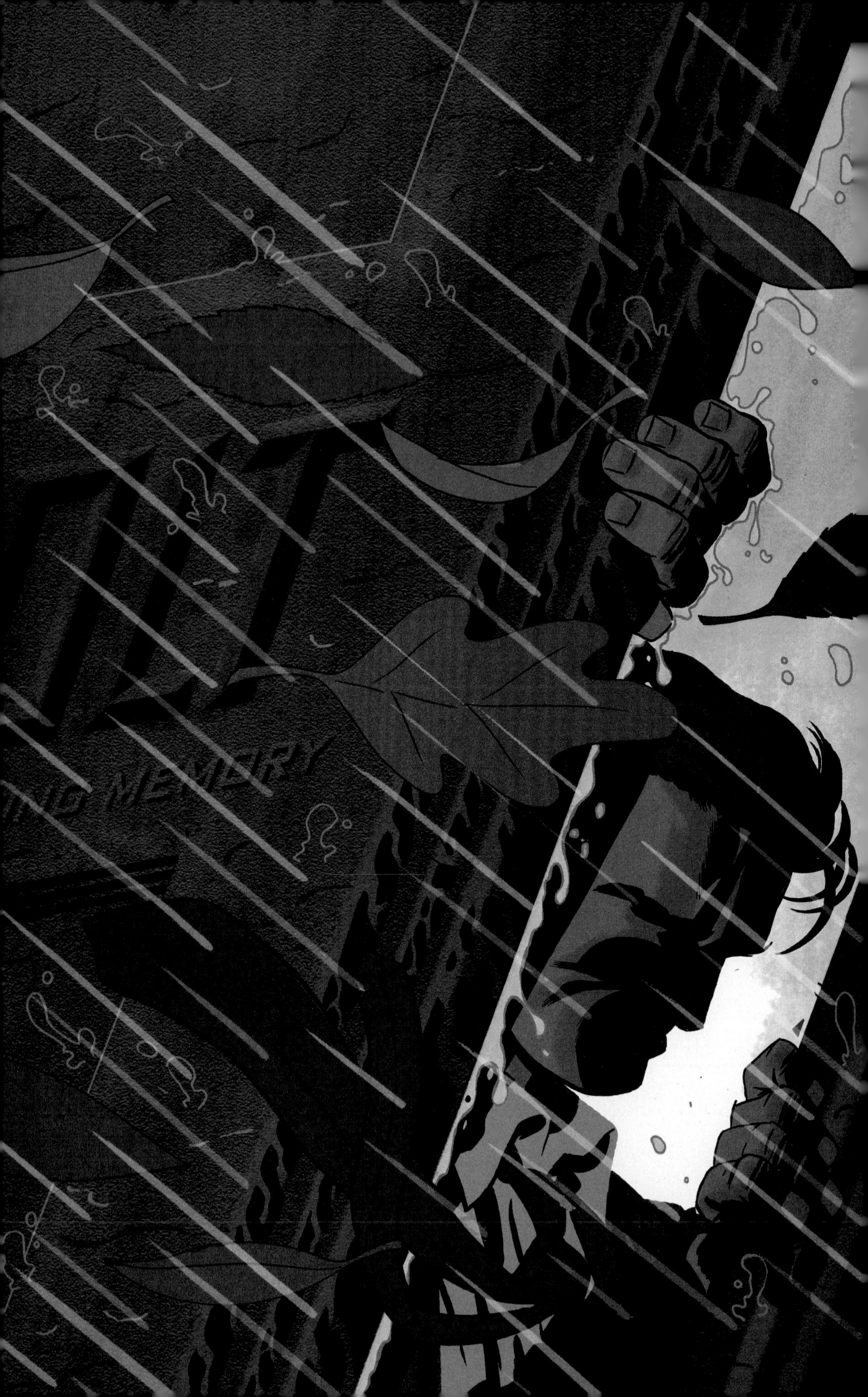
ND MEMORY

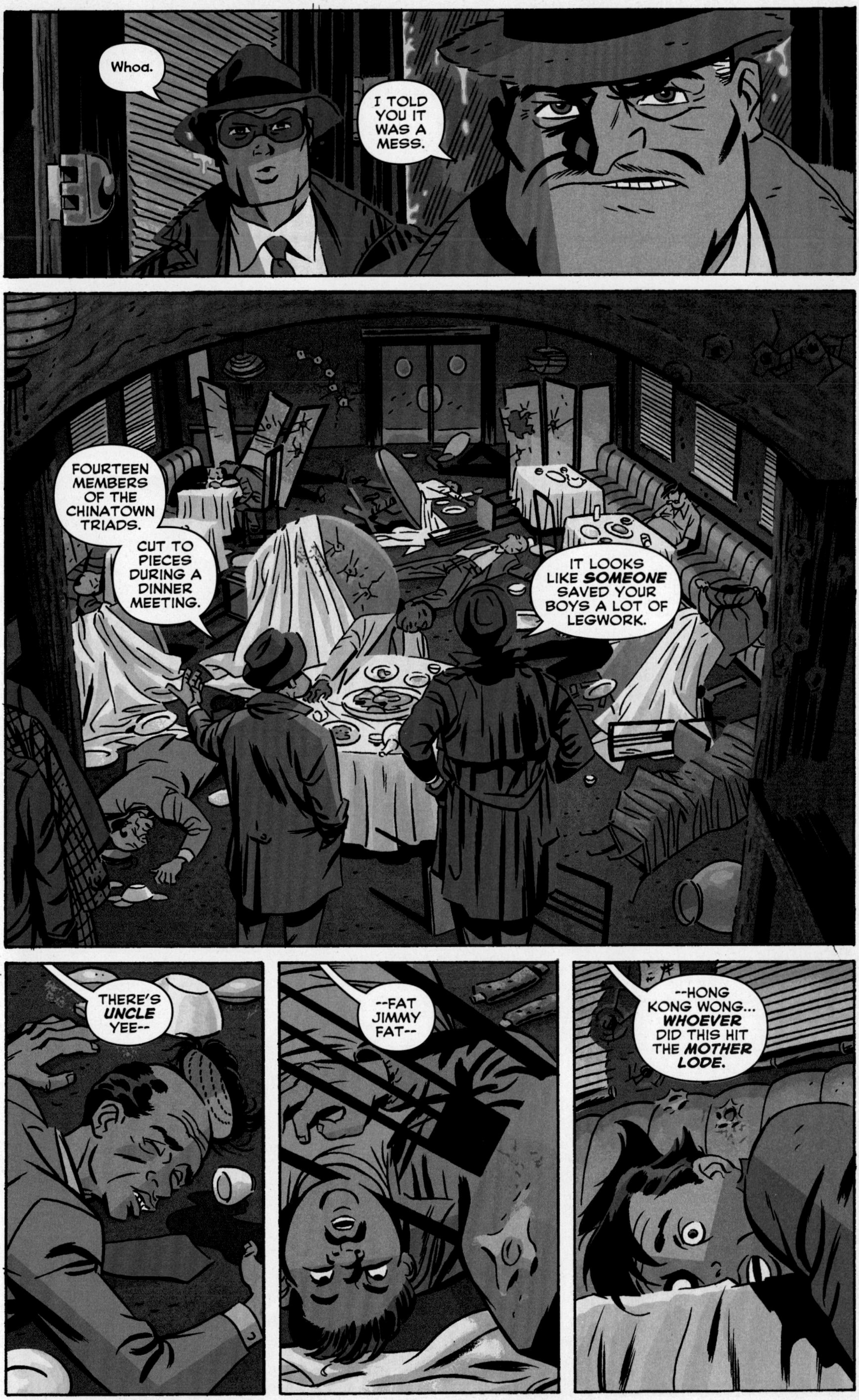
Whoa.
I TOLD YOU IT WAS A MESS.
FOURTEEN MEMBERS OF THE CHINATOWN TRIADS.
CUT TO PIECES DURING A DINNER MEETING.
IT LOOKS LIKE *SOMEONE* SAVED YOUR BOYS A LOT OF LEGWORK.
THERE'S *UNCLE* YEE--
--FAT JIMMY FAT--
--HONG KONG WONG... *WHOEVER* DID THIS HIT THE *MOTHER LODE.*

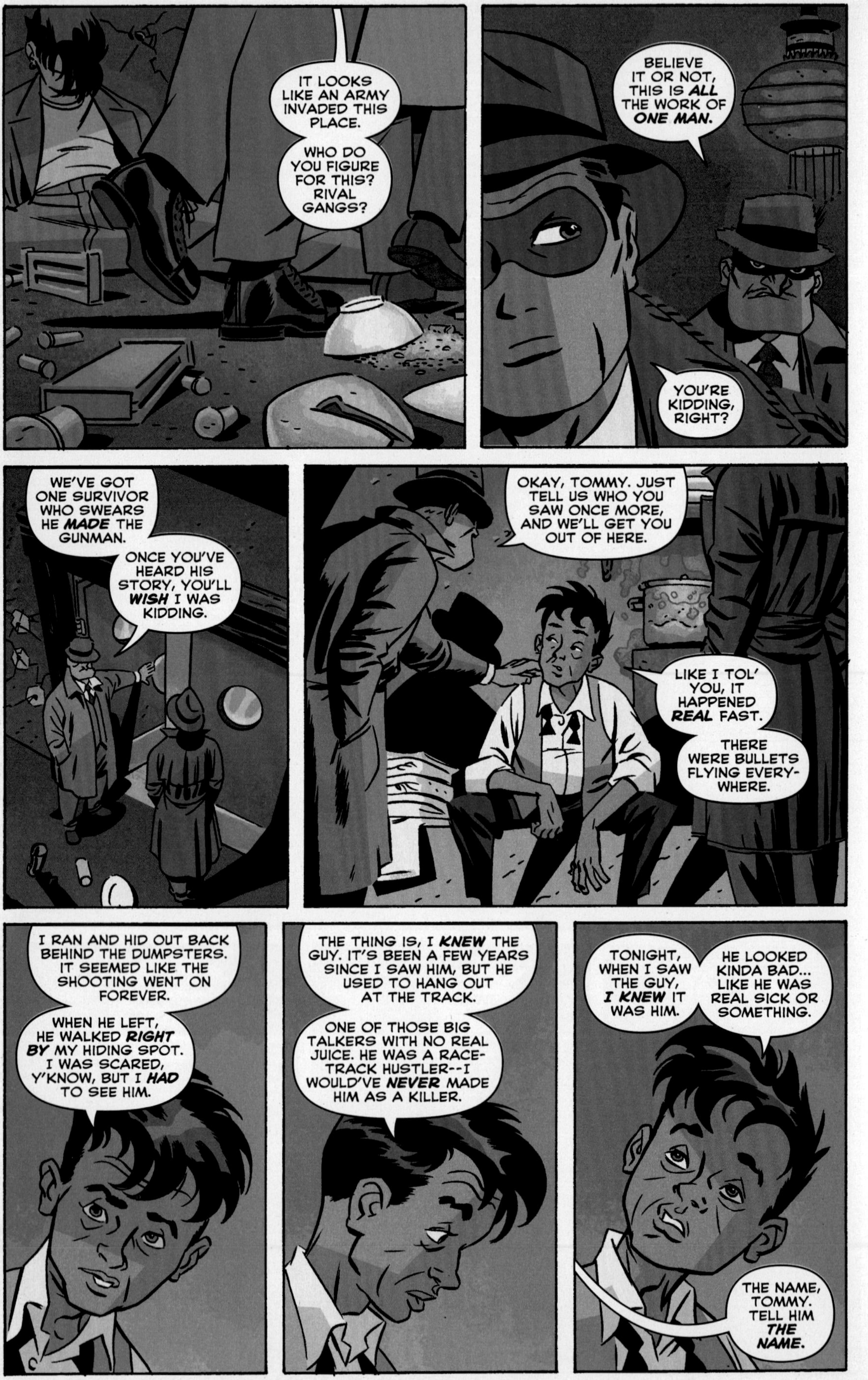
IT LOOKS LIKE AN ARMY INVADED THIS PLACE.
WHO DO YOU FIGURE FOR THIS? RIVAL GANGS?
BELIEVE IT OR NOT, THIS IS ALL THE WORK OF ONE MAN.
YOU'RE KIDDING, RIGHT?
WE'VE GOT ONE SURVIVOR WHO SWEARS HE MADE THE GUNMAN.
ONCE YOU'VE HEARD HIS STORY, YOU'LL WISH I WAS KIDDING.
OKAY, TOMMY. JUST TELL US WHO YOU SAW ONCE MORE, AND WE'LL GET YOU OUT OF HERE.
LIKE I TOL' YOU, IT HAPPENED REAL FAST.
THERE WERE BULLETS FLYING EVERY-WHERE.
I RAN AND HID OUT BACK BEHIND THE DUMPSTERS. IT SEEMED LIKE THE SHOOTING WENT ON FOREVER.
WHEN HE LEFT, HE WALKED RIGHT BY MY HIDING SPOT. I WAS SCARED, Y'KNOW, BUT I HAD TO SEE HIM.
THE THING IS, I KNEW THE GUY. IT'S BEEN A FEW YEARS SINCE I SAW HIM, BUT HE USED TO HANG OUT AT THE TRACK.
ONE OF THOSE BIG TALKERS WITH NO REAL JUICE. HE WAS A RACE-TRACK HUSTLER--I WOULD'VE NEVER MADE HIM AS A KILLER.
TONIGHT, WHEN I SAW THE GUY, I KNEW IT WAS HIM.
HE LOOKED KINDA BAD... LIKE HE WAS REAL SICK OR SOMETHING.
THE NAME, TOMMY. TELL HIM THE NAME.

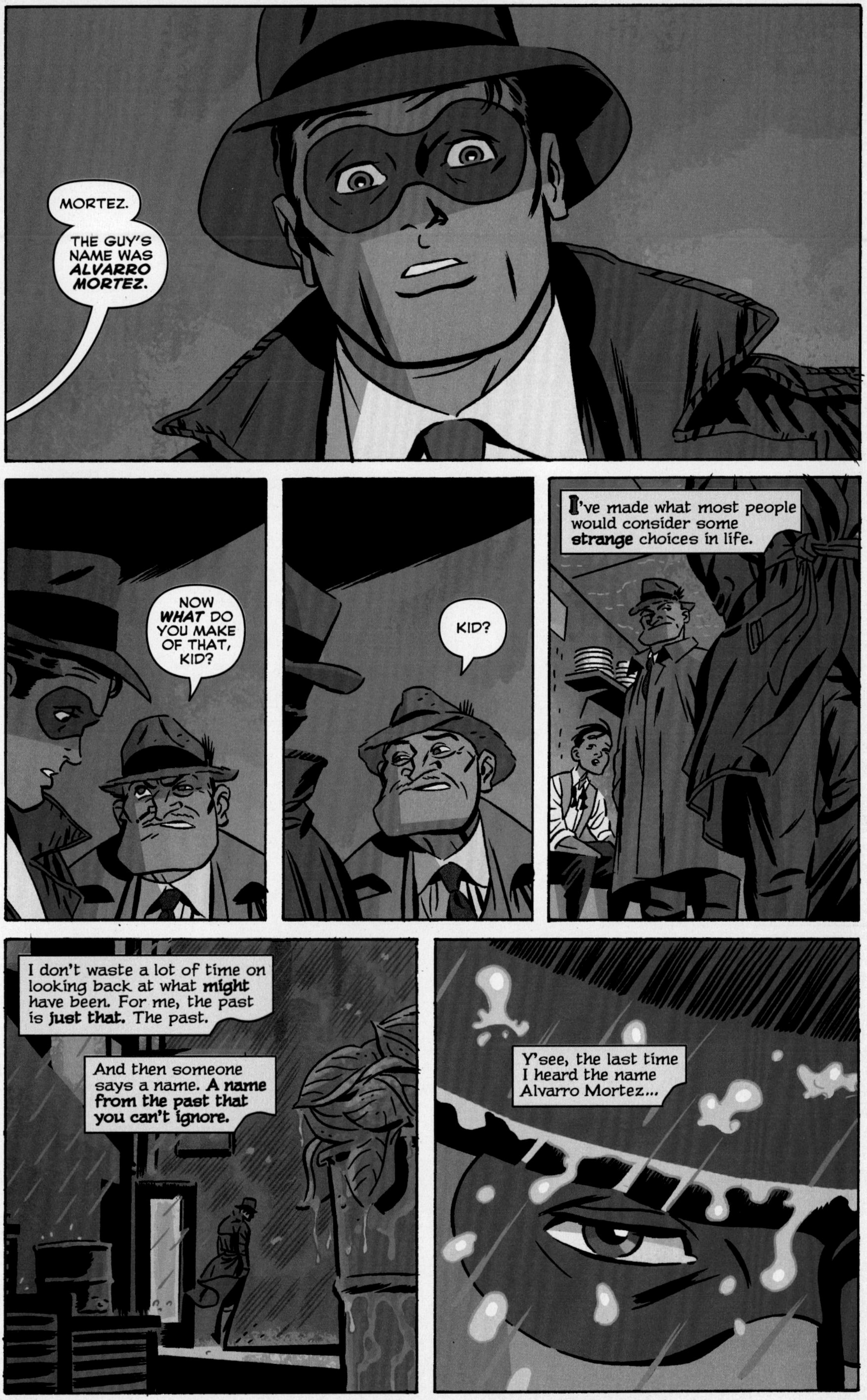
MORTEZ.
THE GUY'S NAME WAS ***ALVARRO MORTEZ.***
NOW ***WHAT*** DO YOU MAKE OF THAT, KID?
KID?
I've made what most people would consider some **strange** choices in life.
I don't waste a lot of time on looking back at what **might** have been. For me, the past is **just that.** The past.
And then someone says a name. **A name from the past that you can't ignore.**
Y'see, the last time I heard the name Alvarro Mortez...

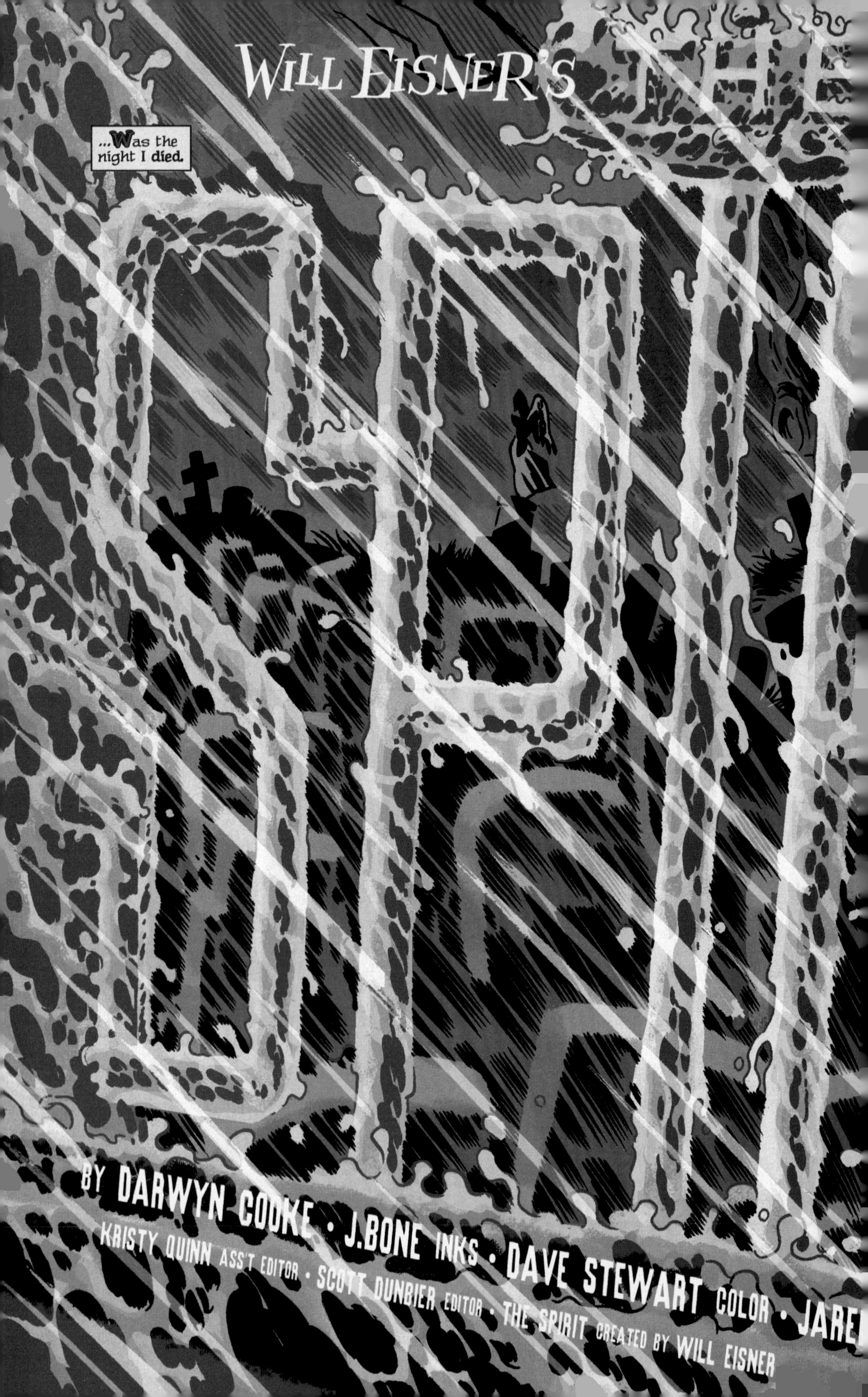
WILL EISNER'S
...Was the night I died.
BY DARWYN COOKE • J.BONE INKS • DAVE STEWART COLOR •
KRISTY QUINN ASS'T EDITOR • SCOTT DUNBIER EDITOR • THE SPIRIT CREATED BY WILL EISNER

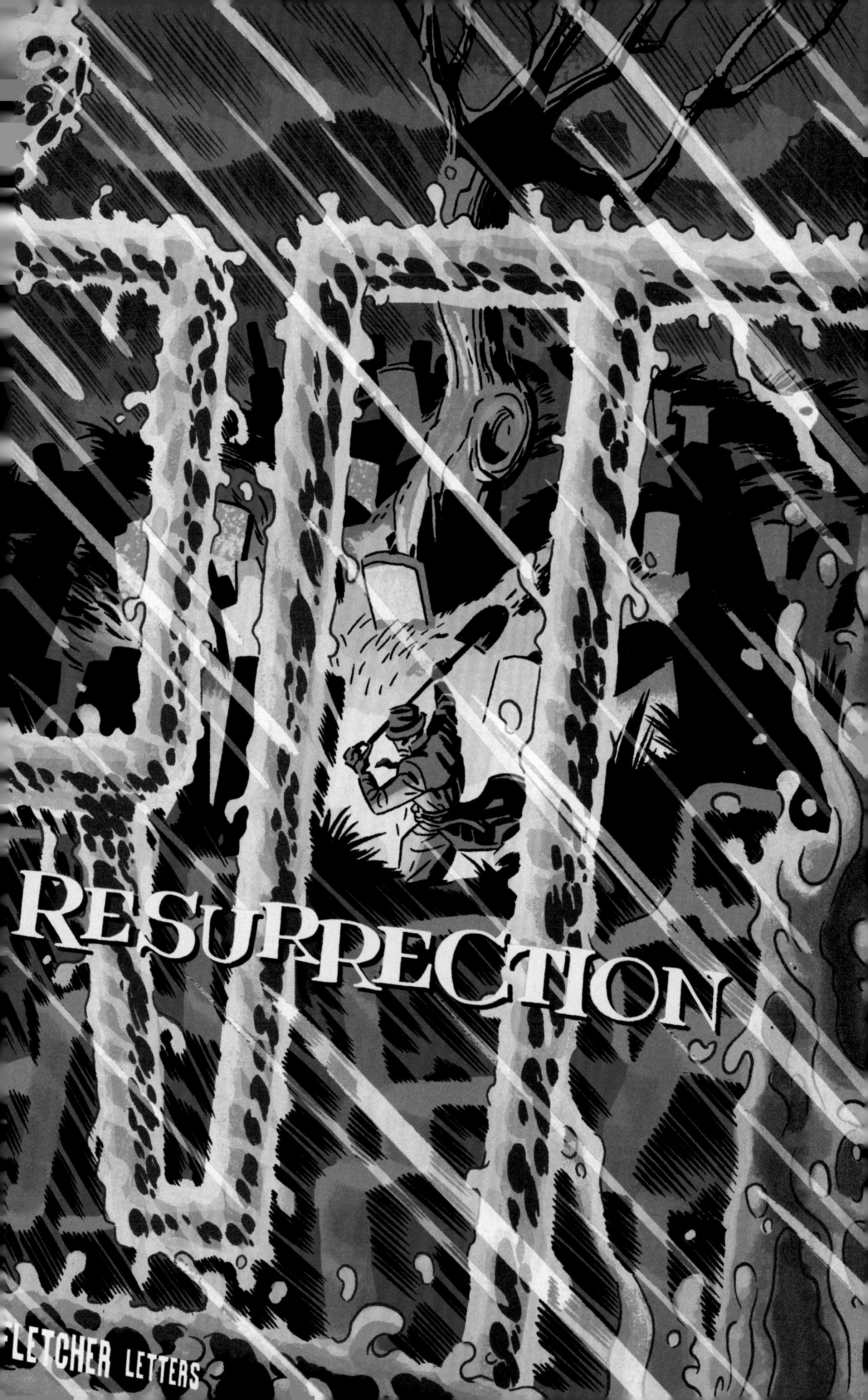
RESURRECTION
FLETCHER LETTERS

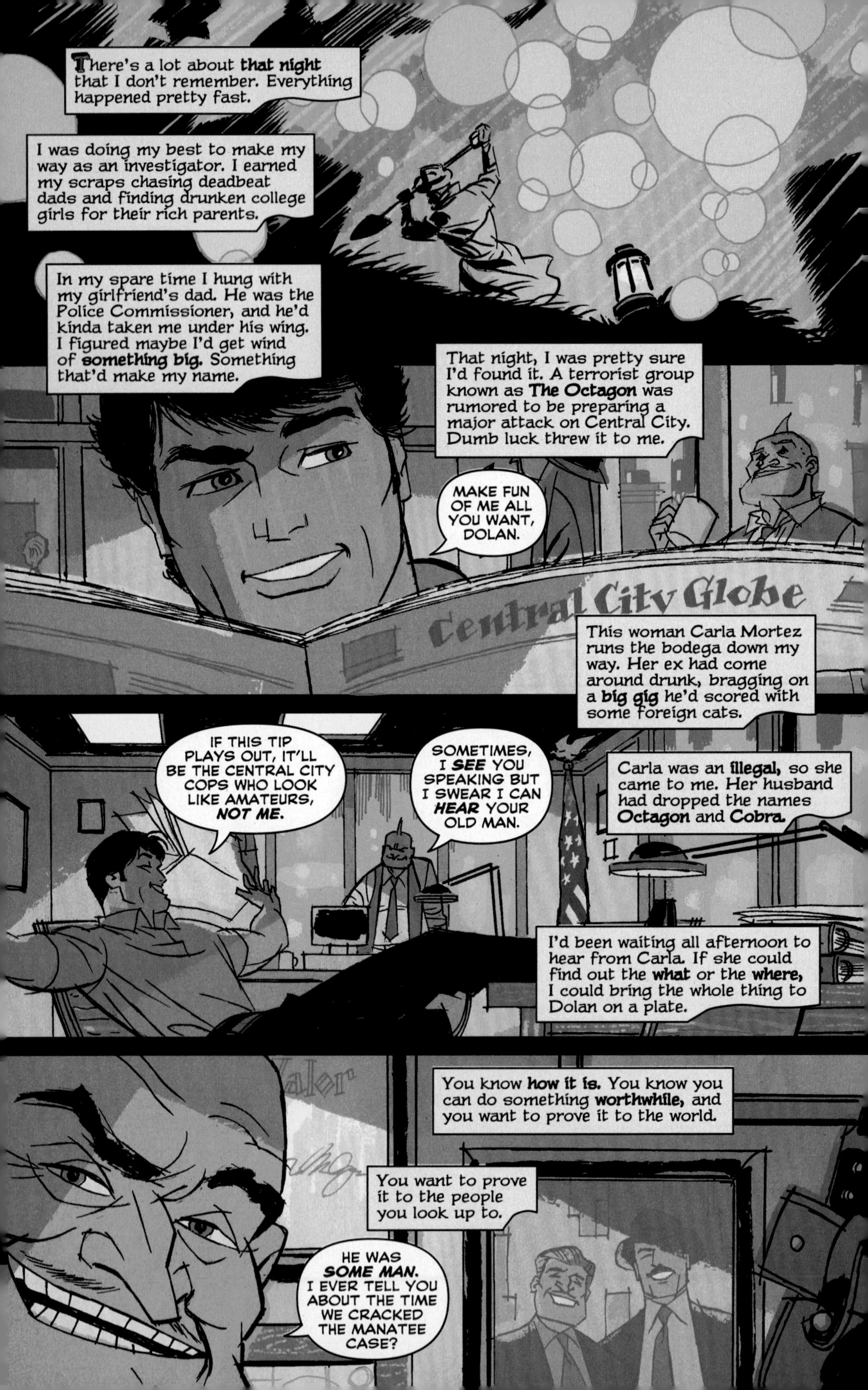
There's a lot about **that night** that I don't remember. Everything happened pretty fast.
I was doing my best to make my way as an investigator. I earned my scraps chasing deadbeat dads and finding drunken college girls for their rich parents.
In my spare time I hung with my girlfriend's dad. He was the Police Commissioner, and he'd kinda taken me under his wing. I figured maybe I'd get wind of **something big.** Something that'd make my name.
That night, I was pretty sure I'd found it. A terrorist group known as **The Octagon** was rumored to be preparing a major attack on Central City. Dumb luck threw it to me.
MAKE FUN OF ME ALL YOU WANT, DOLAN.
Central City Globe
This woman Carla Mortez runs the bodega down my way. Her ex had come around drunk, bragging on a **big gig** he'd scored with some foreign cats.
IF THIS TIP PLAYS OUT, IT'LL BE THE CENTRAL CITY COPS WHO LOOK LIKE AMATEURS, ***NOT ME.***
SOMETIMES, I ***SEE*** YOU SPEAKING BUT I SWEAR I CAN ***HEAR*** YOUR OLD MAN.
Carla was an **illegal,** so she came to me. Her husband had dropped the names **Octagon** and **Cobra.**
I'd been waiting all afternoon to hear from Carla. If she could find out the **what** or the **where,** I could bring the whole thing to Dolan on a plate.
You know **how it is.** You know you can do something **worthwhile,** and you want to prove it to the world.
You want to prove it to the people you look up to.
HE WAS ***SOME MAN.*** I EVER TELL YOU ABOUT THE TIME WE CRACKED THE MANATEE CASE?

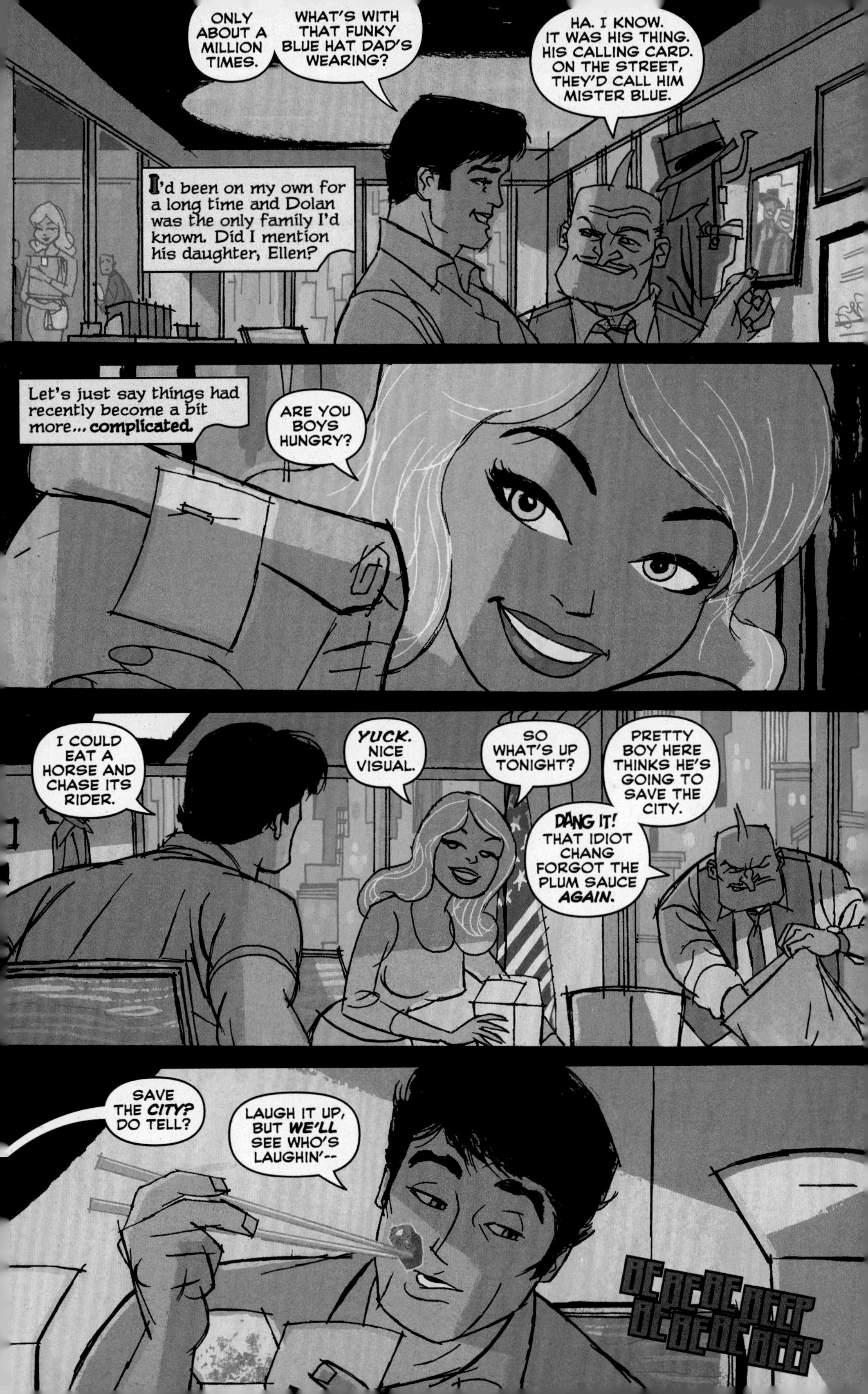
ONLY ABOUT A MILLION TIMES.
WHAT'S WITH THAT FUNKY BLUE HAT DAD'S WEARING?
HA. I KNOW. IT WAS HIS THING. HIS CALLING CARD. ON THE STREET, THEY'D CALL HIM MISTER BLUE.
I'd been on my own for a long time and Dolan was the only family I'd known. Did I mention his daughter, Ellen?
Let's just say things had recently become a bit more... complicated.
ARE YOU BOYS HUNGRY?
I COULD EAT A HORSE AND CHASE ITS RIDER.
YUCK. NICE VISUAL.
SO WHAT'S UP TONIGHT?
PRETTY BOY HERE THINKS HE'S GOING TO SAVE THE CITY.
DANG IT! THAT IDIOT CHANG FORGOT THE PLUM SAUCE AGAIN.
SAVE THE CITY? DO TELL?
LAUGH IT UP, BUT WE'LL SEE WHO'S LAUGHIN'--
BEBEBEBEEP BEBEBEBEEP

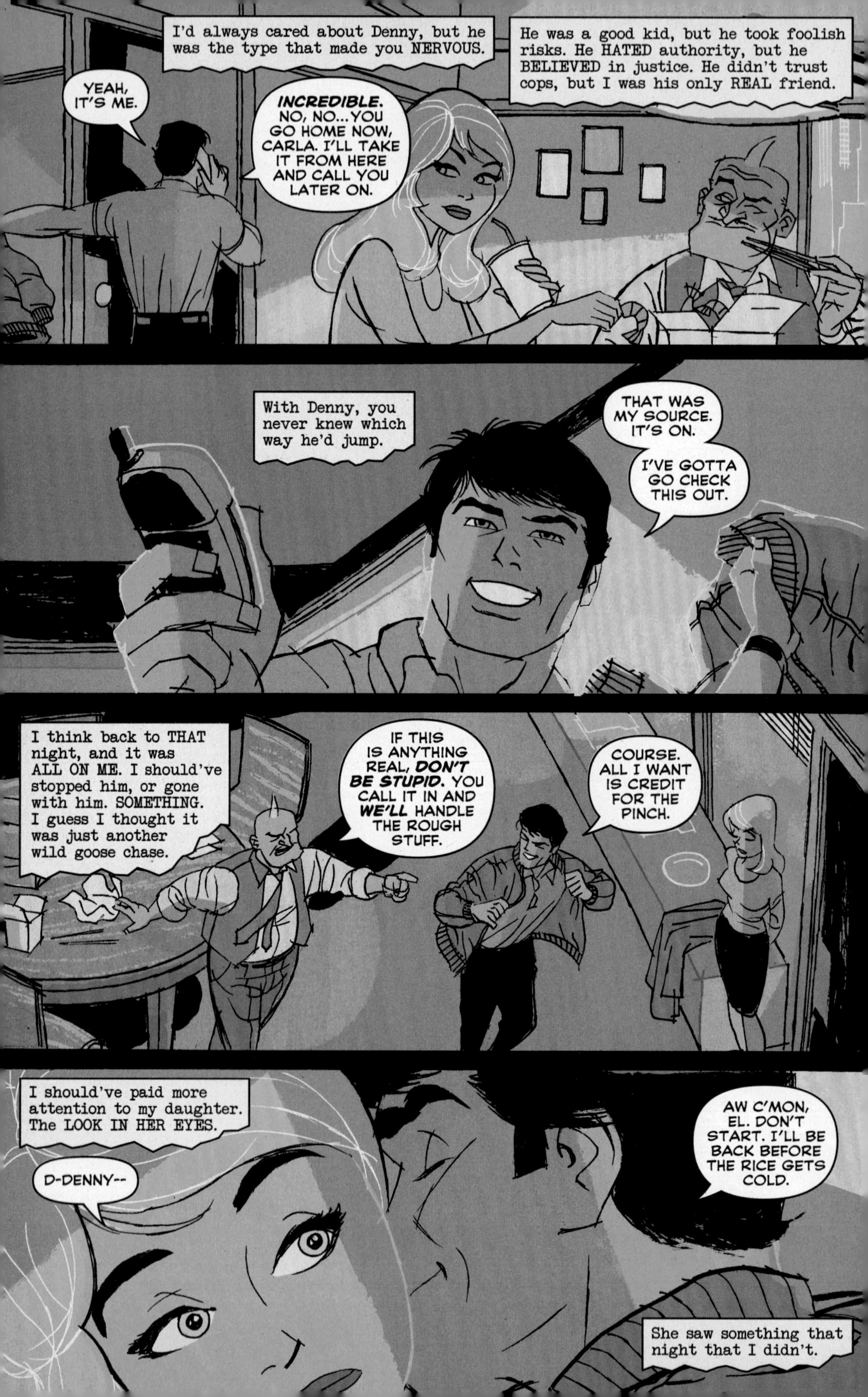
I'd always cared about Denny, but he was the type that made you NERVOUS.
He was a good kid, but he took foolish risks. He HATED authority, but he BELIEVED in justice. He didn't trust cops, but I was his only REAL friend.
YEAH, IT'S ME.
INCREDIBLE. NO, NO...YOU GO HOME NOW, CARLA. I'LL TAKE IT FROM HERE AND CALL YOU LATER ON.
With Denny, you never knew which way he'd jump.
THAT WAS MY SOURCE. IT'S ON.
I'VE GOTTA GO CHECK THIS OUT.
I think back to THAT night, and it was ALL ON ME. I should've stopped him, or gone with him. SOMETHING. I guess I thought it was just another wild goose chase.
IF THIS IS ANYTHING REAL, DON'T BE STUPID. YOU CALL IT IN AND WE'LL HANDLE THE ROUGH STUFF.
COURSE. ALL I WANT IS CREDIT FOR THE PINCH.
I should've paid more attention to my daughter. The LOOK IN HER EYES.
D-DENNY--
AW C'MON, EL. DON'T START. I'LL BE BACK BEFORE THE RICE GETS COLD.
She saw something that night that I didn't.

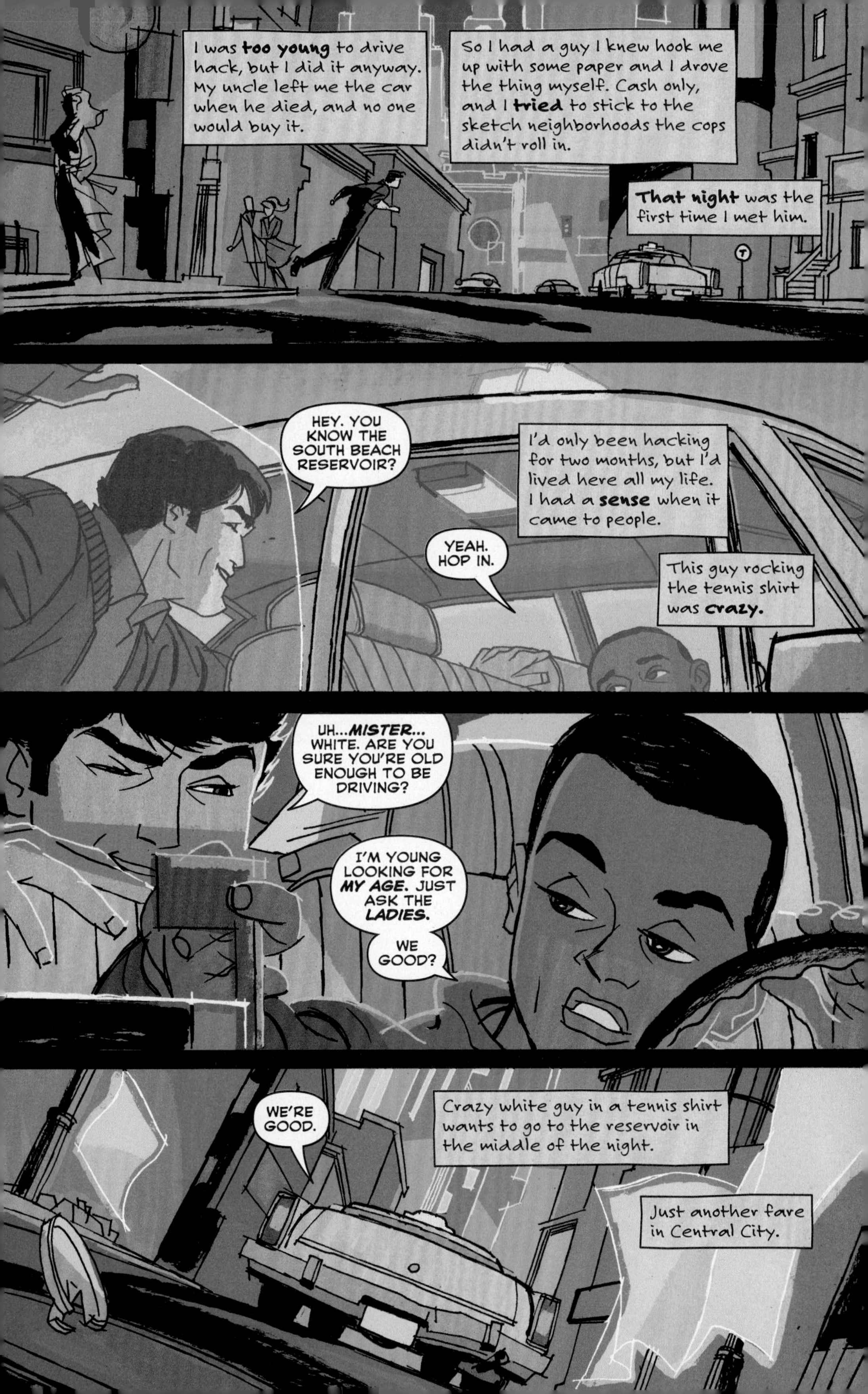
I was **too young** to drive hack, but I did it anyway. My uncle left me the car when he died, and no one would buy it.
So I had a guy I knew hook me up with some paper and I drove the thing myself. Cash only, and I **tried** to stick to the sketch neighborhoods the cops didn't roll in.
**That night** was the first time I met him.
HEY. YOU KNOW THE SOUTH BEACH RESERVOIR?
I'd only been hacking for two months, but I'd lived here all my life. I had a **sense** when it came to people.
YEAH. HOP IN.
This guy rocking the tennis shirt was **crazy.**
UH...*MISTER...* WHITE. ARE YOU SURE YOU'RE OLD ENOUGH TO BE DRIVING?
I'M YOUNG LOOKING FOR *MY AGE.* JUST ASK THE *LADIES.*
WE GOOD?
WE'RE GOOD.
Crazy white guy in a tennis shirt wants to go to the reservoir in the middle of the night.
Just another fare in Central City.

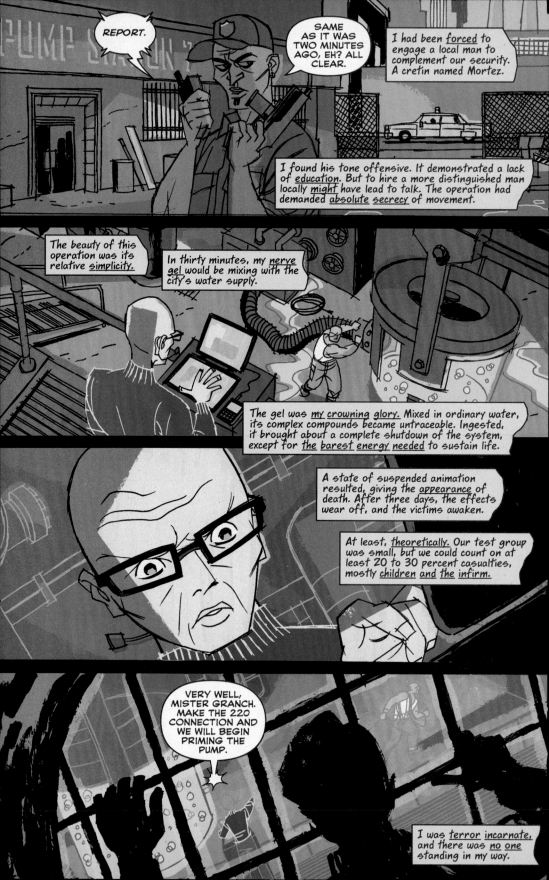

REPORT.

SAME AS IT WAS TWO MINUTES AGO, EH? ALL CLEAR.

I had been *forced* to engage a local man to complement our security. A cretin named Mortez.

I found his tone offensive. It demonstrated a lack of *education*. But to hire a more distinguished man locally *might* have lead to talk. The operation had demanded *absolute secrecy* of movement.

The beauty of this operation was its relative *simplicity*.

In thirty minutes, my *nerve gel* would be mixing with the city's water supply.

The gel was *my crowning glory*. Mixed in ordinary water, its complex compounds became untraceable. Ingested, it brought about a complete shutdown of the system, except for *the barest energy needed* to sustain life.

A state of suspended animation resulted, giving the *appearance* of death. After three days, the effects wear off, and the victims awaken.

At least, *theoretically*. Our test group was small, but we could count on at least 20 to 30 percent casualties, mostly *children* and *the infirm*.

VERY WELL, MISTER GRANCH. MAKE THE 220 CONNECTION AND WE WILL BEGIN PRIMING THE PUMP.

I was *terror incarnate*, and there was *no one* standing in my way.

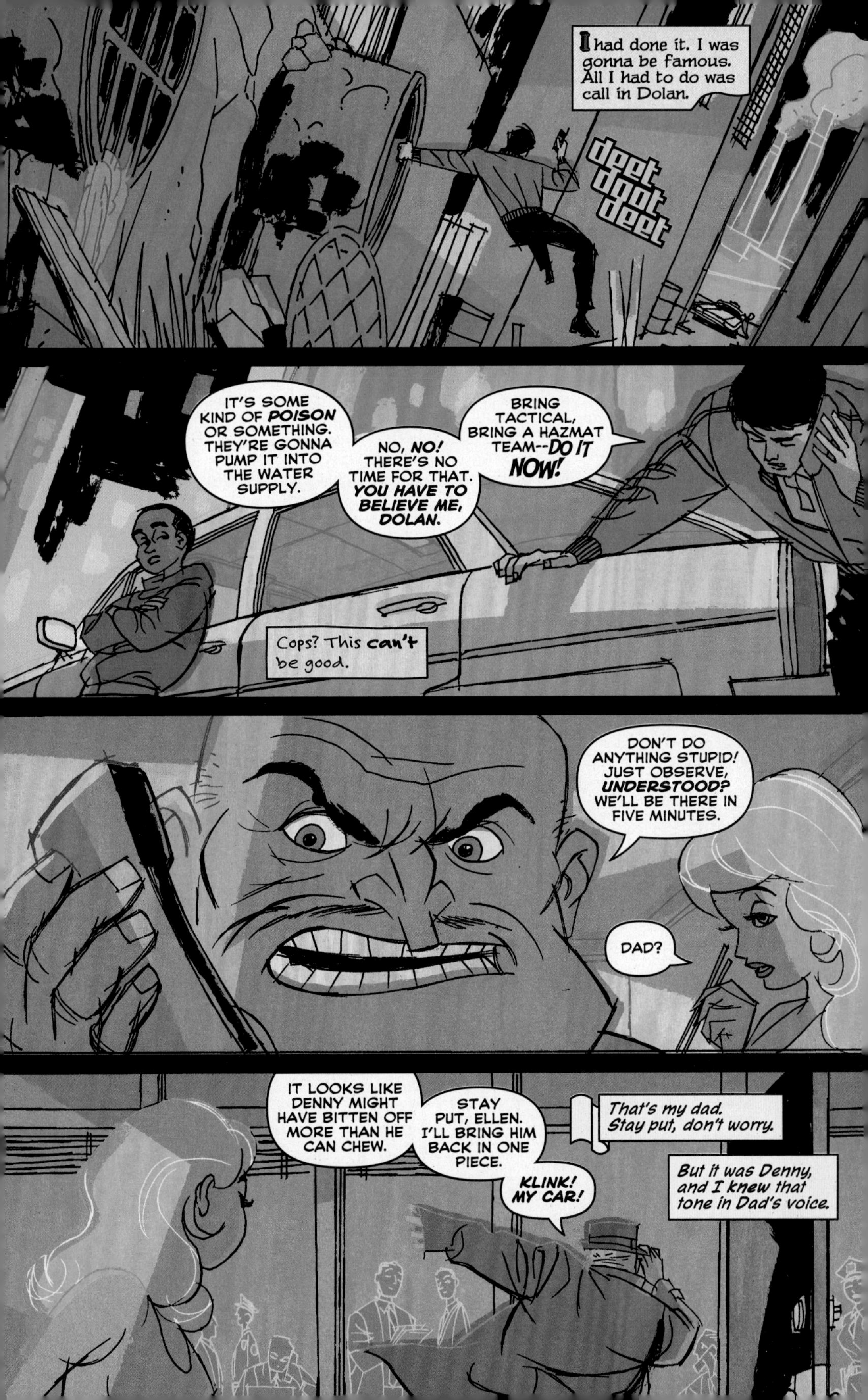
I had done it. I was gonna be famous. All I had to do was call in Dolan.
deet doot deet
IT'S SOME KIND OF POISON OR SOMETHING. THEY'RE GONNA PUMP IT INTO THE WATER SUPPLY.
NO, NO! THERE'S NO TIME FOR THAT. YOU HAVE TO BELIEVE ME, DOLAN.
BRING TACTICAL, BRING A HAZMAT TEAM--DO IT NOW!
Cops? This can't be good.
DON'T DO ANYTHING STUPID! JUST OBSERVE, UNDERSTOOD? WE'LL BE THERE IN FIVE MINUTES.
DAD?
IT LOOKS LIKE DENNY MIGHT HAVE BITTEN OFF MORE THAN HE CAN CHEW.
STAY PUT, ELLEN. I'LL BRING HIM BACK IN ONE PIECE.
KLINK! MY CAR!
That's my dad. Stay put, don't worry.
But it was Denny, and I knew that tone in Dad's voice.

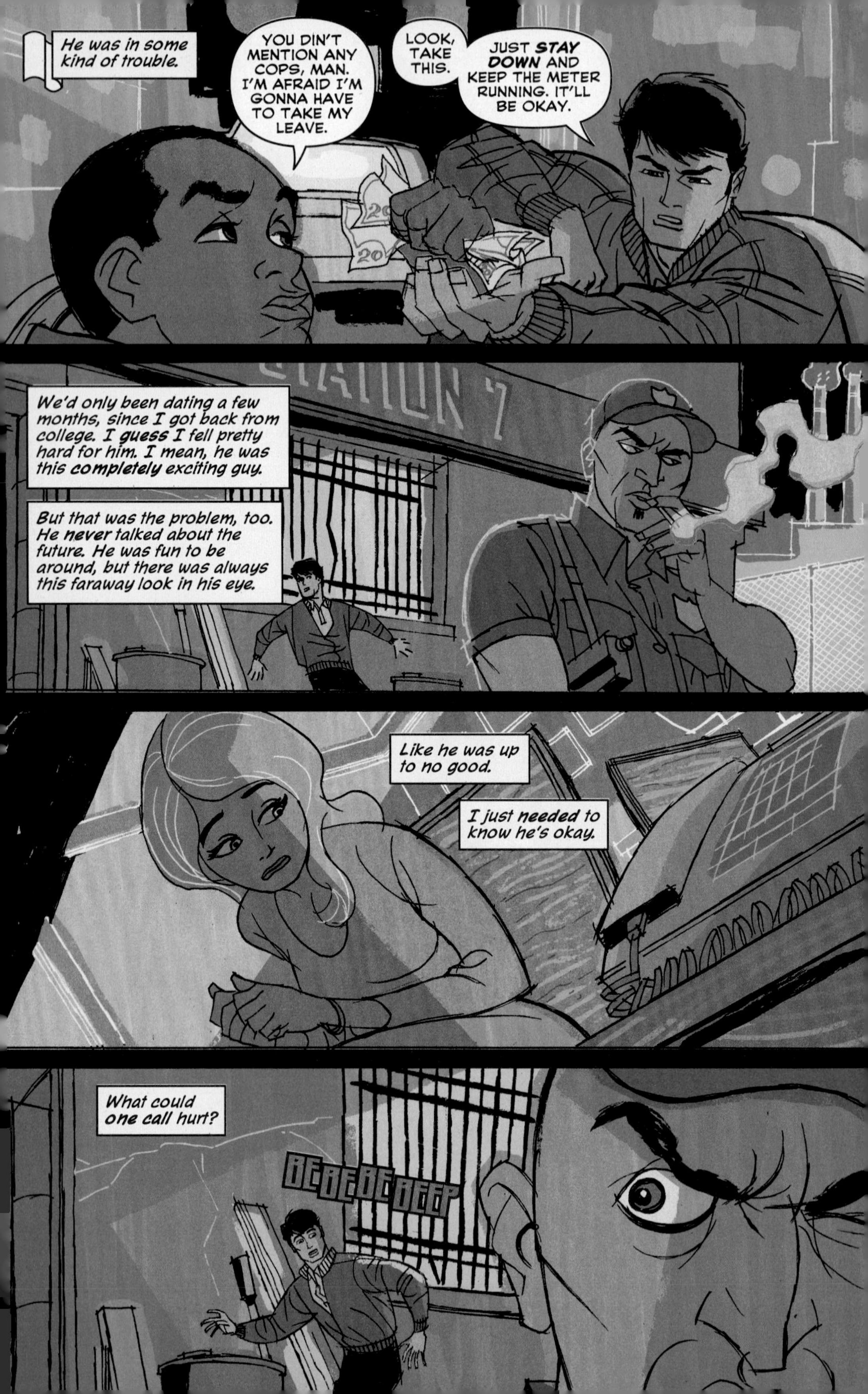
He was in some kind of trouble.
YOU DIN'T MENTION ANY COPS, MAN. I'M AFRAID I'M GONNA HAVE TO TAKE MY LEAVE.
LOOK, TAKE THIS.
JUST STAY DOWN AND KEEP THE METER RUNNING. IT'LL BE OKAY.
STATION 7
We'd only been dating a few months, since I got back from college. I guess I fell pretty hard for him. I mean, he was this completely exciting guy.
But that was the problem, too. He never talked about the future. He was fun to be around, but there was always this faraway look in his eye.
Like he was up to no good.
I just needed to know he's okay.
What could one call hurt?
BEBEBEBEEP

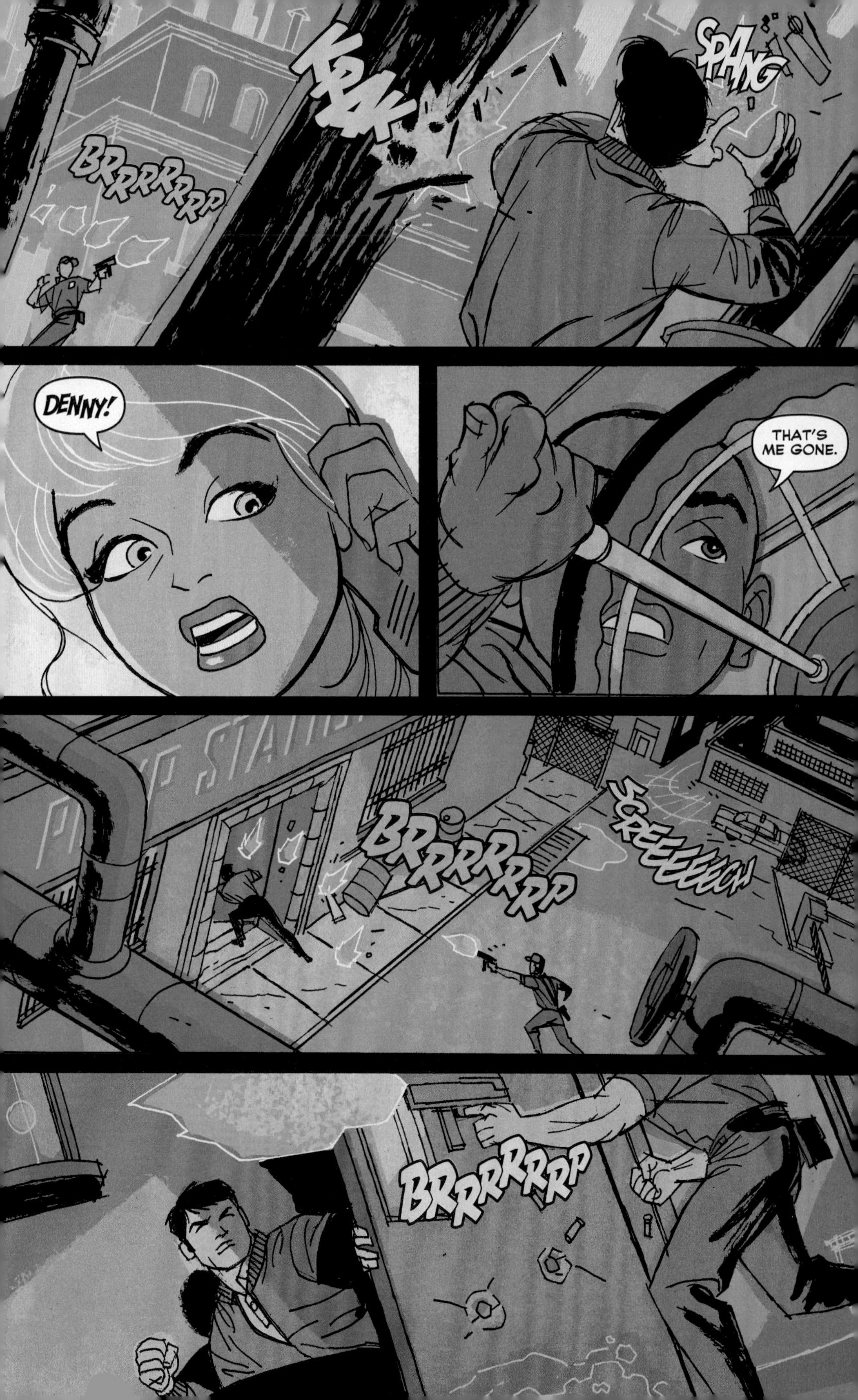
KRAK
SPANG
BRRRRRRP
DENNY!
THAT'S ME GONE.
BRRRRRRRP
SCREEEEEECH
BRRRRRRRP

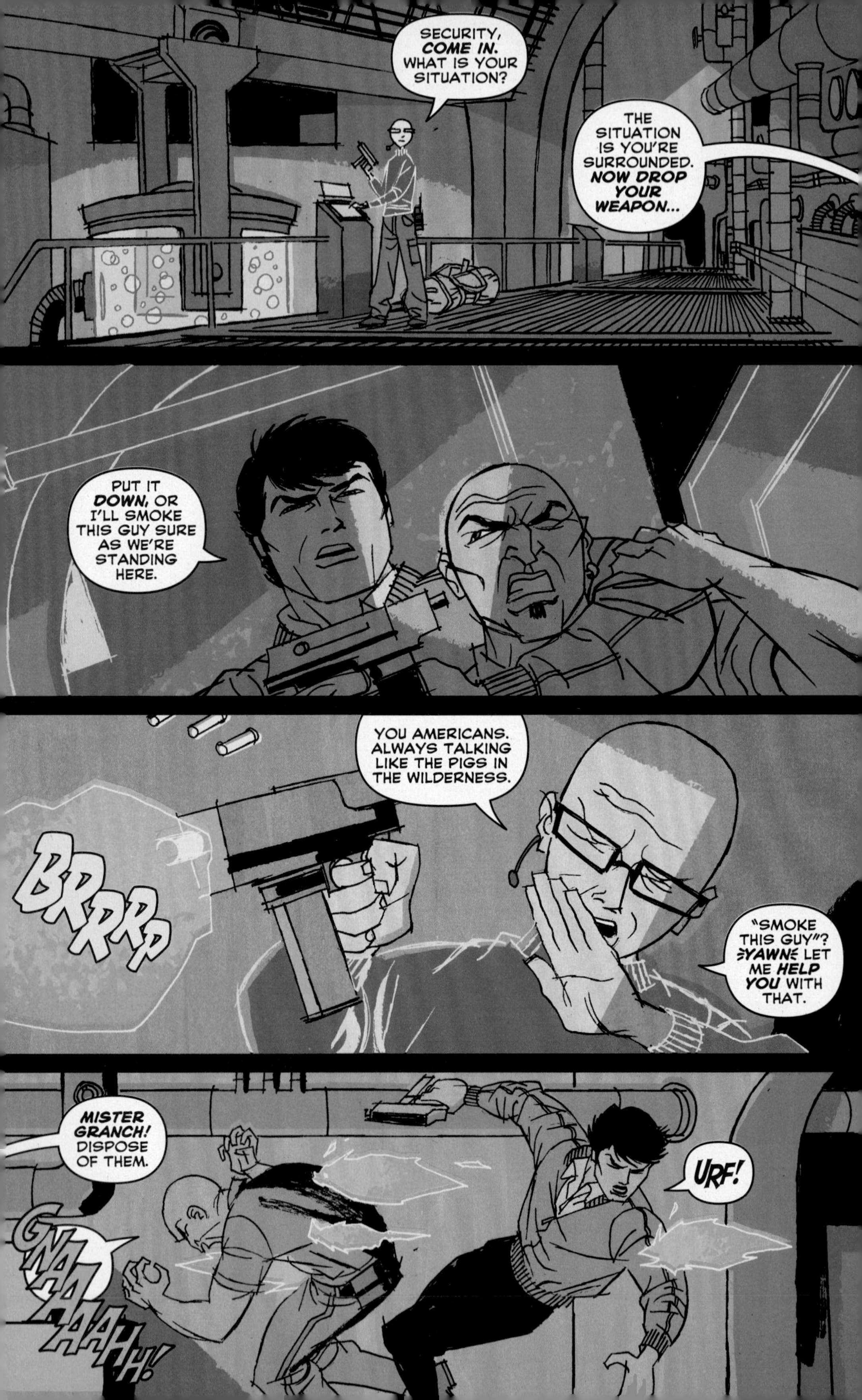
SECURITY, COME IN. WHAT IS YOUR SITUATION?
THE SITUATION IS YOU'RE SURROUNDED. NOW DROP YOUR WEAPON...
PUT IT DOWN, OR I'LL SMOKE THIS GUY SURE AS WE'RE STANDING HERE.
YOU AMERICANS. ALWAYS TALKING LIKE THE PIGS IN THE WILDERNESS.
BRRRP
"SMOKE THIS GUY"? *YAWN* LET ME HELP YOU WITH THAT.
MISTER GRANCH! DISPOSE OF THEM.
URF!
GNAAAAAHH!

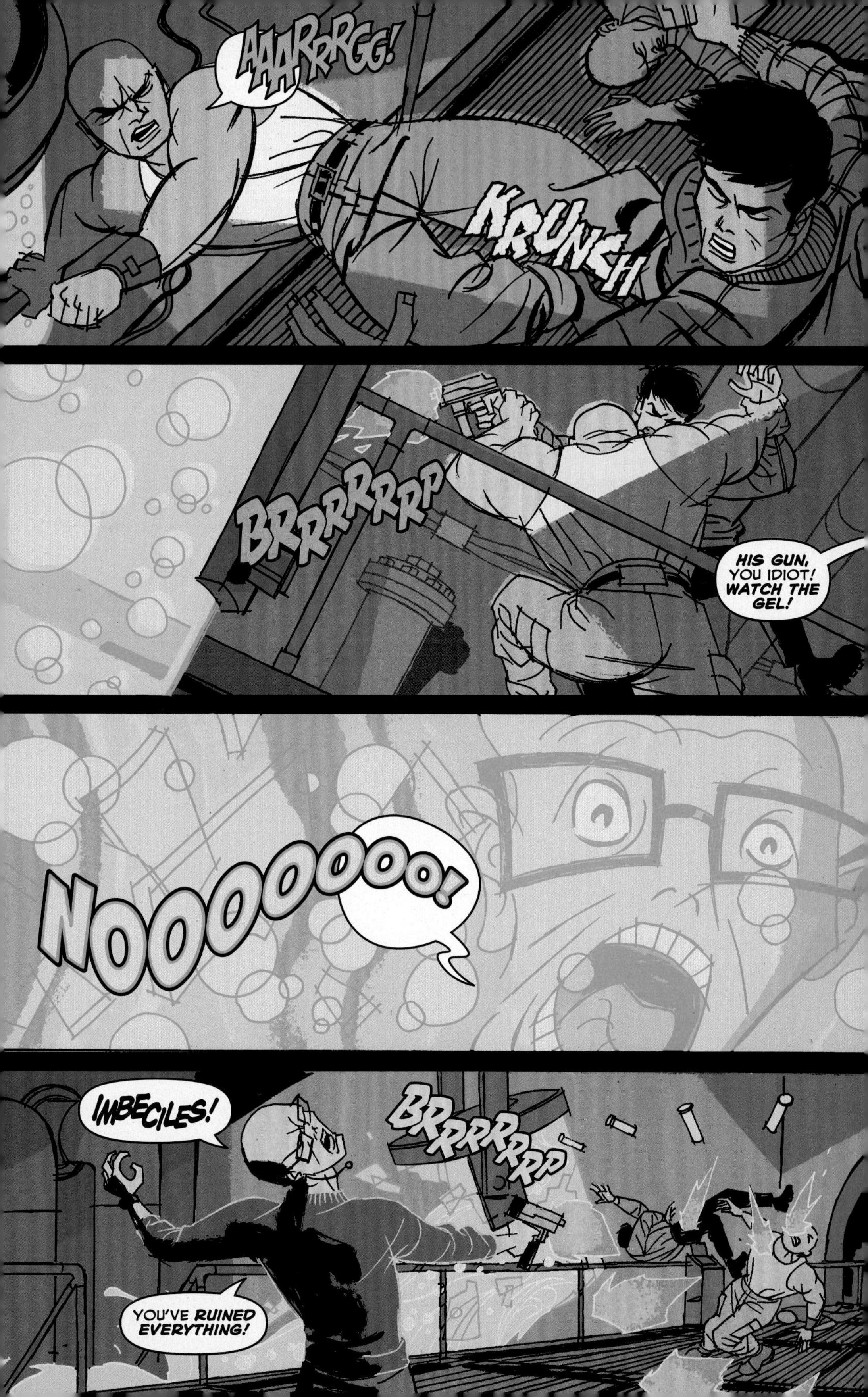
AAARRRGG!
KRUNCH
BRRRRRRP
HIS GUN, YOU IDIOT! WATCH THE GEL!
NOOOOOOOO!
IMBECILES!
BRRRRRRRP
YOU'VE RUINED EVERYTHING!

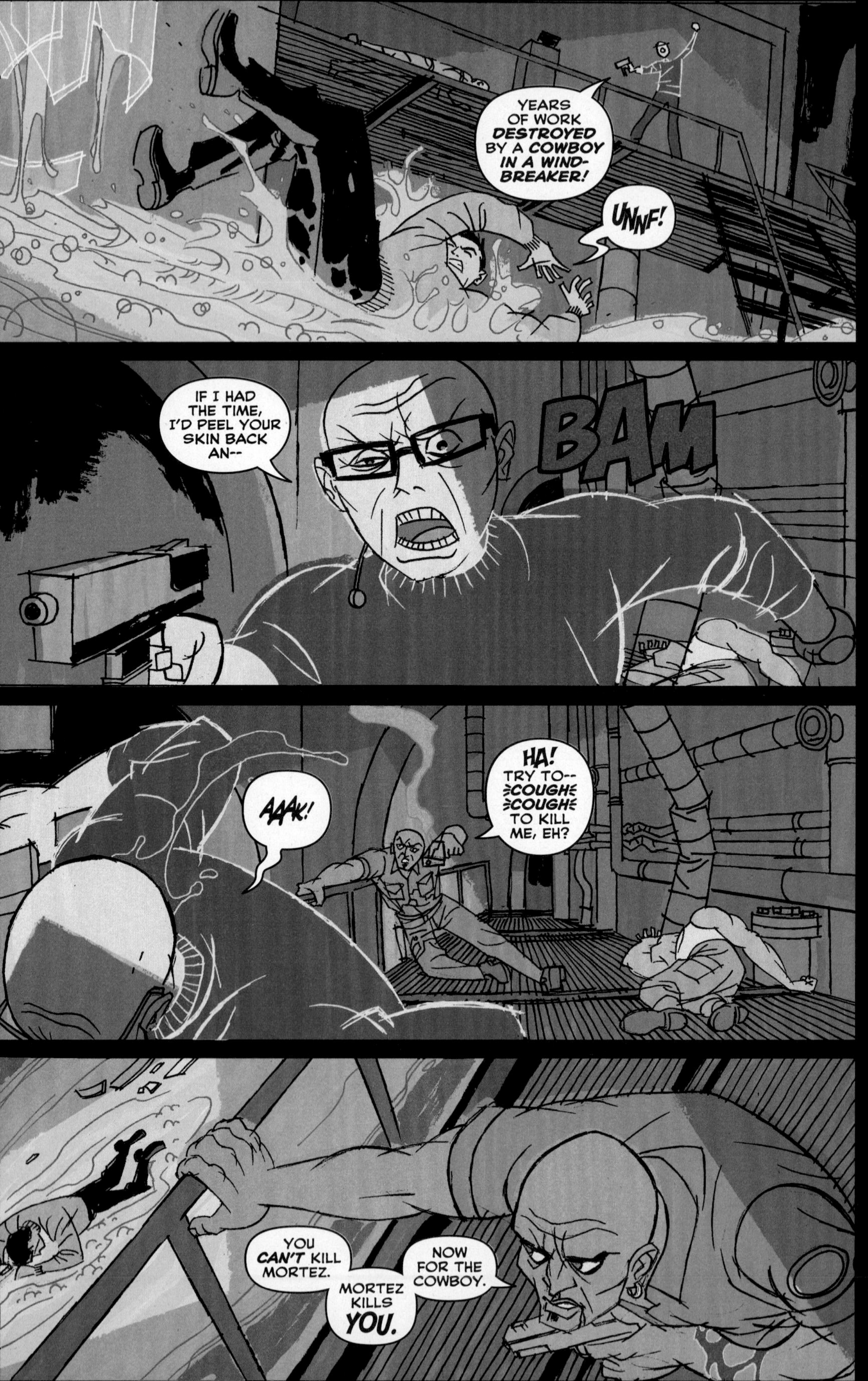

YEARS OF WORK DESTROYED BY A COWBOY IN A WIND-BREAKER!
UNNF!
IF I HAD THE TIME, I'D PEEL YOUR SKIN BACK AN--
BAM
AAAK!
HA! TRY TO-- *COUGH* *COUGH* TO KILL ME, EH?
YOU CAN'T KILL MORTEZ.
MORTEZ KILLS YOU.
NOW FOR THE COWBOY.

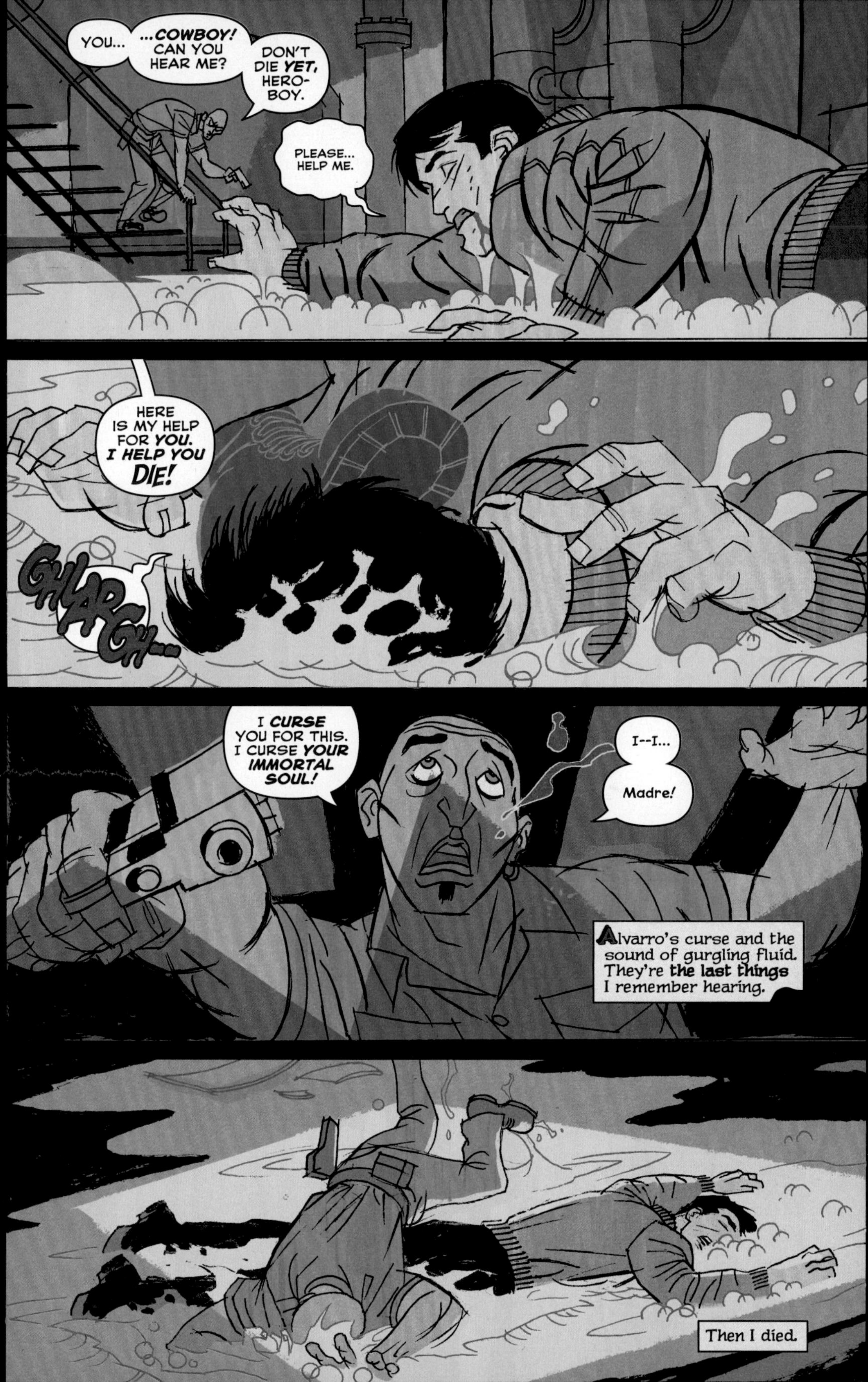
YOU...
...COWBOY! CAN YOU HEAR ME?
DON'T DIE YET, HERO-BOY.
PLEASE... HELP ME.
HERE IS MY HELP FOR YOU. I HELP YOU DIE!
GHLARGH...
I CURSE YOU FOR THIS. I CURSE YOUR IMMORTAL SOUL!
I--I...
Madre!
Alvarro's curse and the sound of gurgling fluid. They're the last things I remember hearing.
Then I died.

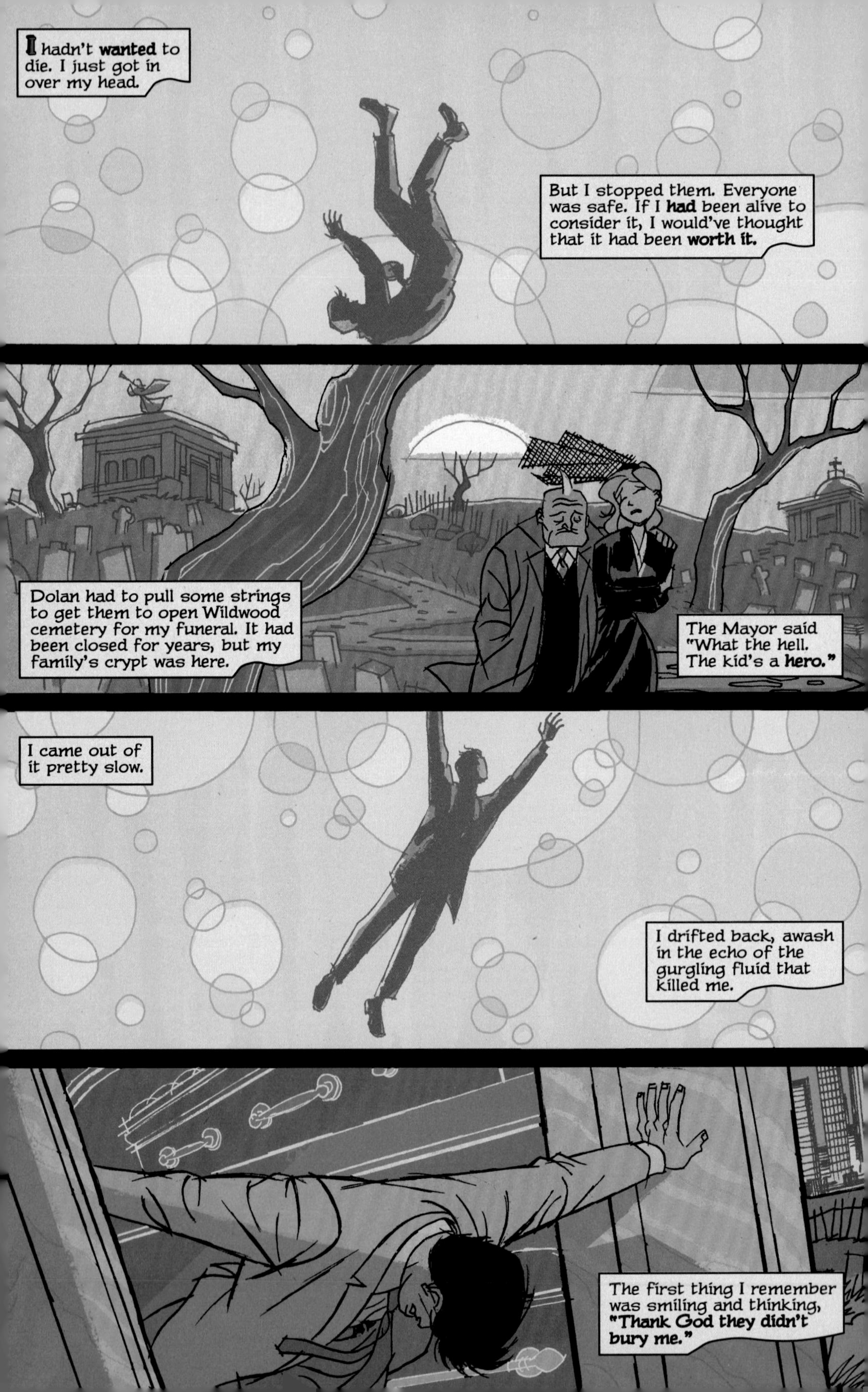
I hadn't wanted to die. I just got in over my head.
But I stopped them. Everyone was safe. If I had been alive to consider it, I would've thought that it had been worth it.
Dolan had to pull some strings to get them to open Wildwood cemetery for my funeral. It had been closed for years, but my family's crypt was here.
The Mayor said "What the hell. The kid's a hero."
I came out of it pretty slow.
I drifted back, awash in the echo of the gurgling fluid that killed me.
The first thing I remember was smiling and thinking, "Thank God they didn't bury me."

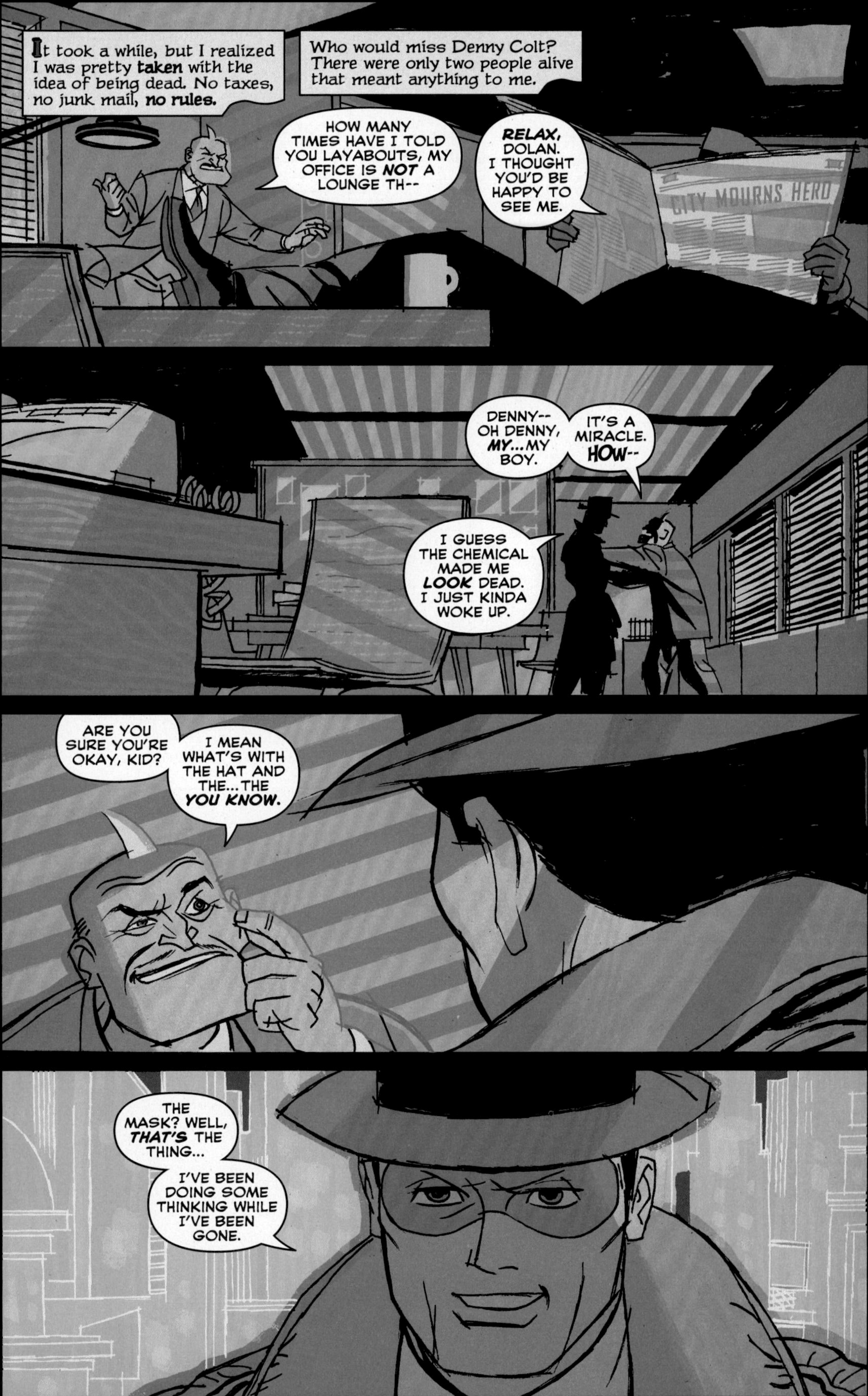
It took a while, but I realized I was pretty **taken** with the idea of being dead. No taxes, no junk mail, **no rules.**
Who would miss Denny Colt? There were only two people alive that meant anything to me.
HOW MANY TIMES HAVE I TOLD YOU LAYABOUTS, MY OFFICE IS ***NOT*** A LOUNGE TH--
***RELAX,*** DOLAN. I THOUGHT YOU'D BE HAPPY TO SEE ME.
CITY MOURNS HERO
DENNY-- OH DENNY, ***MY***...MY BOY.
IT'S A MIRACLE. **HOW**--
I GUESS THE CHEMICAL MADE ME ***LOOK*** DEAD. I JUST KINDA WOKE UP.
ARE YOU SURE YOU'RE OKAY, KID?
I MEAN WHAT'S WITH THE HAT AND THE...THE ***YOU KNOW.***
THE MASK? WELL, ***THAT'S*** THE THING...
I'VE BEEN DOING SOME THINKING WHILE I'VE BEEN GONE.

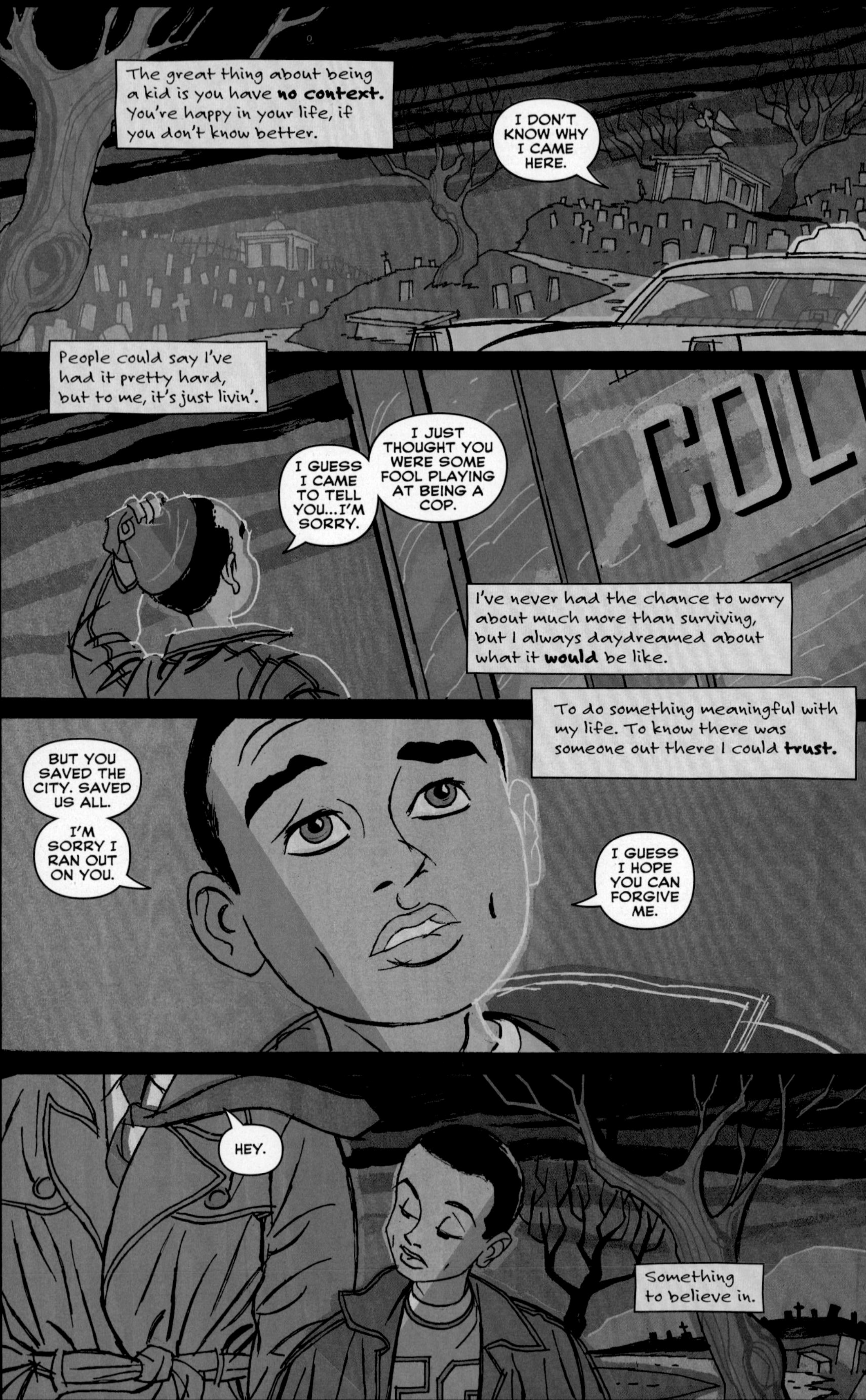
The great thing about being a kid is you have **no context.** You're happy in your life, if you don't know better.
I DON'T KNOW WHY I CAME HERE.
People could say I've had it pretty hard, but to me, it's just livin'.
COL
I GUESS I CAME TO TELL YOU...I'M SORRY.
I JUST THOUGHT YOU WERE SOME FOOL PLAYING AT BEING A COP.
I've never had the chance to worry about much more than surviving, but I always daydreamed about what it **would** be like.
To do something meaningful with my life. To know there was someone out there I could **trust.**
BUT YOU SAVED THE CITY. SAVED US ALL.
I'M SORRY I RAN OUT ON YOU.
I GUESS I HOPE YOU CAN FORGIVE ME.
HEY.
Something to believe in.

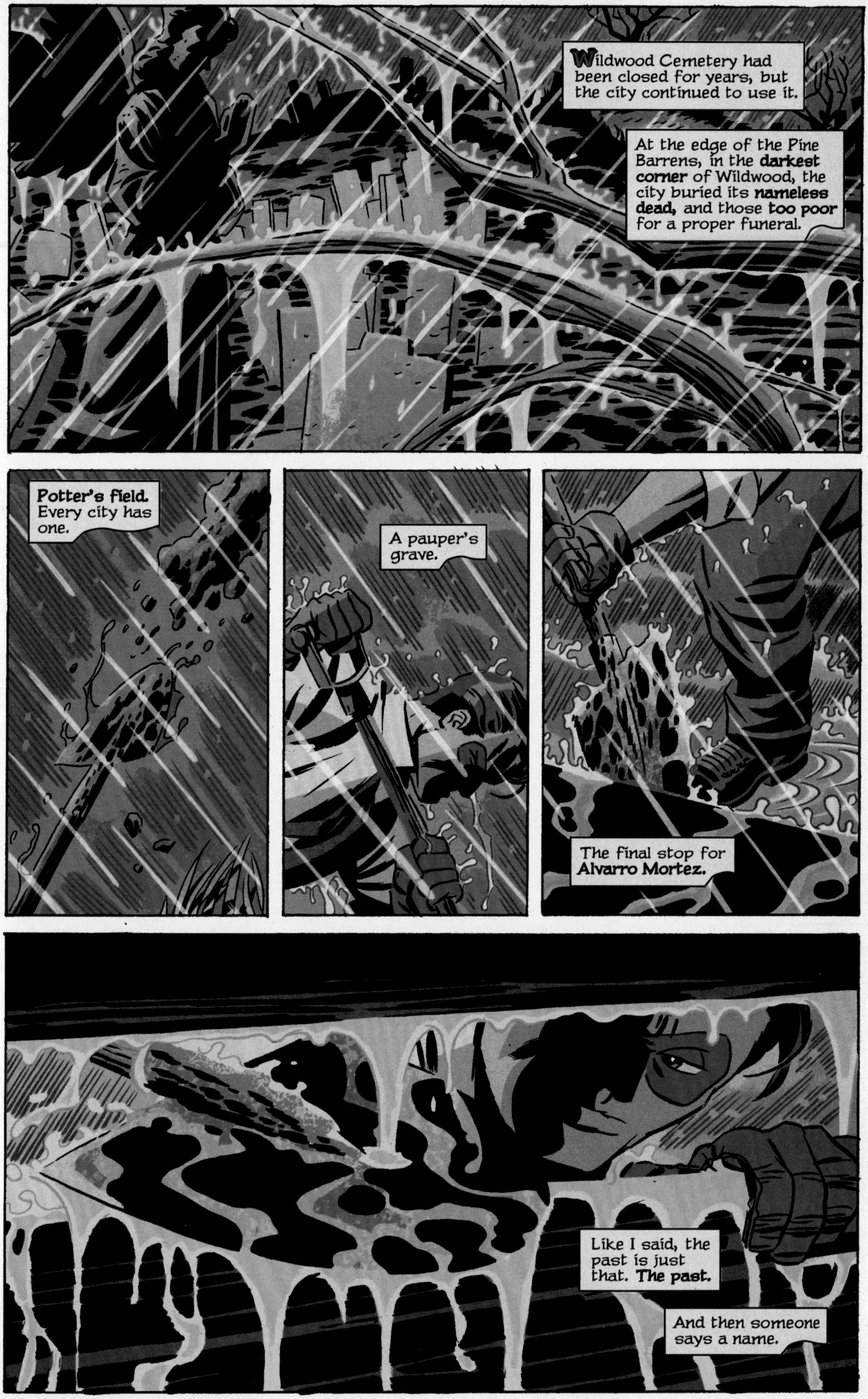
Wildwood Cemetery had been closed for years, but the city continued to use it.
At the edge of the Pine Barrens, in the **darkest corner** of Wildwood, the city buried its **nameless dead,** and those **too poor** for a proper funeral.
**Potter's field.** Every city has one.
A pauper's grave.
The final stop for **Alvarro Mortez.**
Like I said, the past is just that. **The past.**
And then someone says a name.

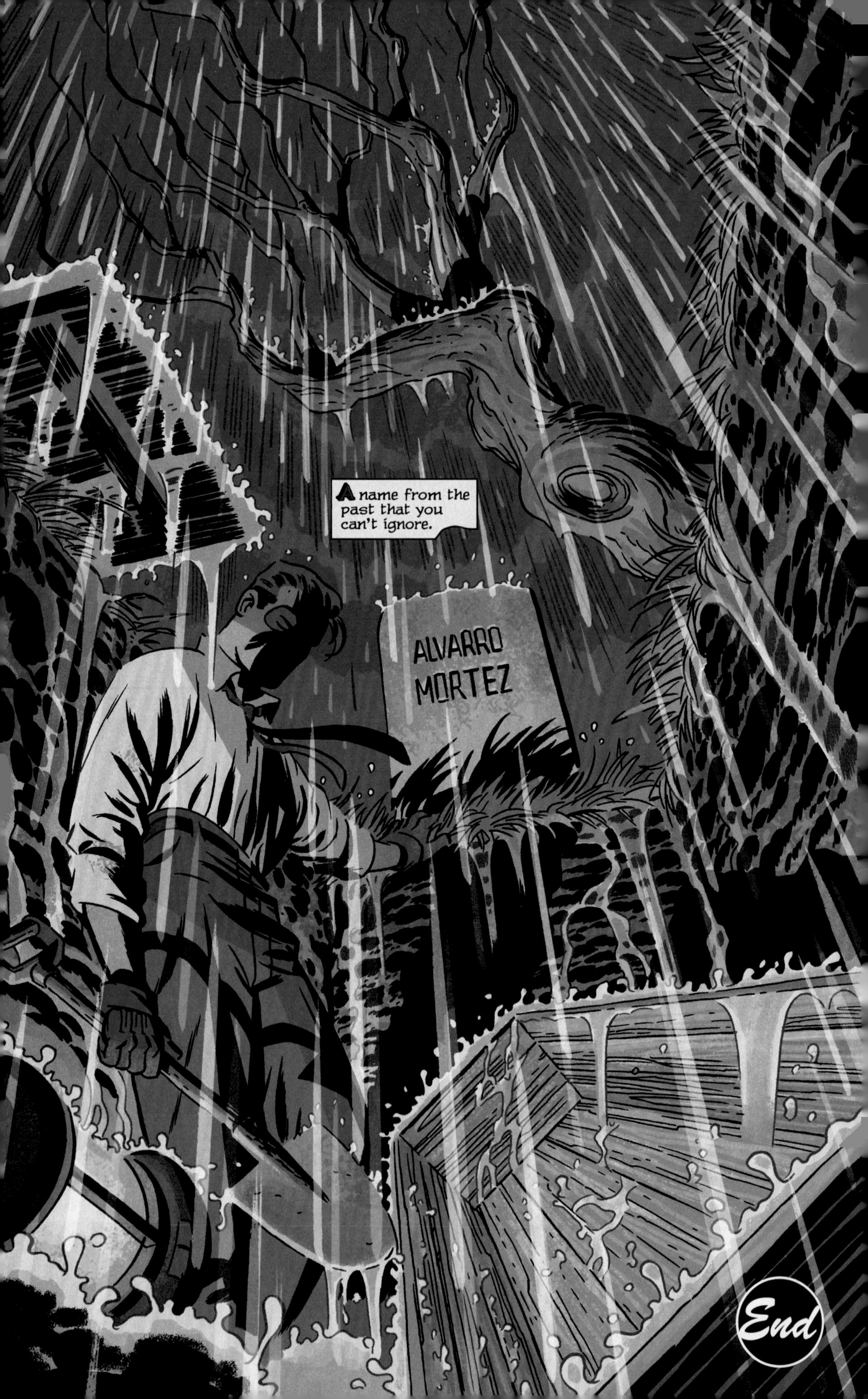
A name from the past that you can't ignore.
ALVARRO MORTEZ
End

# 4

ACTION • Mystery • ADVENTURE

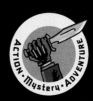

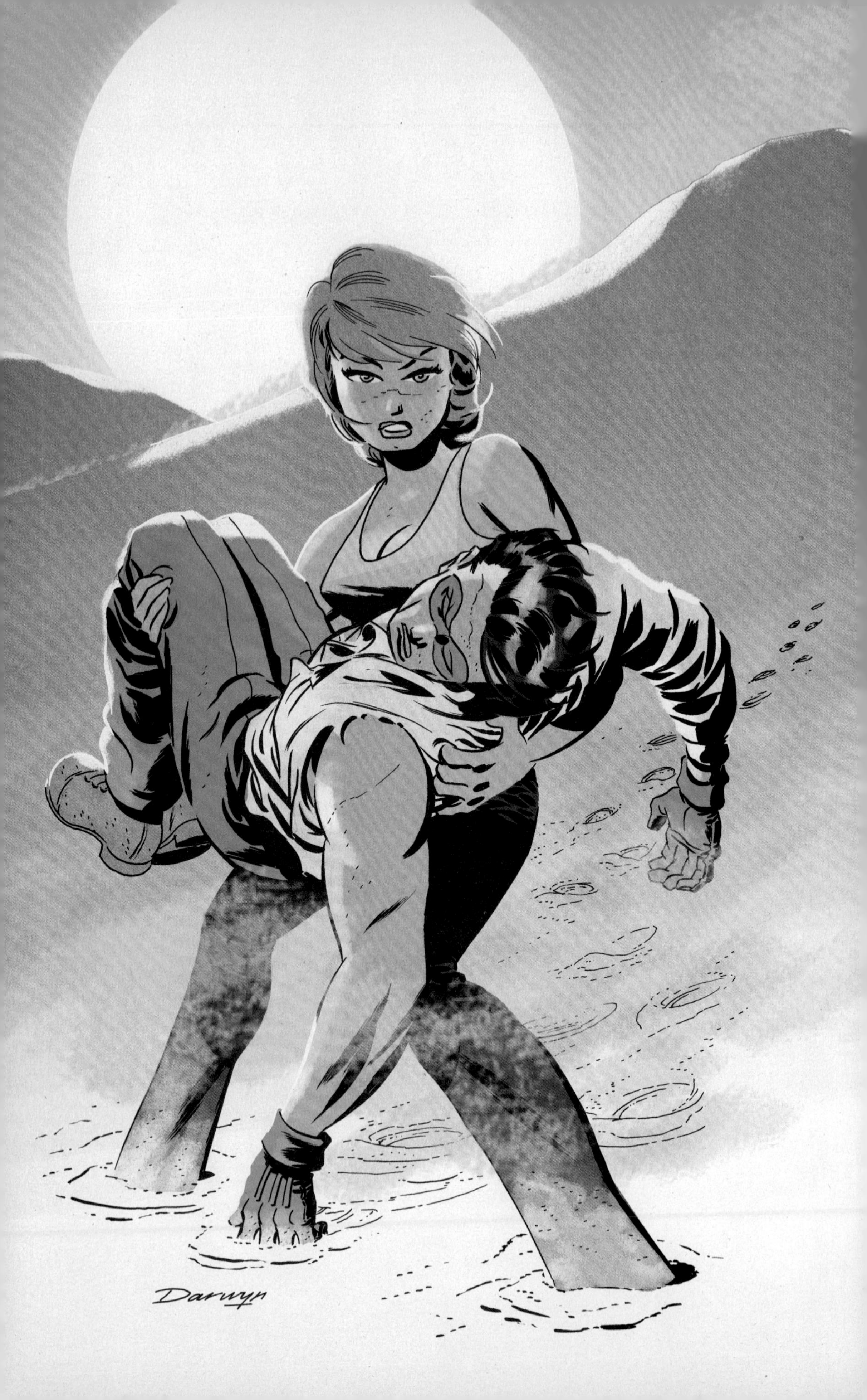
Darwyn

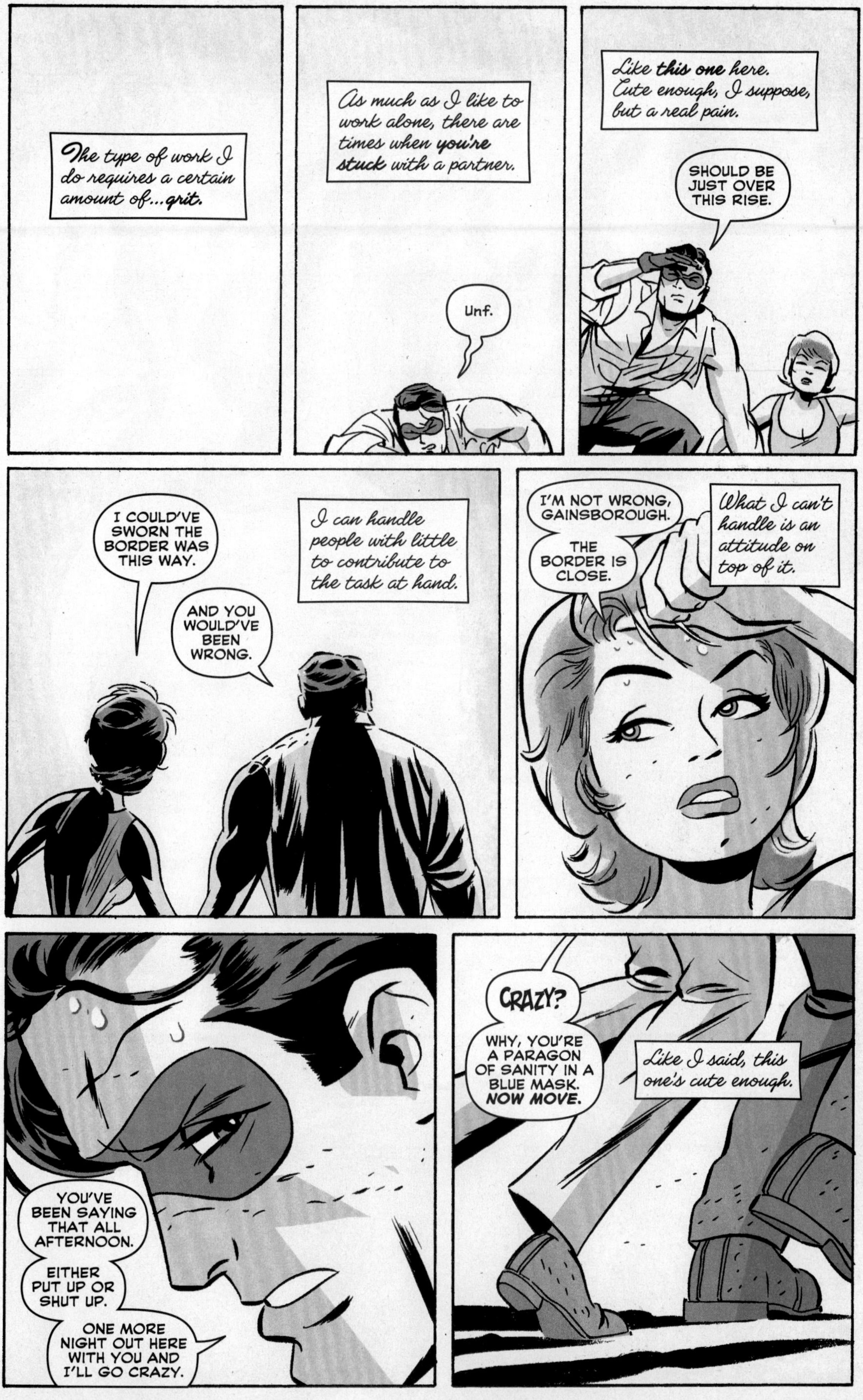
The type of work I do requires a certain amount of...grit.
As much as I like to work alone, there are times when you're stuck with a partner.
Unf.
Like this one here. Cute enough, I suppose, but a real pain.
SHOULD BE JUST OVER THIS RISE.
I COULD'VE SWORN THE BORDER WAS THIS WAY.
I can handle people with little to contribute to the task at hand.
AND YOU WOULD'VE BEEN WRONG.
I'M NOT WRONG, GAINSBOROUGH.
THE BORDER IS CLOSE.
What I can't handle is an attitude on top of it.
YOU'VE BEEN SAYING THAT ALL AFTERNOON.
EITHER PUT UP OR SHUT UP.
ONE MORE NIGHT OUT HERE WITH YOU AND I'LL GO CRAZY.
CRAZY?
WHY, YOU'RE A PARAGON OF SANITY IN A BLUE MASK. NOW MOVE.
Like I said, this one's cute enough.

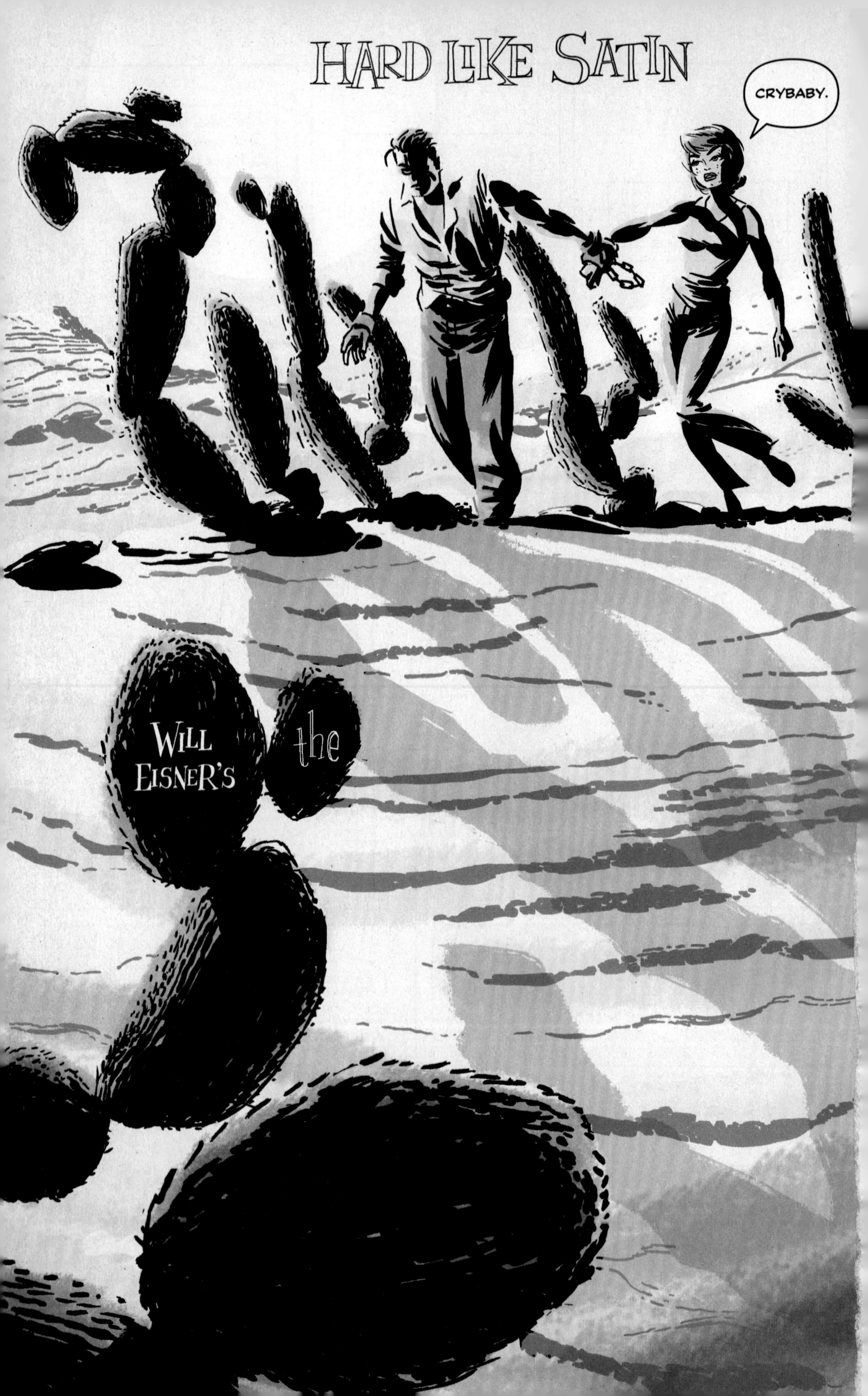
HARD LIKE SATIN
CRYBABY.
WILL EISNER'S
the

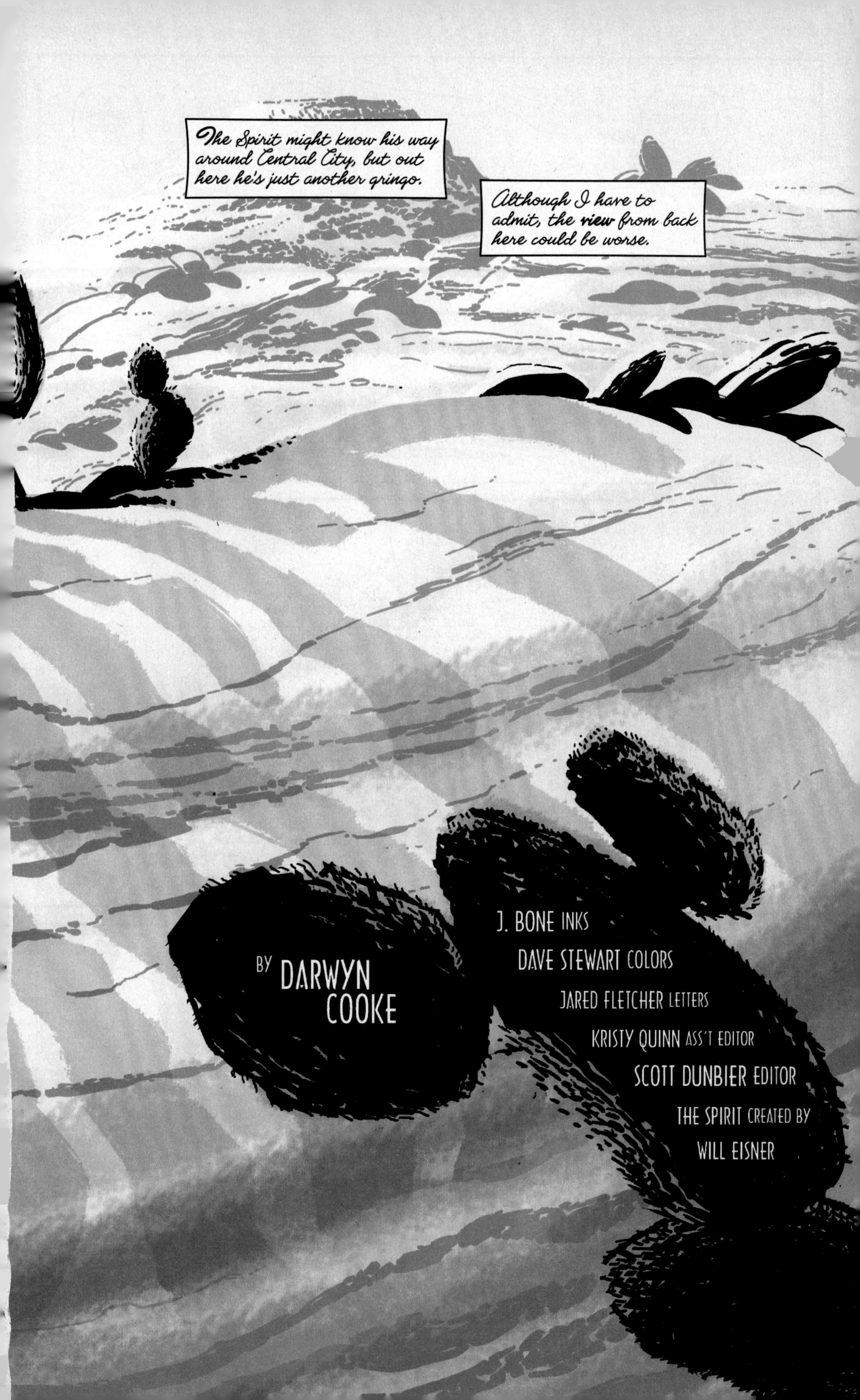
The Spirit might know his way around Central City, but out here he's just another gringo.
Although I have to admit, the view from back here could be worse.
BY DARWYN COOKE
J. BONE INKS
DAVE STEWART COLORS
JARED FLETCHER LETTERS
KRISTY QUINN ASS'T EDITOR
SCOTT DUNBIER EDITOR
THE SPIRIT CREATED BY
WILL EISNER

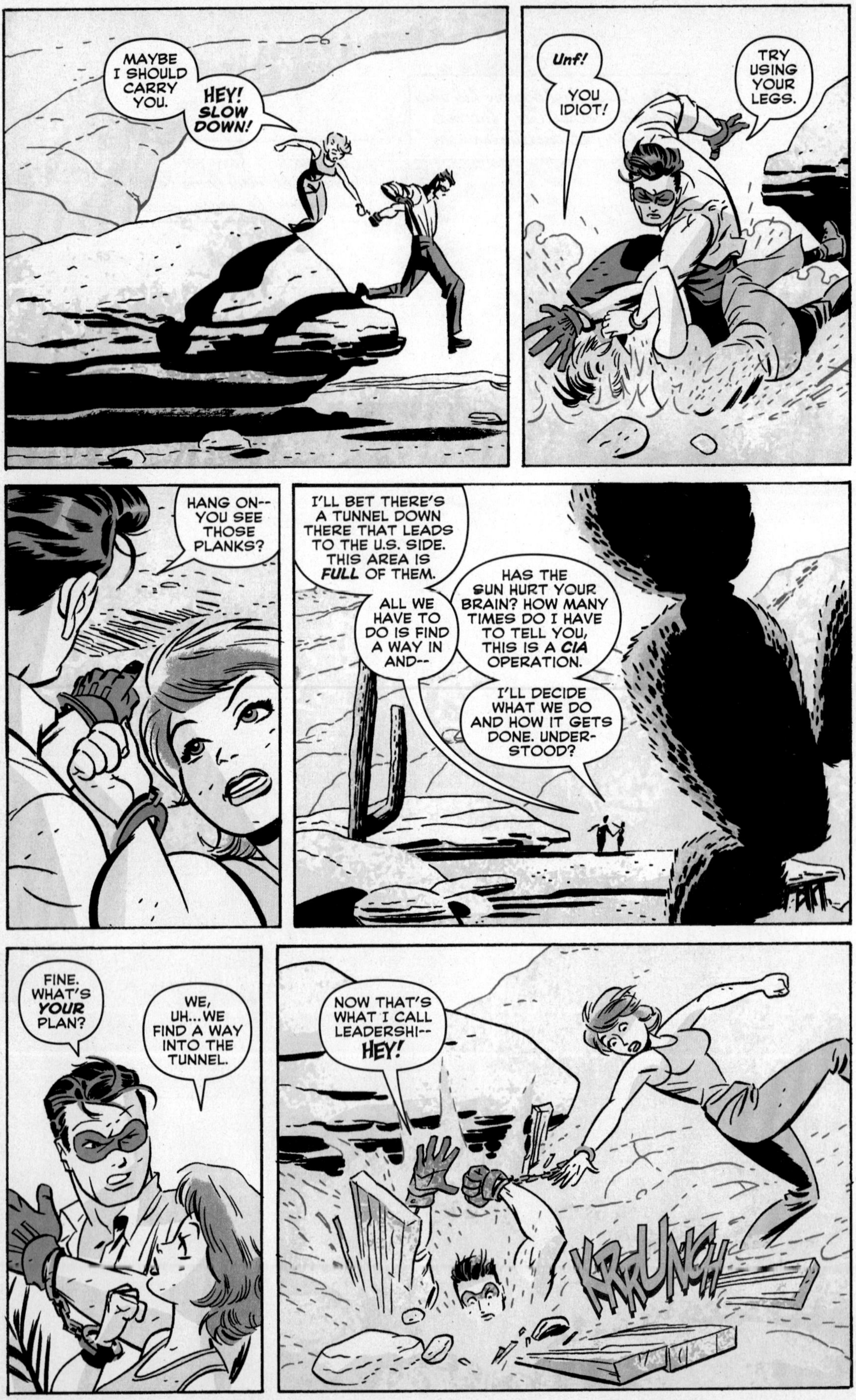
MAYBE I SHOULD CARRY YOU.
HEY! SLOW DOWN!
Unf!
YOU IDIOT!
TRY USING YOUR LEGS.
HANG ON-- YOU SEE THOSE PLANKS?
I'LL BET THERE'S A TUNNEL DOWN THERE THAT LEADS TO THE U.S. SIDE. THIS AREA IS FULL OF THEM.
ALL WE HAVE TO DO IS FIND A WAY IN AND--
HAS THE SUN HURT YOUR BRAIN? HOW MANY TIMES DO I HAVE TO TELL YOU, THIS IS A CIA OPERATION.
I'LL DECIDE WHAT WE DO AND HOW IT GETS DONE. UNDER-STOOD?
FINE. WHAT'S YOUR PLAN?
WE, UH...WE FIND A WAY INTO THE TUNNEL.
NOW THAT'S WHAT I CALL LEADERSHI-- HEY!
KRRUNCH

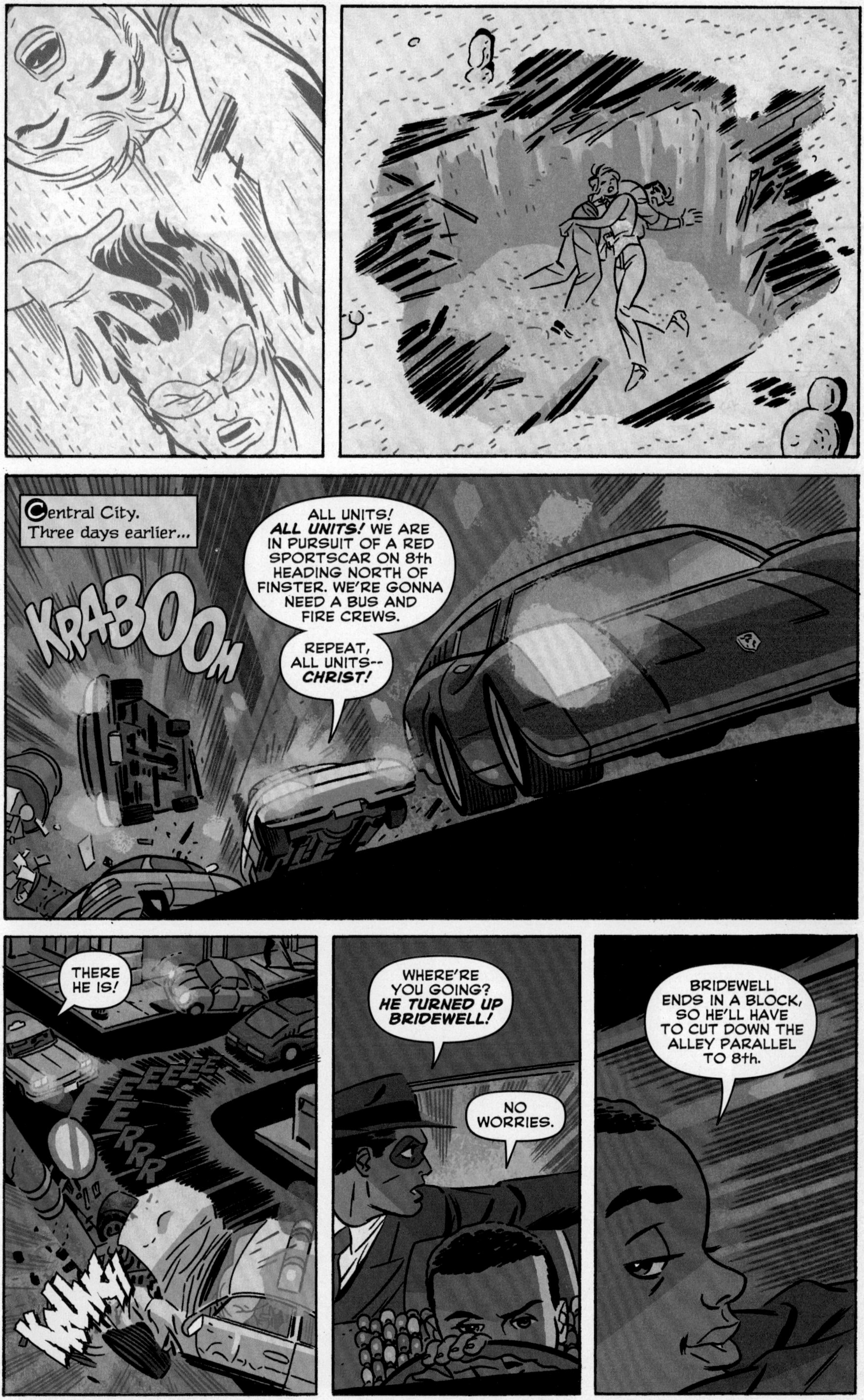

Central City. Three days earlier...
ALL UNITS! ALL UNITS! WE ARE IN PURSUIT OF A RED SPORTSCAR ON 8th HEADING NORTH OF FINSTER. WE'RE GONNA NEED A BUS AND FIRE CREWS.
KRABOOM
REPEAT, ALL UNITS-- CHRIST!
THERE HE IS!
WHERE'RE YOU GOING? HE TURNED UP BRIDEWELL!
NO WORRIES.
BRIDEWELL ENDS IN A BLOCK, SO HE'LL HAVE TO CUT DOWN THE ALLEY PARALLEL TO 8th.

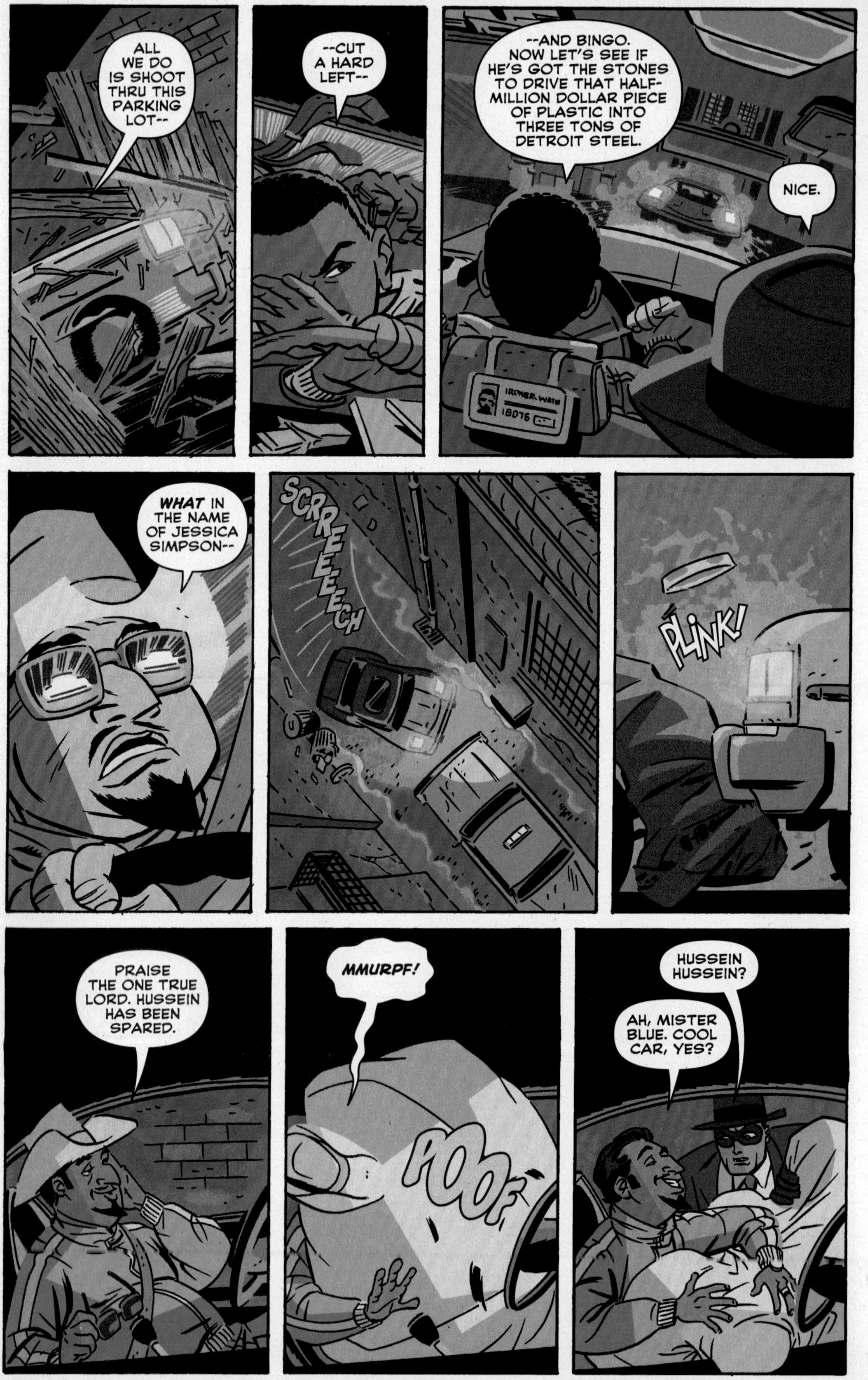
ALL WE DO IS SHOOT THRU THIS PARKING LOT--
--CUT A HARD LEFT--
--AND BINGO. NOW LET'S SEE IF HE'S GOT THE STONES TO DRIVE THAT HALF-MILLION DOLLAR PIECE OF PLASTIC INTO THREE TONS OF DETROIT STEEL.
NICE.
WHAT IN THE NAME OF JESSICA SIMPSON--
SCRREEEEECH
PLINK!
PRAISE THE ONE TRUE LORD. HUSSEIN HAS BEEN SPARED.
MMURPF!
POOF
HUSSEIN HUSSEIN?
AH, MISTER BLUE. COOL CAR, YES?

HOW'D YOU END UP IN THIS?

WE WERE OUT TRYING TO TRACK DOWN LEADS ON ELVARRO MORTEZ. WE CAUGHT THIS ON THE RADIO AND HAPPENED TO BE HANDY.

I KNOW THIS GUY.

HE'S MIDDLE EASTERN, AND HAS SOME INTERESTING CONNECTIONS. LET ME TAKE A CRACK AT HIM.

BE MY GUEST. AS SOON AS THE FEDS SHOW, HE'S OFF OUR PLATE.

THEY TREATING YOU OKAY, HUSSEIN?

AH, MISTER BLUE.

ARE YOU HERE FOR THE SPRINGING? I AM MOST READY TO SPRING.

SORRY, HUSSEIN, BUT THERE'S NO WAY I CAN GET YOU OUT OF THIS.

YOU STOLE THAT CAR, AND THE TRUNK WAS FULL OF GUNS AND MONEY.

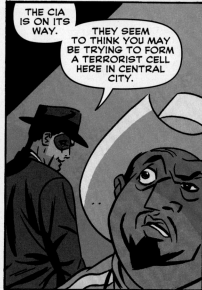

THE CIA IS ON ITS WAY.

THEY SEEM TO THINK YOU MAY BE TRYING TO FORM A TERRORIST CELL HERE IN CENTRAL CITY.

MISTER BLUE, YOU SPEAR MY HEART WITH YOUR POINTY WORDS.

HUSSEIN? A TERRORIST?

IT IS THE HILARIOUS!

I LOVE AMERICA! THE CARS, THE MONEY--

HAVE YOU EVER BEEN TO THIS "PEPPERMINT HIPPO MEN'S CLUB"?

THE WOMEN THERE, MY FRIEND. THAT IS AMERICA.

I KISS HER NOW FOR YOU.

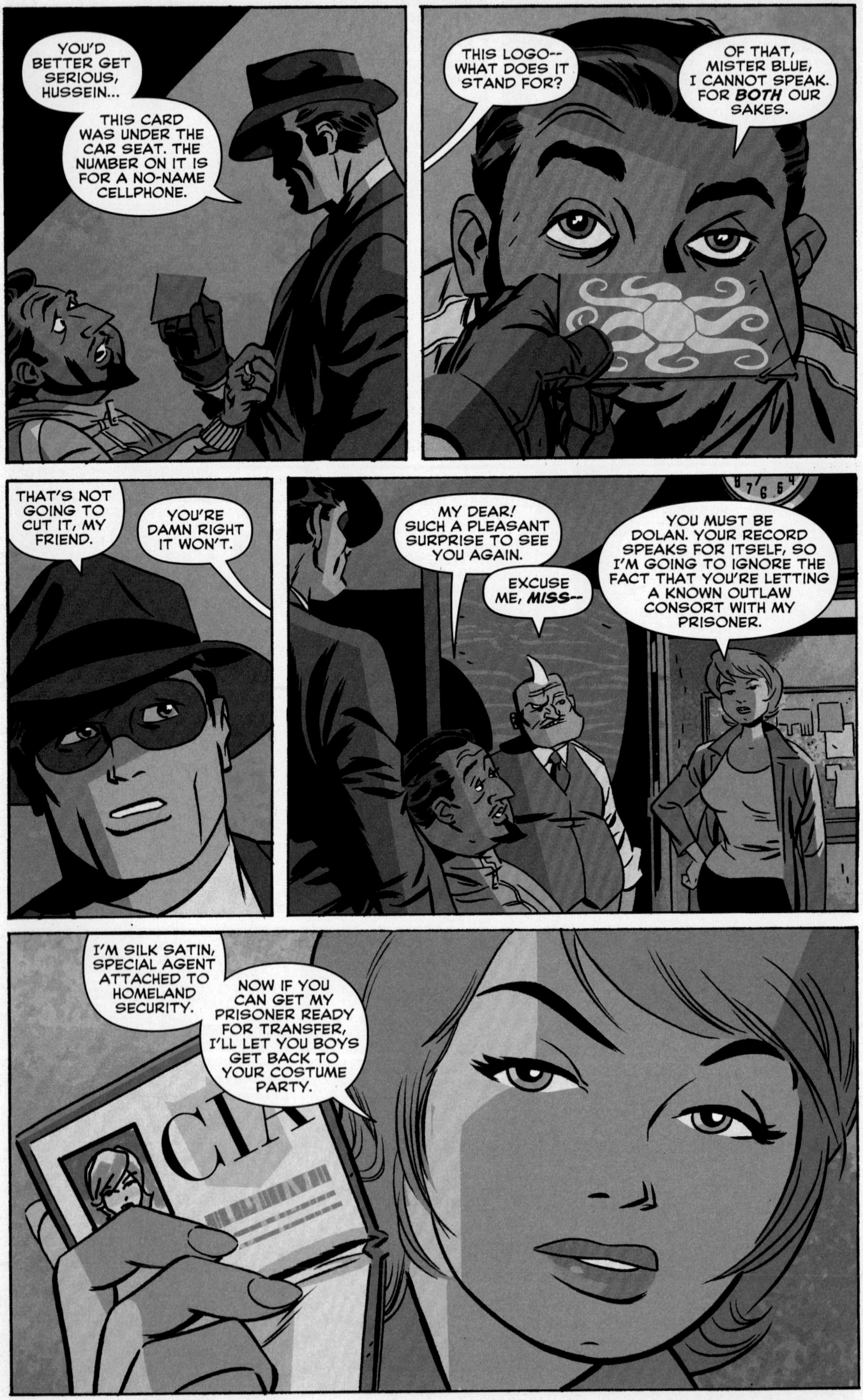
YOU'D BETTER GET SERIOUS, HUSSEIN...
THIS CARD WAS UNDER THE CAR SEAT. THE NUMBER ON IT IS FOR A NO-NAME CELLPHONE.
THIS LOGO--WHAT DOES IT STAND FOR?
OF THAT, MISTER BLUE, I CANNOT SPEAK. FOR BOTH OUR SAKES.
THAT'S NOT GOING TO CUT IT, MY FRIEND.
YOU'RE DAMN RIGHT IT WON'T.
MY DEAR! SUCH A PLEASANT SURPRISE TO SEE YOU AGAIN.
EXCUSE ME, MISS--
YOU MUST BE DOLAN. YOUR RECORD SPEAKS FOR ITSELF, SO I'M GOING TO IGNORE THE FACT THAT YOU'RE LETTING A KNOWN OUTLAW CONSORT WITH MY PRISONER.
I'M SILK SATIN, SPECIAL AGENT ATTACHED TO HOMELAND SECURITY.
NOW IF YOU CAN GET MY PRISONER READY FOR TRANSFER, I'LL LET YOU BOYS GET BACK TO YOUR COSTUME PARTY.
CIA

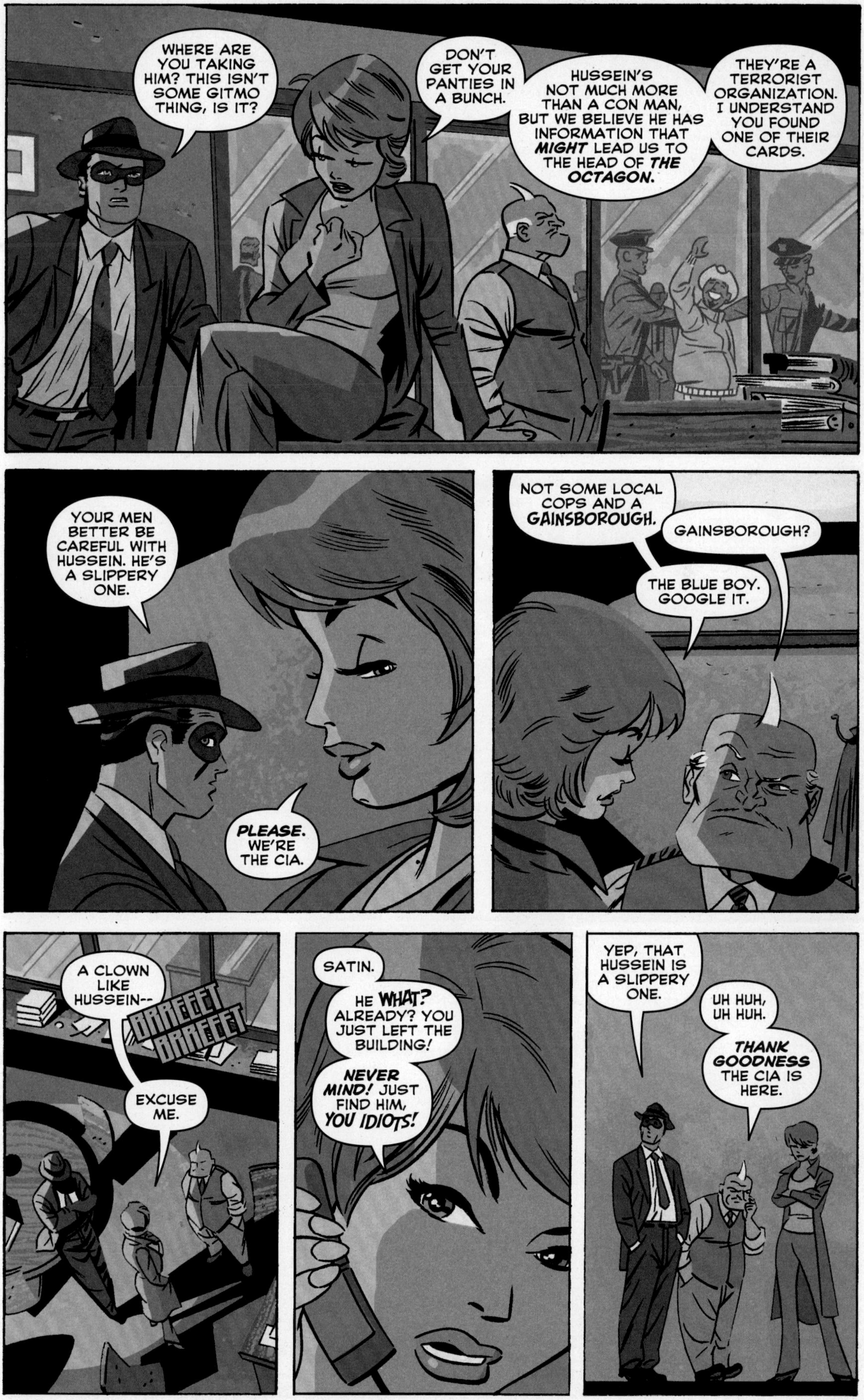
WHERE ARE YOU TAKING HIM? THIS ISN'T SOME GITMO THING, IS IT?
DON'T GET YOUR PANTIES IN A BUNCH.
HUSSEIN'S NOT MUCH MORE THAN A CON MAN, BUT WE BELIEVE HE HAS INFORMATION THAT MIGHT LEAD US TO THE HEAD OF THE OCTAGON.
THEY'RE A TERRORIST ORGANIZATION. I UNDERSTAND YOU FOUND ONE OF THEIR CARDS.
YOUR MEN BETTER BE CAREFUL WITH HUSSEIN. HE'S A SLIPPERY ONE.
PLEASE. WE'RE THE CIA.
NOT SOME LOCAL COPS AND A GAINSBOROUGH.
GAINSBOROUGH?
THE BLUE BOY. GOOGLE IT.
A CLOWN LIKE HUSSEIN--
BRREEET BRREEET
EXCUSE ME.
SATIN.
HE WHAT? ALREADY? YOU JUST LEFT THE BUILDING!
NEVER MIND! JUST FIND HIM, YOU IDIOTS!
YEP, THAT HUSSEIN IS A SLIPPERY ONE.
UH HUH, UH HUH.
THANK GOODNESS THE CIA IS HERE.

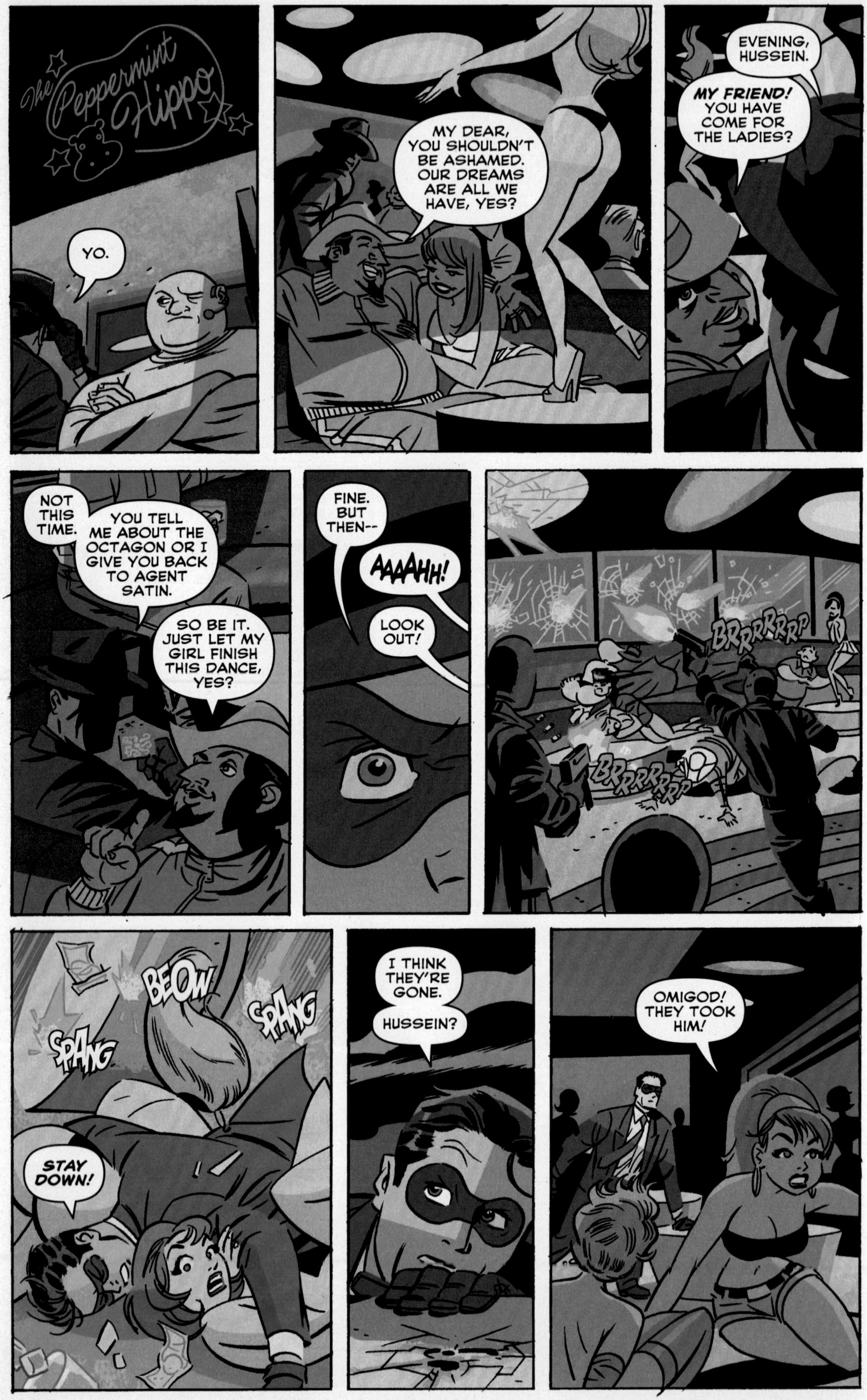
The Peppermint Hippo
YO.
MY DEAR, YOU SHOULDN'T BE ASHAMED. OUR DREAMS ARE ALL WE HAVE, YES?
EVENING, HUSSEIN.
MY FRIEND! YOU HAVE COME FOR THE LADIES?
NOT THIS TIME.
YOU TELL ME ABOUT THE OCTAGON OR I GIVE YOU BACK TO AGENT SATIN.
SO BE IT. JUST LET MY GIRL FINISH THIS DANCE, YES?
FINE. BUT THEN--
AAAAHH!
LOOK OUT!
BRRRRRP
BRRRRRRP
BEOW
SPANG
SPANG
STAY DOWN!
I THINK THEY'RE GONE.
HUSSEIN?
OMIGOD! THEY TOOK HIM!

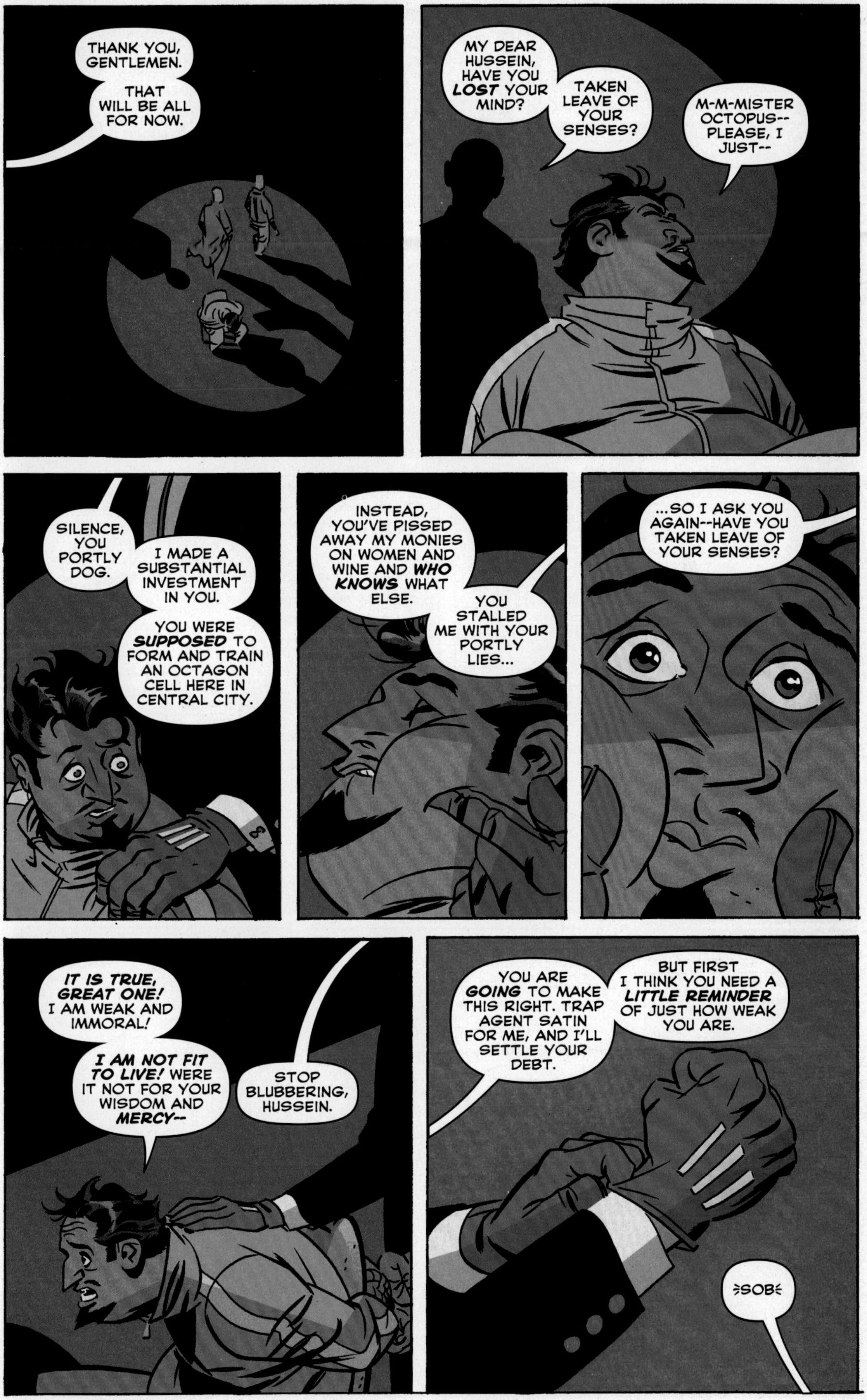
THANK YOU, GENTLEMEN.
THAT WILL BE ALL FOR NOW.
MY DEAR HUSSEIN, HAVE YOU LOST YOUR MIND?
TAKEN LEAVE OF YOUR SENSES?
M-M-MISTER OCTOPUS-- PLEASE, I JUST--
SILENCE, YOU PORTLY DOG.
I MADE A SUBSTANTIAL INVESTMENT IN YOU.
YOU WERE SUPPOSED TO FORM AND TRAIN AN OCTAGON CELL HERE IN CENTRAL CITY.
INSTEAD, YOU'VE PISSED AWAY MY MONIES ON WOMEN AND WINE AND WHO KNOWS WHAT ELSE.
YOU STALLED ME WITH YOUR PORTLY LIES...
...SO I ASK YOU AGAIN--HAVE YOU TAKEN LEAVE OF YOUR SENSES?
IT IS TRUE, GREAT ONE! I AM WEAK AND IMMORAL!
I AM NOT FIT TO LIVE! WERE IT NOT FOR YOUR WISDOM AND MERCY--
STOP BLUBBERING, HUSSEIN.
YOU ARE GOING TO MAKE THIS RIGHT. TRAP AGENT SATIN FOR ME, AND I'LL SETTLE YOUR DEBT.
BUT FIRST I THINK YOU NEED A LITTLE REMINDER OF JUST HOW WEAK YOU ARE.
SOB

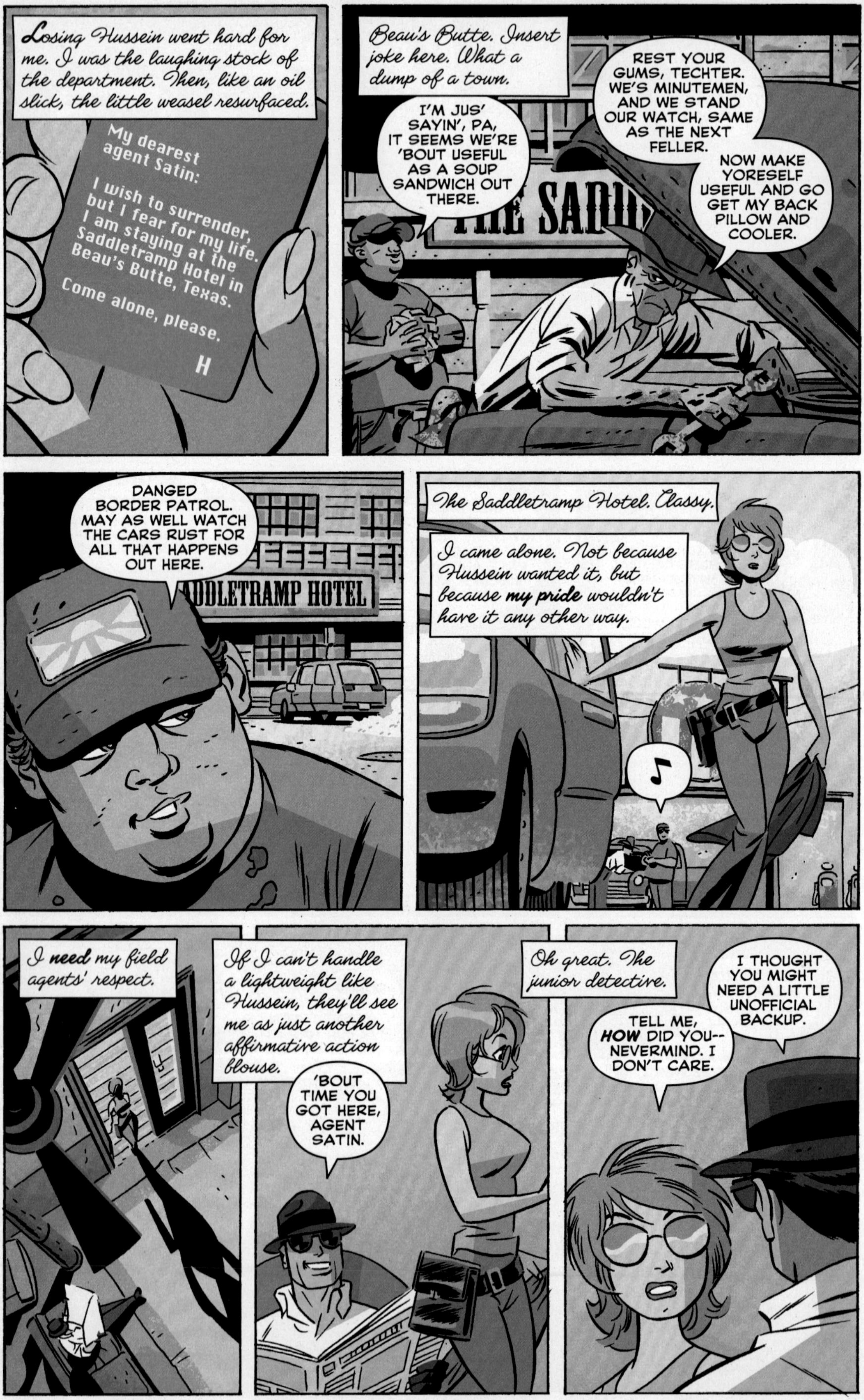
Losing Hussein went hard for me. I was the laughing stock of the department. Then, like an oil slick, the little weasel resurfaced.
My dearest agent Satin:
I wish to surrender, but I fear for my life. I am staying at the Saddletramp Hotel in Beau's Butte, Texas.
Come alone, please.
H
Beau's Butte. Insert joke here. What a dump of a town.
I'M JUS' SAYIN', PA, IT SEEMS WE'RE 'BOUT USEFUL AS A SOUP SANDWICH OUT THERE.
REST YOUR GUMS, TECHTER. WE'S MINUTEMEN, AND WE STAND OUR WATCH, SAME AS THE NEXT FELLER.
NOW MAKE YORESELF USEFUL AND GO GET MY BACK PILLOW AND COOLER.
DANGED BORDER PATROL. MAY AS WELL WATCH THE CARS RUST FOR ALL THAT HAPPENS OUT HERE.
ADDLETRAMP HOTEL
The Saddletramp Hotel. Classy.
I came alone. Not because Hussein wanted it, but because **my pride** wouldn't have it any other way.
♪
I **need** my field agents' respect.
If I can't handle a lightweight like Hussein, they'll see me as just another affirmative action blouse.
'BOUT TIME YOU GOT HERE, AGENT SATIN.
Oh great. The junior detective.
I THOUGHT YOU MIGHT NEED A LITTLE UNOFFICIAL BACKUP.
TELL ME, ***HOW*** DID YOU-- NEVERMIND. I DON'T CARE.

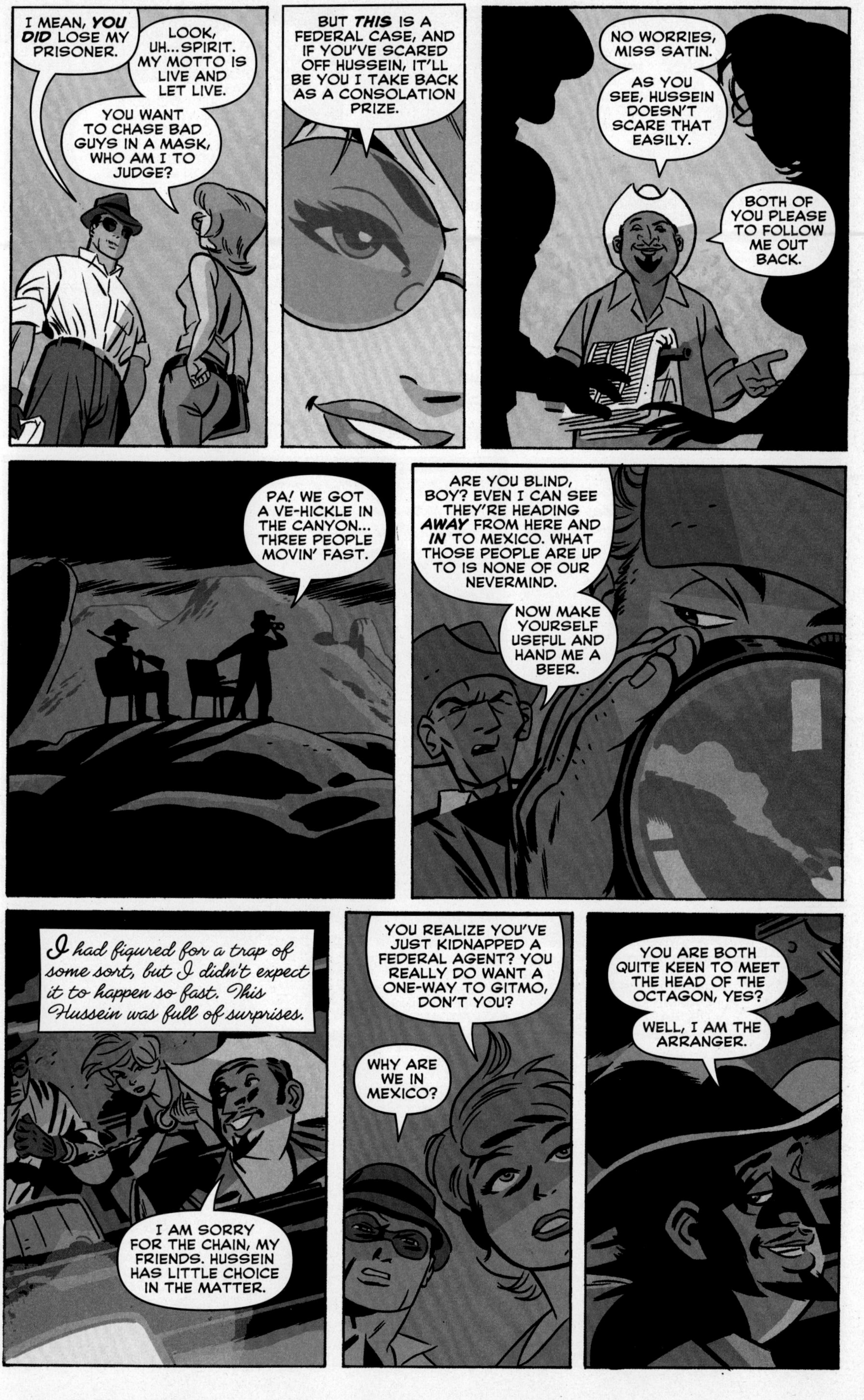
I MEAN, YOU DID LOSE MY PRISONER.
LOOK, UH...SPIRIT. MY MOTTO IS LIVE AND LET LIVE.
YOU WANT TO CHASE BAD GUYS IN A MASK, WHO AM I TO JUDGE?
BUT THIS IS A FEDERAL CASE, AND IF YOU'VE SCARED OFF HUSSEIN, IT'LL BE YOU I TAKE BACK AS A CONSOLATION PRIZE.
NO WORRIES, MISS SATIN.
AS YOU SEE, HUSSEIN DOESN'T SCARE THAT EASILY.
BOTH OF YOU PLEASE TO FOLLOW ME OUT BACK.
PA! WE GOT A VE-HICKLE IN THE CANYON... THREE PEOPLE MOVIN' FAST.
ARE YOU BLIND, BOY? EVEN I CAN SEE THEY'RE HEADING AWAY FROM HERE AND IN TO MEXICO. WHAT THOSE PEOPLE ARE UP TO IS NONE OF OUR NEVERMIND.
NOW MAKE YOURSELF USEFUL AND HAND ME A BEER.
I had figured for a trap of some sort, but I didn't expect it to happen so fast. This Hussein was full of surprises.
I AM SORRY FOR THE CHAIN, MY FRIENDS. HUSSEIN HAS LITTLE CHOICE IN THE MATTER.
YOU REALIZE YOU'VE JUST KIDNAPPED A FEDERAL AGENT? YOU REALLY DO WANT A ONE-WAY TO GITMO, DON'T YOU?
WHY ARE WE IN MEXICO?
YOU ARE BOTH QUITE KEEN TO MEET THE HEAD OF THE OCTAGON, YES?
WELL, I AM THE ARRANGER.

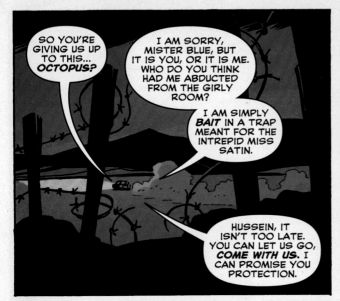

SO YOU'RE GIVING US UP TO THIS... *OCTOPUS?*

I AM SORRY, MISTER BLUE, BUT IT IS YOU, OR IT IS ME. WHO DO YOU THINK HAD ME ABDUCTED FROM THE GIRLY ROOM?

I AM SIMPLY *BAIT* IN A TRAP MEANT FOR THE INTREPID MISS SATIN.

HUSSEIN, IT ISN'T TOO LATE. YOU CAN LET US GO, *COME WITH US.* I CAN PROMISE YOU PROTECTION.

MISS SATIN, HUSSEIN WAS NOT BORN YESTERDAY.

IF I DO NOT DELIVER YOU TO THE OCTOPUS, I WILL BE *HUNTED DOWN AND KILLED*, NO MATTER WHERE I HIDE.

*Pitch black, and I'm chained to Gainsborough. This does not look good.*

OUT PLEASE.

MOVE TO THE FRONT OF THE TRUCK.

*Need a plan. Need it fast. The question is, will beefcake foul me up?*

KA-CHUNK

*Great. Now I'm blind as well.*

FREEZE, AGENT SATIN.

SILK SATIN. THE PRIDE OF THE CIA.

COUNTER-TERRORIST EXPERT. SINGLE. ONE DAUGHTER, DECEASED.

THEY SAY THAT THE BOSNIANS WORKED ON YOU FOR *TEN DAYS* OVER THAT KESSLER THING. YOU NEVER TALKED, AND IN THE END YOU *KILLED EVERY ONE OF THEM* AND MADE YOUR WAY TO THE BORDER ON FOOT.

IN THE DEAD OF WINTER, *NO LESS.* YOU ARE A FORCE OF NATURE, MY DEAR.

WHY NOT START A FANSITE.

IF YOU BROUGHT ME OUT HERE FOR INFORMATION, YOU AREN'T GOING TO GET IT. THE SPIRIT--

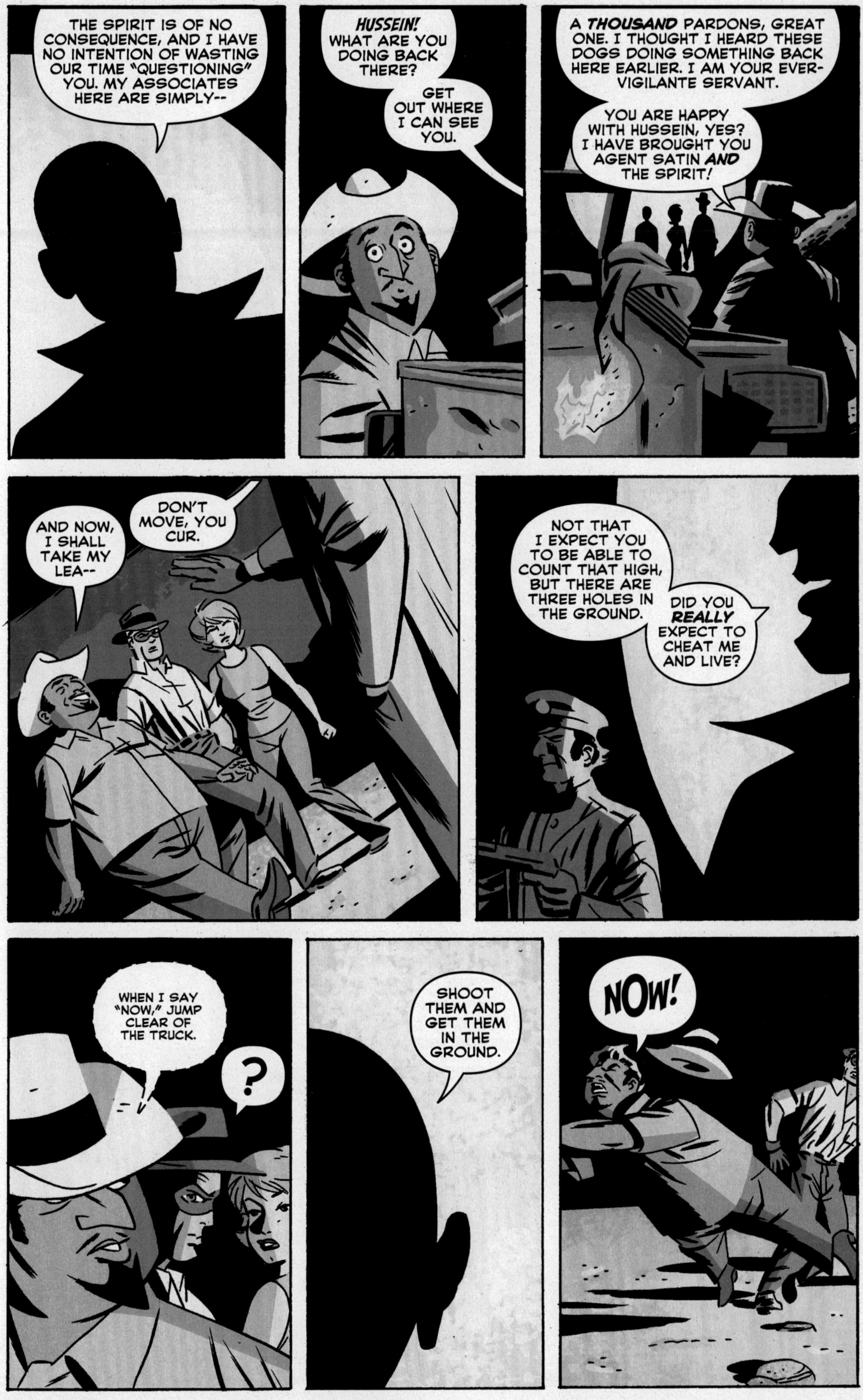
THE SPIRIT IS OF NO CONSEQUENCE, AND I HAVE NO INTENTION OF WASTING OUR TIME "QUESTIONING" YOU. MY ASSOCIATES HERE ARE SIMPLY--
HUSSEIN! WHAT ARE YOU DOING BACK THERE?
GET OUT WHERE I CAN SEE YOU.
A THOUSAND PARDONS, GREAT ONE. I THOUGHT I HEARD THESE DOGS DOING SOMETHING BACK HERE EARLIER. I AM YOUR EVER-VIGILANTE SERVANT.
YOU ARE HAPPY WITH HUSSEIN, YES? I HAVE BROUGHT YOU AGENT SATIN AND THE SPIRIT!
AND NOW, I SHALL TAKE MY LEA--
DON'T MOVE, YOU CUR.
NOT THAT I EXPECT YOU TO BE ABLE TO COUNT THAT HIGH, BUT THERE ARE THREE HOLES IN THE GROUND.
DID YOU REALLY EXPECT TO CHEAT ME AND LIVE?
WHEN I SAY "NOW," JUMP CLEAR OF THE TRUCK.
?
SHOOT THEM AND GET THEM IN THE GROUND.
NOW!

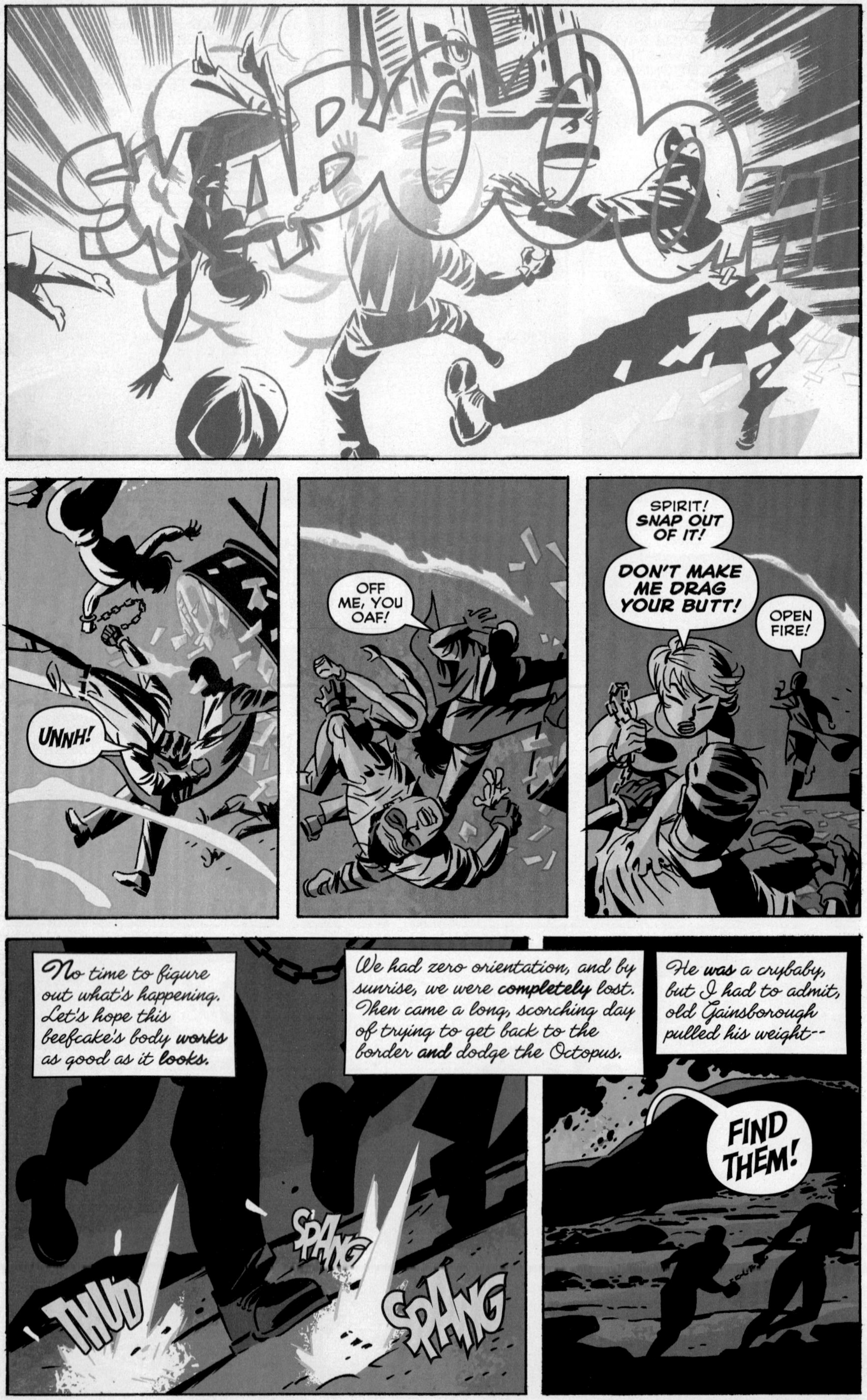
SKABOOOM
UNNH!
OFF ME, YOU OAF!
SPIRIT! SNAP OUT OF IT!
DON'T MAKE ME DRAG YOUR BUTT!
OPEN FIRE!
No time to figure out what's happening. Let's hope this beefcake's body works as good as it looks.
We had zero orientation, and by sunrise, we were completely lost. Then came a long, scorching day of trying to get back to the border and dodge the Octopus.
He was a crybaby, but I had to admit, old Gainsborough pulled his weight--
FIND THEM!
SPANG
THUD
SPANG

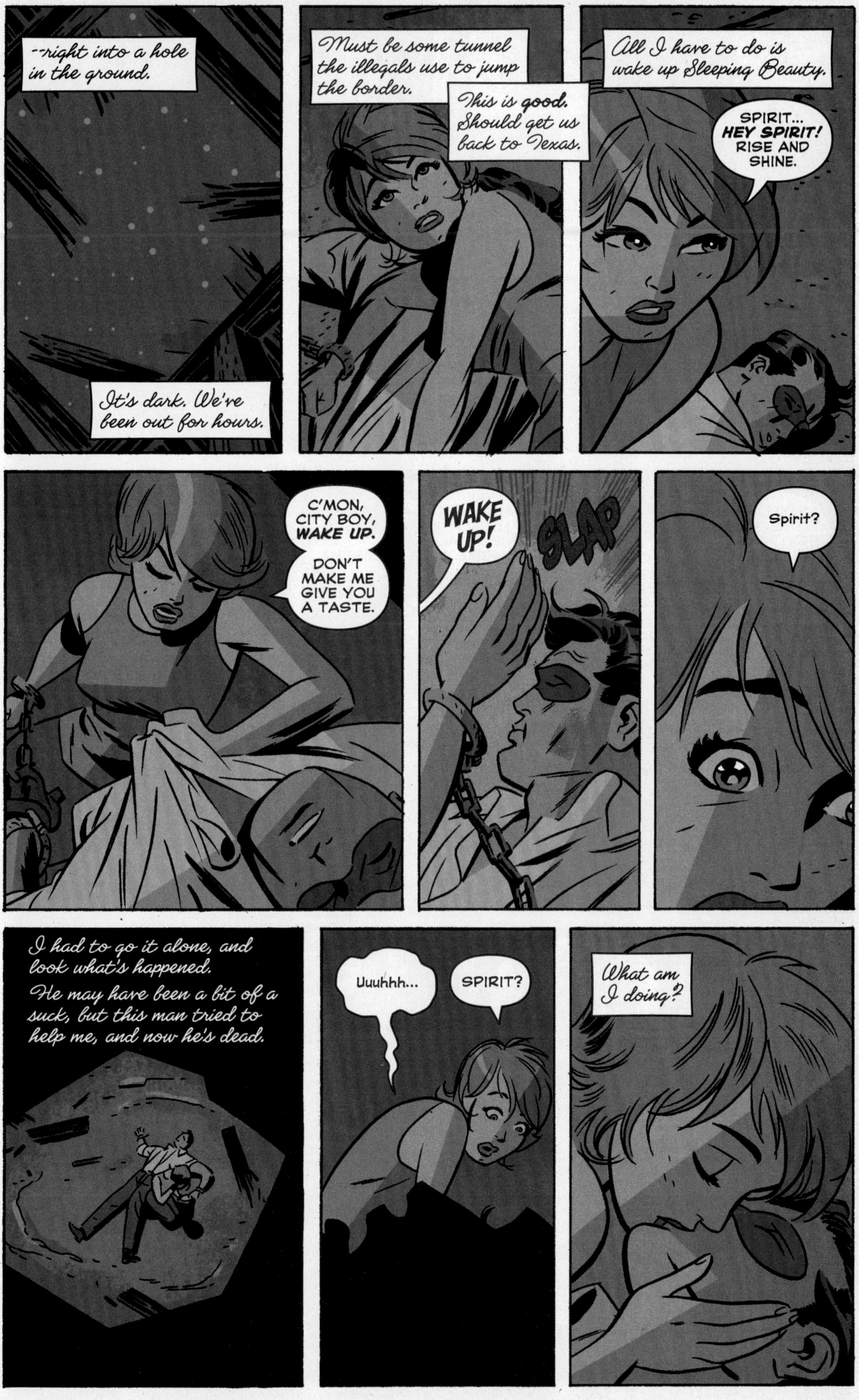
--right into a hole in the ground.
It's dark. We've been out for hours.
Must be some tunnel the illegals use to jump the border.
This is good. Should get us back to Texas.
All I have to do is wake up Sleeping Beauty.
SPIRIT... HEY SPIRIT! RISE AND SHINE.
C'MON, CITY BOY, WAKE UP.
DON'T MAKE ME GIVE YOU A TASTE.
WAKE UP!
SLAP
Spirit?
I had to go it alone, and look what's happened.
He may have been a bit of a suck, but this man tried to help me, and now he's dead.
Uuuhhh...
SPIRIT?
What am I doing?

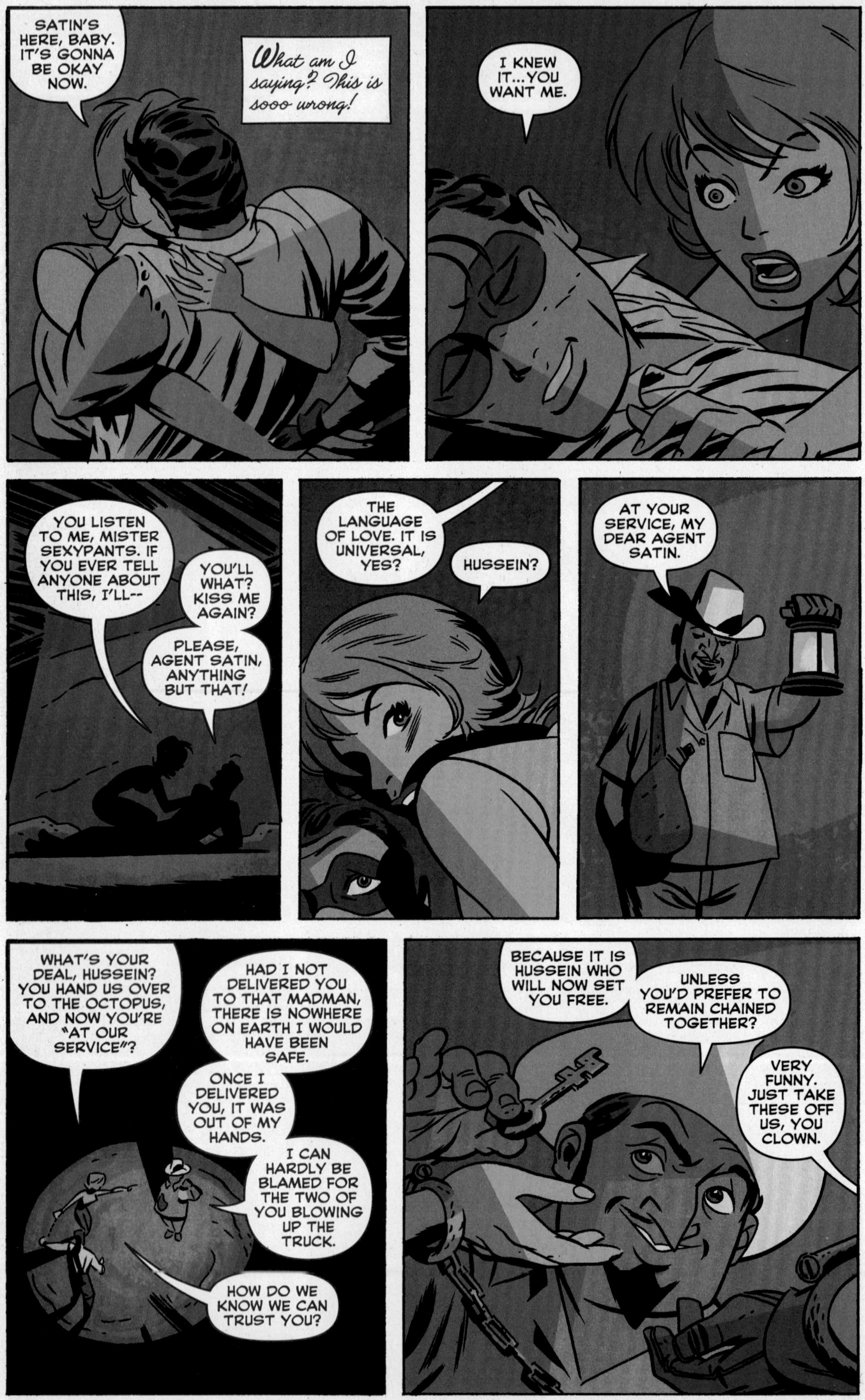
SATIN'S HERE, BABY. IT'S GONNA BE OKAY NOW.
What am I saying? This is sooo wrong!
I KNEW IT...YOU WANT ME.
YOU LISTEN TO ME, MISTER SEXYPANTS. IF YOU EVER TELL ANYONE ABOUT THIS, I'LL--
YOU'LL WHAT? KISS ME AGAIN?
PLEASE, AGENT SATIN, ANYTHING BUT THAT!
THE LANGUAGE OF LOVE. IT IS UNIVERSAL, YES?
HUSSEIN?
AT YOUR SERVICE, MY DEAR AGENT SATIN.
WHAT'S YOUR DEAL, HUSSEIN? YOU HAND US OVER TO THE OCTOPUS, AND NOW YOU'RE "AT OUR SERVICE"?
HAD I NOT DELIVERED YOU TO THAT MADMAN, THERE IS NOWHERE ON EARTH I WOULD HAVE BEEN SAFE.
ONCE I DELIVERED YOU, IT WAS OUT OF MY HANDS.
I CAN HARDLY BE BLAMED FOR THE TWO OF YOU BLOWING UP THE TRUCK.
HOW DO WE KNOW WE CAN TRUST YOU?
BECAUSE IT IS HUSSEIN WHO WILL NOW SET YOU FREE.
UNLESS YOU'D PREFER TO REMAIN CHAINED TOGETHER?
VERY FUNNY. JUST TAKE THESE OFF US, YOU CLOWN.

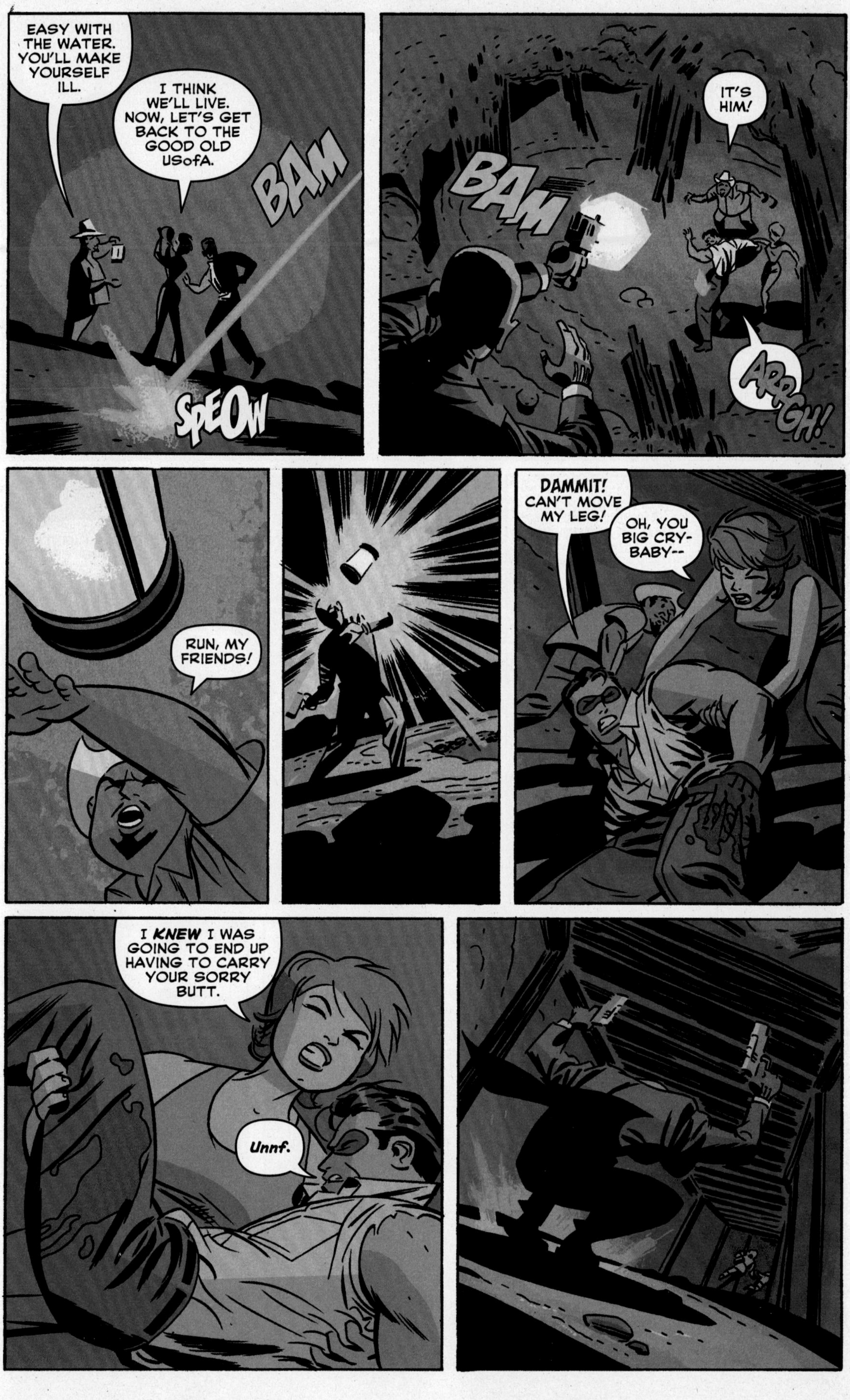
EASY WITH THE WATER. YOU'LL MAKE YOURSELF ILL.
I THINK WE'LL LIVE. NOW, LET'S GET BACK TO THE GOOD OLD USofA.
BAM
SPEOW
IT'S HIM!
BAM
ARRGH!
RUN, MY FRIENDS!
DAMMIT! CAN'T MOVE MY LEG!
OH, YOU BIG CRY-BABY--
I *KNEW* I WAS GOING TO END UP HAVING TO CARRY YOUR SORRY BUTT.
*Unnf.*

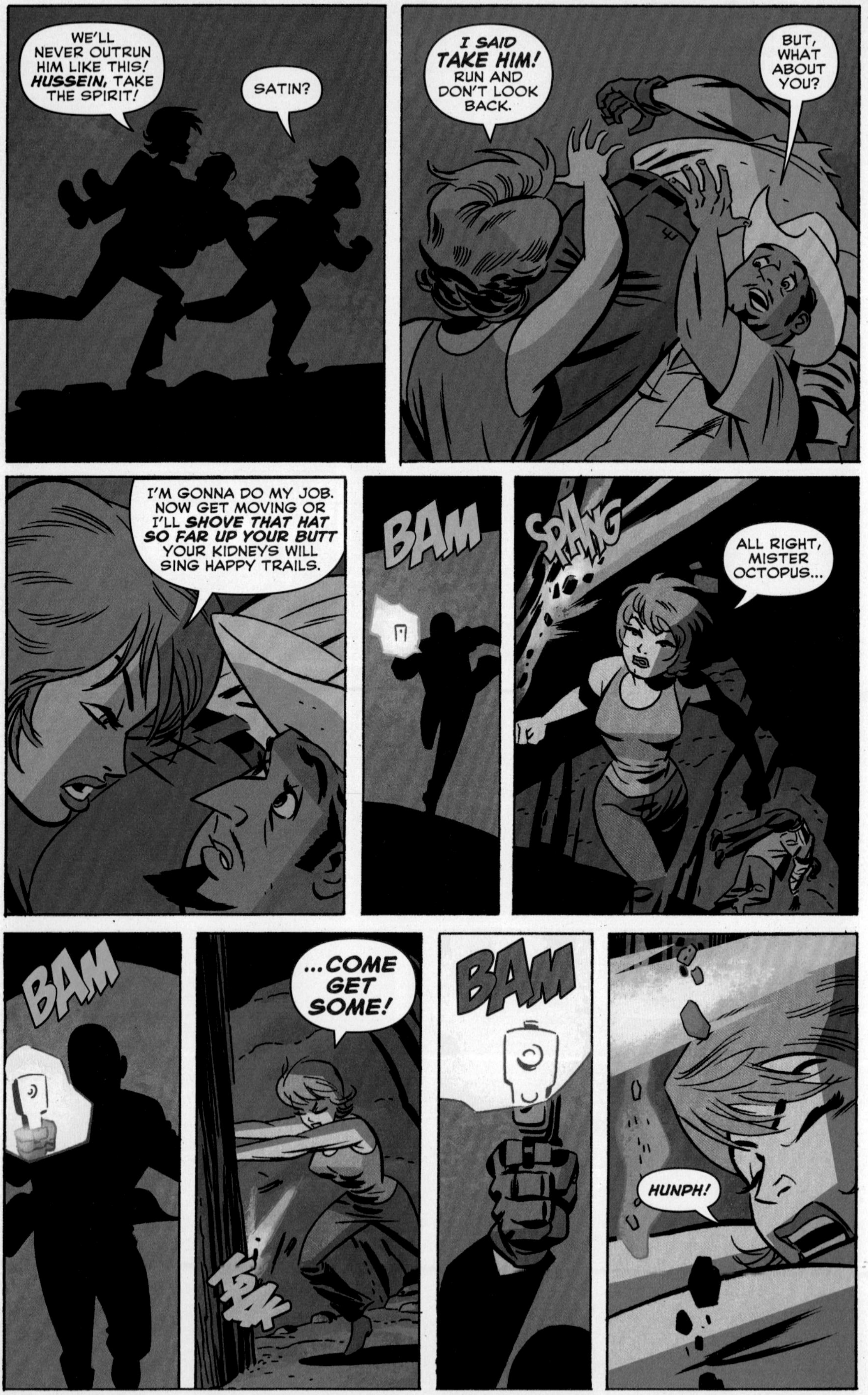

WE'LL NEVER OUTRUN HIM LIKE THIS! HUSSEIN, TAKE THE SPIRIT!
SATIN?
I SAID TAKE HIM! RUN AND DON'T LOOK BACK.
BUT, WHAT ABOUT YOU?
I'M GONNA DO MY JOB. NOW GET MOVING OR I'LL SHOVE THAT HAT SO FAR UP YOUR BUTT YOUR KIDNEYS WILL SING HAPPY TRAILS.
BAM
SPANG
ALL RIGHT, MISTER OCTOPUS...
BAM
...COME GET SOME!
KLANK
BAM
HUNPH!

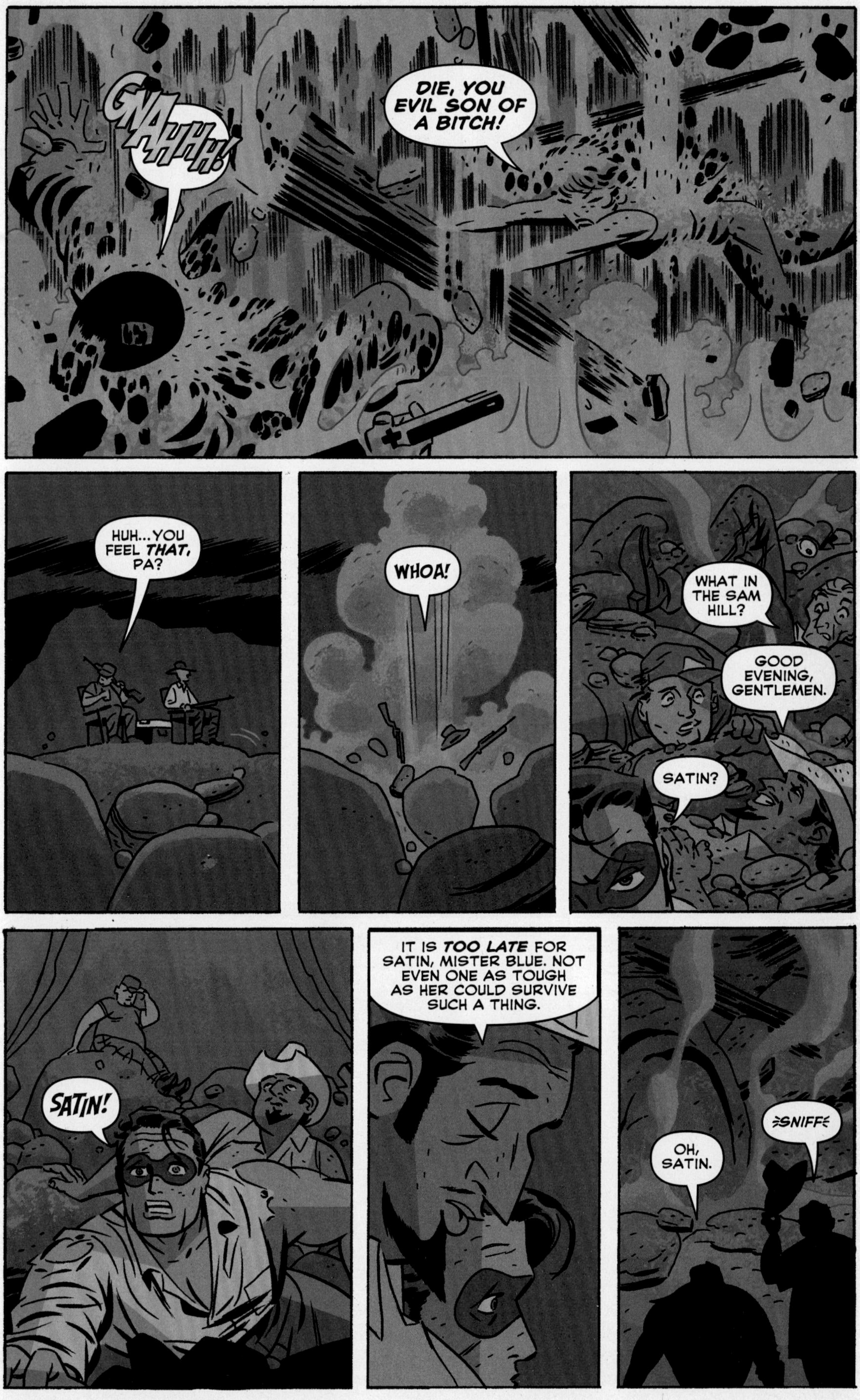
GNAHHH!
DIE, YOU EVIL SON OF A BITCH!
HUH...YOU FEEL THAT, PA?
WHOA!
WHAT IN THE SAM HILL?
GOOD EVENING, GENTLEMEN.
SATIN?
SATIN!
IT IS TOO LATE FOR SATIN, MISTER BLUE. NOT EVEN ONE AS TOUGH AS HER COULD SURVIVE SUCH A THING.
OH, SATIN.
SNIFF

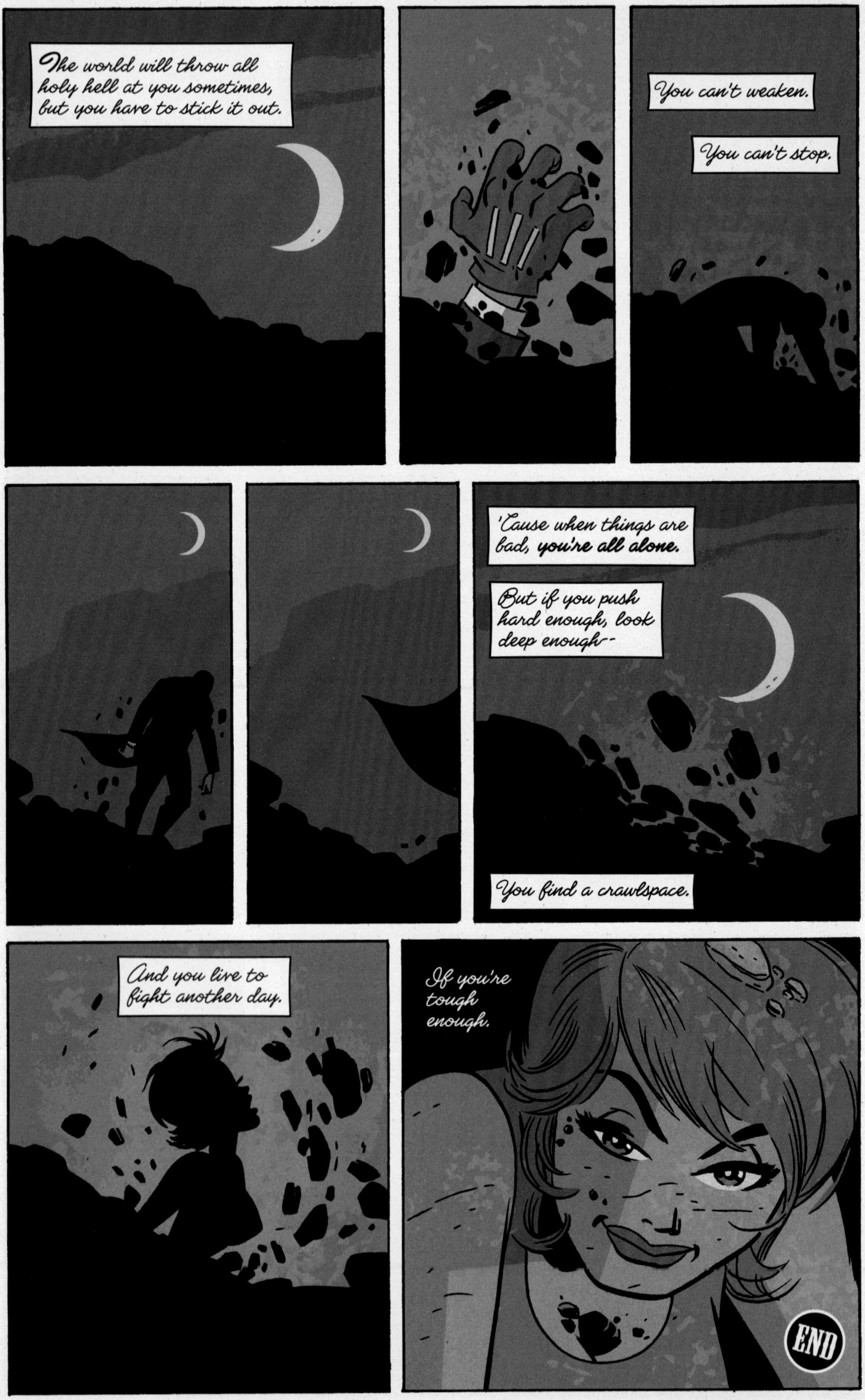
The world will throw all holy hell at you sometimes, but you have to stick it out.
You can't weaken.
You can't stop.
'Cause when things are bad, you're all alone.
But if you push hard enough, look deep enough--
You find a crawlspace.
And you live to fight another day.
If you're tough enough.
END

# 5

ACTION • Mystery • ADVENTURE

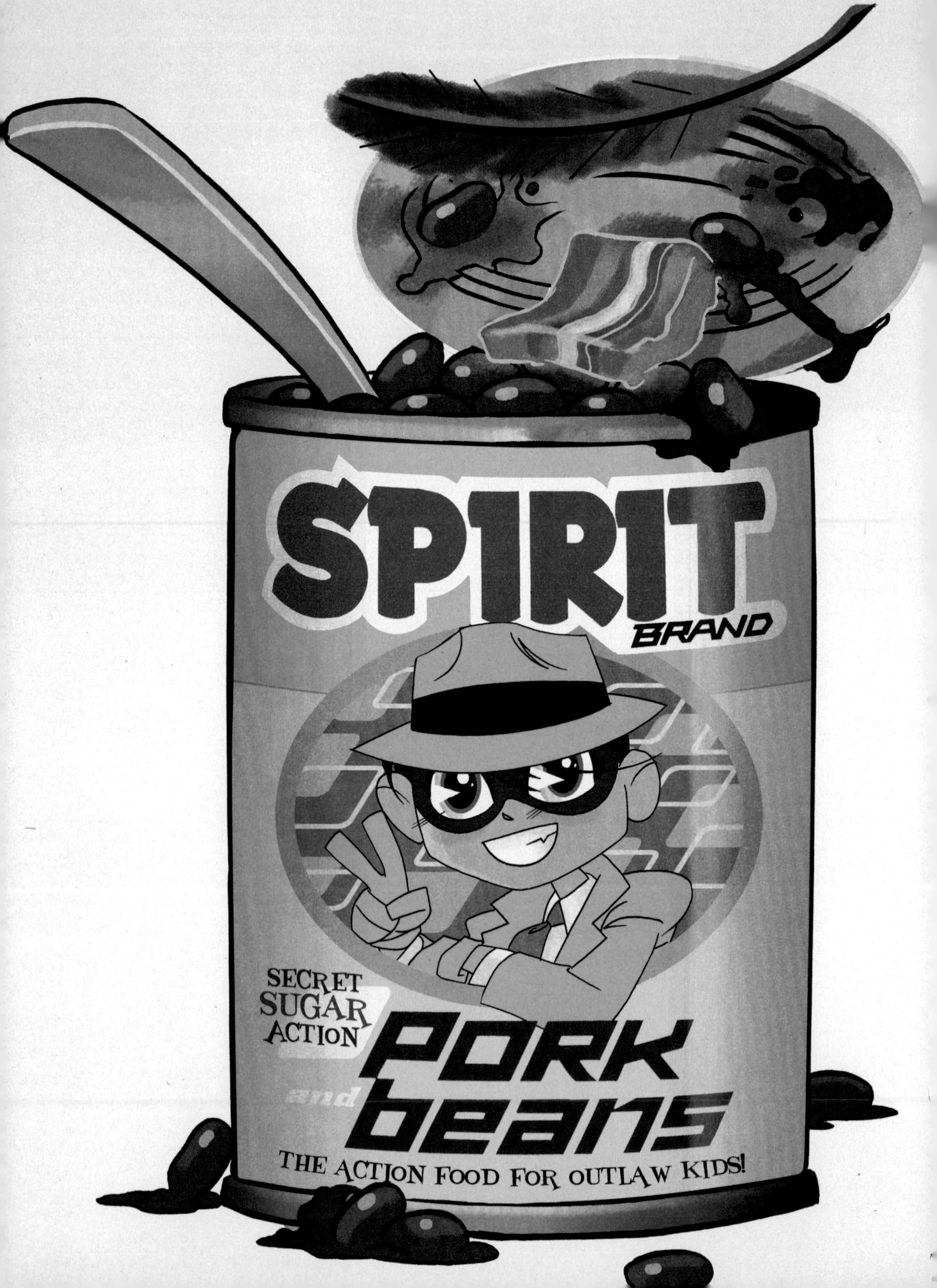
SPIRIT
BRAND
SECRET SUGAR ACTION
PORK and beans
THE ACTION FOOD FOR OUTLAW KIDS!

IT'S LIKE DÉJÀ VU ALL OVER AGAIN.

ANY WITNESSES THIS TIME?

SO FAR, JUST THE LADY WHO CALLED IT IN.

MY MEN ARE CANVASSING THE NEARBY BUILDINGS.

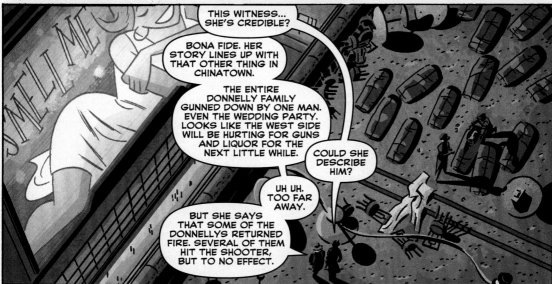

THIS WITNESS... SHE'S CREDIBLE?

BONA FIDE. HER STORY LINES UP WITH THAT OTHER THING IN CHINATOWN.

THE ENTIRE DONNELLY FAMILY GUNNED DOWN BY ONE MAN. EVEN THE WEDDING PARTY. LOOKS LIKE THE WEST SIDE WILL BE HURTING FOR GUNS AND LIQUOR FOR THE NEXT LITTLE WHILE.

COULD SHE DESCRIBE HIM?

UH UH. TOO FAR AWAY.

BUT SHE SAYS THAT SOME OF THE DONNELLYS RETURNED FIRE. SEVERAL OF THEM HIT THE SHOOTER, BUT TO NO EFFECT.

MUST'VE BEEN WEARING BODY ARMOR. IF IT WAS MORTEZ--

?

NO WAY.

DEAR *GOD!*

WILL EISNER'S
SP
THIS CAN'T BE GOOD.
DAVE STEWART color JARED FLETCHER letters KRISTY QUINN as'st editor
by DARWYN COOKE • J. BONE finishes

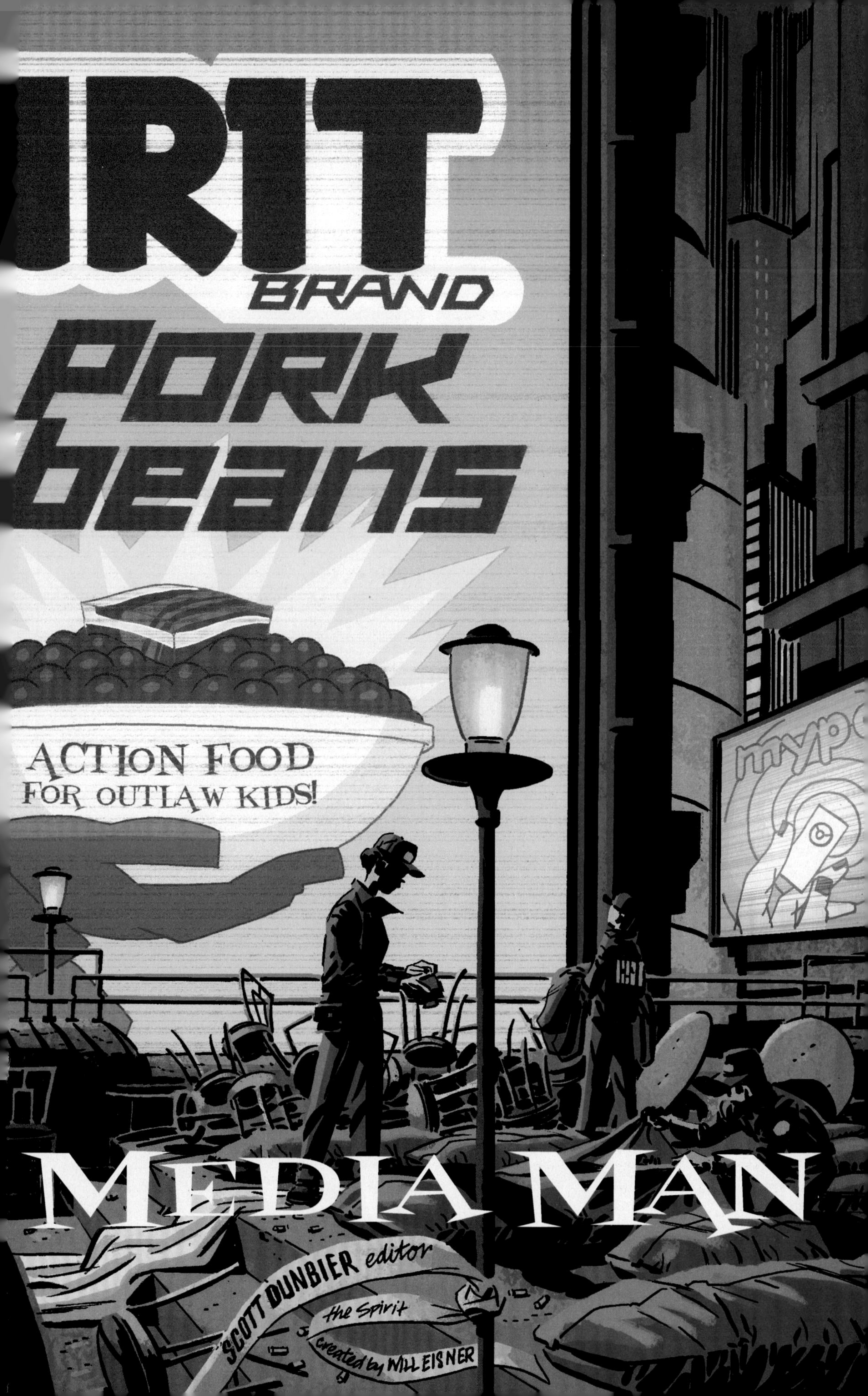
BRAND
PORK beans
ACTION FOOD
FOR OUTLAW KIDS!
MEDIA MAN
SCOTT DUNBIER editor
the Spirit
created by WILL EISNER

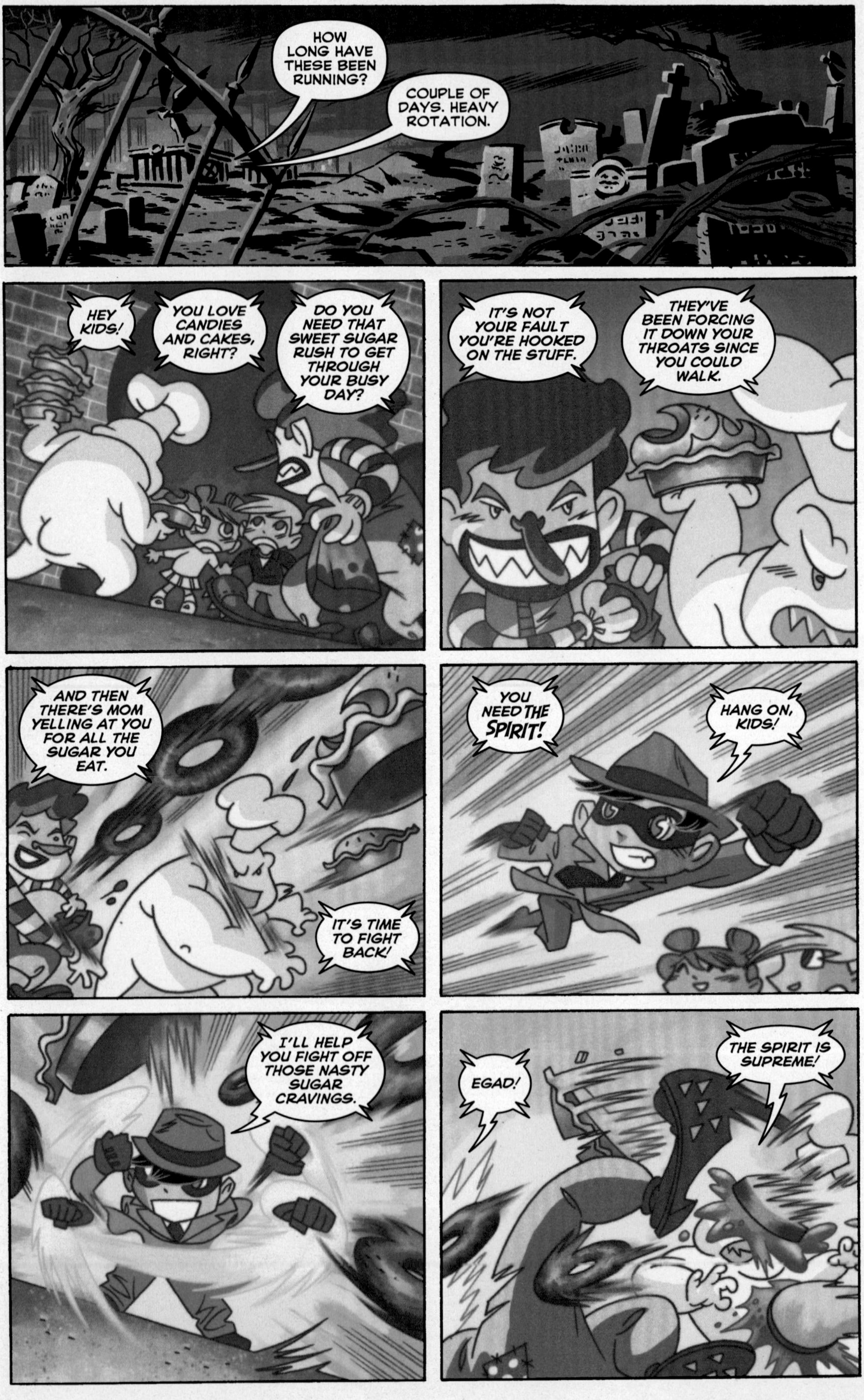
HOW LONG HAVE THESE BEEN RUNNING?
COUPLE OF DAYS. HEAVY ROTATION.
HEY KIDS!
YOU LOVE CANDIES AND CAKES, RIGHT?
DO YOU NEED THAT SWEET SUGAR RUSH TO GET THROUGH YOUR BUSY DAY?
IT'S NOT YOUR FAULT YOU'RE HOOKED ON THE STUFF.
THEY'VE BEEN FORCING IT DOWN YOUR THROATS SINCE YOU COULD WALK.
AND THEN THERE'S MOM YELLING AT YOU FOR ALL THE SUGAR YOU EAT.
IT'S TIME TO FIGHT BACK!
YOU NEED THE SPIRIT!
HANG ON, KIDS!
I'LL HELP YOU FIGHT OFF THOSE NASTY SUGAR CRAVINGS.
EGAD!
THE SPIRIT IS SUPREME!

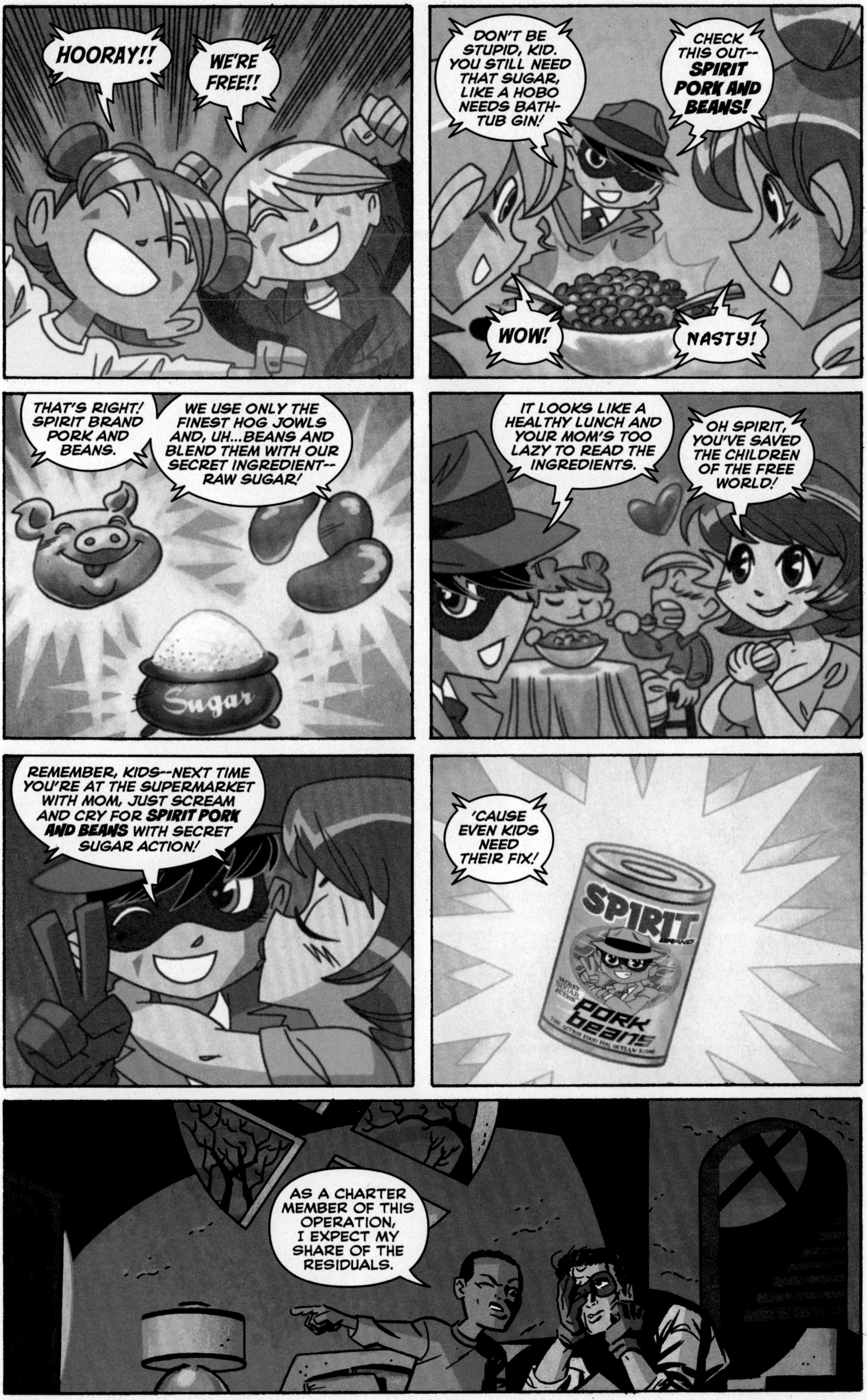
HOORAY!!
WE'RE FREE!!
DON'T BE STUPID, KID. YOU STILL NEED THAT SUGAR, LIKE A HOBO NEEDS BATH-TUB GIN!
CHECK THIS OUT-- SPIRIT PORK AND BEANS!
WOW!
NASTY!
THAT'S RIGHT! SPIRIT BRAND PORK AND BEANS.
WE USE ONLY THE FINEST HOG JOWLS AND, UH...BEANS AND BLEND THEM WITH OUR SECRET INGREDIENT-- RAW SUGAR!
Sugar
IT LOOKS LIKE A HEALTHY LUNCH AND YOUR MOM'S TOO LAZY TO READ THE INGREDIENTS.
OH SPIRIT, YOU'VE SAVED THE CHILDREN OF THE FREE WORLD!
REMEMBER, KIDS--NEXT TIME YOU'RE AT THE SUPERMARKET WITH MOM, JUST SCREAM AND CRY FOR SPIRIT PORK AND BEANS WITH SECRET SUGAR ACTION!
'CAUSE EVEN KIDS NEED THEIR FIX!
SPIRIT BRAND
PORK beans
AS A CHARTER MEMBER OF THIS OPERATION, I EXPECT MY SHARE OF THE RESIDUALS.

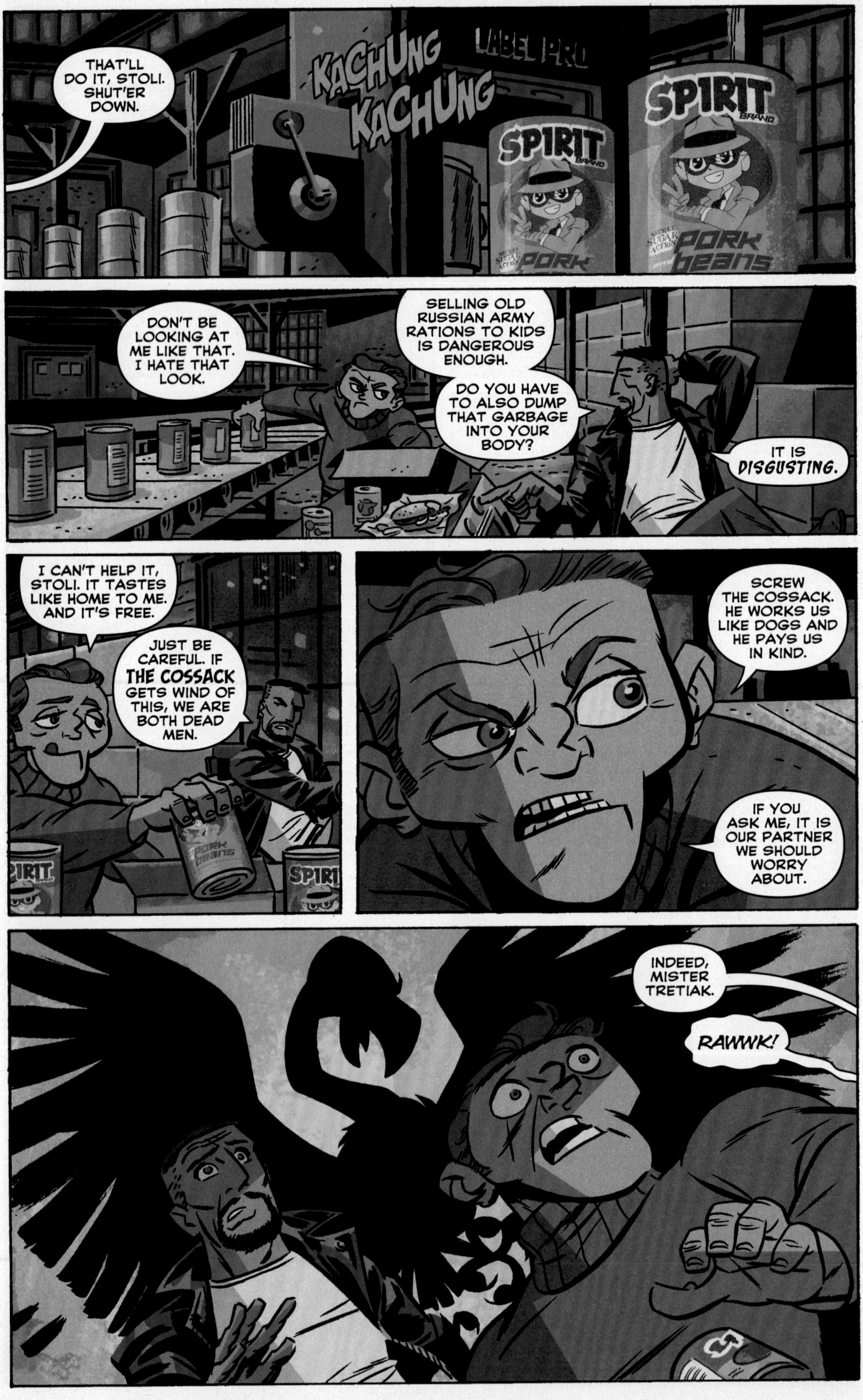
THAT'LL DO IT, STOLI. SHUT'ER DOWN.
KACHUNG KACHUNG
LABEL PRO
SPIRIT BRAND
SECRET SUGAR ACTION PORK
SPIRIT BRAND
SECRET SUGAR ACTION PORK beans
DON'T BE LOOKING AT ME LIKE THAT. I HATE THAT LOOK.
SELLING OLD RUSSIAN ARMY RATIONS TO KIDS IS DANGEROUS ENOUGH.
DO YOU HAVE TO ALSO DUMP THAT GARBAGE INTO YOUR BODY?
IT IS DISGUSTING.
I CAN'T HELP IT, STOLI. IT TASTES LIKE HOME TO ME. AND IT'S FREE.
JUST BE CAREFUL. IF THE COSSACK GETS WIND OF THIS, WE ARE BOTH DEAD MEN.
SCREW THE COSSACK. HE WORKS US LIKE DOGS AND HE PAYS US IN KIND.
IF YOU ASK ME, IT IS OUR PARTNER WE SHOULD WORRY ABOUT.
INDEED, MISTER TRETIAK.
RAWWK!

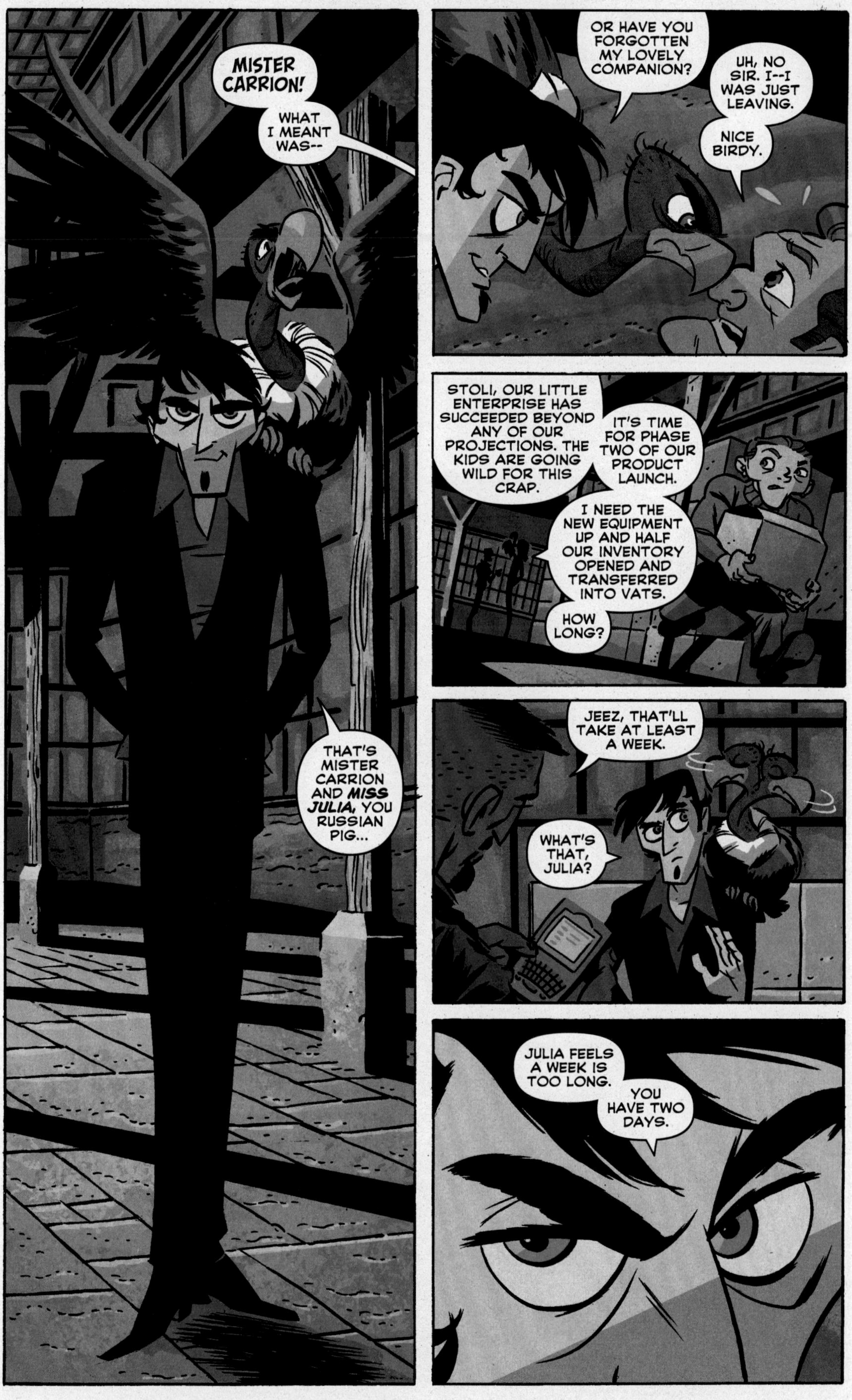
MISTER CARRION!
WHAT I MEANT WAS--
THAT'S MISTER CARRION AND MISS JULIA, YOU RUSSIAN PIG...
OR HAVE YOU FORGOTTEN MY LOVELY COMPANION?
UH, NO SIR. I--I WAS JUST LEAVING.
NICE BIRDY.
STOLI, OUR LITTLE ENTERPRISE HAS SUCCEEDED BEYOND ANY OF OUR PROJECTIONS. THE KIDS ARE GOING WILD FOR THIS CRAP.
IT'S TIME FOR PHASE TWO OF OUR PRODUCT LAUNCH.
I NEED THE NEW EQUIPMENT UP AND HALF OUR INVENTORY OPENED AND TRANSFERRED INTO VATS.
HOW LONG?
JEEZ, THAT'LL TAKE AT LEAST A WEEK.
WHAT'S THAT, JULIA?
JULIA FEELS A WEEK IS TOO LONG.
YOU HAVE TWO DAYS.

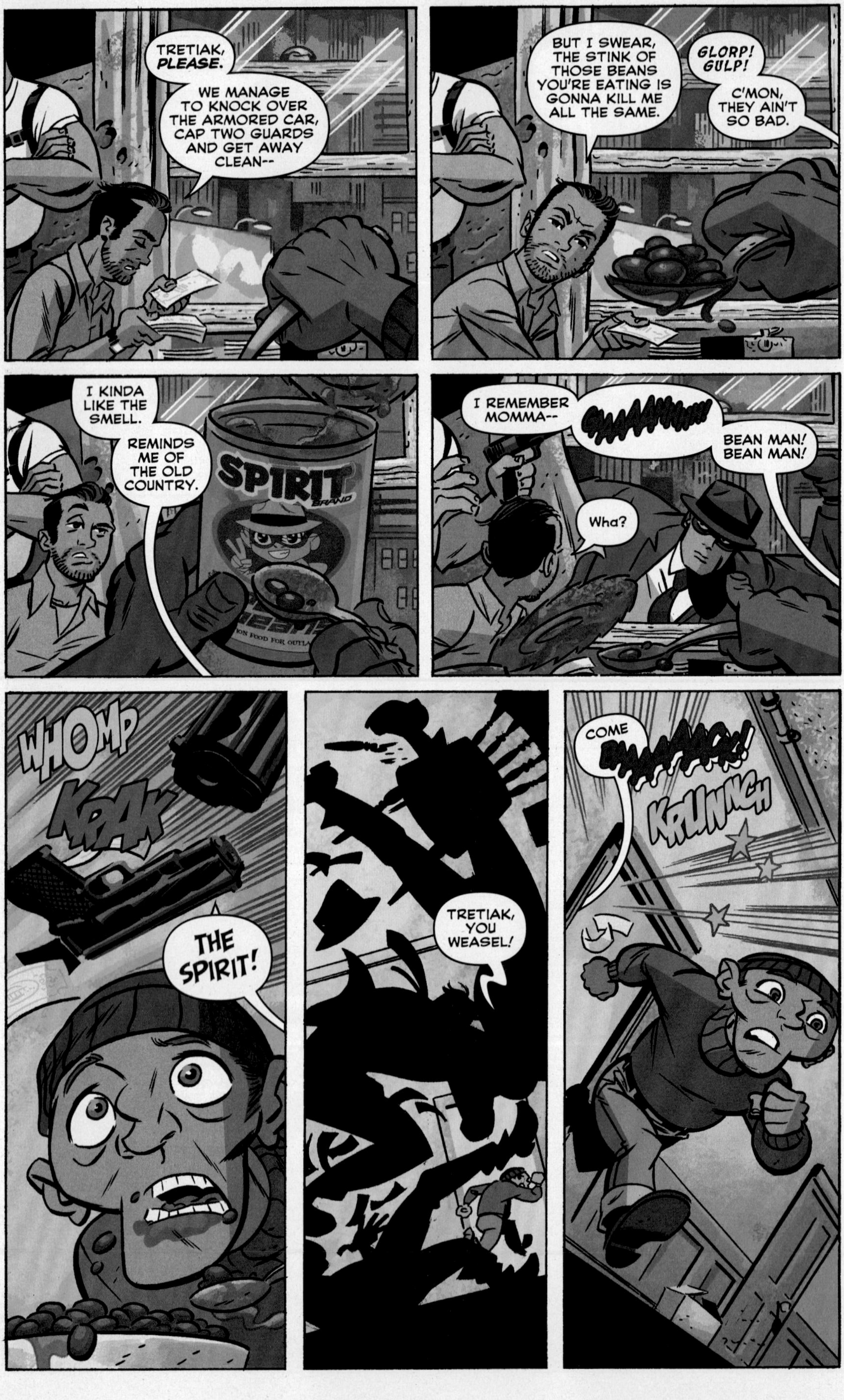
TRETIAK, *PLEASE.*
WE MANAGE TO KNOCK OVER THE ARMORED CAR, CAP TWO GUARDS AND GET AWAY CLEAN--
BUT I SWEAR, THE STINK OF THOSE BEANS YOU'RE EATING IS GONNA KILL ME ALL THE SAME.
*GLORP! GULP!*
C'MON, THEY AIN'T SO BAD.
I KINDA LIKE THE SMELL.
REMINDS ME OF THE OLD COUNTRY.
SPIRIT BRAND
BEANS
ION FOOD FOR OUTLA
I REMEMBER MOMMA--
BEAN MAN! BEAN MAN!
Wha?
WHOMP
KRAK
THE SPIRIT!
TRETIAK, YOU WEASEL!
COME
KRUNNCH

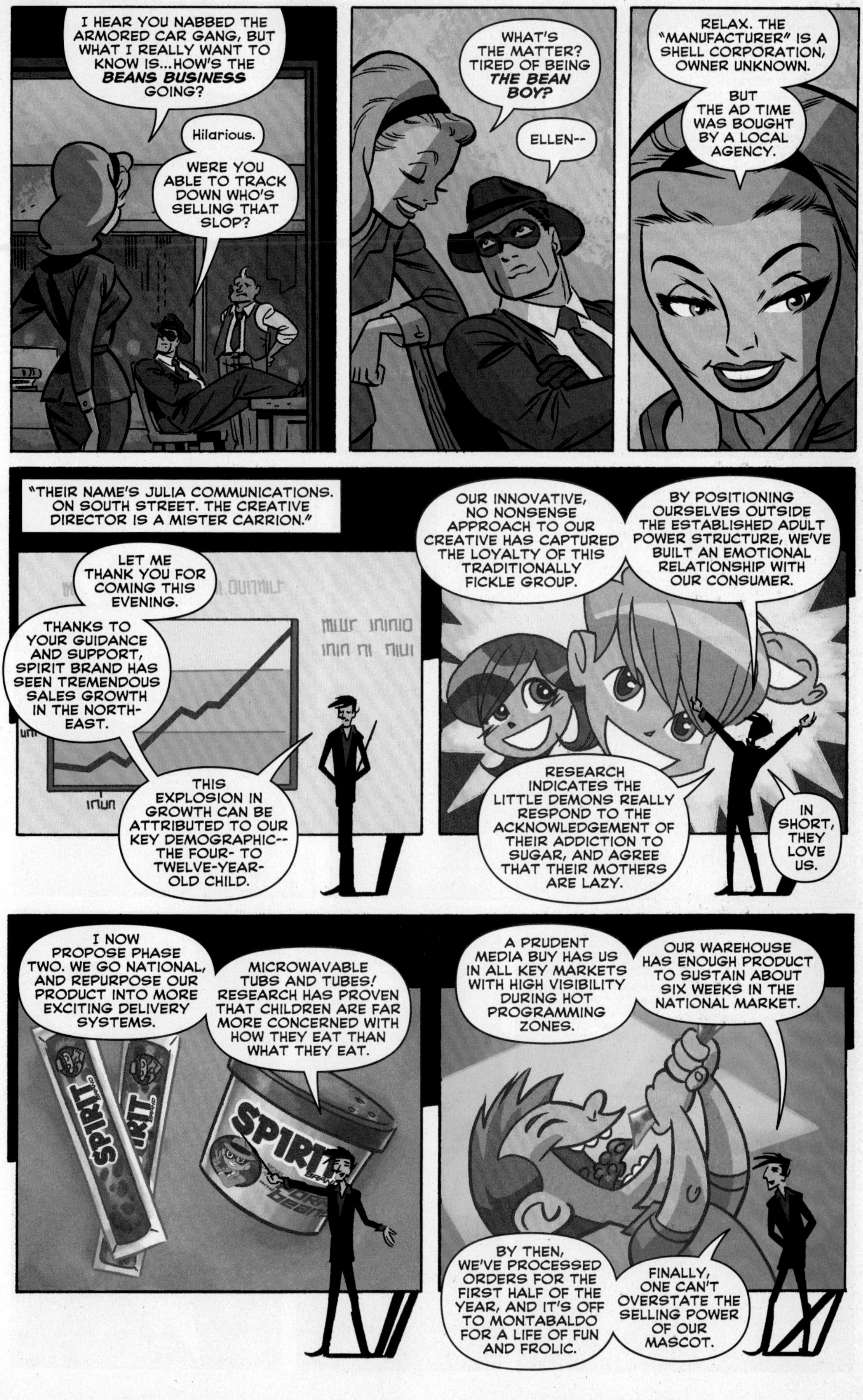
I HEAR YOU NABBED THE ARMORED CAR GANG, BUT WHAT I REALLY WANT TO KNOW IS...HOW'S THE ***BEANS BUSINESS*** GOING?
Hilarious.
WERE YOU ABLE TO TRACK DOWN WHO'S SELLING THAT SLOP?
WHAT'S THE MATTER? TIRED OF BEING ***THE BEAN BOY?***
ELLEN--
RELAX. THE "MANUFACTURER" IS A SHELL CORPORATION, OWNER UNKNOWN.
BUT THE AD TIME WAS BOUGHT BY A LOCAL AGENCY.
"THEIR NAME'S JULIA COMMUNICATIONS. ON SOUTH STREET. THE CREATIVE DIRECTOR IS A MISTER CARRION."
LET ME THANK YOU FOR COMING THIS EVENING.
THANKS TO YOUR GUIDANCE AND SUPPORT, SPIRIT BRAND HAS SEEN TREMENDOUS SALES GROWTH IN THE NORTH-EAST.
THIS EXPLOSION IN GROWTH CAN BE ATTRIBUTED TO OUR KEY DEMOGRAPHIC-- THE FOUR- TO TWELVE-YEAR-OLD CHILD.
OUR INNOVATIVE, NO NONSENSE APPROACH TO OUR CREATIVE HAS CAPTURED THE LOYALTY OF THIS TRADITIONALLY FICKLE GROUP.
BY POSITIONING OURSELVES OUTSIDE THE ESTABLISHED ADULT POWER STRUCTURE, WE'VE BUILT AN EMOTIONAL RELATIONSHIP WITH OUR CONSUMER.
RESEARCH INDICATES THE LITTLE DEMONS REALLY RESPOND TO THE ACKNOWLEDGEMENT OF THEIR ADDICTION TO SUGAR, AND AGREE THAT THEIR MOTHERS ARE LAZY.
IN SHORT, THEY LOVE US.
I NOW PROPOSE PHASE TWO. WE GO NATIONAL, AND REPURPOSE OUR PRODUCT INTO MORE EXCITING DELIVERY SYSTEMS.
MICROWAVABLE TUBS AND TUBES! RESEARCH HAS PROVEN THAT CHILDREN ARE FAR MORE CONCERNED WITH HOW THEY EAT THAN WHAT THEY EAT.
SPIRIT BRAND
SPIRIT BRAND
SPIRIT BRAND
A PRUDENT MEDIA BUY HAS US IN ALL KEY MARKETS WITH HIGH VISIBILITY DURING HOT PROGRAMMING ZONES.
OUR WAREHOUSE HAS ENOUGH PRODUCT TO SUSTAIN ABOUT SIX WEEKS IN THE NATIONAL MARKET.
BY THEN, WE'VE PROCESSED ORDERS FOR THE FIRST HALF OF THE YEAR, AND IT'S OFF TO MONTABALDO FOR A LIFE OF FUN AND FROLIC.
FINALLY, ONE CAN'T OVERSTATE THE SELLING POWER OF OUR MASCOT.

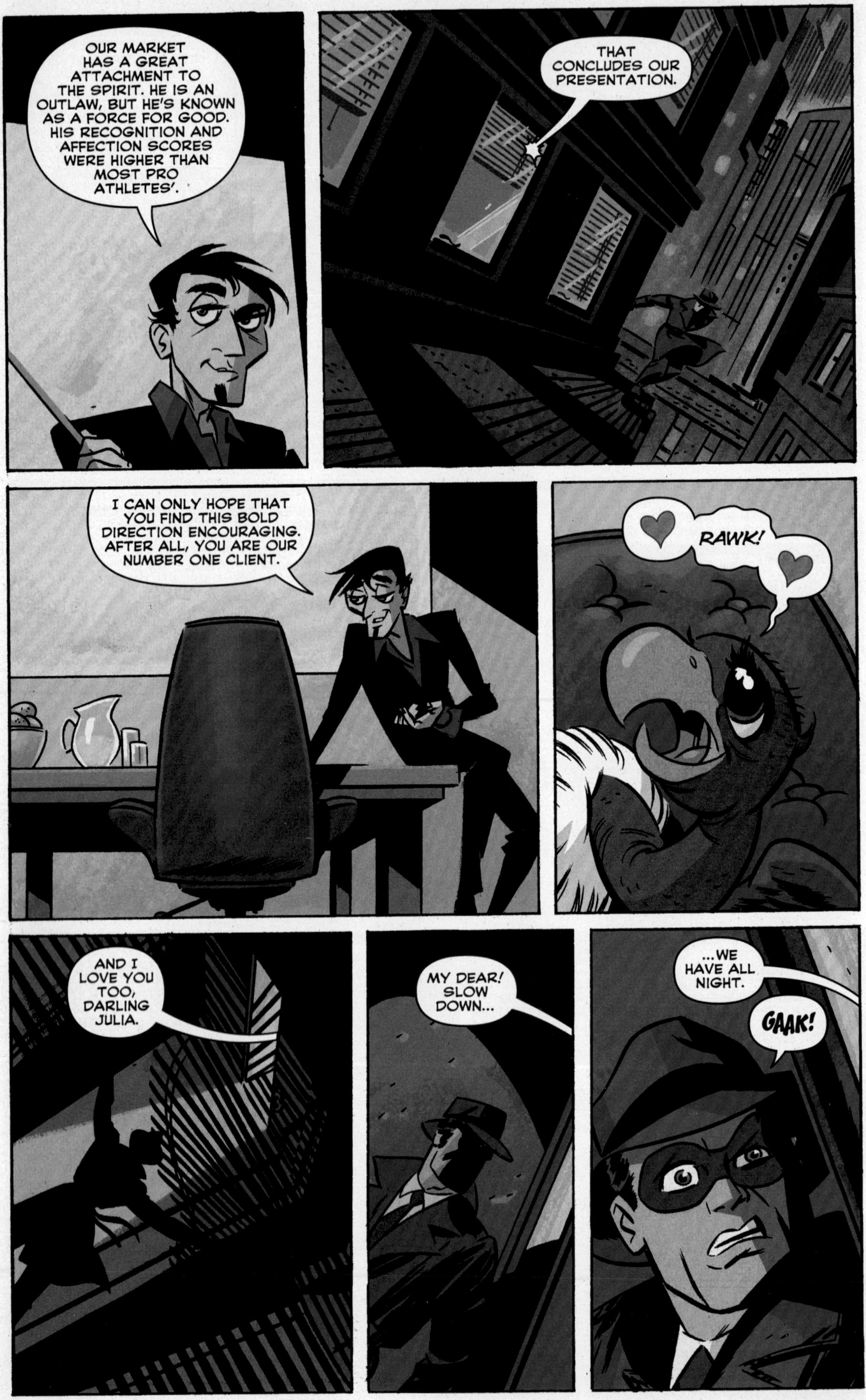
OUR MARKET HAS A GREAT ATTACHMENT TO THE SPIRIT. HE IS AN OUTLAW, BUT HE'S KNOWN AS A FORCE FOR GOOD. HIS RECOGNITION AND AFFECTION SCORES WERE HIGHER THAN MOST PRO ATHLETES'.
THAT CONCLUDES OUR PRESENTATION.
I CAN ONLY HOPE THAT YOU FIND THIS BOLD DIRECTION ENCOURAGING. AFTER ALL, YOU ARE OUR NUMBER ONE CLIENT.
RAWK!
AND I LOVE YOU TOO, DARLING JULIA.
MY DEAR! SLOW DOWN...
...WE HAVE ALL NIGHT.
GAAK!

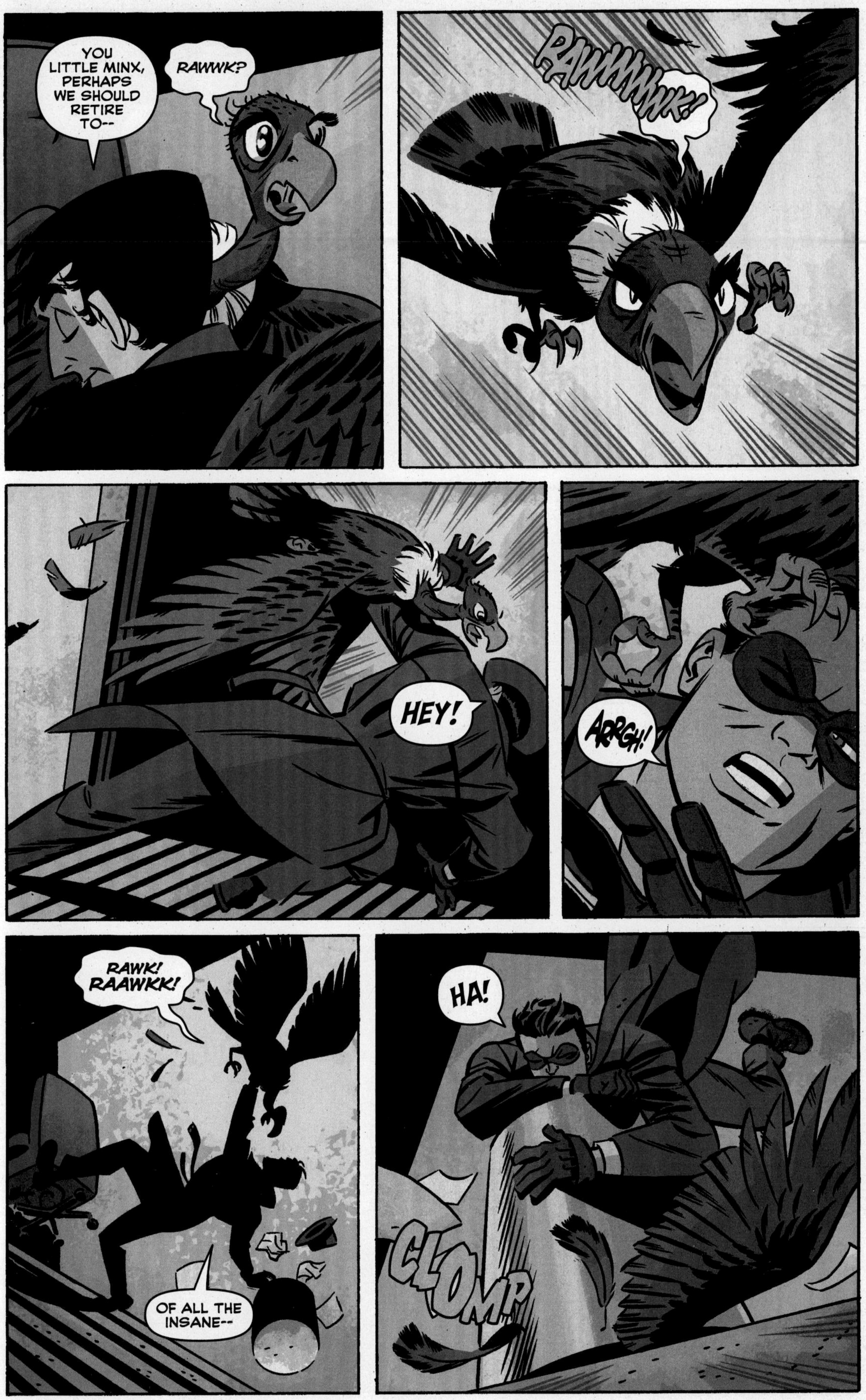
YOU LITTLE MINX, PERHAPS WE SHOULD RETIRE TO--
RAWWK?
RAWWWWWK!
HEY!
ARRGH!
RAWK! RAAWKK!
OF ALL THE INSANE--
HA!
CLOMP

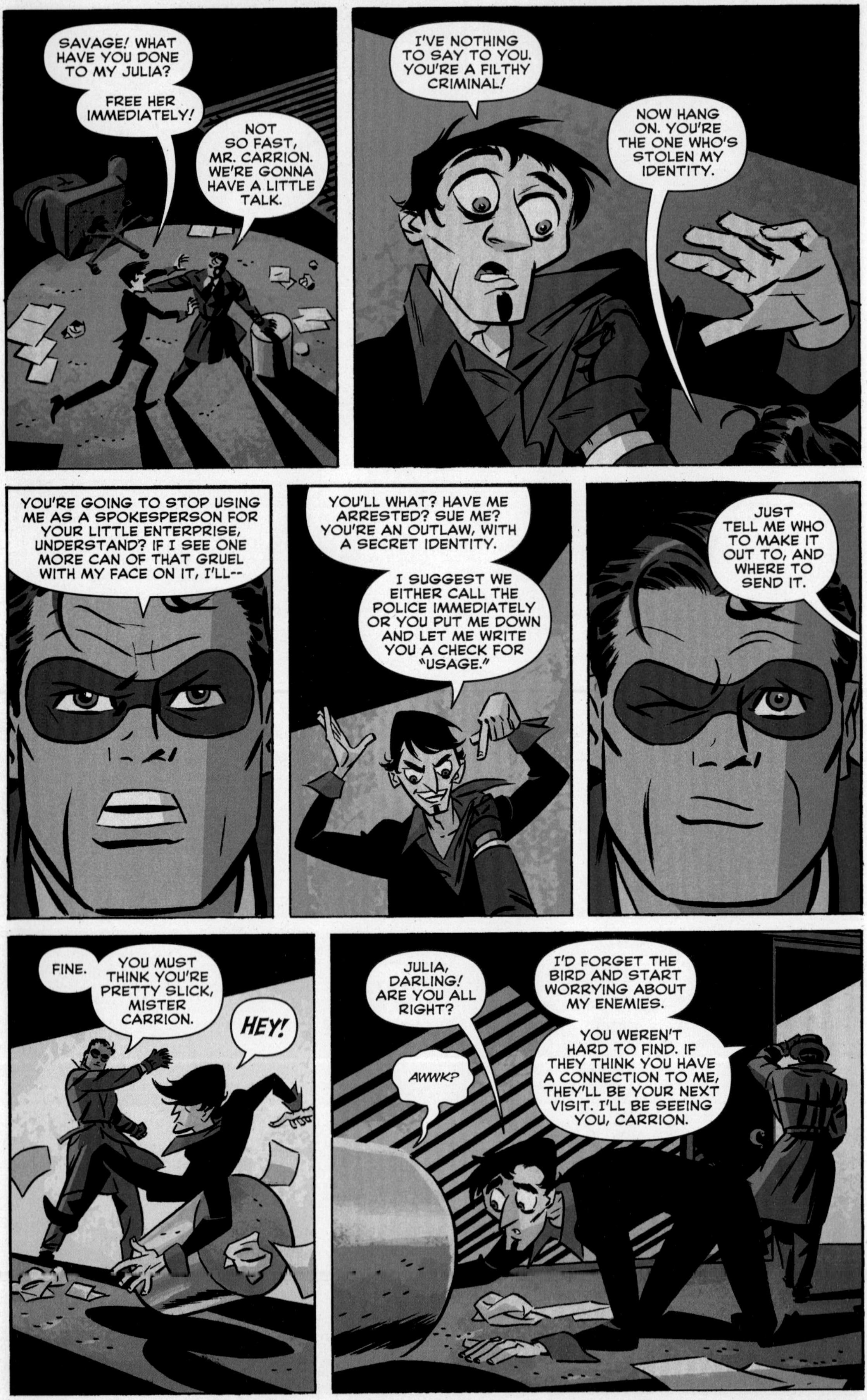
SAVAGE! WHAT HAVE YOU DONE TO MY JULIA?
FREE HER IMMEDIATELY!
NOT SO FAST, MR. CARRION. WE'RE GONNA HAVE A LITTLE TALK.
I'VE NOTHING TO SAY TO YOU. YOU'RE A FILTHY CRIMINAL!
NOW HANG ON. YOU'RE THE ONE WHO'S STOLEN MY IDENTITY.
YOU'RE GOING TO STOP USING ME AS A SPOKESPERSON FOR YOUR LITTLE ENTERPRISE, UNDERSTAND? IF I SEE ONE MORE CAN OF THAT GRUEL WITH MY FACE ON IT, I'LL--
YOU'LL WHAT? HAVE ME ARRESTED? SUE ME? YOU'RE AN OUTLAW, WITH A SECRET IDENTITY.
I SUGGEST WE EITHER CALL THE POLICE IMMEDIATELY OR YOU PUT ME DOWN AND LET ME WRITE YOU A CHECK FOR "USAGE."
JUST TELL ME WHO TO MAKE IT OUT TO, AND WHERE TO SEND IT.
FINE.
YOU MUST THINK YOU'RE PRETTY SLICK, MISTER CARRION.
HEY!
JULIA, DARLING! ARE YOU ALL RIGHT?
AWWK?
I'D FORGET THE BIRD AND START WORRYING ABOUT MY ENEMIES.
YOU WEREN'T HARD TO FIND. IF THEY THINK YOU HAVE A CONNECTION TO ME, THEY'LL BE YOUR NEXT VISIT. I'LL BE SEEING YOU, CARRION.

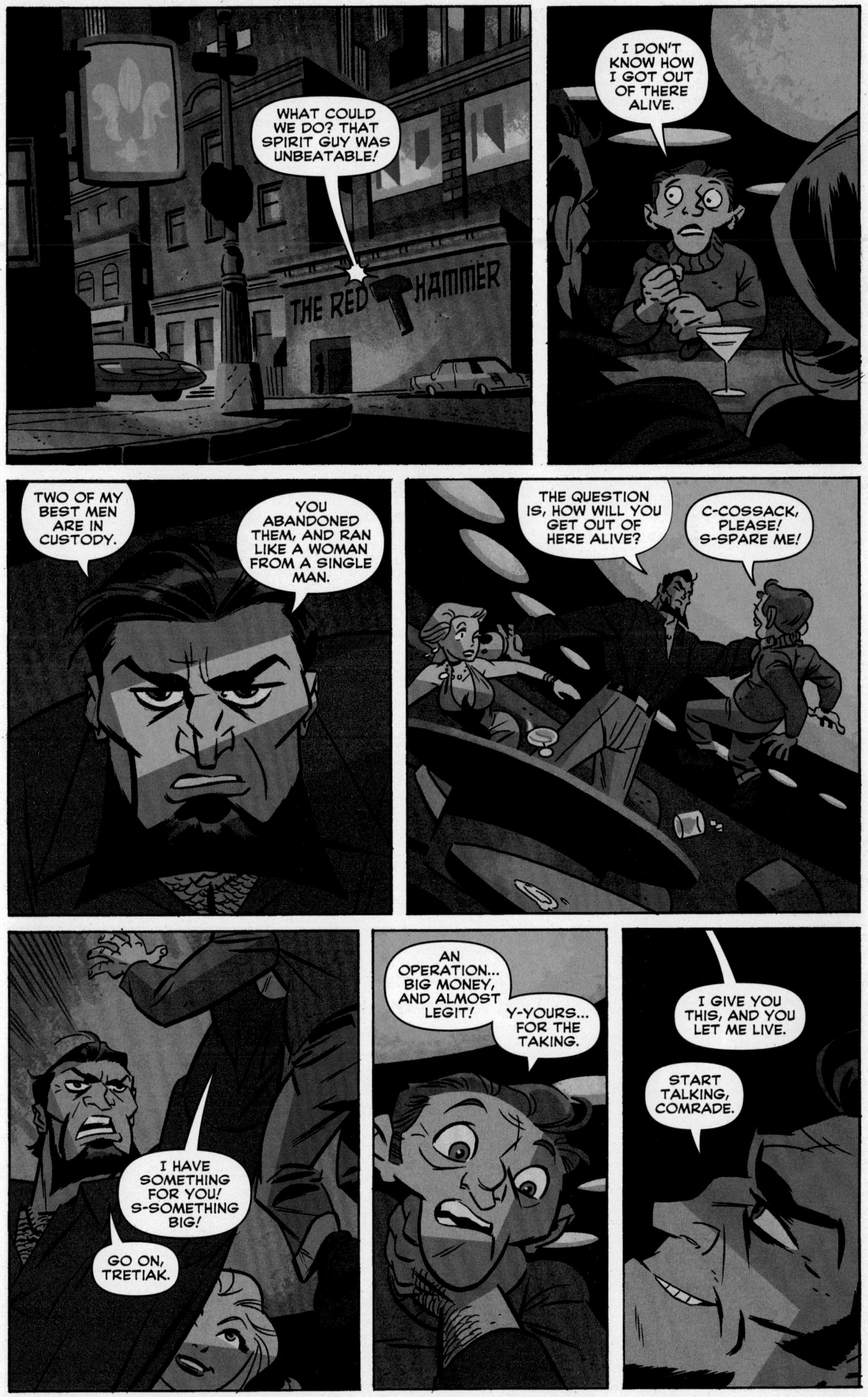
THE RED HAMMER
WHAT COULD WE DO? THAT SPIRIT GUY WAS UNBEATABLE!
I DON'T KNOW HOW I GOT OUT OF THERE ALIVE.
TWO OF MY BEST MEN ARE IN CUSTODY.
YOU ABANDONED THEM, AND RAN LIKE A WOMAN FROM A SINGLE MAN.
THE QUESTION IS, HOW WILL YOU GET OUT OF HERE ALIVE?
C-COSSACK, PLEASE! S-SPARE ME!
I HAVE SOMETHING FOR YOU! S-SOMETHING BIG!
GO ON, TRETIAK.
AN OPERATION... BIG MONEY, AND ALMOST LEGIT!
Y-YOURS... FOR THE TAKING.
I GIVE YOU THIS, AND YOU LET ME LIVE.
START TALKING, COMRADE.

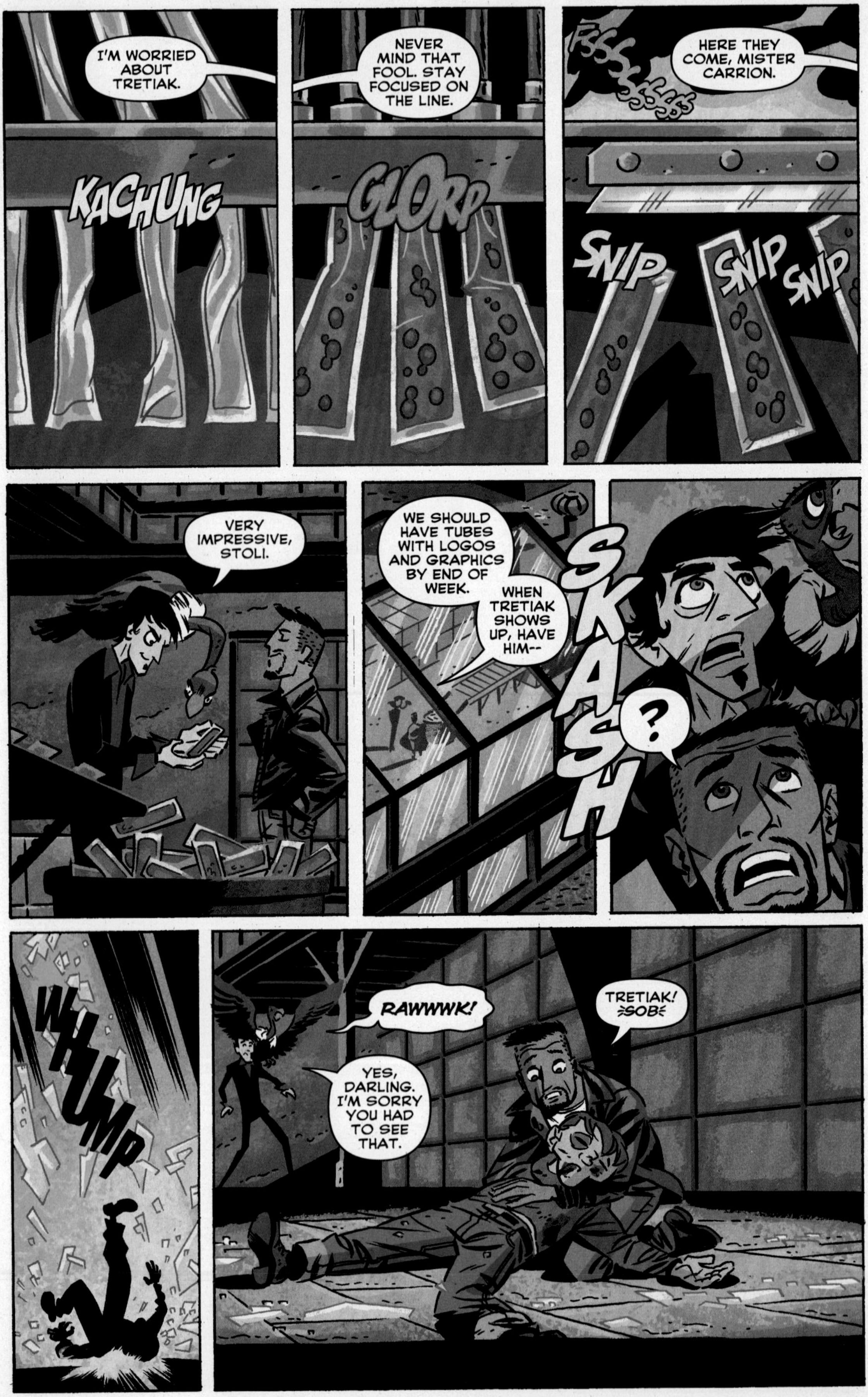

I'M WORRIED ABOUT TRETIAK.
KACHUNG
NEVER MIND THAT FOOL. STAY FOCUSED ON THE LINE.
GLORP
FSSSSSSSS
HERE THEY COME, MISTER CARRION.
SNIP
SNIP
SNIP
VERY IMPRESSIVE, STOLI.
WE SHOULD HAVE TUBES WITH LOGOS AND GRAPHICS BY END OF WEEK.
WHEN TRETIAK SHOWS UP, HAVE HIM--
SKASH
?
WHUMP
RAWWWK!
YES, DARLING. I'M SORRY YOU HAD TO SEE THAT.
TRETIAK! SOB

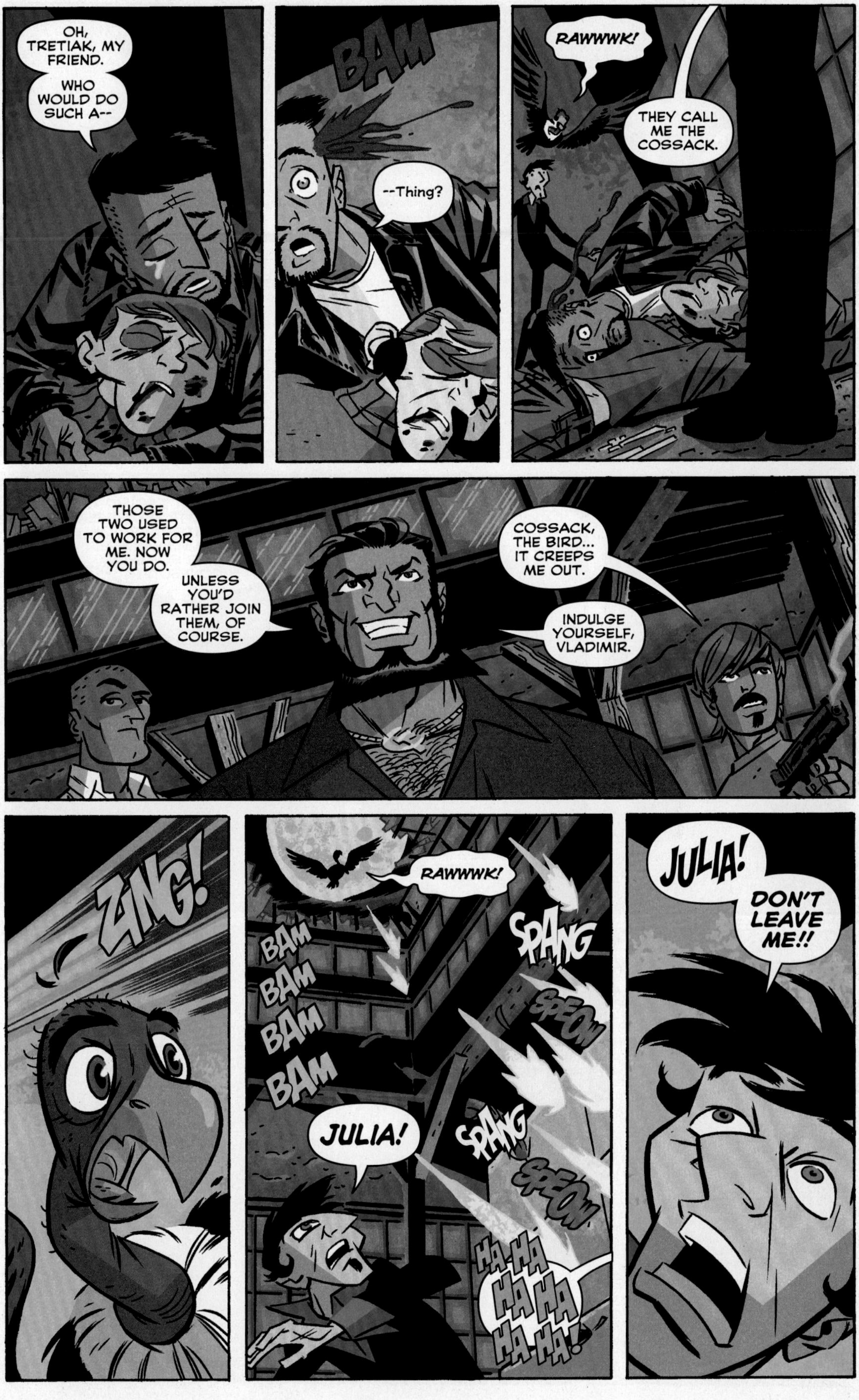
OH, TRETIAK, MY FRIEND.
WHO WOULD DO SUCH A--
BAM
--Thing?
RAWWWK!
THEY CALL ME THE COSSACK.
THOSE TWO USED TO WORK FOR ME. NOW YOU DO.
UNLESS YOU'D RATHER JOIN THEM, OF COURSE.
COSSACK, THE BIRD... IT CREEPS ME OUT.
INDULGE YOURSELF, VLADIMIR.
ZING!
RAWWWK!
BAM BAM BAM BAM
SPANG
SPEOW
JULIA!
SPANG
SPEOW
HA HA HA HA HA HA!
JULIA!
DON'T LEAVE ME!!

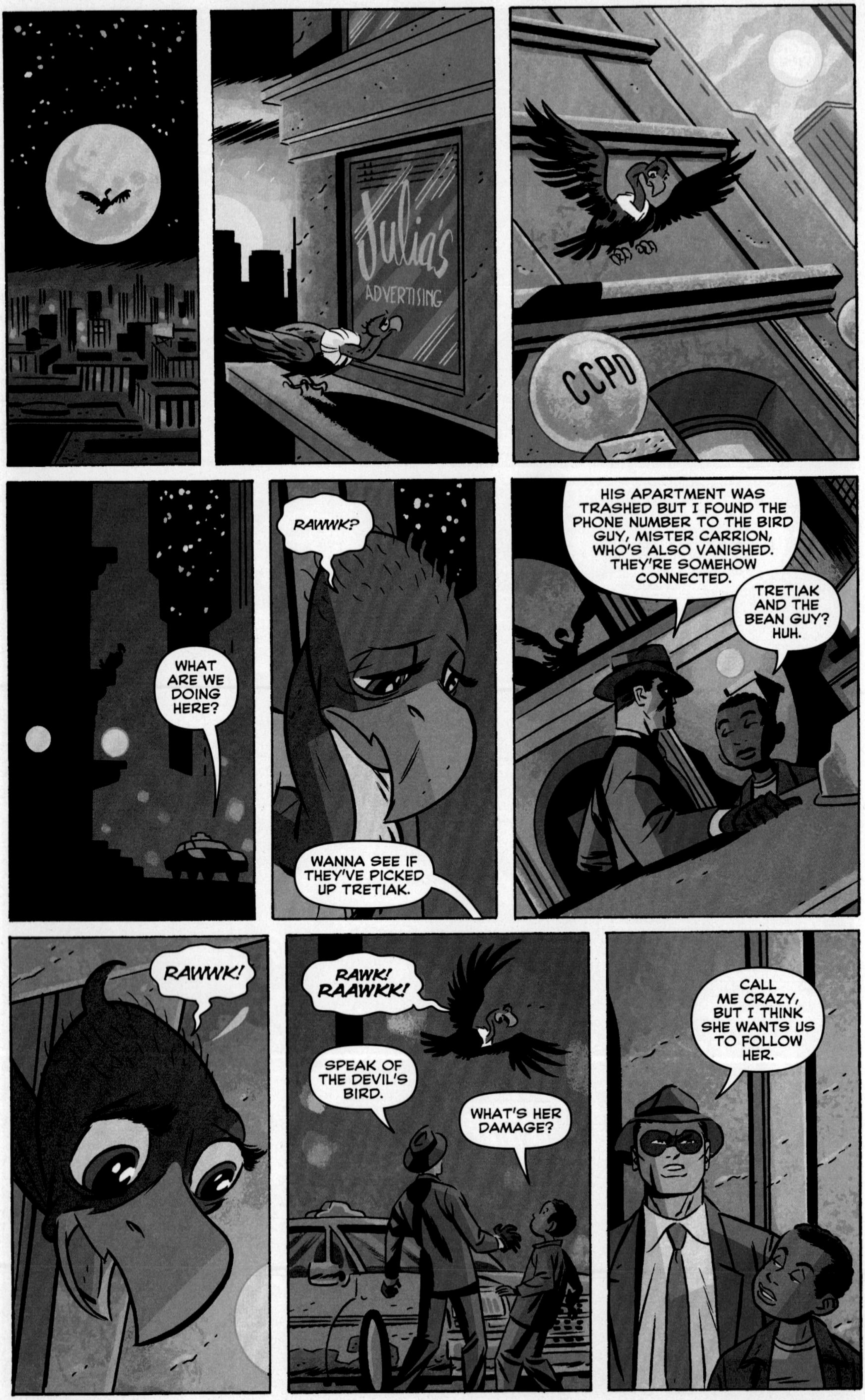

Julia's
ADVERTISING
CCPD
WHAT ARE WE DOING HERE?
RAWWK?
WANNA SEE IF THEY'VE PICKED UP TRETIAK.
HIS APARTMENT WAS TRASHED BUT I FOUND THE PHONE NUMBER TO THE BIRD GUY, MISTER CARRION, WHO'S ALSO VANISHED. THEY'RE SOMEHOW CONNECTED.
TRETIAK AND THE BEAN GUY? HUH.
RAWWK!
RAWK! RAAWKK!
SPEAK OF THE DEVIL'S BIRD.
WHAT'S HER DAMAGE?
CALL ME CRAZY, BUT I THINK SHE WANTS US TO FOLLOW HER.

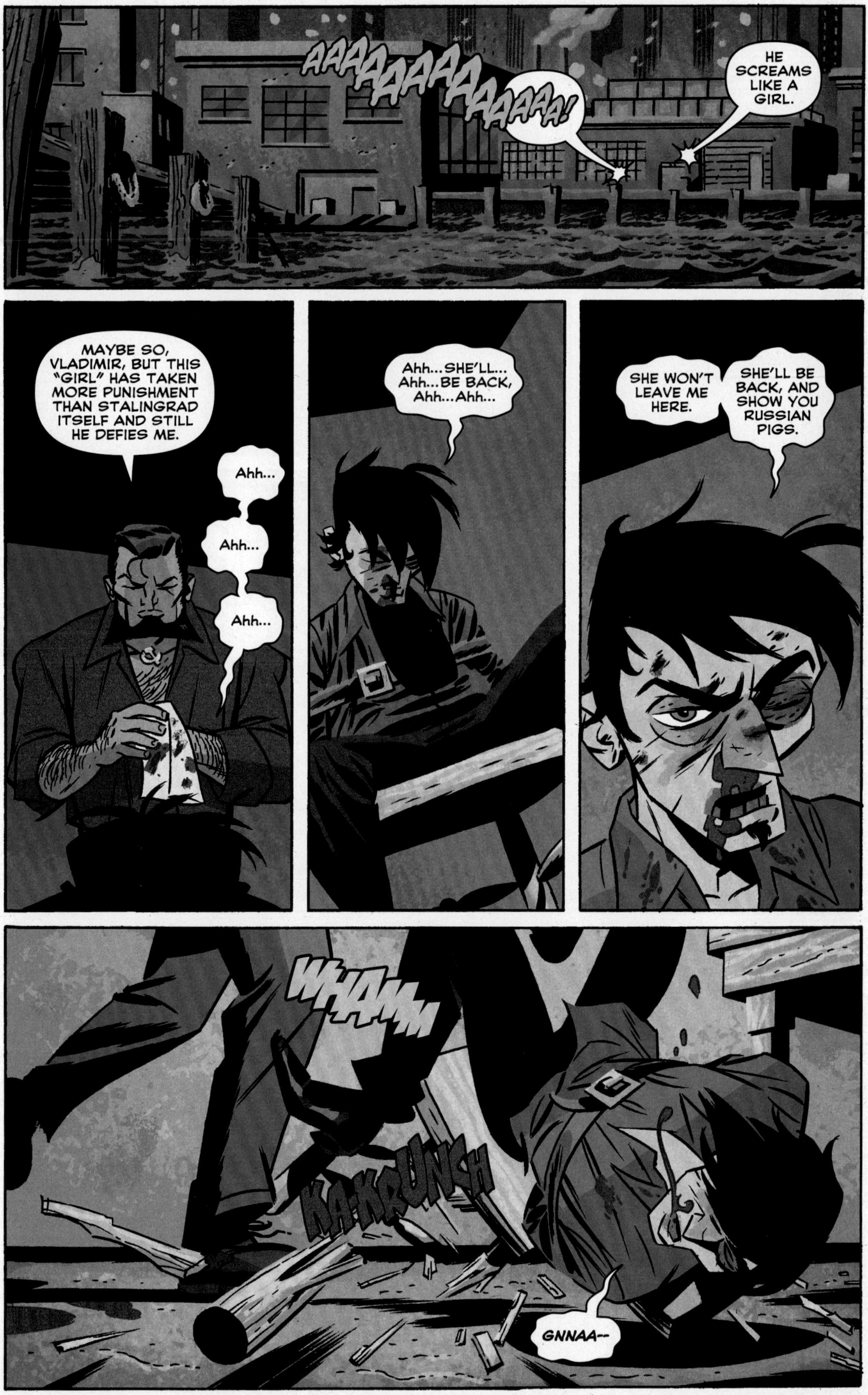
AAAAAAAAAAAAAAAA!
HE SCREAMS LIKE A GIRL.
MAYBE SO, VLADIMIR, BUT THIS "GIRL" HAS TAKEN MORE PUNISHMENT THAN STALINGRAD ITSELF AND STILL HE DEFIES ME.
Ahh...
Ahh...
Ahh...
Ahh...SHE'LL... Ahh...BE BACK, Ahh...Ahh...
SHE WON'T LEAVE ME HERE.
SHE'LL BE BACK, AND SHOW YOU RUSSIAN PIGS.
WHAMM
KA-KRUNCH
GNNAA--

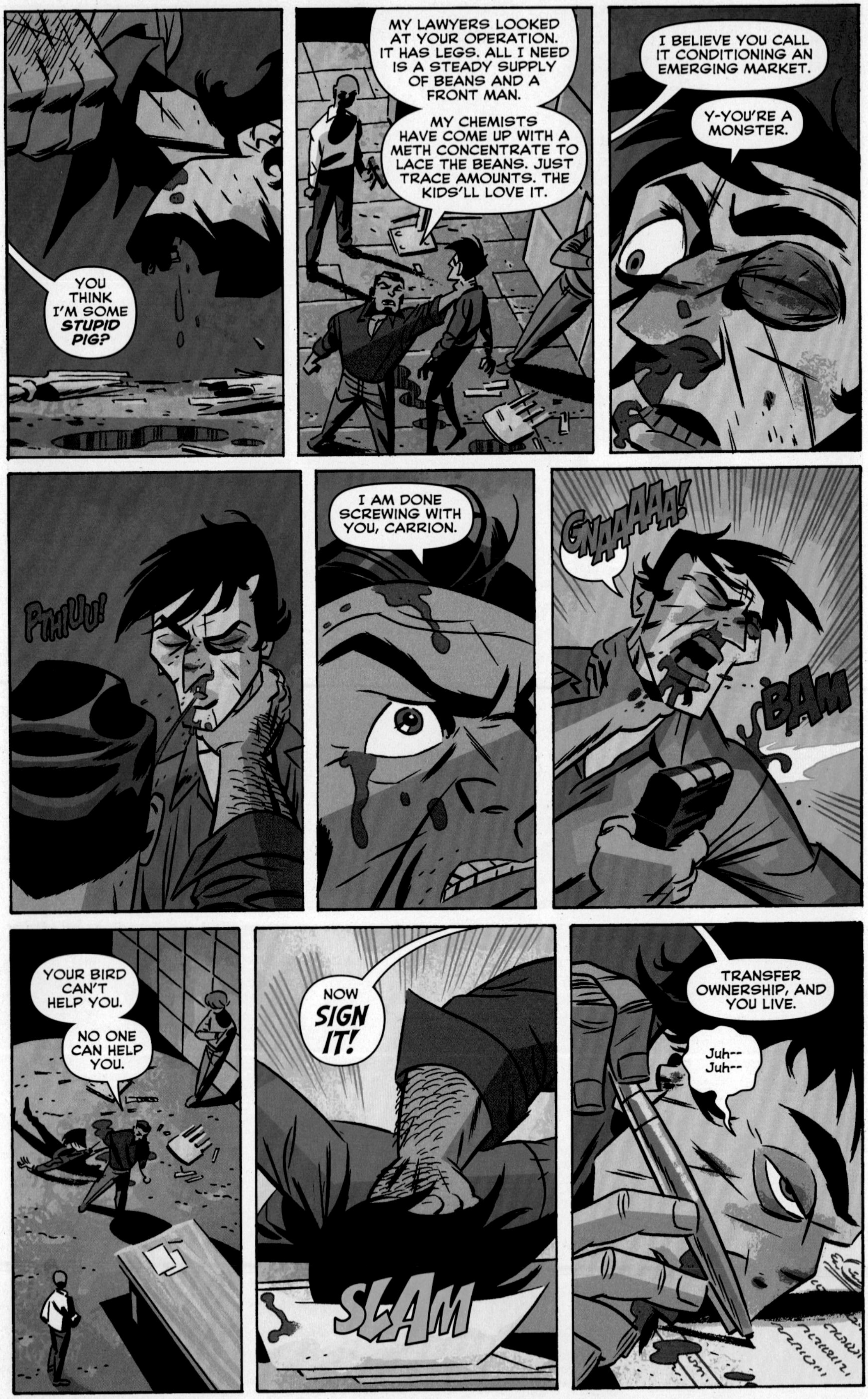
YOU THINK I'M SOME STUPID PIG?
MY LAWYERS LOOKED AT YOUR OPERATION. IT HAS LEGS. ALL I NEED IS A STEADY SUPPLY OF BEANS AND A FRONT MAN.
MY CHEMISTS HAVE COME UP WITH A METH CONCENTRATE TO LACE THE BEANS. JUST TRACE AMOUNTS. THE KIDS'LL LOVE IT.
I BELIEVE YOU CALL IT CONDITIONING AN EMERGING MARKET.
Y-YOU'RE A MONSTER.
PTHUU!
I AM DONE SCREWING WITH YOU, CARRION.
GNAAAAA!
BAM
YOUR BIRD CAN'T HELP YOU.
NO ONE CAN HELP YOU.
NOW SIGN IT!
SLAM
TRANSFER OWNERSHIP, AND YOU LIVE.
Juh-- Juh--

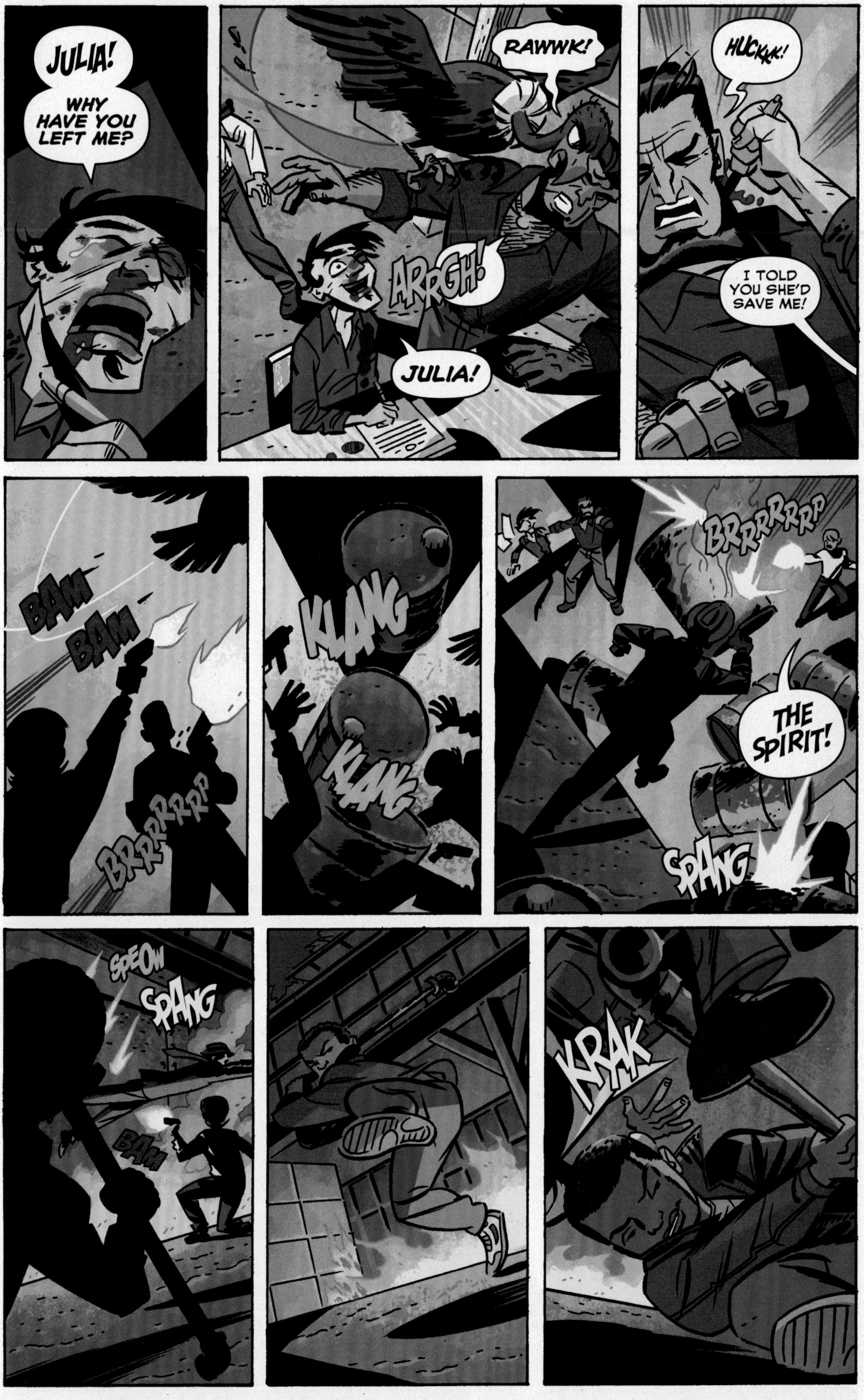
JULIA!
WHY HAVE YOU LEFT ME?
RAWWK!
ARRGH!
JULIA!
HUCKKK!
I TOLD YOU SHE'D SAVE ME!
BAM
BAM
BRRRRRRP
KLANG
KLANG
BRRRRRRP
THE SPIRIT!
SPANG
SPEOW
SPANG
BAM
KRAK

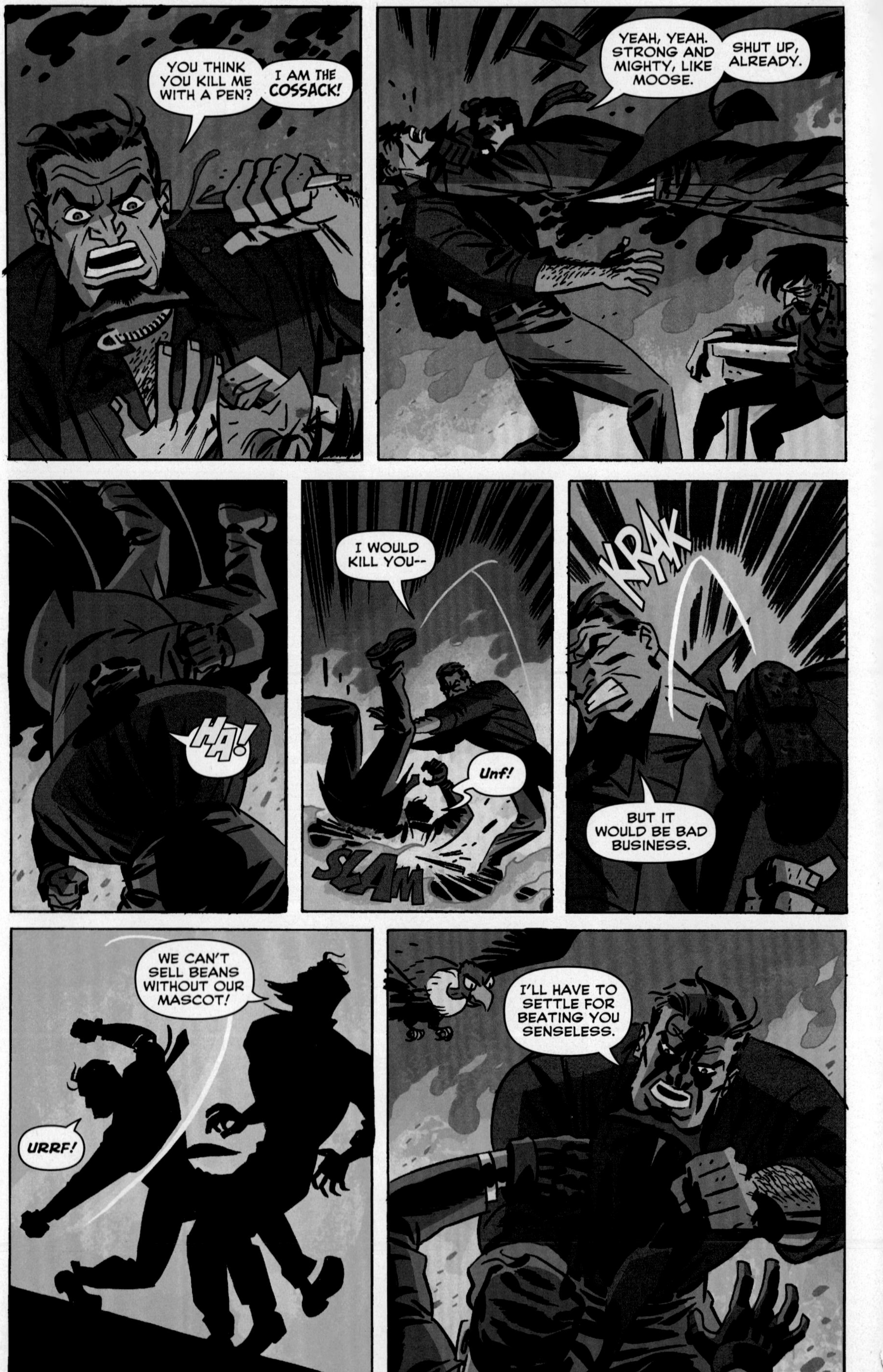
YOU THINK YOU KILL ME WITH A PEN?
I AM THE COSSACK!
YEAH, YEAH. STRONG AND MIGHTY, LIKE MOOSE.
SHUT UP, ALREADY.
HA!
I WOULD KILL YOU--
Unf!
SLAM
KRAK
BUT IT WOULD BE BAD BUSINESS.
WE CAN'T SELL BEANS WITHOUT OUR MASCOT!
URRF!
I'LL HAVE TO SETTLE FOR BEATING YOU SENSELESS.

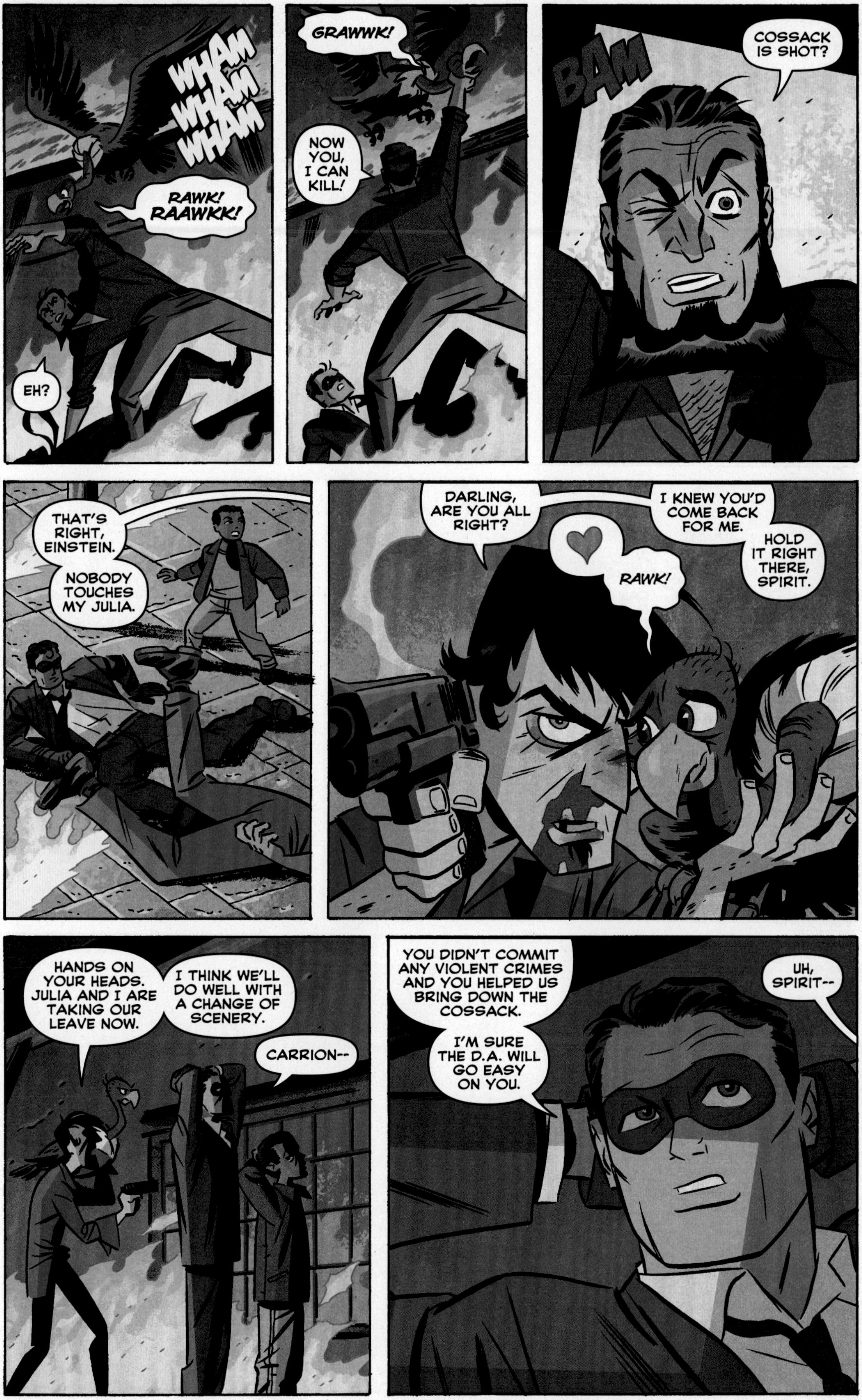
WHAM WHAM WHAM
RAWK! RAAWKK!
EH?
GRAWWK!
NOW YOU, I CAN KILL!
BAM
COSSACK IS SHOT?
THAT'S RIGHT, EINSTEIN.
NOBODY TOUCHES MY JULIA.
DARLING, ARE YOU ALL RIGHT?
I KNEW YOU'D COME BACK FOR ME.
RAWK!
HOLD IT RIGHT THERE, SPIRIT.
HANDS ON YOUR HEADS. JULIA AND I ARE TAKING OUR LEAVE NOW.
I THINK WE'LL DO WELL WITH A CHANGE OF SCENERY.
CARRION--
YOU DIDN'T COMMIT ANY VIOLENT CRIMES AND YOU HELPED US BRING DOWN THE COSSACK.
I'M SURE THE D.A. WILL GO EASY ON YOU.
UH, SPIRIT--

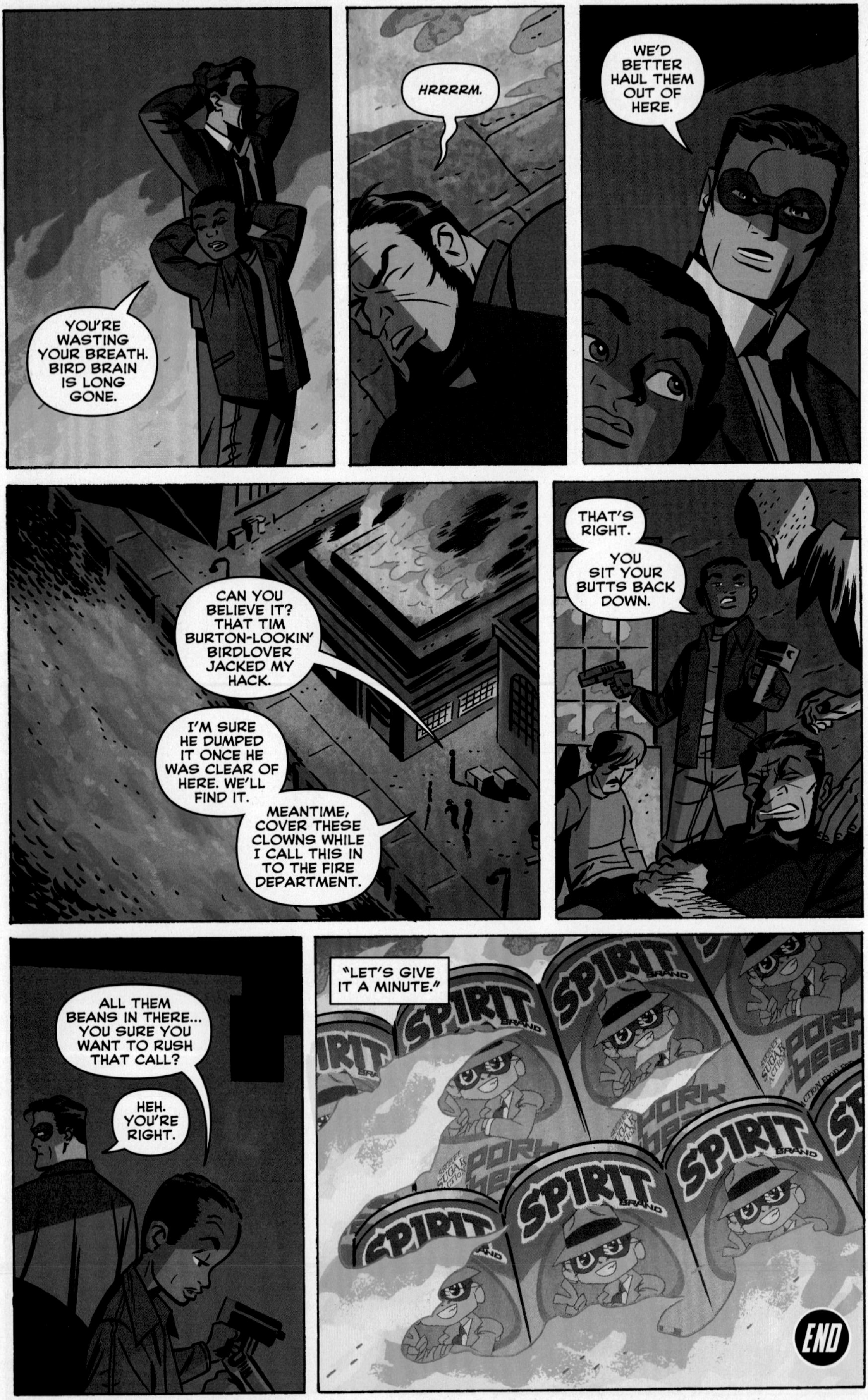
YOU'RE WASTING YOUR BREATH. BIRD BRAIN IS LONG GONE.
HRRRRM.
WE'D BETTER HAUL THEM OUT OF HERE.
CAN YOU BELIEVE IT? THAT TIM BURTON-LOOKIN' BIRDLOVER JACKED MY HACK.
I'M SURE HE DUMPED IT ONCE HE WAS CLEAR OF HERE. WE'LL FIND IT.
MEANTIME, COVER THESE CLOWNS WHILE I CALL THIS IN TO THE FIRE DEPARTMENT.
THAT'S RIGHT.
YOU SIT YOUR BUTTS BACK DOWN.
ALL THEM BEANS IN THERE... YOU SURE YOU WANT TO RUSH THAT CALL?
HEH. YOU'RE RIGHT.
"LET'S GIVE IT A MINUTE."
SPIRIT BRAND
PORK beans
SECRET SUGAR ACTION
END

6

ACTION · Mystery · ADVENTURE

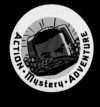

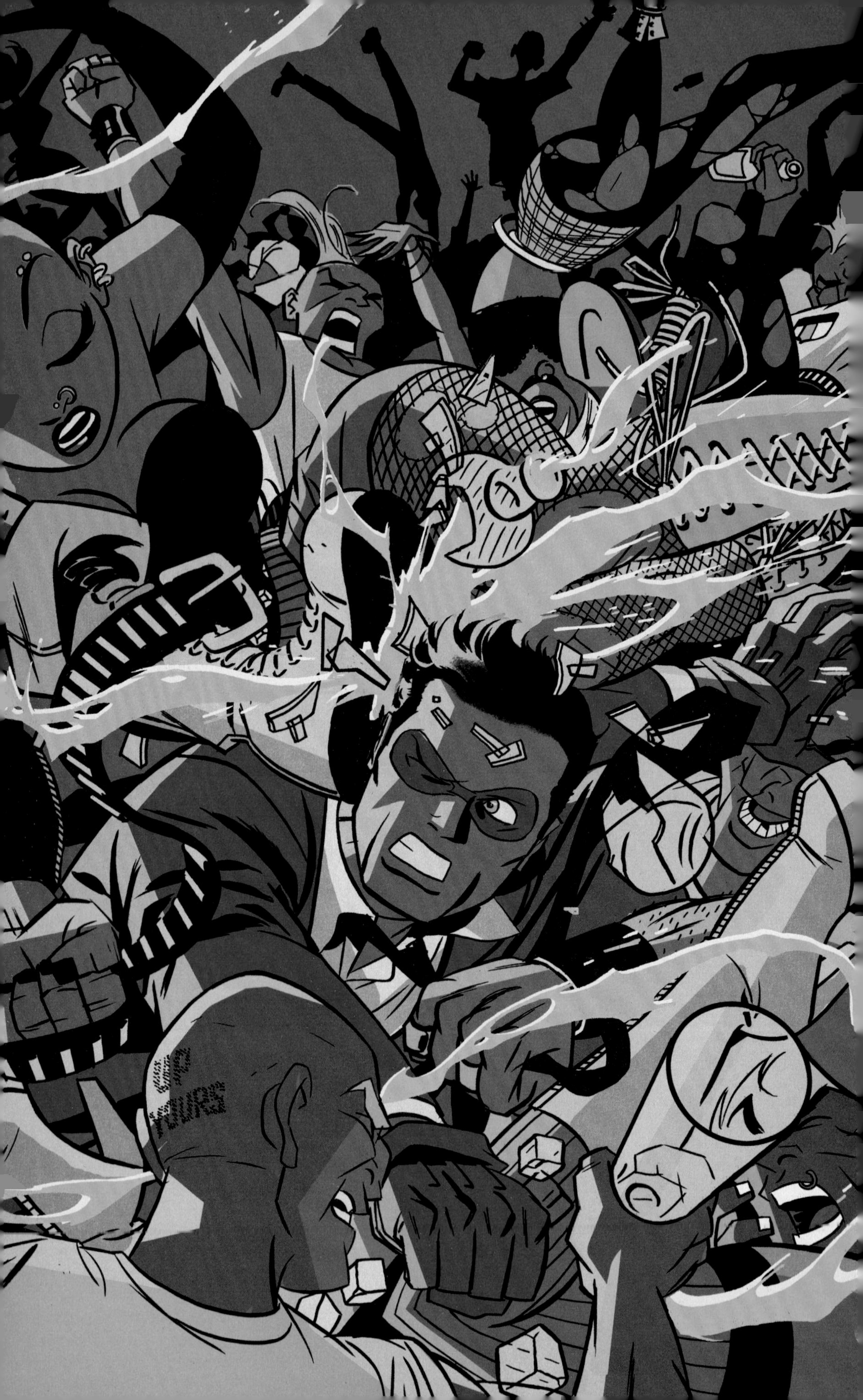

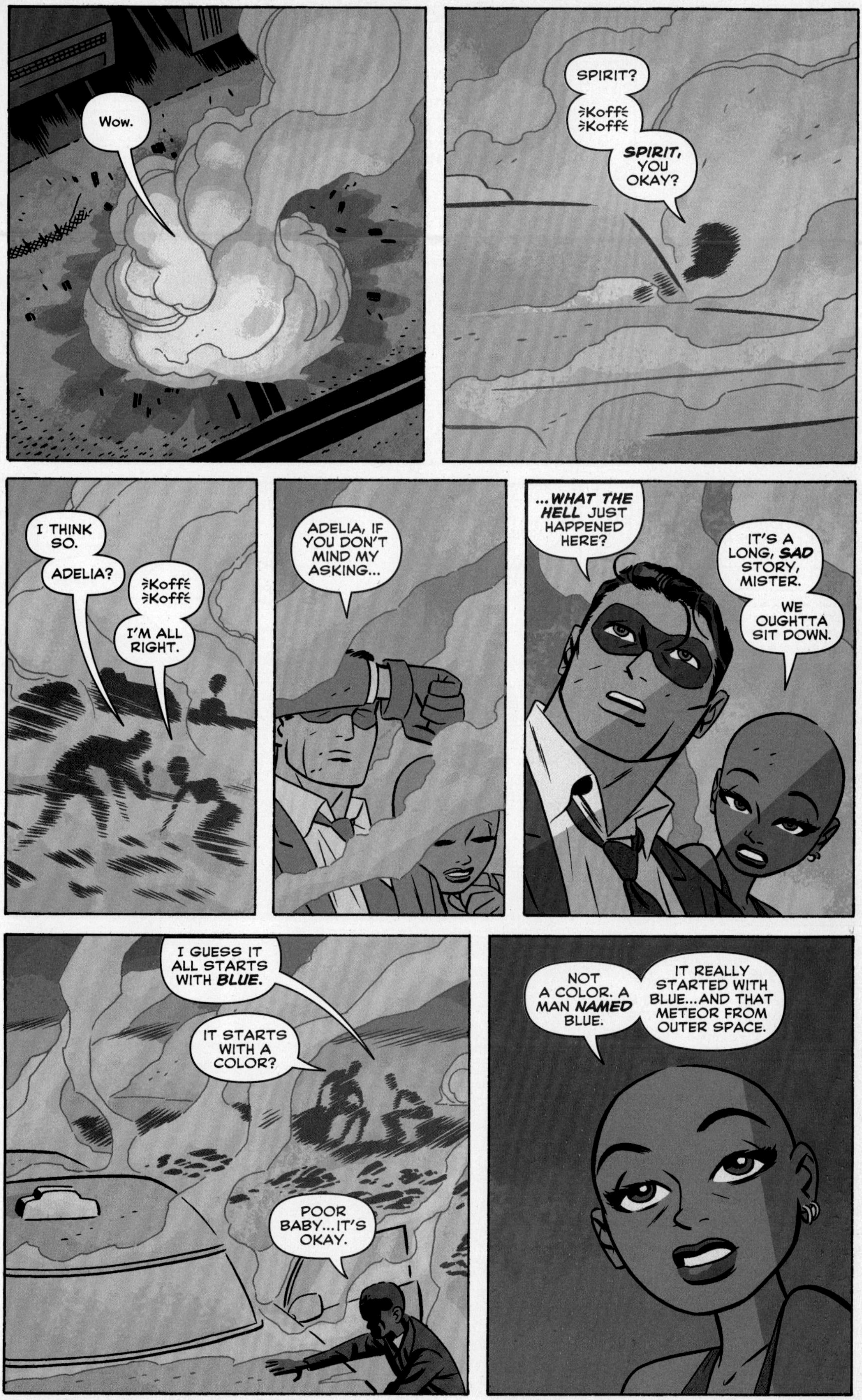
Wow.
SPIRIT?
Koff Koff
SPIRIT, YOU OKAY?
I THINK SO.
ADELIA?
Koff Koff
I'M ALL RIGHT.
ADELIA, IF YOU DON'T MIND MY ASKING...
...WHAT THE HELL JUST HAPPENED HERE?
IT'S A LONG, SAD STORY, MISTER.
WE OUGHTTA SIT DOWN.
I GUESS IT ALL STARTS WITH BLUE.
IT STARTS WITH A COLOR?
POOR BABY...IT'S OKAY.
NOT A COLOR. A MAN NAMED BLUE.
IT REALLY STARTED WITH BLUE...AND THAT METEOR FROM OUTER SPACE.

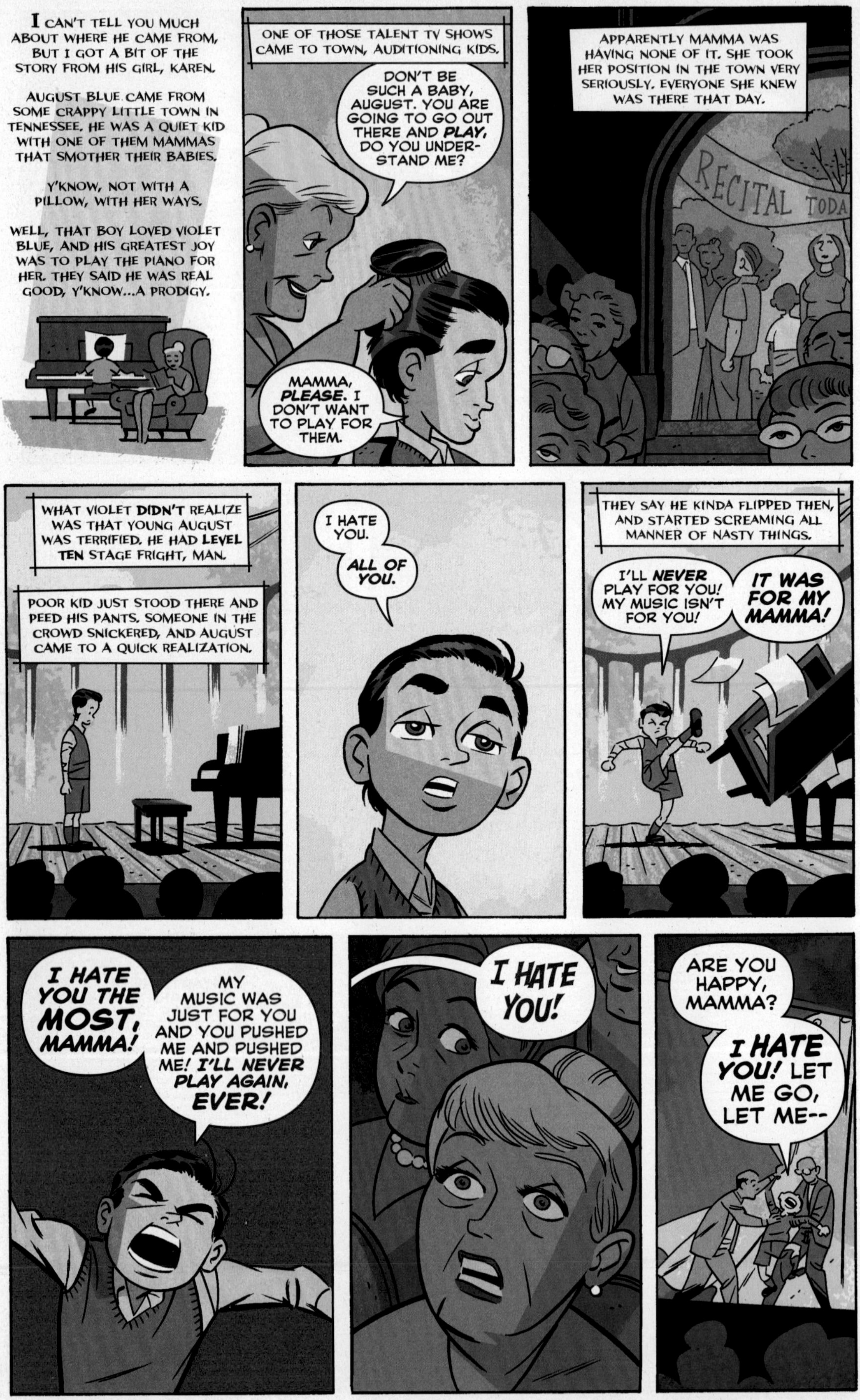
I CAN'T TELL YOU MUCH ABOUT WHERE HE CAME FROM, BUT I GOT A BIT OF THE STORY FROM HIS GIRL, KAREN.
AUGUST BLUE CAME FROM SOME CRAPPY LITTLE TOWN IN TENNESSEE. HE WAS A QUIET KID WITH ONE OF THEM MAMMAS THAT SMOTHER THEIR BABIES.
Y'KNOW, NOT WITH A PILLOW, WITH HER WAYS.
WELL, THAT BOY LOVED VIOLET BLUE, AND HIS GREATEST JOY WAS TO PLAY THE PIANO FOR HER. THEY SAID HE WAS REAL GOOD, Y'KNOW...A PRODIGY.
ONE OF THOSE TALENT TV SHOWS CAME TO TOWN, AUDITIONING KIDS.
DON'T BE SUCH A BABY, AUGUST. YOU ARE GOING TO GO OUT THERE AND PLAY, DO YOU UNDER-STAND ME?
MAMMA, PLEASE. I DON'T WANT TO PLAY FOR THEM.
APPARENTLY MAMMA WAS HAVING NONE OF IT. SHE TOOK HER POSITION IN THE TOWN VERY SERIOUSLY. EVERYONE SHE KNEW WAS THERE THAT DAY.
RECITAL TODA
WHAT VIOLET DIDN'T REALIZE WAS THAT YOUNG AUGUST WAS TERRIFIED. HE HAD LEVEL TEN STAGE FRIGHT, MAN.
POOR KID JUST STOOD THERE AND PEED HIS PANTS. SOMEONE IN THE CROWD SNICKERED, AND AUGUST CAME TO A QUICK REALIZATION.
I HATE YOU.
ALL OF YOU.
THEY SAY HE KINDA FLIPPED THEN, AND STARTED SCREAMING ALL MANNER OF NASTY THINGS.
I'LL NEVER PLAY FOR YOU! MY MUSIC ISN'T FOR YOU!
IT WAS FOR MY MAMMA!
I HATE YOU THE MOST, MAMMA!
MY MUSIC WAS JUST FOR YOU AND YOU PUSHED ME AND PUSHED ME! I'LL NEVER PLAY AGAIN, EVER!
I HATE YOU!
ARE YOU HAPPY, MAMMA?
I HATE YOU! LET ME GO, LET ME--

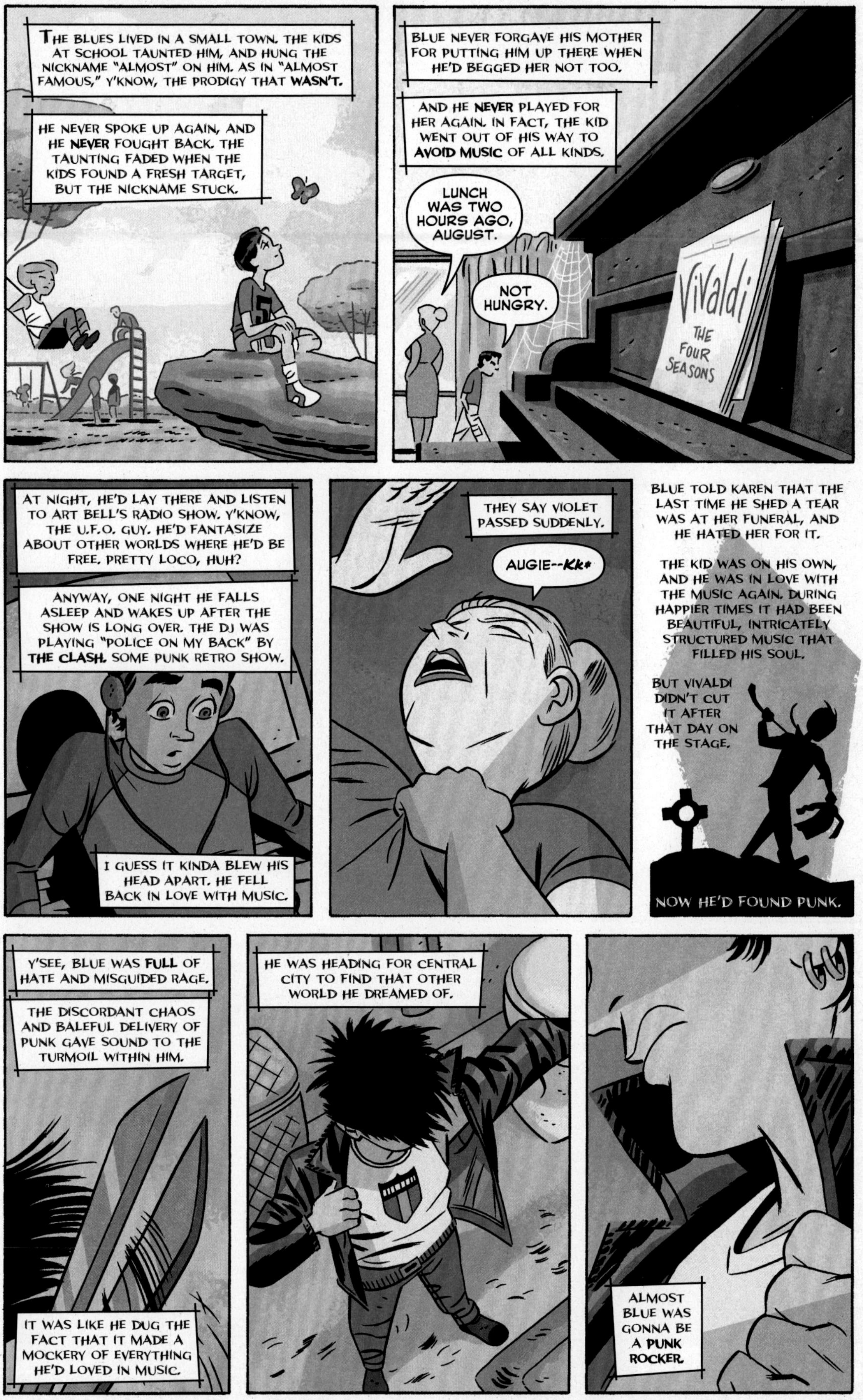
THE BLUES LIVED IN A SMALL TOWN. THE KIDS AT SCHOOL TAUNTED HIM, AND HUNG THE NICKNAME "ALMOST" ON HIM. AS IN "ALMOST FAMOUS," Y'KNOW, THE PRODIGY THAT WASN'T.
HE NEVER SPOKE UP AGAIN, AND HE NEVER FOUGHT BACK. THE TAUNTING FADED WHEN THE KIDS FOUND A FRESH TARGET, BUT THE NICKNAME STUCK.
BLUE NEVER FORGAVE HIS MOTHER FOR PUTTING HIM UP THERE WHEN HE'D BEGGED HER NOT TOO.
AND HE NEVER PLAYED FOR HER AGAIN. IN FACT, THE KID WENT OUT OF HIS WAY TO AVOID MUSIC OF ALL KINDS.
LUNCH WAS TWO HOURS AGO, AUGUST.
NOT HUNGRY.
VIVALDI THE FOUR SEASONS
AT NIGHT, HE'D LAY THERE AND LISTEN TO ART BELL'S RADIO SHOW. Y'KNOW, THE U.F.O. GUY. HE'D FANTASIZE ABOUT OTHER WORLDS WHERE HE'D BE FREE. PRETTY LOCO, HUH?
ANYWAY, ONE NIGHT HE FALLS ASLEEP AND WAKES UP AFTER THE SHOW IS LONG OVER. THE DJ WAS PLAYING "POLICE ON MY BACK" BY THE CLASH. SOME PUNK RETRO SHOW.
I GUESS IT KINDA BLEW HIS HEAD APART. HE FELL BACK IN LOVE WITH MUSIC.
THEY SAY VIOLET PASSED SUDDENLY.
AUGIE--Kk*
BLUE TOLD KAREN THAT THE LAST TIME HE SHED A TEAR WAS AT HER FUNERAL, AND HE HATED HER FOR IT.
THE KID WAS ON HIS OWN, AND HE WAS IN LOVE WITH THE MUSIC AGAIN. DURING HAPPIER TIMES IT HAD BEEN BEAUTIFUL, INTRICATELY STRUCTURED MUSIC THAT FILLED HIS SOUL.
BUT VIVALDI DIDN'T CUT IT AFTER THAT DAY ON THE STAGE.
NOW HE'D FOUND PUNK.
Y'SEE, BLUE WAS FULL OF HATE AND MISGUIDED RAGE.
THE DISCORDANT CHAOS AND BALEFUL DELIVERY OF PUNK GAVE SOUND TO THE TURMOIL WITHIN HIM.
IT WAS LIKE HE DUG THE FACT THAT IT MADE A MOCKERY OF EVERYTHING HE'D LOVED IN MUSIC.
HE WAS HEADING FOR CENTRAL CITY TO FIND THAT OTHER WORLD HE DREAMED OF.
ALMOST BLUE WAS GONNA BE A PUNK ROCKER.

# Will Eisner's the
# spi

PRESENTED IN
HIGH FIDELITY

BY
DARWYN
COOKE

INKS
J. BONE

COLOR
DAVE STEWART

# rit

## Almost Blue

LETTERING            ASS'T EDITOR      EDITOR
JARED FLETCHER   KRISTY QUINN   SCOTT DUNBIER

THE SPIRIT CREATED BY WILL EISNER

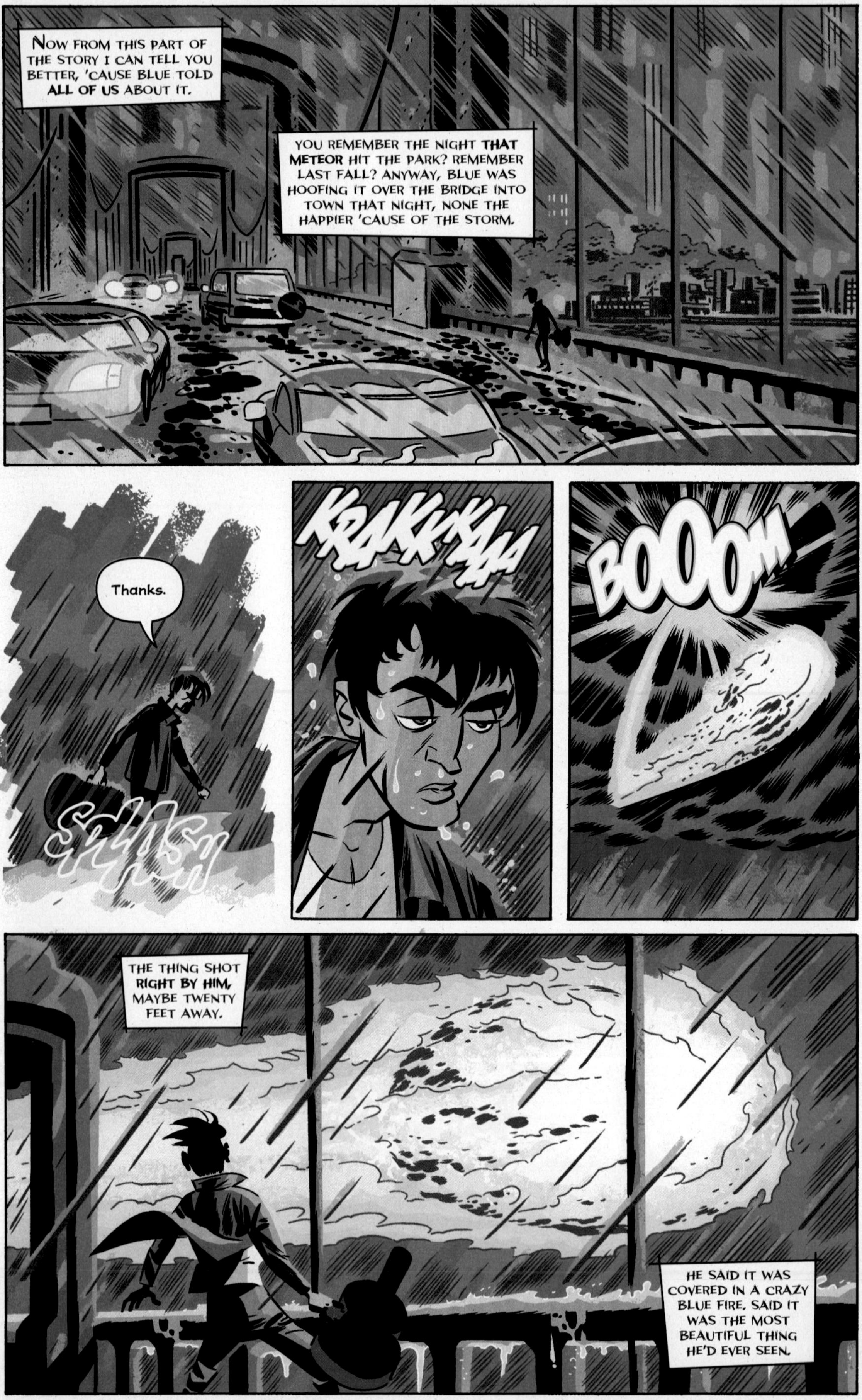
NOW FROM THIS PART OF THE STORY I CAN TELL YOU BETTER, 'CAUSE BLUE TOLD ALL OF US ABOUT IT.
YOU REMEMBER THE NIGHT THAT METEOR HIT THE PARK? REMEMBER LAST FALL? ANYWAY, BLUE WAS HOOFING IT OVER THE BRIDGE INTO TOWN THAT NIGHT, NONE THE HAPPIER 'CAUSE OF THE STORM.
Thanks.
SPLASH
KRAKKKAAA
BOOOOM
THE THING SHOT RIGHT BY HIM, MAYBE TWENTY FEET AWAY.
HE SAID IT WAS COVERED IN A CRAZY BLUE FIRE, SAID IT WAS THE MOST BEAUTIFUL THING HE'D EVER SEEN.

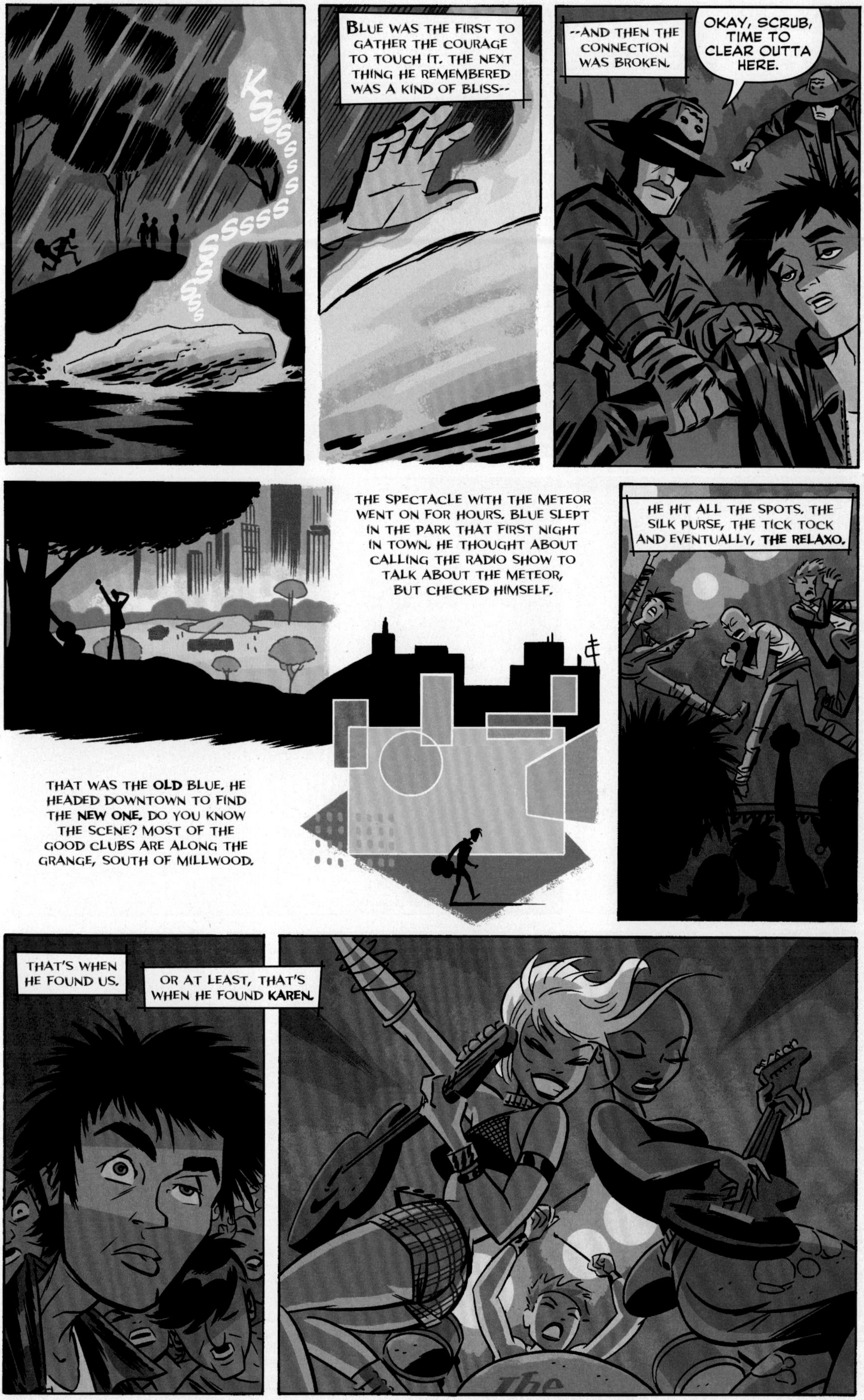
KSSSSSSSSSSSS
BLUE WAS THE FIRST TO GATHER THE COURAGE TO TOUCH IT. THE NEXT THING HE REMEMBERED WAS A KIND OF BLISS--
--AND THEN THE CONNECTION WAS BROKEN.
OKAY, SCRUB, TIME TO CLEAR OUTTA HERE.
THE SPECTACLE WITH THE METEOR WENT ON FOR HOURS. BLUE SLEPT IN THE PARK THAT FIRST NIGHT IN TOWN. HE THOUGHT ABOUT CALLING THE RADIO SHOW TO TALK ABOUT THE METEOR, BUT CHECKED HIMSELF.
THAT WAS THE OLD BLUE. HE HEADED DOWNTOWN TO FIND THE NEW ONE. DO YOU KNOW THE SCENE? MOST OF THE GOOD CLUBS ARE ALONG THE GRANGE, SOUTH OF MILLWOOD.
HE HIT ALL THE SPOTS. THE SILK PURSE, THE TICK TOCK AND EVENTUALLY, THE RELAXO.
THAT'S WHEN HE FOUND US.
OR AT LEAST, THAT'S WHEN HE FOUND KAREN.

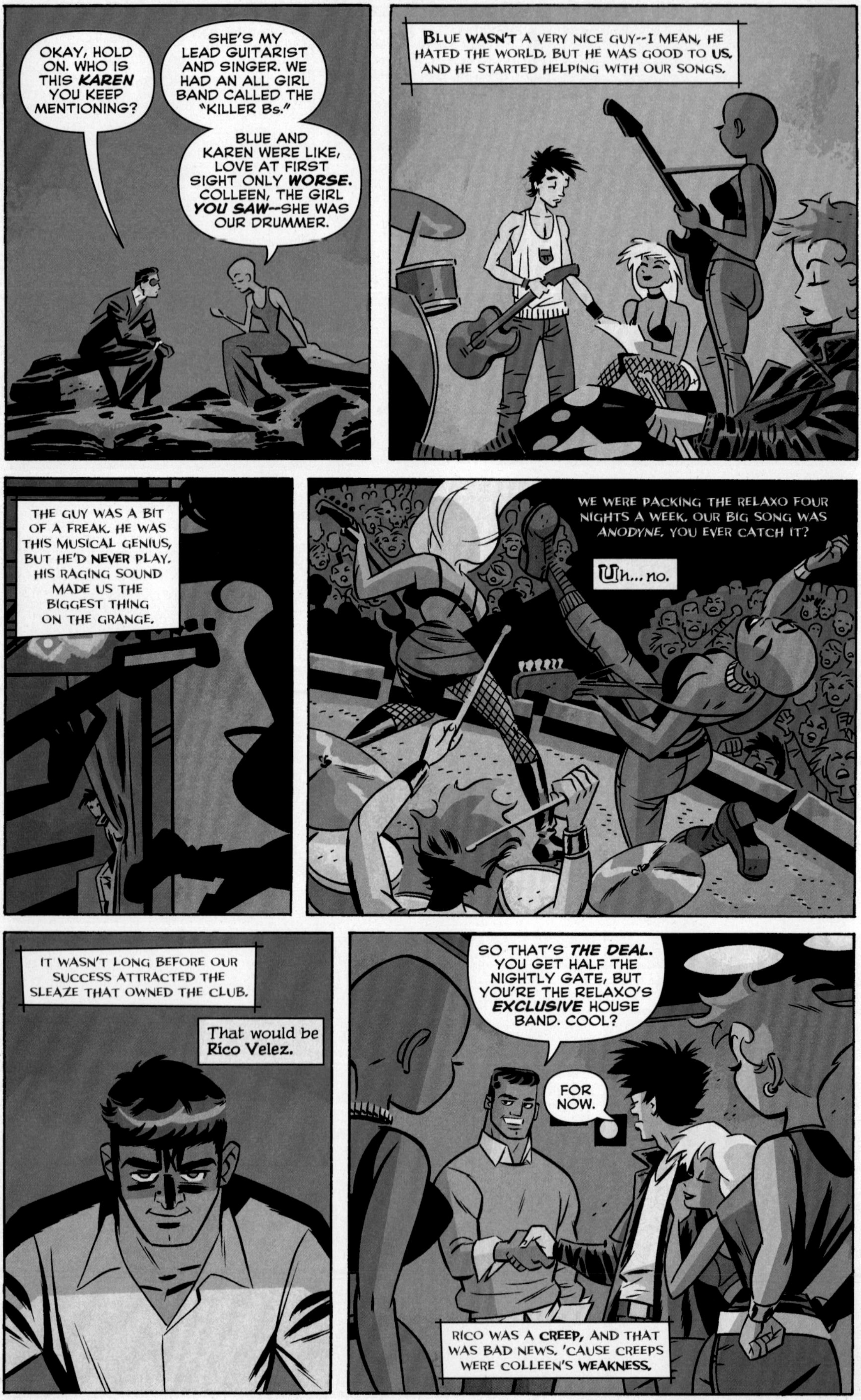
OKAY, HOLD ON. WHO IS THIS KAREN YOU KEEP MENTIONING?
SHE'S MY LEAD GUITARIST AND SINGER. WE HAD AN ALL GIRL BAND CALLED THE "KILLER Bs."
BLUE AND KAREN WERE LIKE, LOVE AT FIRST SIGHT ONLY WORSE. COLLEEN, THE GIRL YOU SAW--SHE WAS OUR DRUMMER.
BLUE WASN'T A VERY NICE GUY--I MEAN, HE HATED THE WORLD. BUT HE WAS GOOD TO US. AND HE STARTED HELPING WITH OUR SONGS.
THE GUY WAS A BIT OF A FREAK. HE WAS THIS MUSICAL GENIUS, BUT HE'D NEVER PLAY. HIS RAGING SOUND MADE US THE BIGGEST THING ON THE GRANGE.
WE WERE PACKING THE RELAXO FOUR NIGHTS A WEEK. OUR BIG SONG WAS ANODYNE. YOU EVER CATCH IT?
Uh... no.
IT WASN'T LONG BEFORE OUR SUCCESS ATTRACTED THE SLEAZE THAT OWNED THE CLUB.
That would be Rico Velez.
SO THAT'S THE DEAL. YOU GET HALF THE NIGHTLY GATE, BUT YOU'RE THE RELAXO'S EXCLUSIVE HOUSE BAND. COOL?
FOR NOW.
RICO WAS A CREEP, AND THAT WAS BAD NEWS. 'CAUSE CREEPS WERE COLLEEN'S WEAKNESS.

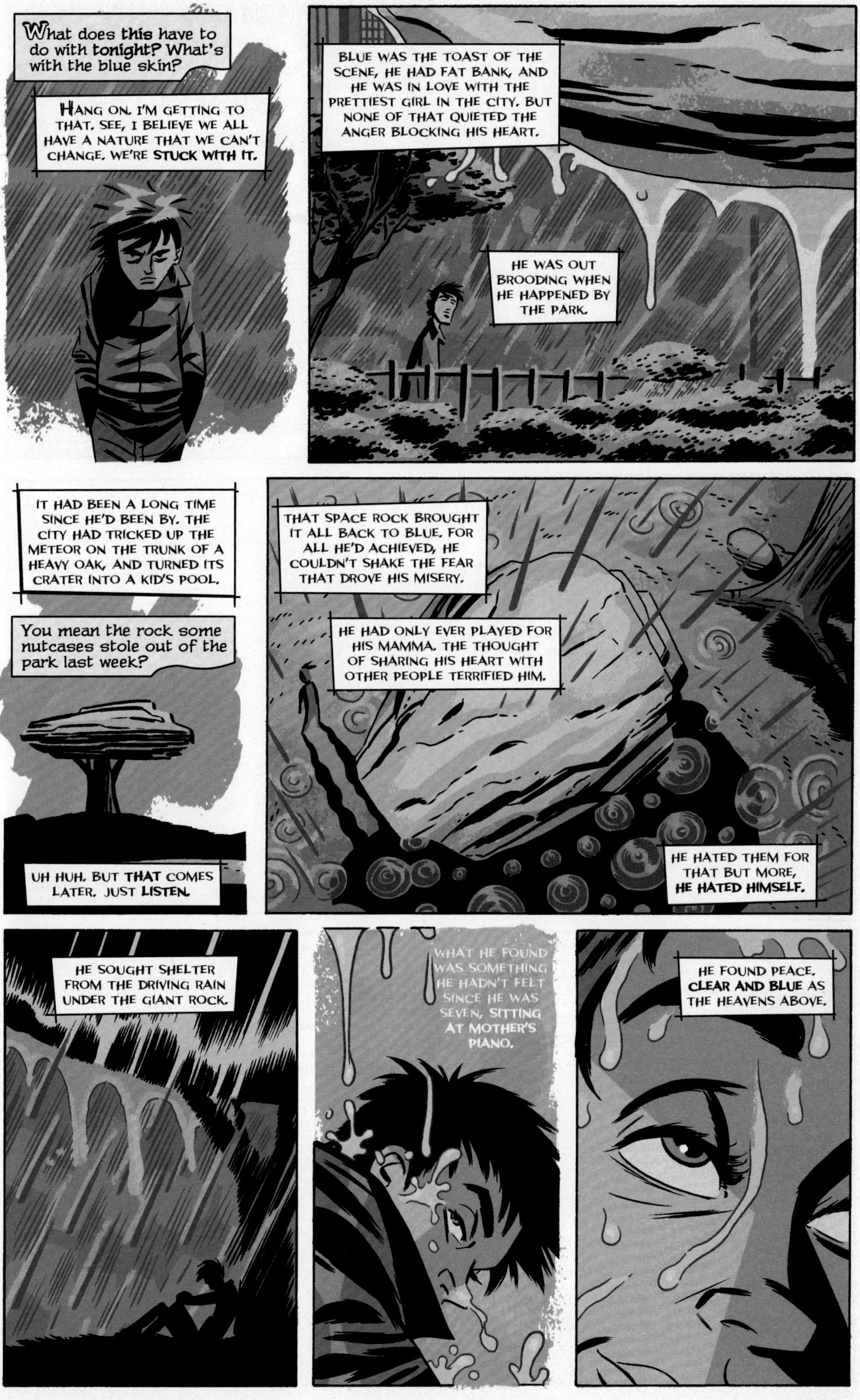

What does this have to do with tonight? What's with the blue skin?
HANG ON. I'M GETTING TO THAT. SEE, I BELIEVE WE ALL HAVE A NATURE THAT WE CAN'T CHANGE. WE'RE STUCK WITH IT.
BLUE WAS THE TOAST OF THE SCENE, HE HAD FAT BANK, AND HE WAS IN LOVE WITH THE PRETTIEST GIRL IN THE CITY. BUT NONE OF THAT QUIETED THE ANGER BLOCKING HIS HEART.
HE WAS OUT BROODING WHEN HE HAPPENED BY THE PARK.
IT HAD BEEN A LONG TIME SINCE HE'D BEEN BY. THE CITY HAD TRICKED UP THE METEOR ON THE TRUNK OF A HEAVY OAK, AND TURNED ITS CRATER INTO A KID'S POOL.
You mean the rock some nutcases stole out of the park last week?
UH HUH. BUT THAT COMES LATER. JUST LISTEN.
THAT SPACE ROCK BROUGHT IT ALL BACK TO BLUE. FOR ALL HE'D ACHIEVED, HE COULDN'T SHAKE THE FEAR THAT DROVE HIS MISERY.
HE HAD ONLY EVER PLAYED FOR HIS MAMMA. THE THOUGHT OF SHARING HIS HEART WITH OTHER PEOPLE TERRIFIED HIM.
HE HATED THEM FOR THAT BUT MORE, HE HATED HIMSELF.
HE SOUGHT SHELTER FROM THE DRIVING RAIN UNDER THE GIANT ROCK.
WHAT HE FOUND WAS SOMETHING HE HADN'T FELT SINCE HE WAS SEVEN, SITTING AT MOTHER'S PIANO.
HE FOUND PEACE. CLEAR AND BLUE AS THE HEAVENS ABOVE.

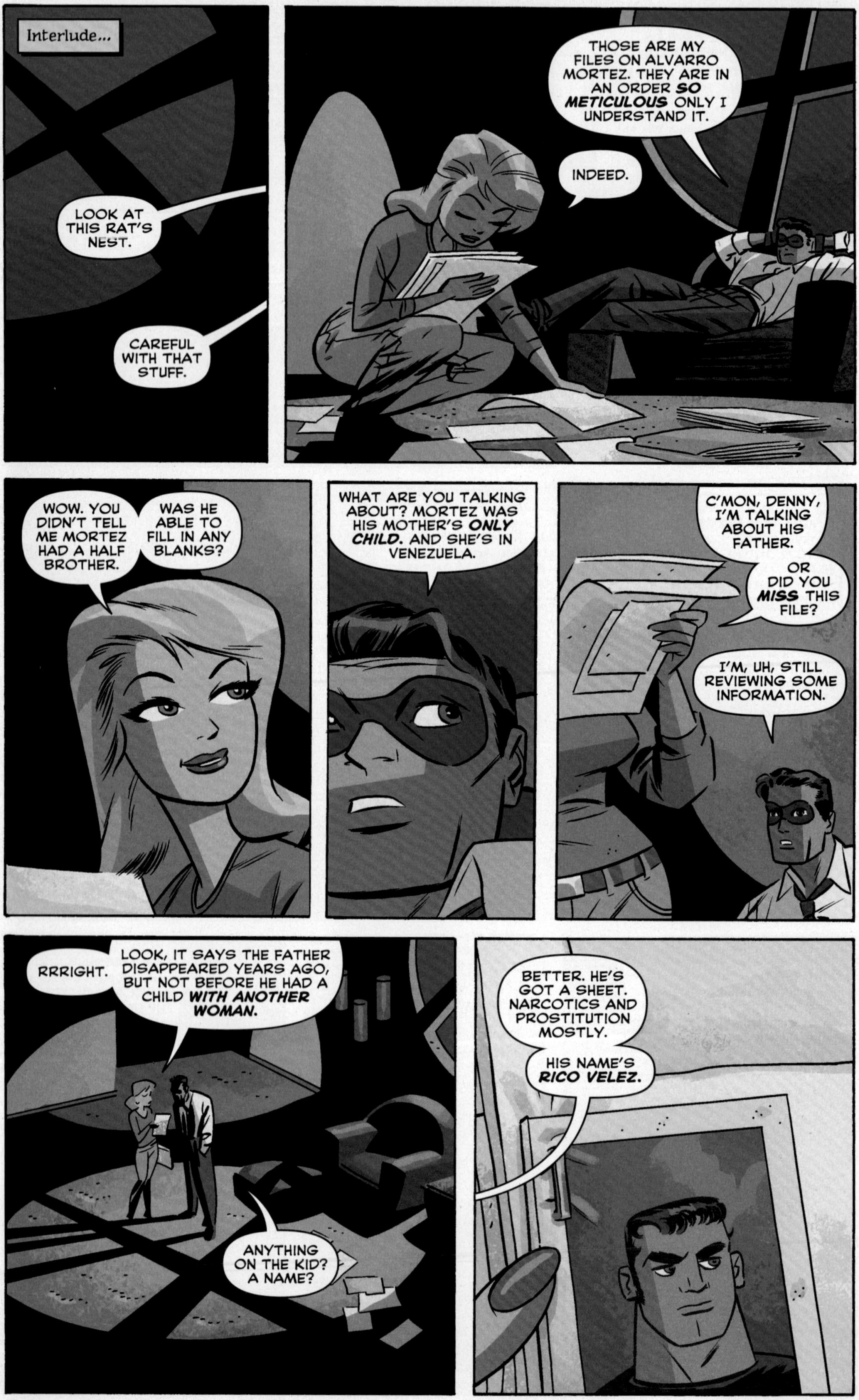
Interlude...
LOOK AT THIS RAT'S NEST.
CAREFUL WITH THAT STUFF.
THOSE ARE MY FILES ON ALVARRO MORTEZ. THEY ARE IN AN ORDER SO METICULOUS ONLY I UNDERSTAND IT.
INDEED.
WOW. YOU DIDN'T TELL ME MORTEZ HAD A HALF BROTHER.
WAS HE ABLE TO FILL IN ANY BLANKS?
WHAT ARE YOU TALKING ABOUT? MORTEZ WAS HIS MOTHER'S ONLY CHILD. AND SHE'S IN VENEZUELA.
C'MON, DENNY, I'M TALKING ABOUT HIS FATHER.
OR DID YOU MISS THIS FILE?
I'M, UH, STILL REVIEWING SOME INFORMATION.
RRRIGHT.
LOOK, IT SAYS THE FATHER DISAPPEARED YEARS AGO, BUT NOT BEFORE HE HAD A CHILD WITH ANOTHER WOMAN.
ANYTHING ON THE KID? A NAME?
BETTER. HE'S GOT A SHEET. NARCOTICS AND PROSTITUTION MOSTLY.
HIS NAME'S RICO VELEZ.

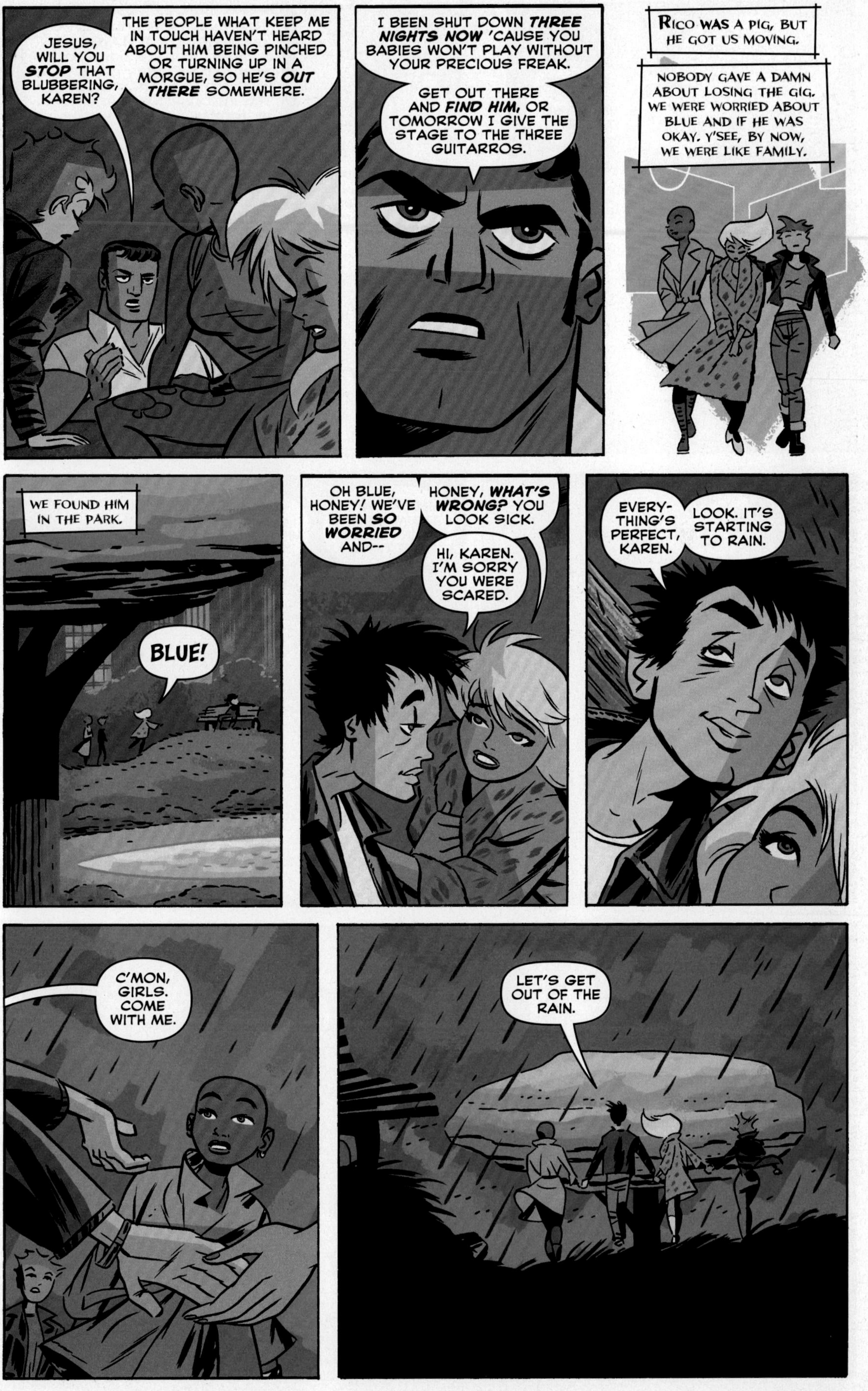
JESUS, WILL YOU STOP THAT BLUBBERING, KAREN?
THE PEOPLE WHAT KEEP ME IN TOUCH HAVEN'T HEARD ABOUT HIM BEING PINCHED OR TURNING UP IN A MORGUE, SO HE'S OUT THERE SOMEWHERE.
I BEEN SHUT DOWN THREE NIGHTS NOW 'CAUSE YOU BABIES WON'T PLAY WITHOUT YOUR PRECIOUS FREAK.
GET OUT THERE AND FIND HIM, OR TOMORROW I GIVE THE STAGE TO THE THREE GUITARROS.
RICO WAS A PIG, BUT HE GOT US MOVING.
NOBODY GAVE A DAMN ABOUT LOSING THE GIG. WE WERE WORRIED ABOUT BLUE AND IF HE WAS OKAY. Y'SEE, BY NOW, WE WERE LIKE FAMILY.
WE FOUND HIM IN THE PARK.
BLUE!
OH BLUE, HONEY! WE'VE BEEN SO WORRIED AND--
HONEY, WHAT'S WRONG? YOU LOOK SICK.
HI, KAREN. I'M SORRY YOU WERE SCARED.
EVERY-THING'S PERFECT, KAREN.
LOOK. IT'S STARTING TO RAIN.
C'MON, GIRLS. COME WITH ME.
LET'S GET OUT OF THE RAIN.

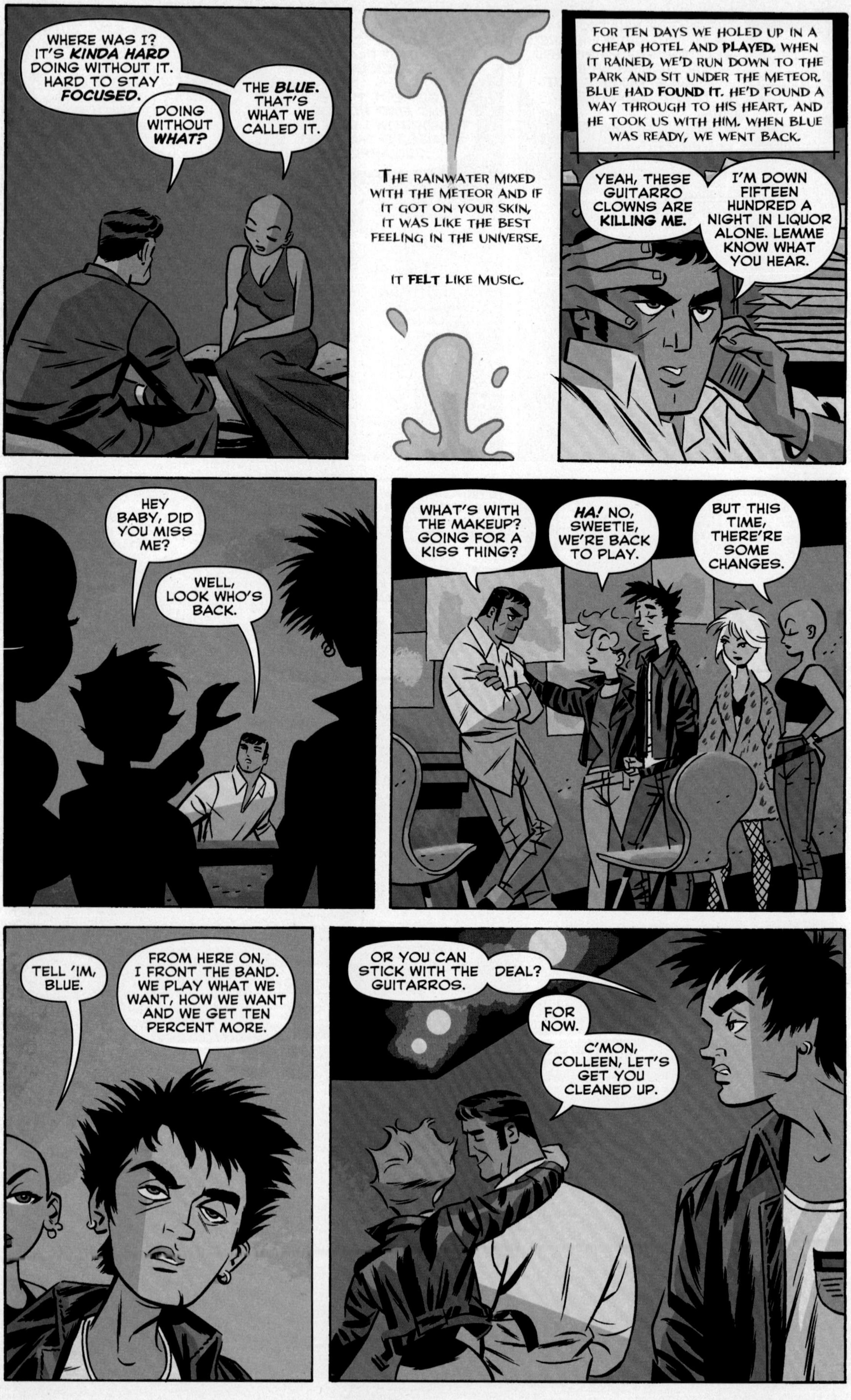
WHERE WAS I? IT'S KINDA HARD DOING WITHOUT IT. HARD TO STAY FOCUSED.
DOING WITHOUT WHAT?
THE BLUE. THAT'S WHAT WE CALLED IT.
THE RAINWATER MIXED WITH THE METEOR AND IF IT GOT ON YOUR SKIN, IT WAS LIKE THE BEST FEELING IN THE UNIVERSE.
IT FELT LIKE MUSIC.
FOR TEN DAYS WE HOLED UP IN A CHEAP HOTEL AND PLAYED. WHEN IT RAINED, WE'D RUN DOWN TO THE PARK AND SIT UNDER THE METEOR. BLUE HAD FOUND IT. HE'D FOUND A WAY THROUGH TO HIS HEART, AND HE TOOK US WITH HIM. WHEN BLUE WAS READY, WE WENT BACK.
YEAH, THESE GUITARRO CLOWNS ARE KILLING ME.
I'M DOWN FIFTEEN HUNDRED A NIGHT IN LIQUOR ALONE. LEMME KNOW WHAT YOU HEAR.
HEY BABY, DID YOU MISS ME?
WELL, LOOK WHO'S BACK.
WHAT'S WITH THE MAKEUP? GOING FOR A KISS THING?
HA! NO, SWEETIE, WE'RE BACK TO PLAY.
BUT THIS TIME, THERE'RE SOME CHANGES.
TELL 'IM, BLUE.
FROM HERE ON, I FRONT THE BAND. WE PLAY WHAT WE WANT, HOW WE WANT AND WE GET TEN PERCENT MORE.
OR YOU CAN STICK WITH THE GUITARROS.
DEAL?
FOR NOW.
C'MON, COLLEEN, LET'S GET YOU CLEANED UP.

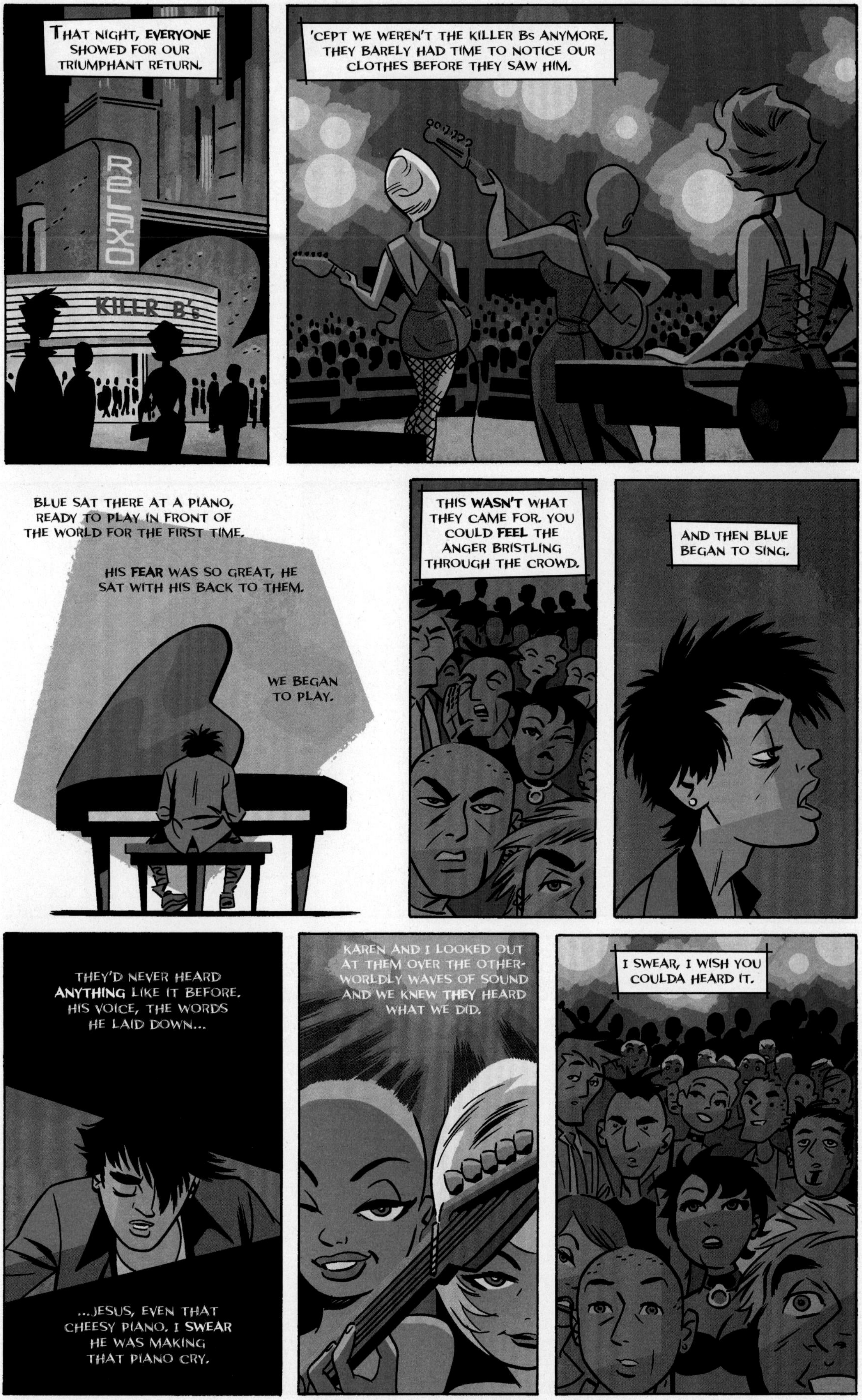
THAT NIGHT, EVERYONE SHOWED FOR OUR TRIUMPHANT RETURN.
RELAXO
KILLER B's
'CEPT WE WEREN'T THE KILLER Bs ANYMORE. THEY BARELY HAD TIME TO NOTICE OUR CLOTHES BEFORE THEY SAW HIM.
BLUE SAT THERE AT A PIANO, READY TO PLAY IN FRONT OF THE WORLD FOR THE FIRST TIME.
HIS FEAR WAS SO GREAT, HE SAT WITH HIS BACK TO THEM.
WE BEGAN TO PLAY.
THIS WASN'T WHAT THEY CAME FOR. YOU COULD FEEL THE ANGER BRISTLING THROUGH THE CROWD.
AND THEN BLUE BEGAN TO SING.
THEY'D NEVER HEARD ANYTHING LIKE IT BEFORE. HIS VOICE, THE WORDS HE LAID DOWN...
...JESUS, EVEN THAT CHEESY PIANO. I SWEAR HE WAS MAKING THAT PIANO CRY.
KAREN AND I LOOKED OUT AT THEM OVER THE OTHER-WORLDLY WAVES OF SOUND AND WE KNEW THEY HEARD WHAT WE DID.
I SWEAR, I WISH YOU COULDA HEARD IT.

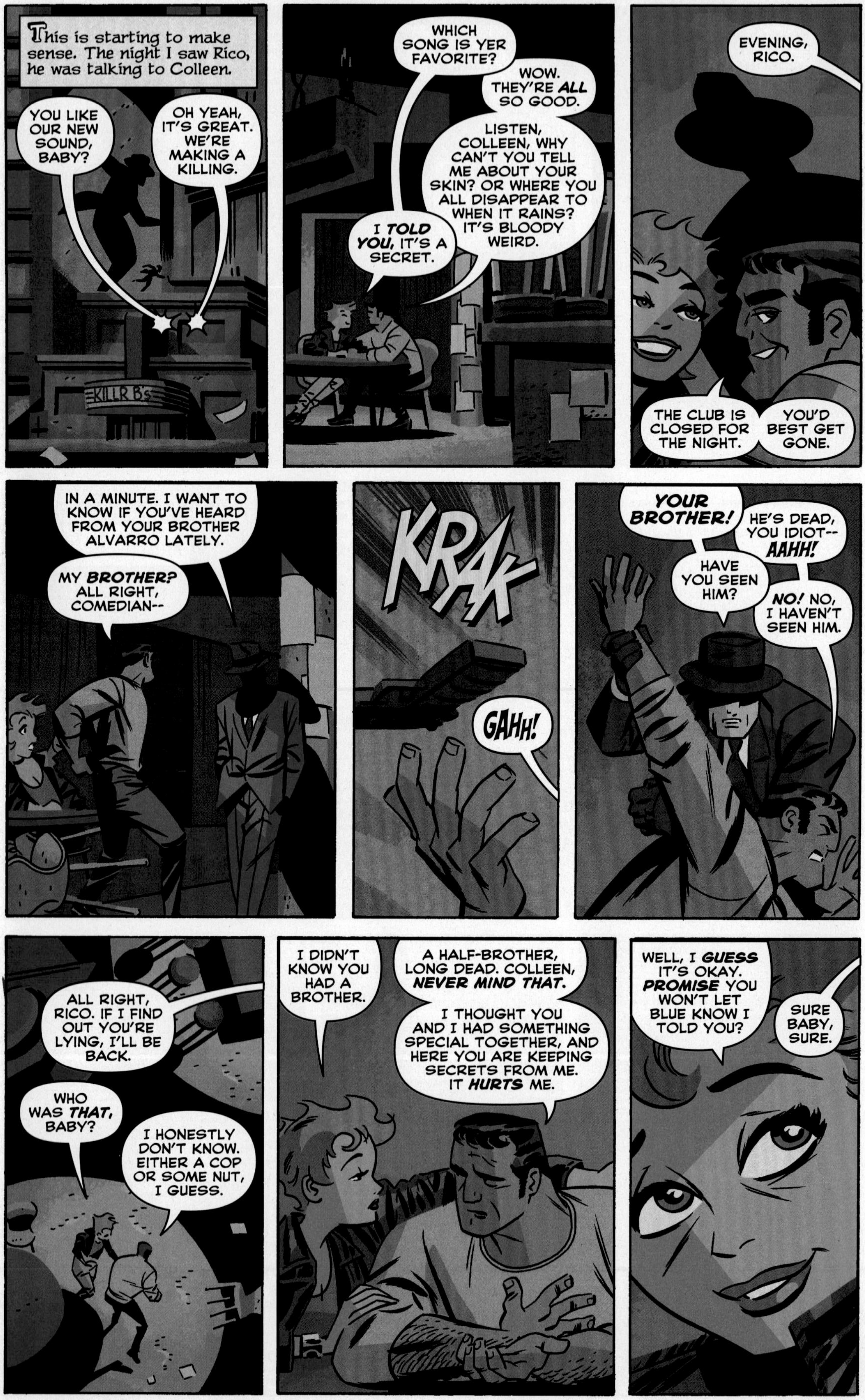
This is starting to make sense. The night I saw Rico, he was talking to Colleen.
YOU LIKE OUR NEW SOUND, BABY?
OH YEAH, IT'S GREAT. WE'RE MAKING A KILLING.
KILLR B's
WHICH SONG IS YER FAVORITE?
WOW. THEY'RE ALL SO GOOD.
LISTEN, COLLEEN, WHY CAN'T YOU TELL ME ABOUT YOUR SKIN? OR WHERE YOU ALL DISAPPEAR TO WHEN IT RAINS? IT'S BLOODY WEIRD.
I TOLD YOU, IT'S A SECRET.
EVENING, RICO.
THE CLUB IS CLOSED FOR THE NIGHT.
YOU'D BEST GET GONE.
IN A MINUTE. I WANT TO KNOW IF YOU'VE HEARD FROM YOUR BROTHER ALVARRO LATELY.
MY BROTHER? ALL RIGHT, COMEDIAN--
KRAK
GAHH!
YOUR BROTHER!
HE'S DEAD, YOU IDIOT-- AAHH!
HAVE YOU SEEN HIM?
NO! NO, I HAVEN'T SEEN HIM.
ALL RIGHT, RICO. IF I FIND OUT YOU'RE LYING, I'LL BE BACK.
WHO WAS THAT, BABY?
I HONESTLY DON'T KNOW. EITHER A COP OR SOME NUT, I GUESS.
I DIDN'T KNOW YOU HAD A BROTHER.
A HALF-BROTHER, LONG DEAD. COLLEEN, NEVER MIND THAT.
I THOUGHT YOU AND I HAD SOMETHING SPECIAL TOGETHER, AND HERE YOU ARE KEEPING SECRETS FROM ME. IT HURTS ME.
WELL, I GUESS IT'S OKAY. PROMISE YOU WON'T LET BLUE KNOW I TOLD YOU?
SURE BABY, SURE.

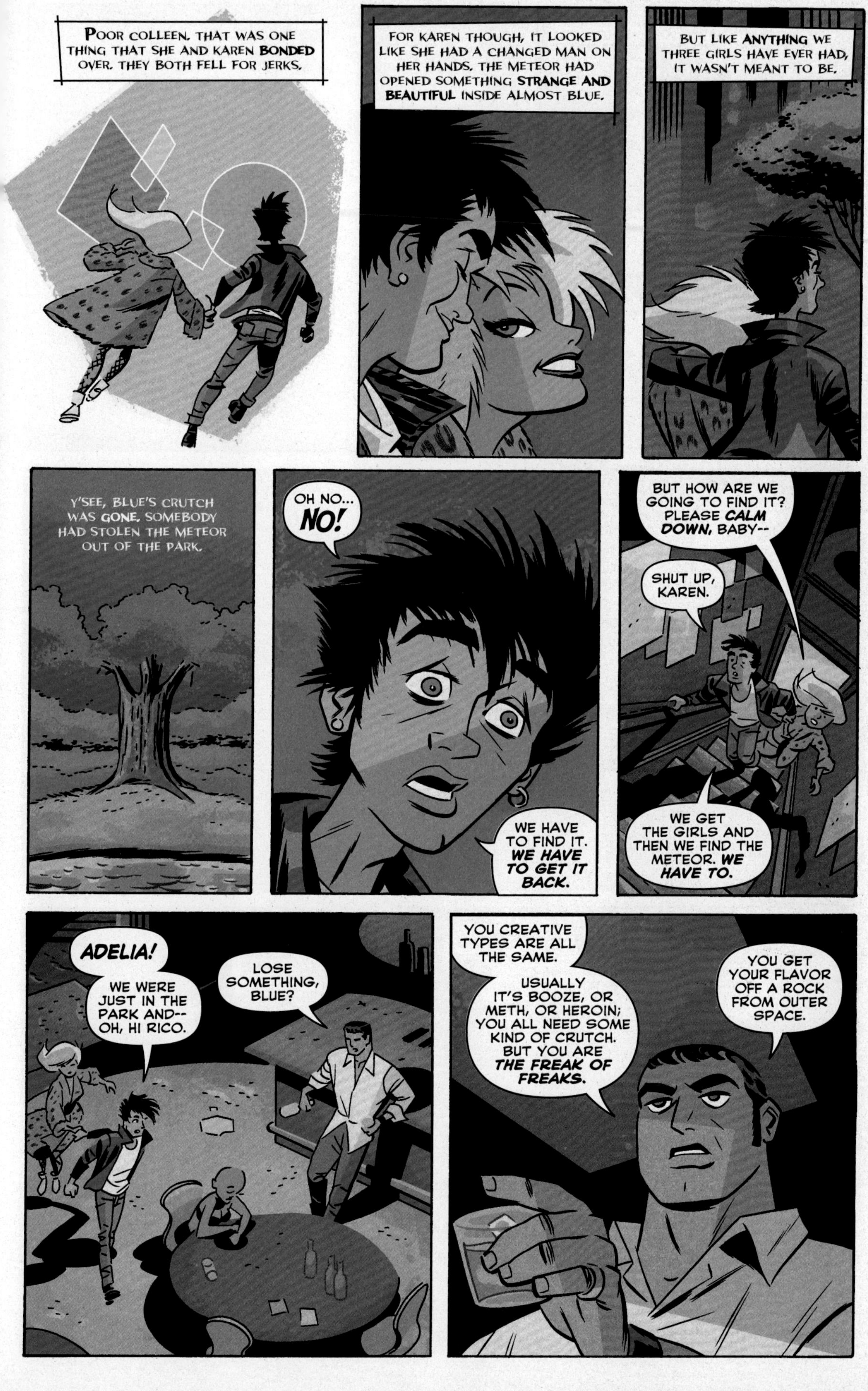
Poor colleen. That was one thing that she and Karen **bonded** over. They both fell for jerks.
For Karen though, it looked like she had a changed man on her hands. The meteor had opened something **strange and beautiful** inside Almost Blue.
But like **anything** we three girls have ever had, it wasn't meant to be.
Y'see, Blue's crutch was **gone**. Somebody had stolen the meteor out of the park.
OH NO... ***NO!***
WE HAVE TO FIND IT. ***WE HAVE TO GET IT BACK.***
BUT HOW ARE WE GOING TO FIND IT? PLEASE ***CALM DOWN,*** BABY--
SHUT UP, KAREN.
WE GET THE GIRLS AND THEN WE FIND THE METEOR. ***WE HAVE TO.***
***ADELIA!***
WE WERE JUST IN THE PARK AND-- OH, HI RICO.
LOSE SOMETHING, BLUE?
YOU CREATIVE TYPES ARE ALL THE SAME.
USUALLY IT'S BOOZE, OR METH, OR HEROIN; YOU ALL NEED SOME KIND OF CRUTCH. BUT YOU ARE ***THE FREAK OF FREAKS.***
YOU GET YOUR FLAVOR OFF A ROCK FROM OUTER SPACE.

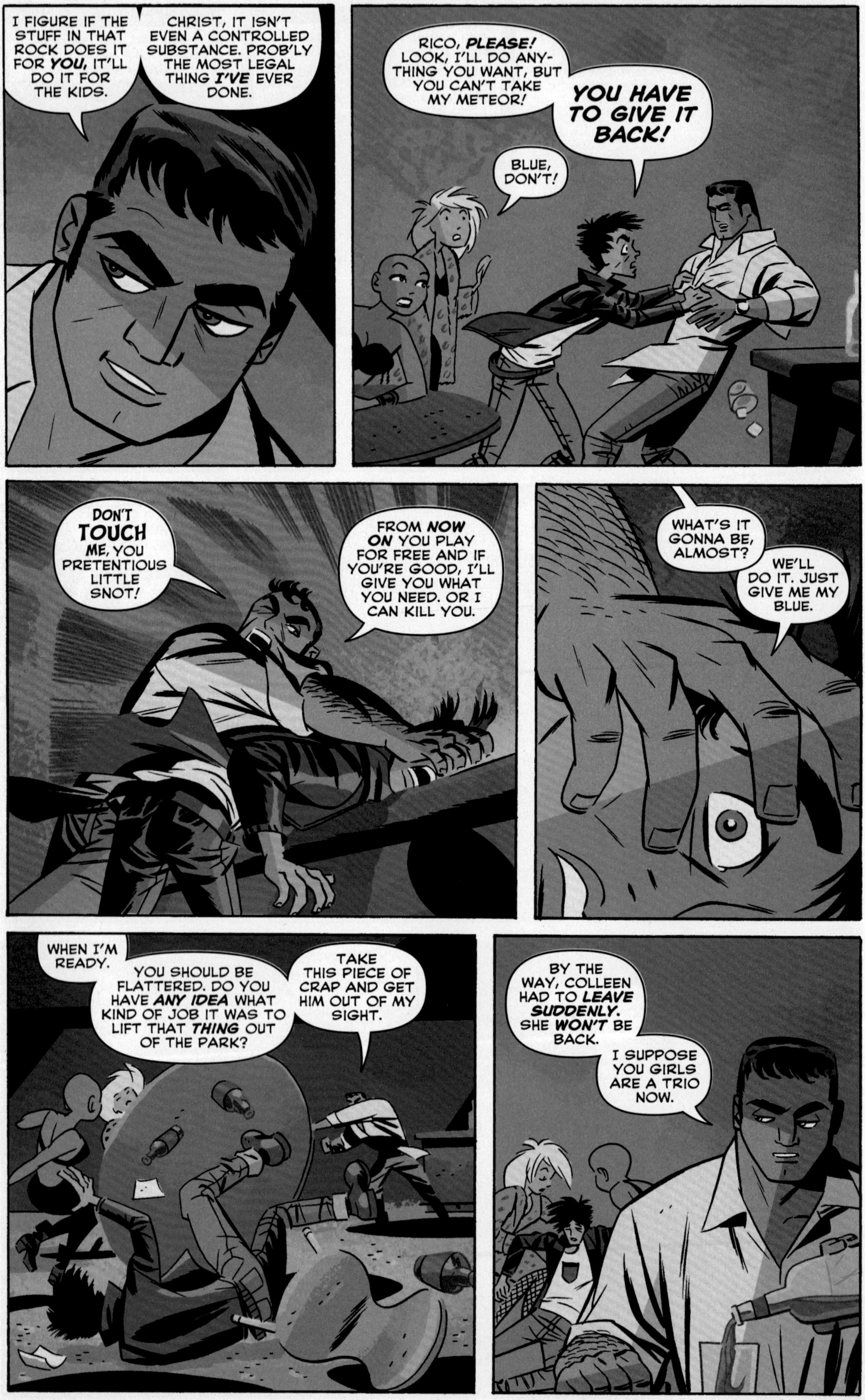
I FIGURE IF THE STUFF IN THAT ROCK DOES IT FOR *YOU*, IT'LL DO IT FOR THE KIDS.
CHRIST, IT ISN'T EVEN A CONTROLLED SUBSTANCE. PROB'LY THE MOST LEGAL THING *I'VE* EVER DONE.
RICO, *PLEASE!* LOOK, I'LL DO ANYTHING YOU WANT, BUT YOU CAN'T TAKE MY METEOR!
*YOU HAVE TO GIVE IT BACK!*
BLUE, DON'T!
DON'T **TOUCH ME**, YOU PRETENTIOUS LITTLE SNOT!
FROM *NOW ON* YOU PLAY FOR FREE AND IF YOU'RE GOOD, I'LL GIVE YOU WHAT YOU NEED. OR I CAN KILL YOU.
WHAT'S IT GONNA BE, ALMOST?
WE'LL DO IT. JUST GIVE ME MY BLUE.
WHEN I'M READY.
YOU SHOULD BE FLATTERED. DO YOU HAVE *ANY IDEA* WHAT KIND OF JOB IT WAS TO LIFT THAT *THING* OUT OF THE PARK?
TAKE THIS PIECE OF CRAP AND GET HIM OUT OF MY SIGHT.
BY THE WAY, COLLEEN HAD TO *LEAVE SUDDENLY*. SHE *WON'T* BE BACK.
I SUPPOSE YOU GIRLS ARE A TRIO NOW.

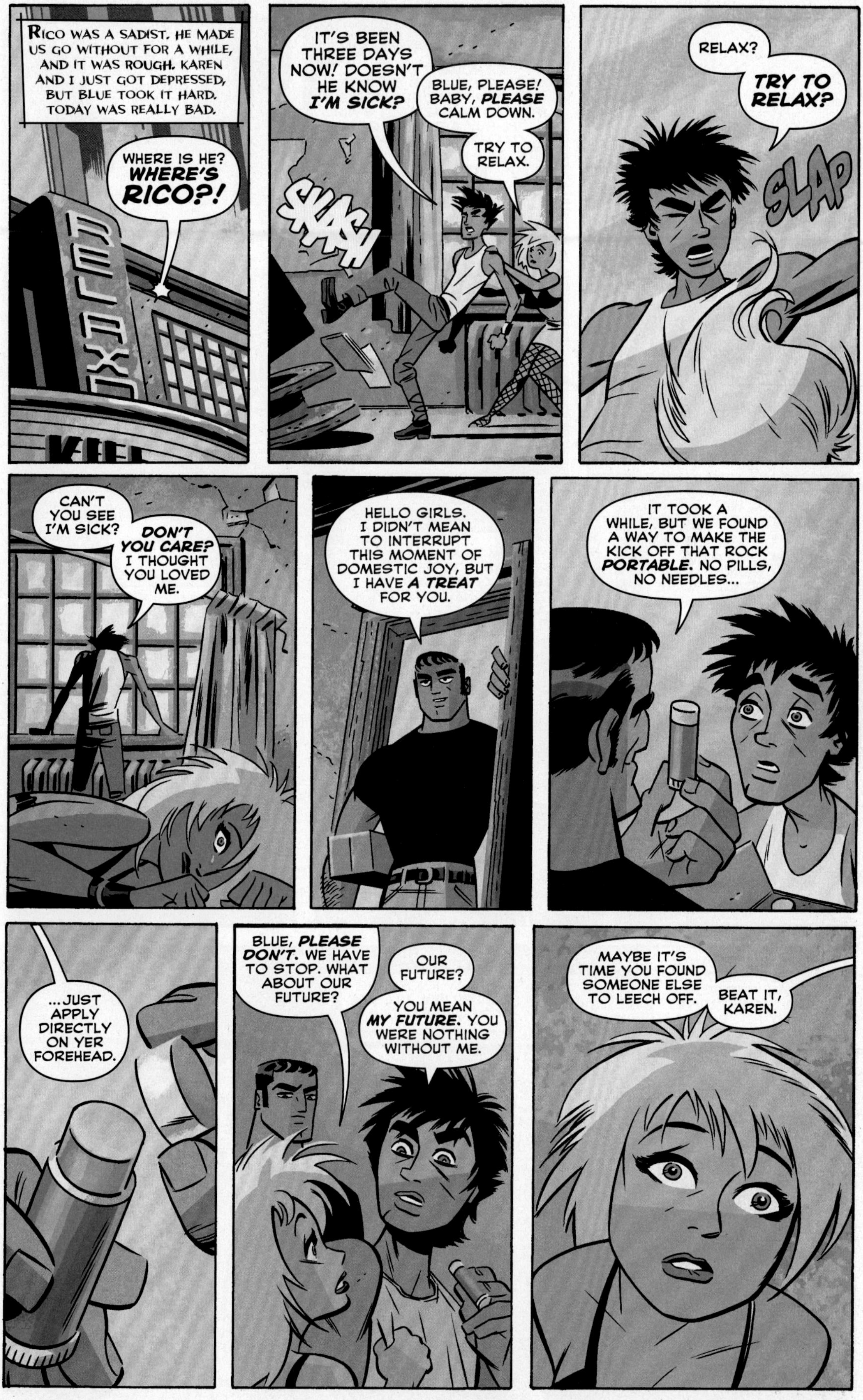
RICO WAS A SADIST. HE MADE US GO WITHOUT FOR A WHILE, AND IT WAS ROUGH. KAREN AND I JUST GOT DEPRESSED, BUT BLUE TOOK IT HARD. TODAY WAS REALLY BAD.
WHERE IS HE? WHERE'S RICO?!
RELAXO
IT'S BEEN THREE DAYS NOW! DOESN'T HE KNOW I'M SICK?
BLUE, PLEASE! BABY, PLEASE CALM DOWN.
TRY TO RELAX.
SMASH
RELAX?
TRY TO RELAX?
SLAP
CAN'T YOU SEE I'M SICK?
DON'T YOU CARE? I THOUGHT YOU LOVED ME.
HELLO GIRLS. I DIDN'T MEAN TO INTERRUPT THIS MOMENT OF DOMESTIC JOY, BUT I HAVE A TREAT FOR YOU.
IT TOOK A WHILE, BUT WE FOUND A WAY TO MAKE THE KICK OFF THAT ROCK PORTABLE. NO PILLS, NO NEEDLES...
...JUST APPLY DIRECTLY ON YER FOREHEAD.
BLUE, PLEASE DON'T. WE HAVE TO STOP. WHAT ABOUT OUR FUTURE?
OUR FUTURE?
YOU MEAN MY FUTURE. YOU WERE NOTHING WITHOUT ME.
MAYBE IT'S TIME YOU FOUND SOMEONE ELSE TO LEECH OFF.
BEAT IT, KAREN.

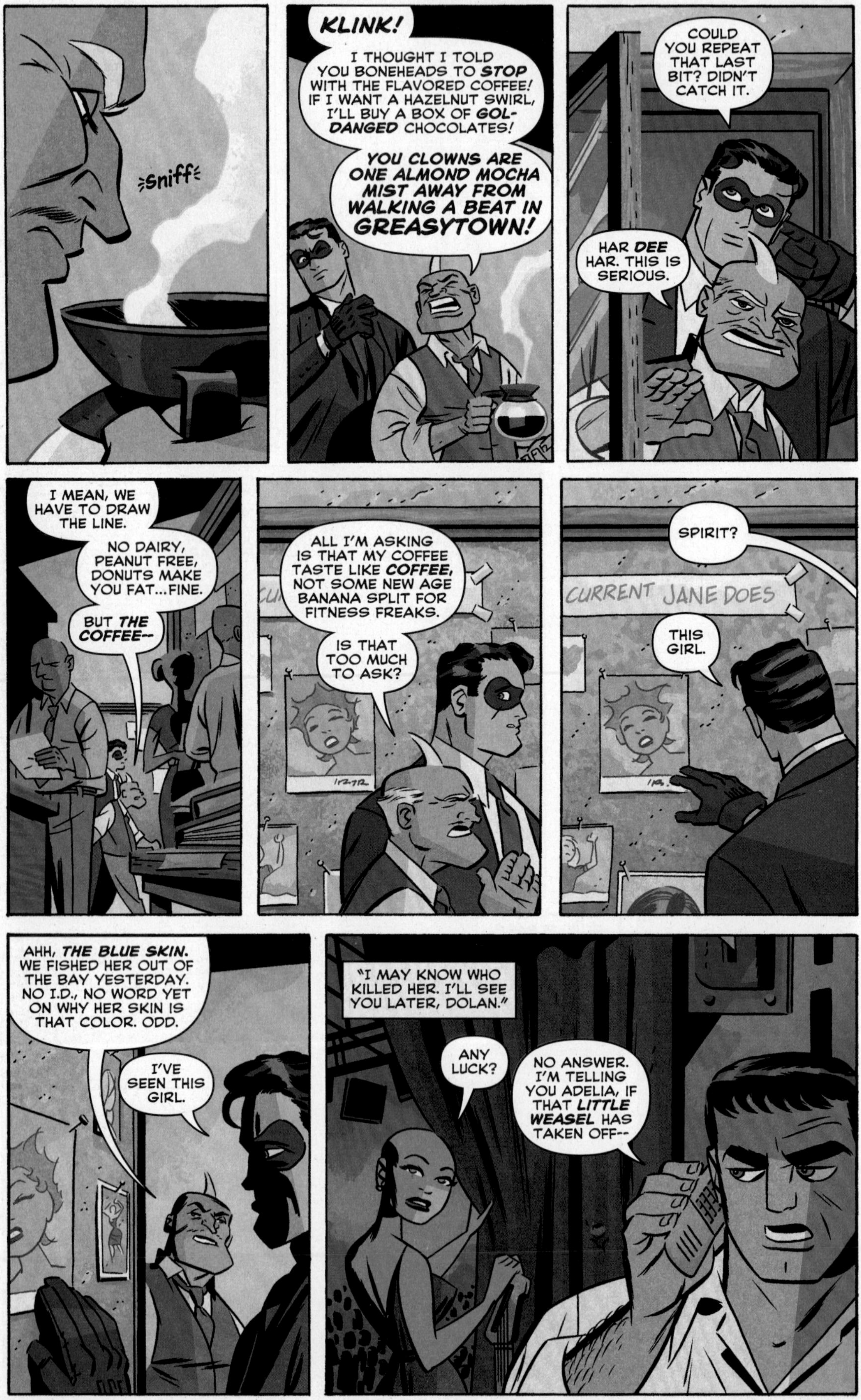
SNIFF
KLINK!
I THOUGHT I TOLD YOU BONEHEADS TO STOP WITH THE FLAVORED COFFEE! IF I WANT A HAZELNUT SWIRL, I'LL BUY A BOX OF GOL-DANGED CHOCOLATES!
YOU CLOWNS ARE ONE ALMOND MOCHA MIST AWAY FROM WALKING A BEAT IN GREASYTOWN!
COULD YOU REPEAT THAT LAST BIT? DIDN'T CATCH IT.
HAR DEE HAR. THIS IS SERIOUS.
I MEAN, WE HAVE TO DRAW THE LINE.
NO DAIRY, PEANUT FREE, DONUTS MAKE YOU FAT...FINE.
BUT THE COFFEE--
ALL I'M ASKING IS THAT MY COFFEE TASTE LIKE COFFEE, NOT SOME NEW AGE BANANA SPLIT FOR FITNESS FREAKS.
IS THAT TOO MUCH TO ASK?
SPIRIT?
CURRENT JANE DOES
THIS GIRL.
AHH, THE BLUE SKIN. WE FISHED HER OUT OF THE BAY YESTERDAY. NO I.D., NO WORD YET ON WHY HER SKIN IS THAT COLOR. ODD.
I'VE SEEN THIS GIRL.
"I MAY KNOW WHO KILLED HER. I'LL SEE YOU LATER, DOLAN."
ANY LUCK?
NO ANSWER. I'M TELLING YOU ADELIA, IF THAT LITTLE WEASEL HAS TAKEN OFF--

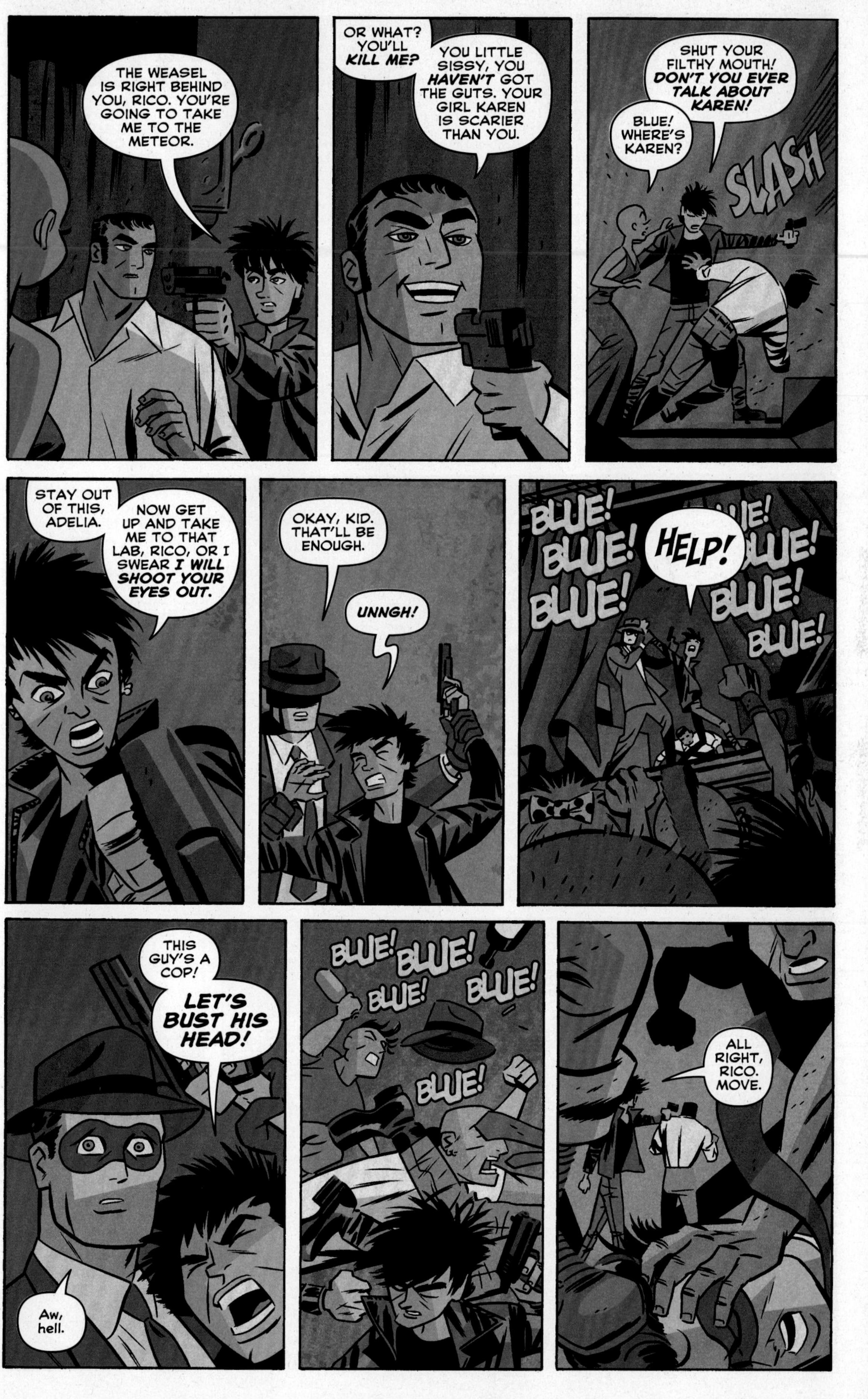
THE WEASEL IS RIGHT BEHIND YOU, RICO. YOU'RE GOING TO TAKE ME TO THE METEOR.
OR WHAT? YOU'LL KILL ME?
YOU LITTLE SISSY, YOU HAVEN'T GOT THE GUTS. YOUR GIRL KAREN IS SCARIER THAN YOU.
SHUT YOUR FILTHY MOUTH! DON'T YOU EVER TALK ABOUT KAREN!
BLUE! WHERE'S KAREN?
SLASH
STAY OUT OF THIS, ADELIA.
NOW GET UP AND TAKE ME TO THAT LAB, RICO, OR I SWEAR I WILL SHOOT YOUR EYES OUT.
OKAY, KID. THAT'LL BE ENOUGH.
UNNGH!
BLUE! BLUE! BLUE!
HELP!
BLUE! BLUE! BLUE! BLUE!
THIS GUY'S A COP!
LET'S BUST HIS HEAD!
Aw, hell.
BLUE! BLUE! BLUE! BLUE!
BLUE!
ALL RIGHT, RICO. MOVE.

THAT'S RIGHT!

EVERYBODY OUT!

BAM BAM

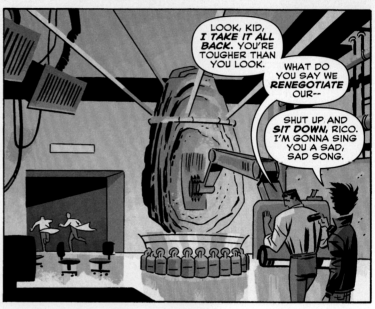

LOOK, KID, I TAKE IT ALL BACK. YOU'RE TOUGHER THAN YOU LOOK.

WHAT DO YOU SAY WE RENEGOTIATE OUR--

SHUT UP AND SIT DOWN, RICO. I'M GONNA SING YOU A SAD, SAD SONG.

KRAK

Amazing.

HOW DID YOU DO THAT?

PLEASE. THEY'RE JUST PUNKS.

THAT KID WITH SKIN LIKE YOURS--

I NEED TO KNOW WHERE HE TOOK RICO.

HE WAS SCREAMING ABOUT GOING TO RICO'S LAB IN THE NORTH END. I USED TO COP METH THERE.

THIS AFTERNOON I TOOK THAT BLUE YOU GAVE ME AND WENT DOWN TO THE PARK TO BE ALONE.

BUT I COULDN'T USE IT.

Y'SEE, FOR A SECOND THERE, MY MISERABLE, SELFISH MIND HAD A MOMENT OF CLARITY.

IT WASN'T THE BLUE I NEEDED.

IT WAS KAREN.

AND I'D THROWN HER AWAY. I DECIDED TO GO HOME TO HER.

TO TRY TO GET HER TO FORGIVE ME.

"BUT IT WAS TOO LATE.

"THE MAN SHE'D DEPENDED ON, THE MAN SHE'D GIVEN HER BATTERED HEART TO...HE HAD TURNED OUT TO BE A SOULLESS CREEP.

"AND SHE COULDN'T LIVE WITH THAT."

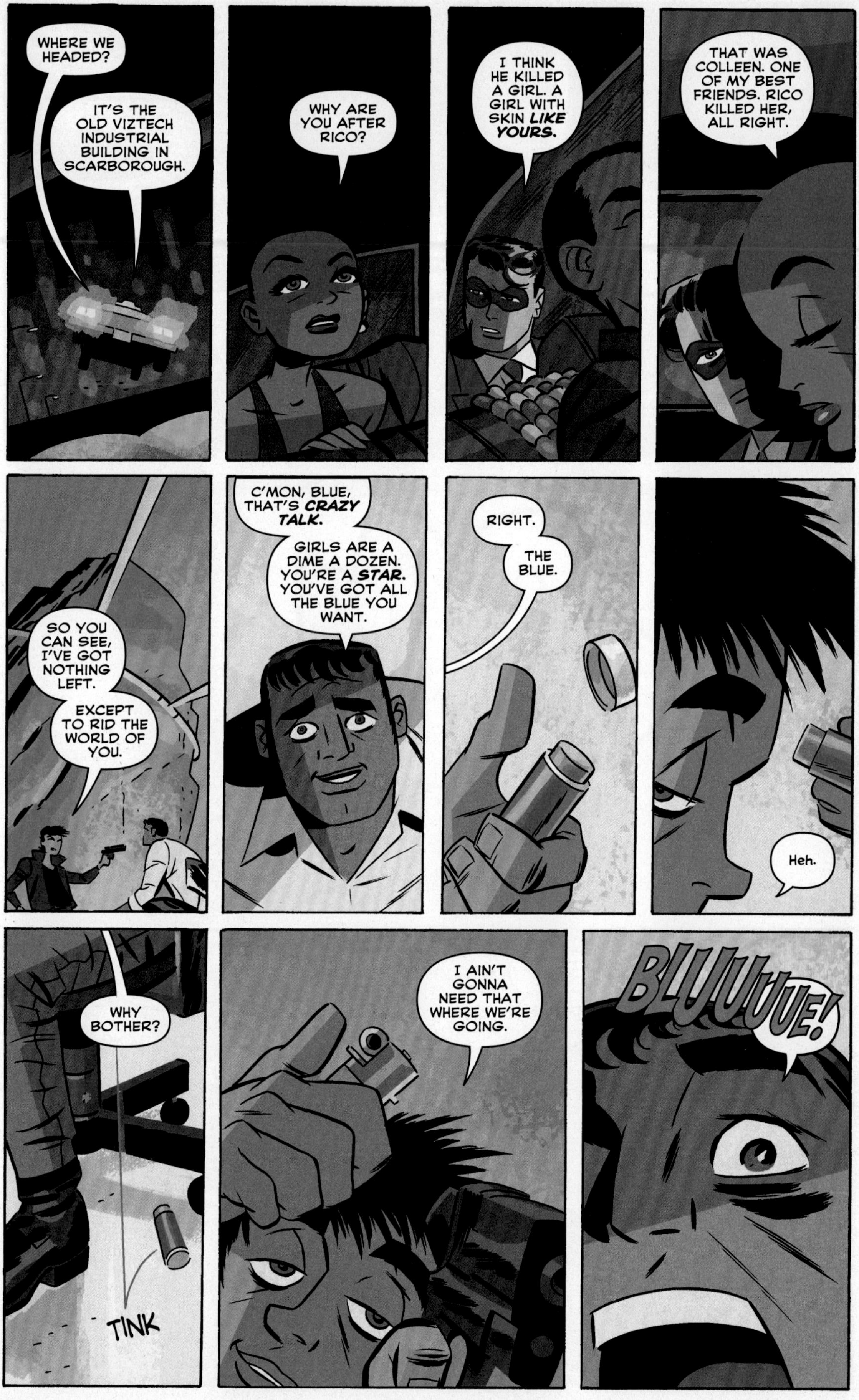

WHERE WE HEADED?
IT'S THE OLD VIZTECH INDUSTRIAL BUILDING IN SCARBOROUGH.
WHY ARE YOU AFTER RICO?
I THINK HE KILLED A GIRL. A GIRL WITH SKIN **LIKE YOURS.**
THAT WAS COLLEEN. ONE OF MY BEST FRIENDS. RICO KILLED HER, ALL RIGHT.
SO YOU CAN SEE, I'VE GOT NOTHING LEFT.
EXCEPT TO RID THE WORLD OF YOU.
C'MON, BLUE, THAT'S **CRAZY TALK.**
GIRLS ARE A DIME A DOZEN. YOU'RE A **STAR.** YOU'VE GOT ALL THE BLUE YOU WANT.
RIGHT.
THE BLUE.
Heh.
WHY BOTHER?
TINK
I AIN'T GONNA NEED THAT WHERE WE'RE GOING.
BLUUUUUE!

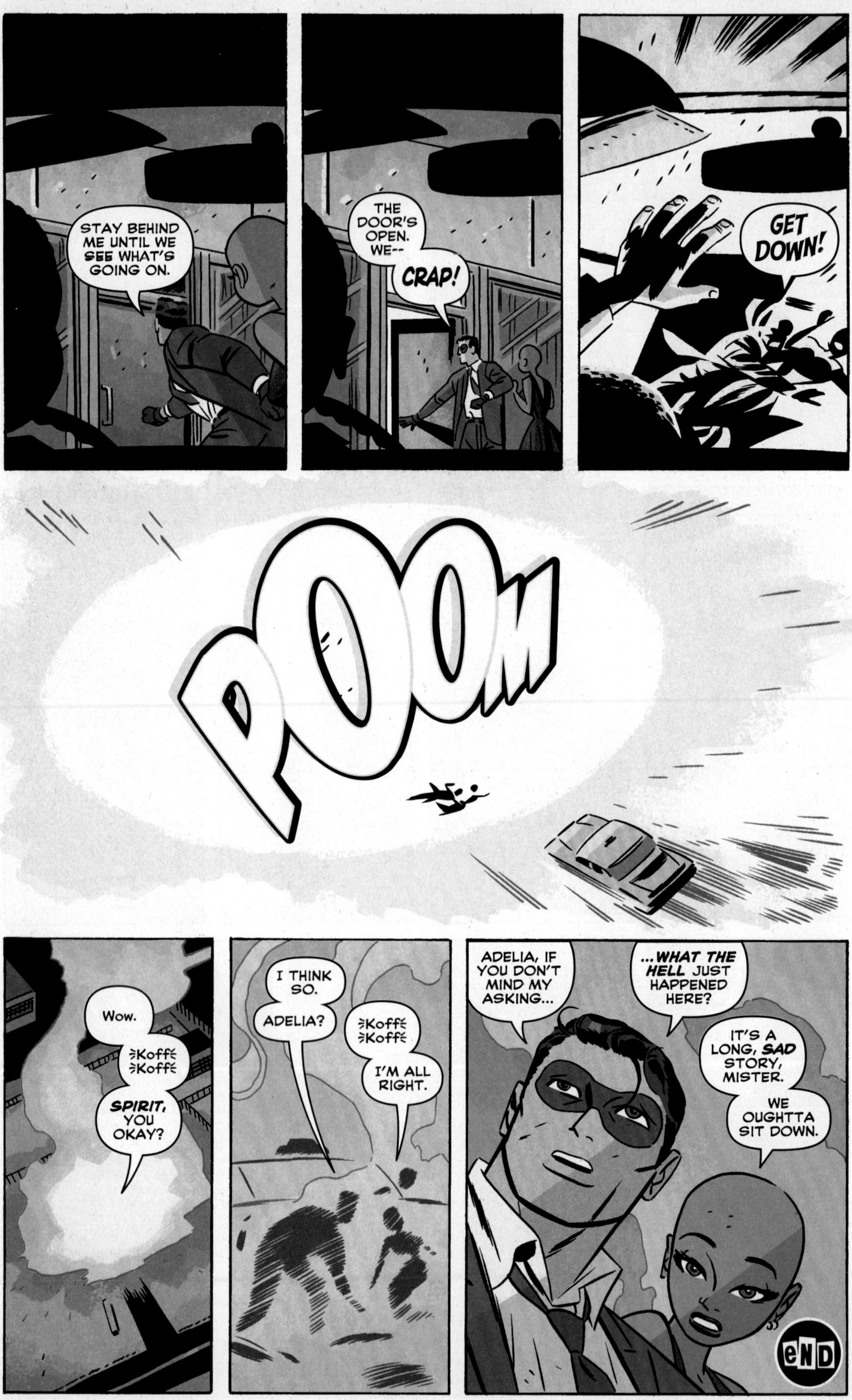
STAY BEHIND ME UNTIL WE SEE WHAT'S GOING ON.
THE DOOR'S OPEN. WE--
CRAP!
GET DOWN!
POOM
Wow.
Koff Koff
SPIRIT, YOU OKAY?
I THINK SO.
ADELIA?
Koff Koff
I'M ALL RIGHT.
ADELIA, IF YOU DON'T MIND MY ASKING...
...WHAT THE HELL JUST HAPPENED HERE?
IT'S A LONG, SAD STORY, MISTER.
WE OUGHTTA SIT DOWN.
END

# 7: Batman/ The Spirit

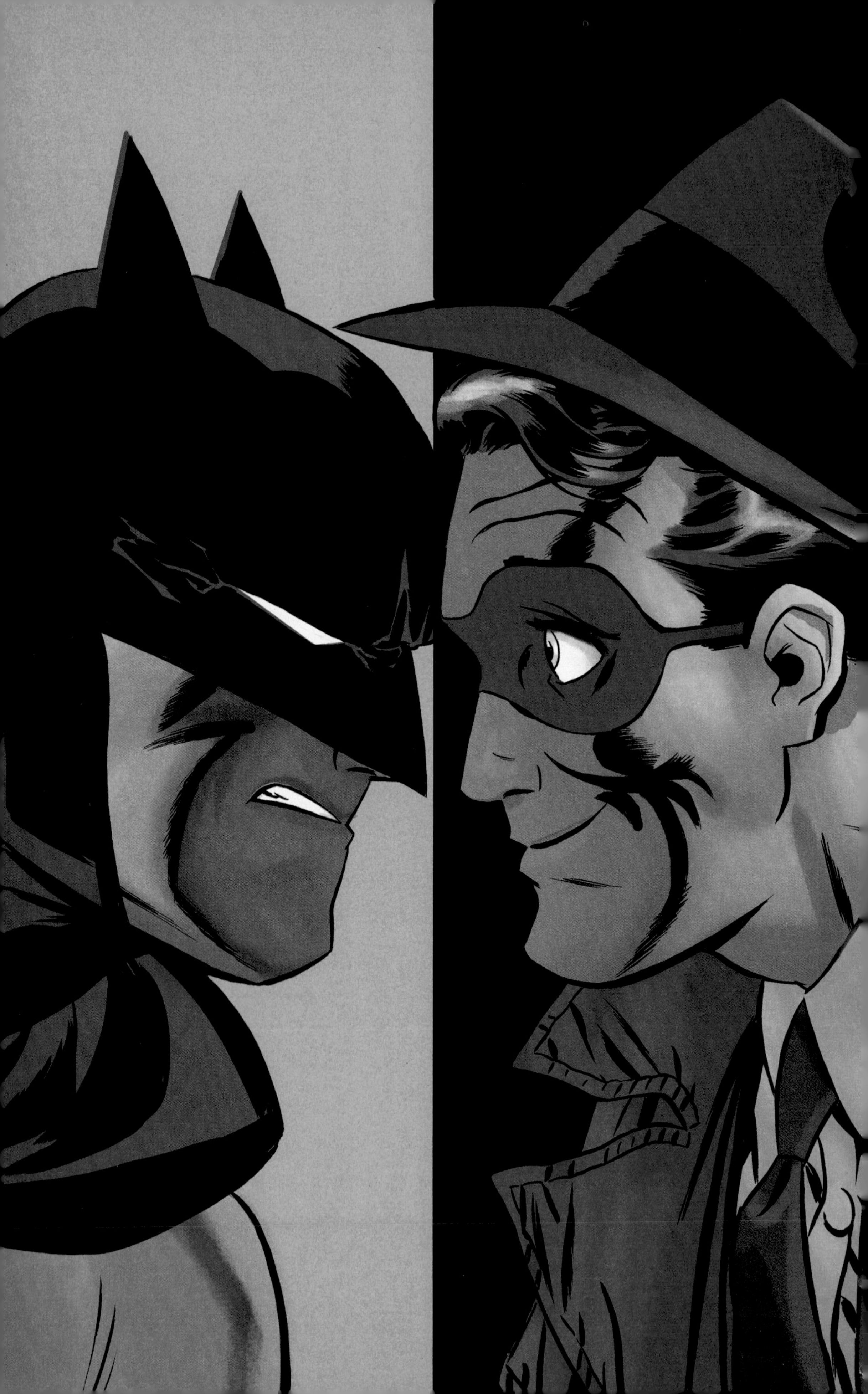

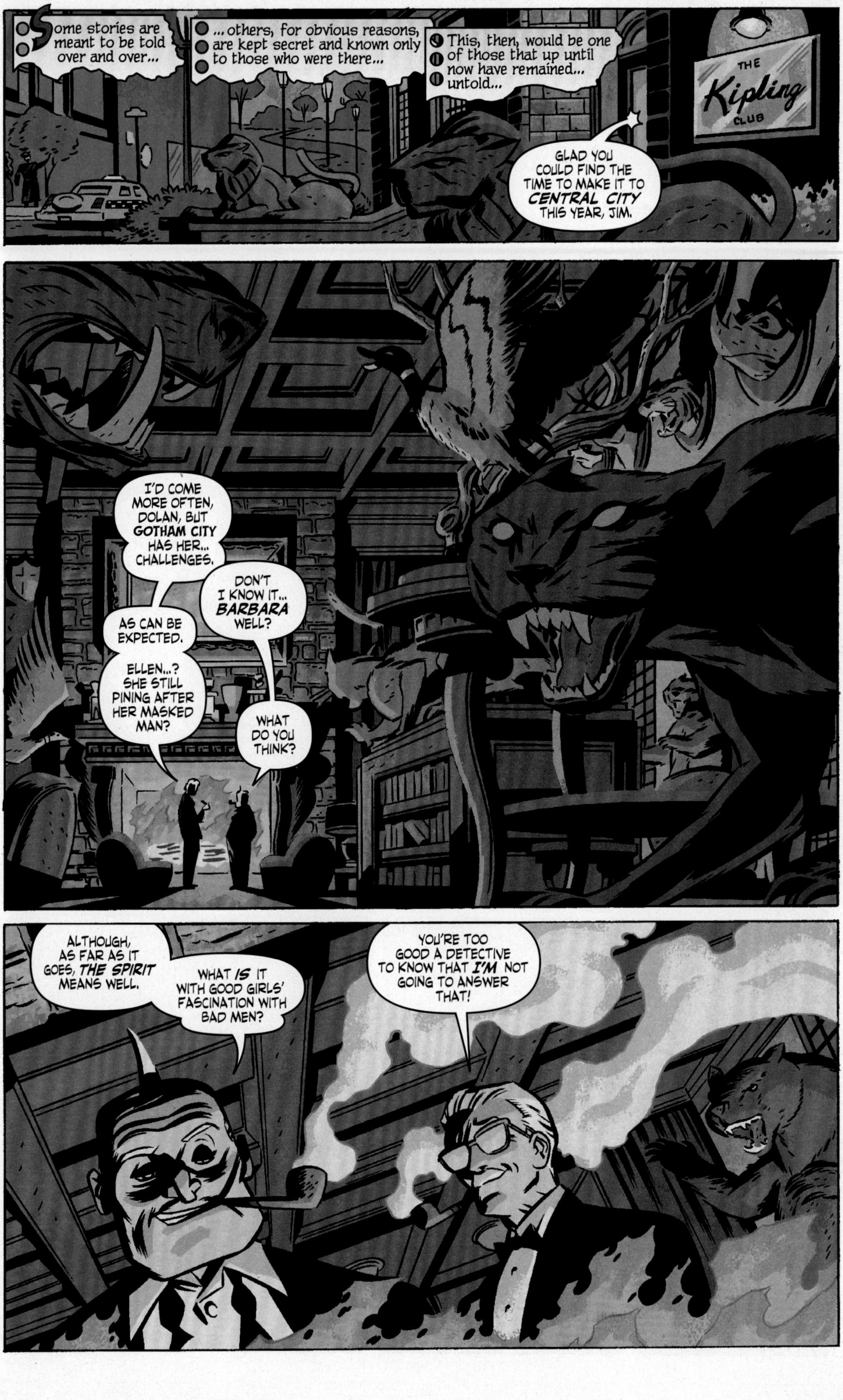
Some stories are meant to be told over and over...
...others, for obvious reasons, are kept secret and known only to those who were there...
This, then, would be one of those that up until now have remained... untold...
THE Kipling CLUB
GLAD YOU COULD FIND THE TIME TO MAKE IT TO CENTRAL CITY THIS YEAR, JIM.
I'D COME MORE OFTEN, DOLAN, BUT GOTHAM CITY HAS HER... CHALLENGES.
DON'T I KNOW IT... BARBARA WELL?
AS CAN BE EXPECTED.
ELLEN...? SHE STILL PINING AFTER HER MASKED MAN?
WHAT DO YOU THINK?
ALTHOUGH, AS FAR AS IT GOES, THE SPIRIT MEANS WELL.
WHAT IS IT WITH GOOD GIRLS' FASCINATION WITH BAD MEN?
YOU'RE TOO GOOD A DETECTIVE TO KNOW THAT I'M NOT GOING TO ANSWER THAT!

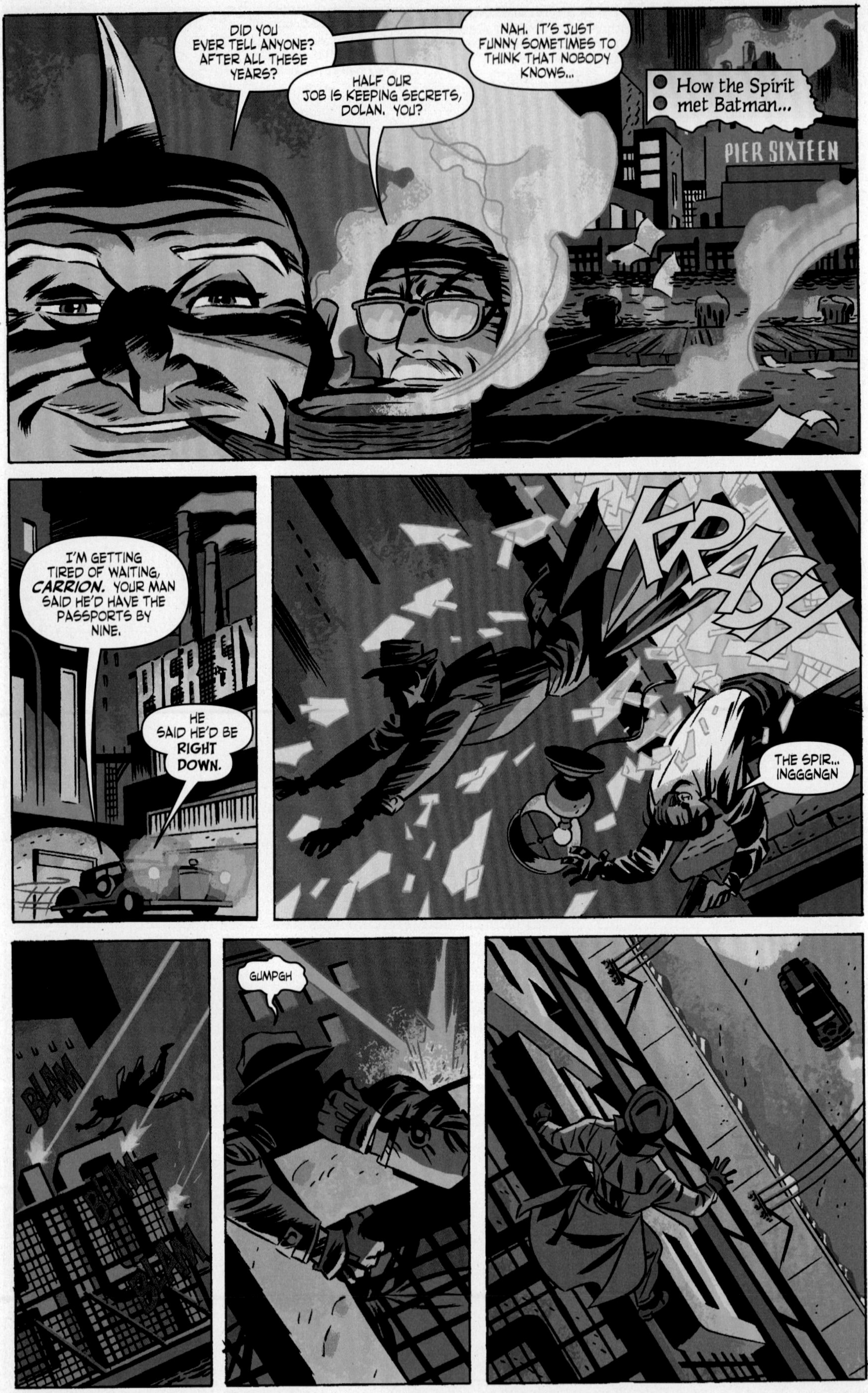
DID YOU EVER TELL ANYONE? AFTER ALL THESE YEARS?
HALF OUR JOB IS KEEPING SECRETS, DOLAN. YOU?
NAH. IT'S JUST FUNNY SOMETIMES TO THINK THAT NOBODY KNOWS...
How the Spirit met Batman...
PIER SIXTEEN
I'M GETTING TIRED OF WAITING, CARRION. YOUR MAN SAID HE'D HAVE THE PASSPORTS BY NINE.
HE SAID HE'D BE RIGHT DOWN.
KRASH
THE SPIR... INGGGNGN
BLAM
GUMPGH

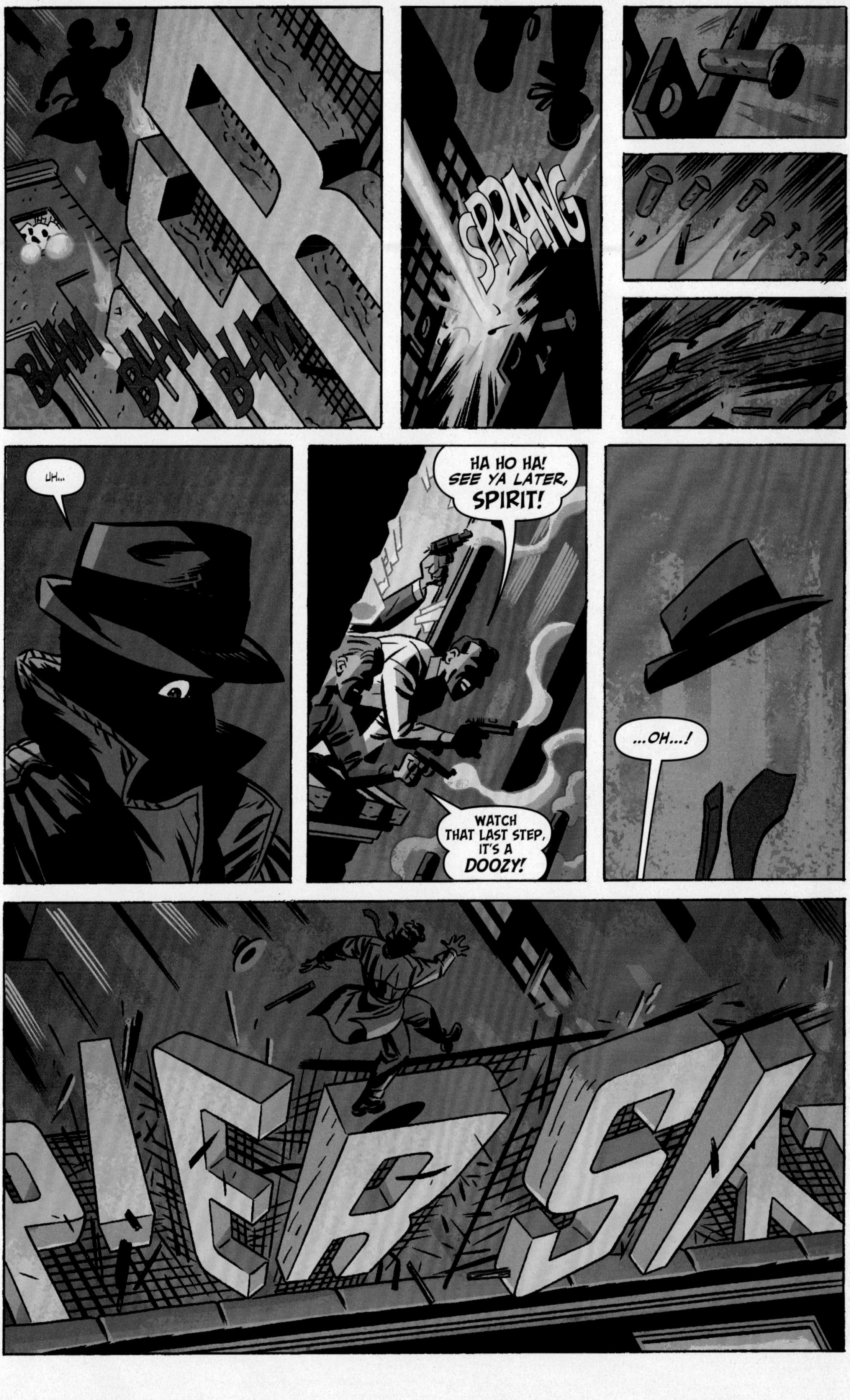
BLAM BLAM BLAM
SPRANG
UH...
HA HO HA! SEE YA LATER, SPIRIT!
WATCH THAT LAST STEP, IT'S A DOOZY!
...OH...!

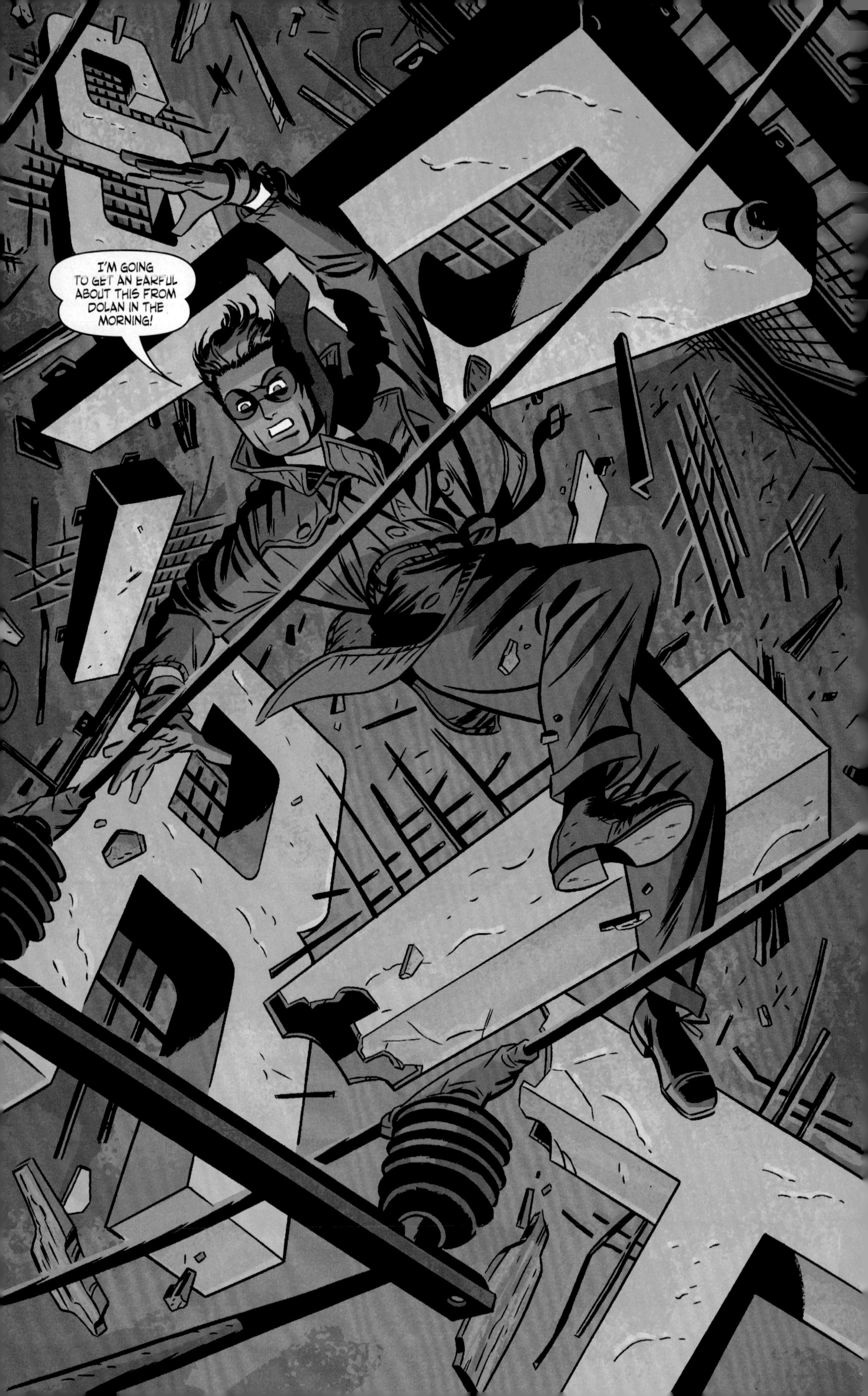
I'M GOING TO GET AN EARFUL ABOUT THIS FROM DOLAN IN THE MORNING!

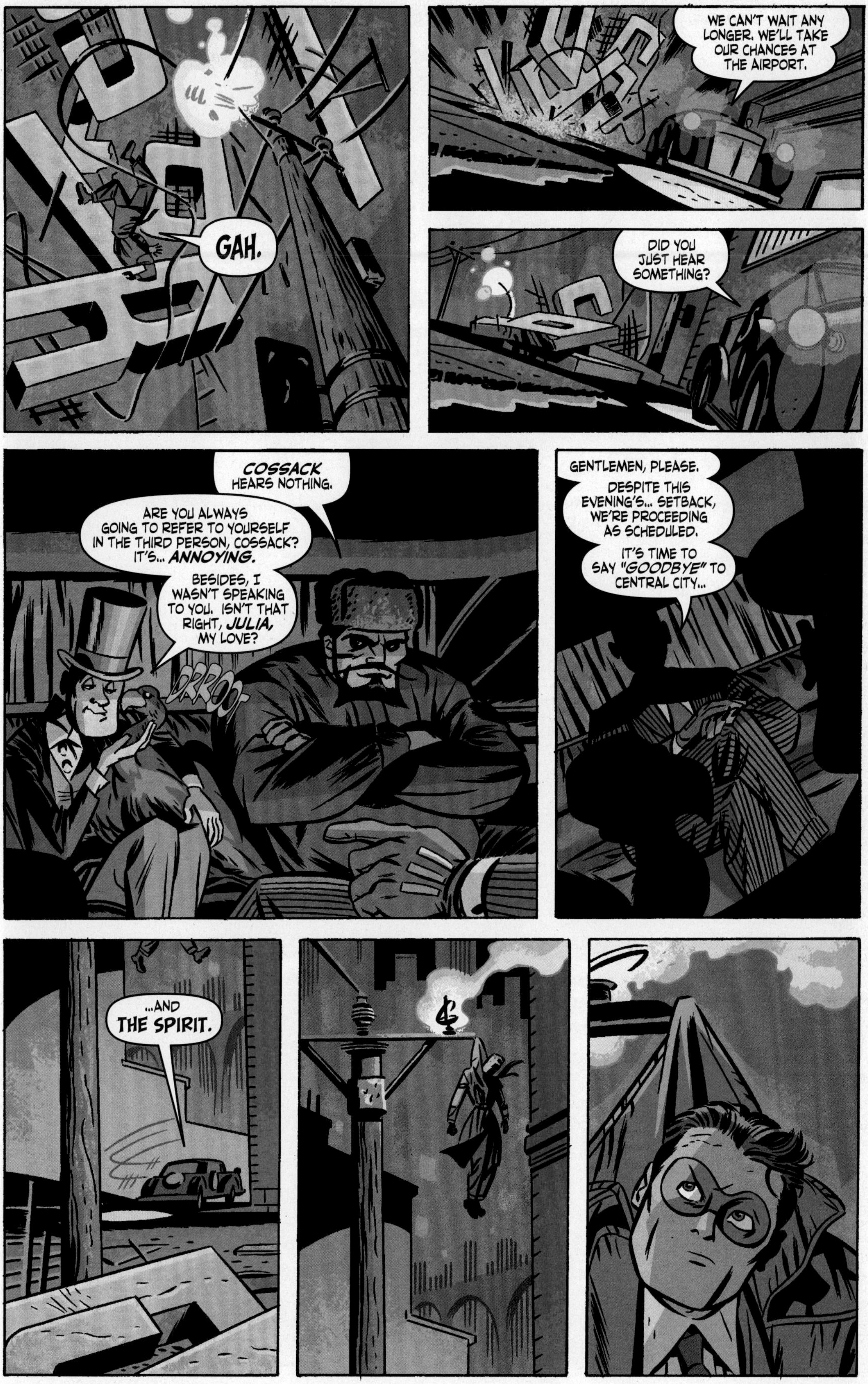
GAH.
WE CAN'T WAIT ANY LONGER. WE'LL TAKE OUR CHANCES AT THE AIRPORT.
DID YOU JUST HEAR SOMETHING?
COSSACK HEARS NOTHING.
ARE YOU ALWAYS GOING TO REFER TO YOURSELF IN THE THIRD PERSON, COSSACK? IT'S... ANNOYING.
BESIDES, I WASN'T SPEAKING TO YOU. ISN'T THAT RIGHT, JULIA, MY LOVE?
BRRROOT
GENTLEMEN, PLEASE.
DESPITE THIS EVENING'S... SETBACK, WE'RE PROCEEDING AS SCHEDULED.
IT'S TIME TO SAY "GOODBYE" TO CENTRAL CITY...
...AND THE SPIRIT.

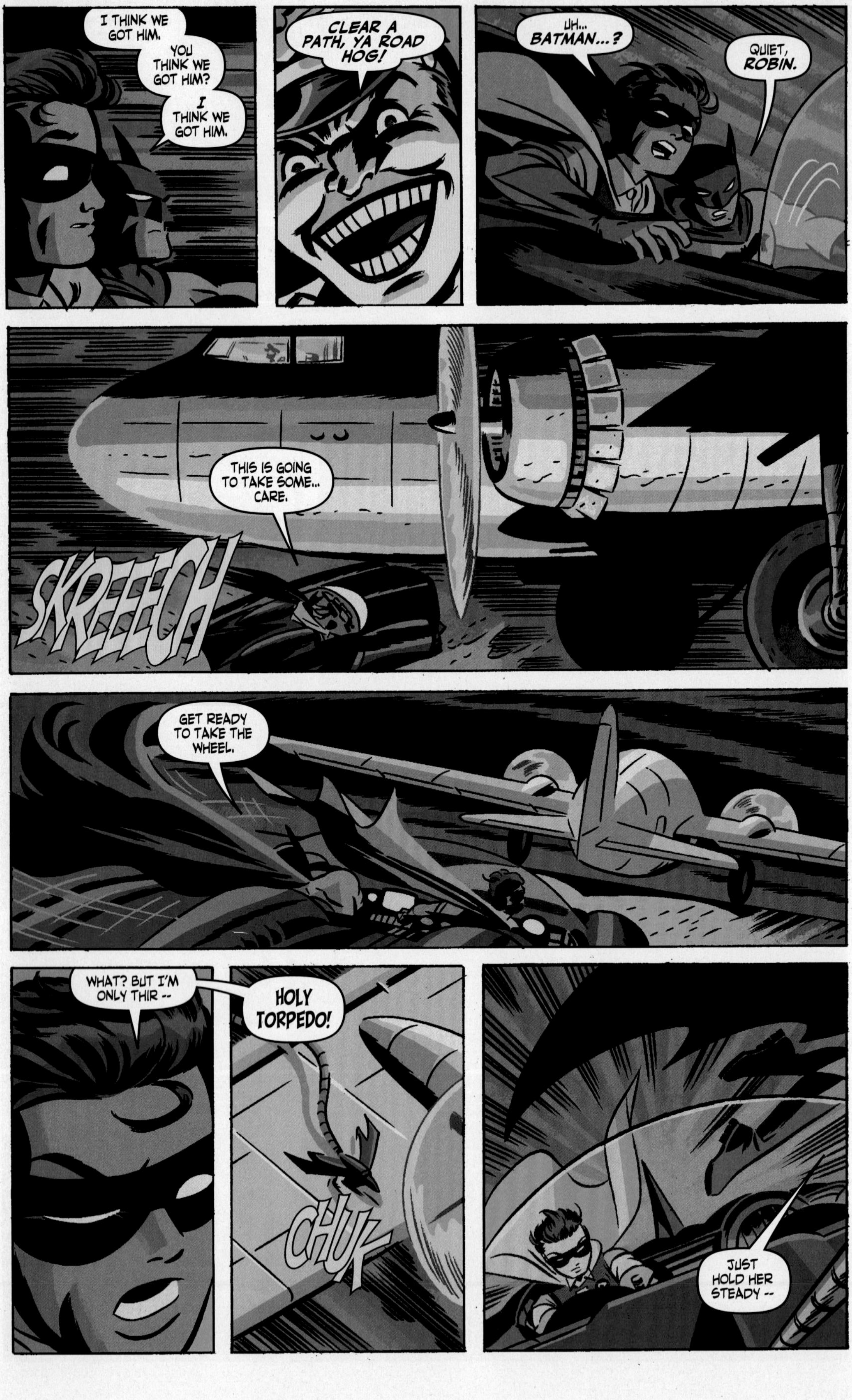
I THINK WE GOT HIM.
YOU THINK WE GOT HIM?
I THINK WE GOT HIM.
CLEAR A PATH, YA ROAD HOG!
UH... BATMAN...?
QUIET, ROBIN.
THIS IS GOING TO TAKE SOME... CARE.
SKREEECH
GET READY TO TAKE THE WHEEL.
WHAT? BUT I'M ONLY THIR --
HOLY TORPEDO!
CHUK
JUST HOLD HER STEADY --

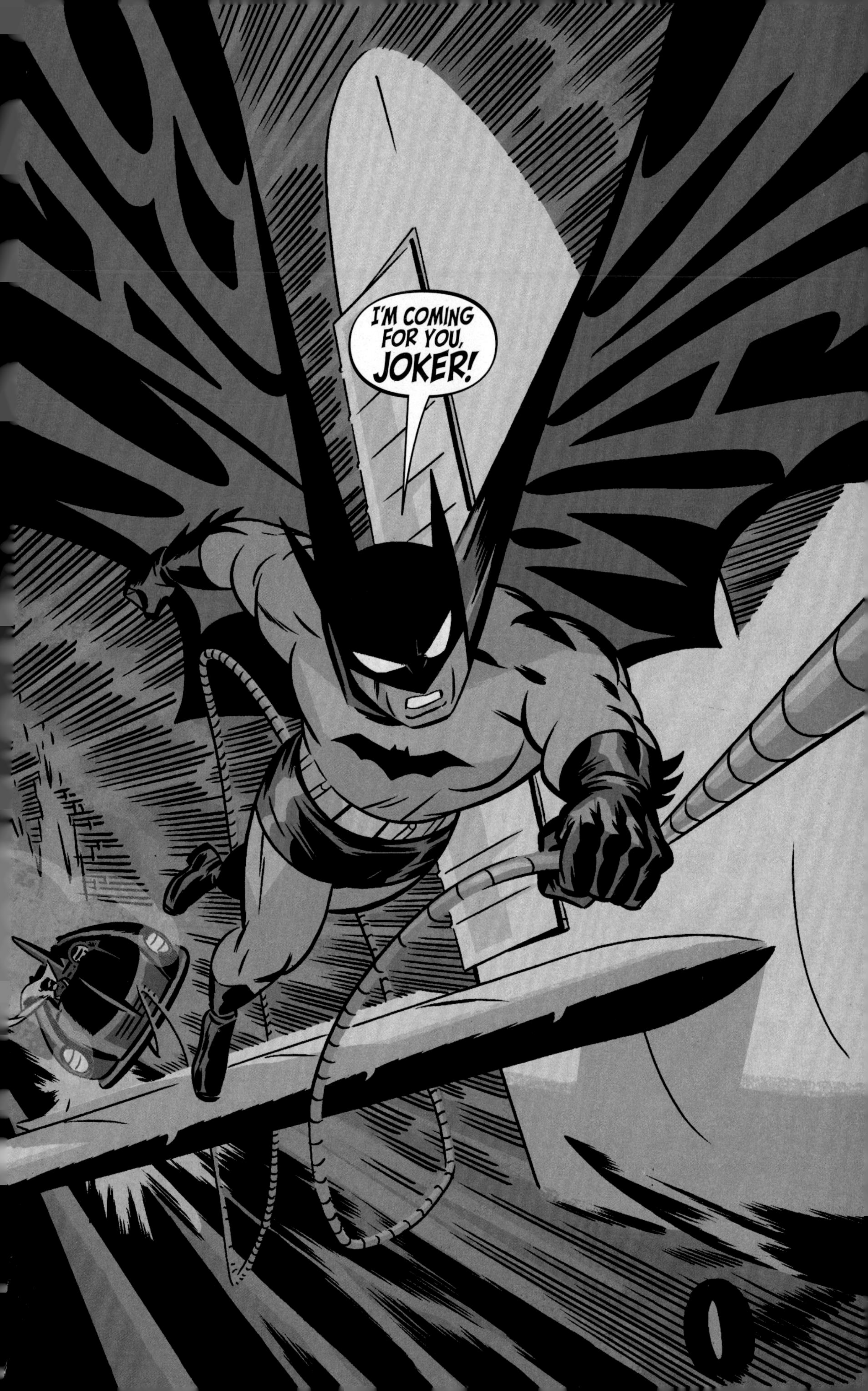
I'M COMING FOR YOU, JOKER!

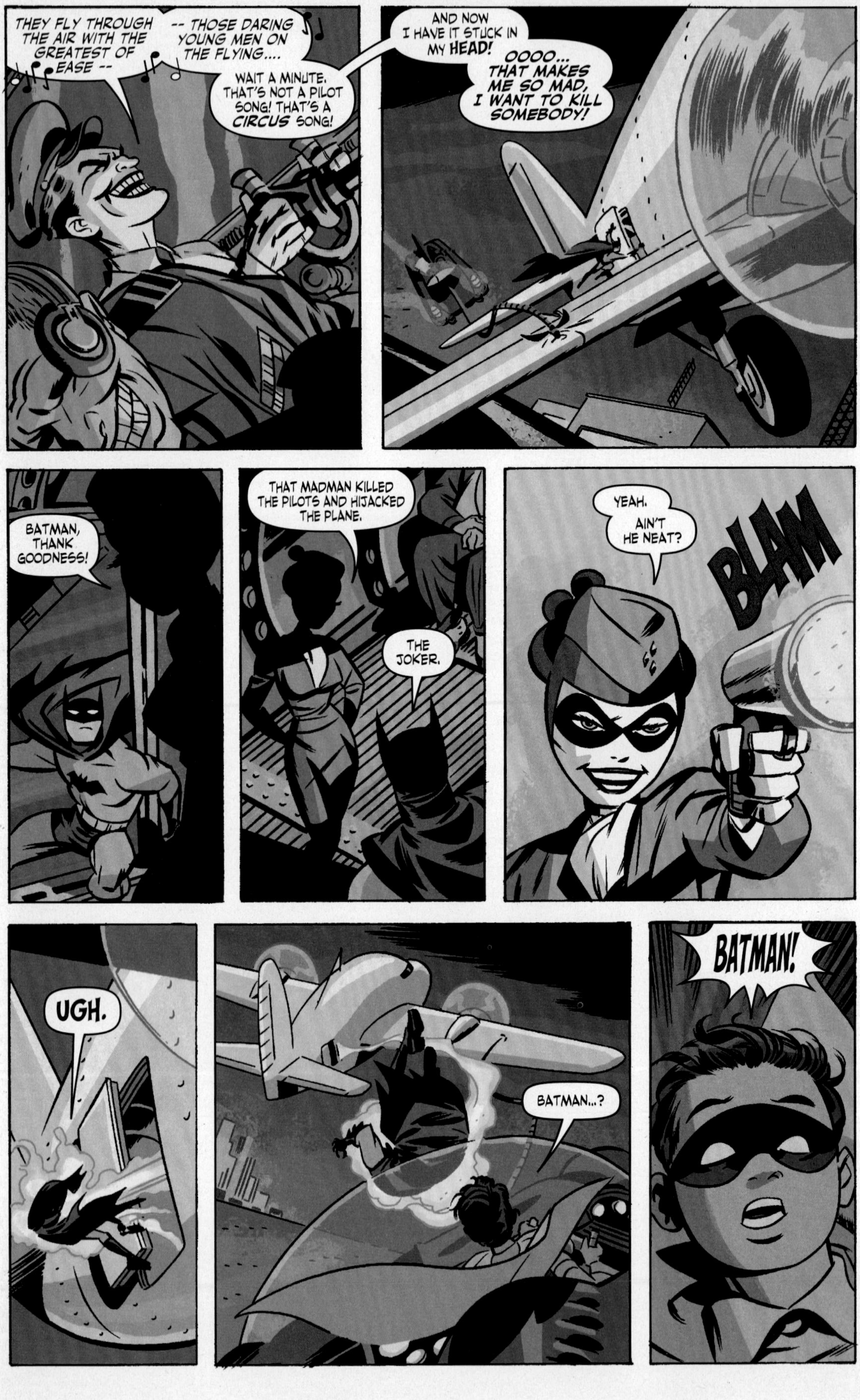
THEY FLY THROUGH THE AIR WITH THE GREATEST OF EASE --
-- THOSE DARING YOUNG MEN ON THE FLYING....
WAIT A MINUTE. THAT'S NOT A PILOT SONG! THAT'S A CIRCUS SONG!
AND NOW I HAVE IT STUCK IN MY HEAD!
OOOO... THAT MAKES ME SO MAD, I WANT TO KILL SOMEBODY!
BATMAN, THANK GOODNESS!
THAT MADMAN KILLED THE PILOTS AND HIJACKED THE PLANE.
THE JOKER.
YEAH. AIN'T HE NEAT?
BLAM
UGH.
BATMAN...?
BATMAN!

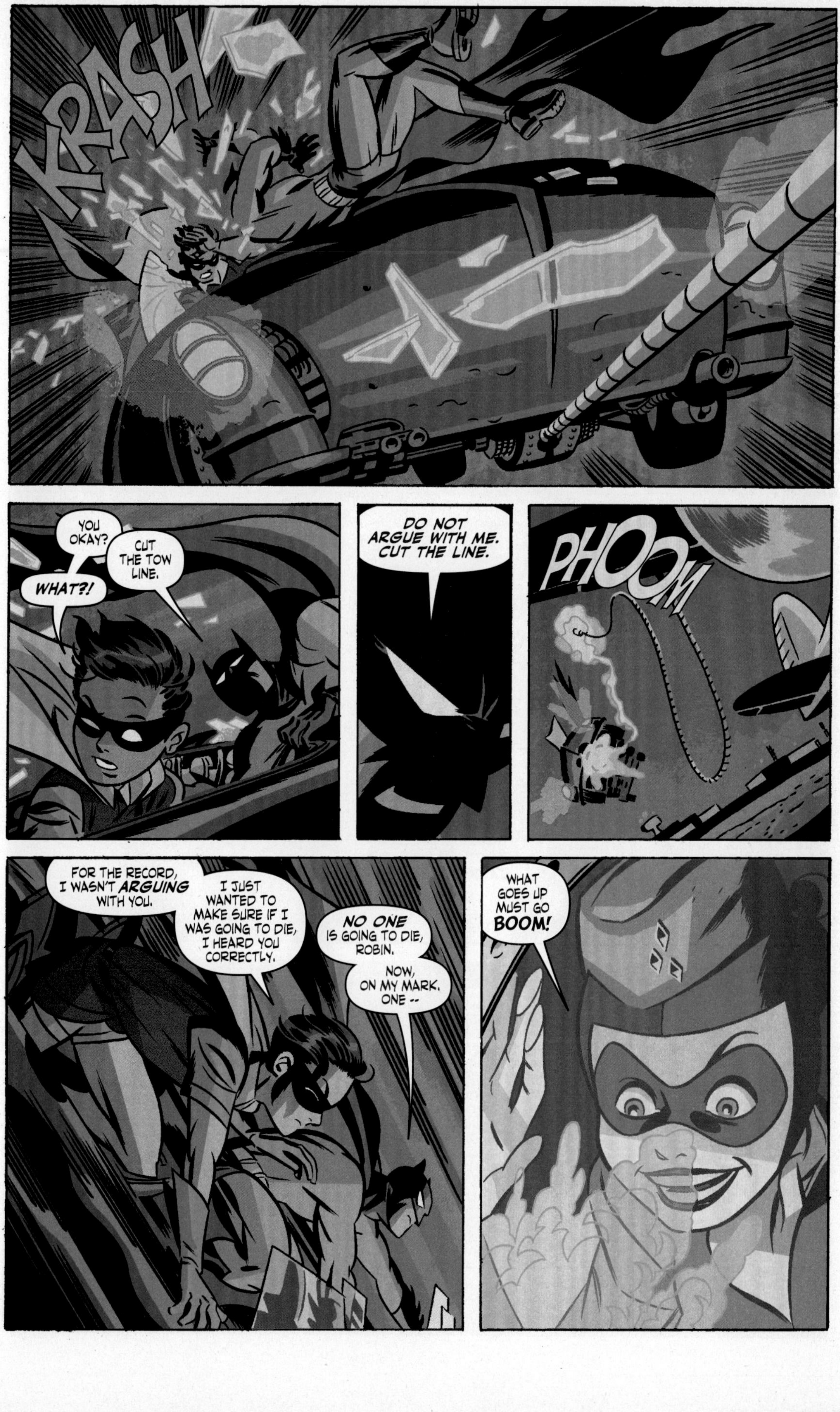
KRASH
YOU OKAY?
CUT THE TOW LINE.
WHAT?!
DO NOT ARGUE WITH ME. CUT THE LINE.
PHOOM
FOR THE RECORD, I WASN'T ARGUING WITH YOU.
I JUST WANTED TO MAKE SURE IF I WAS GOING TO DIE, I HEARD YOU CORRECTLY.
NO ONE IS GOING TO DIE, ROBIN.
NOW, ON MY MARK. ONE --
WHAT GOES UP MUST GO BOOM!

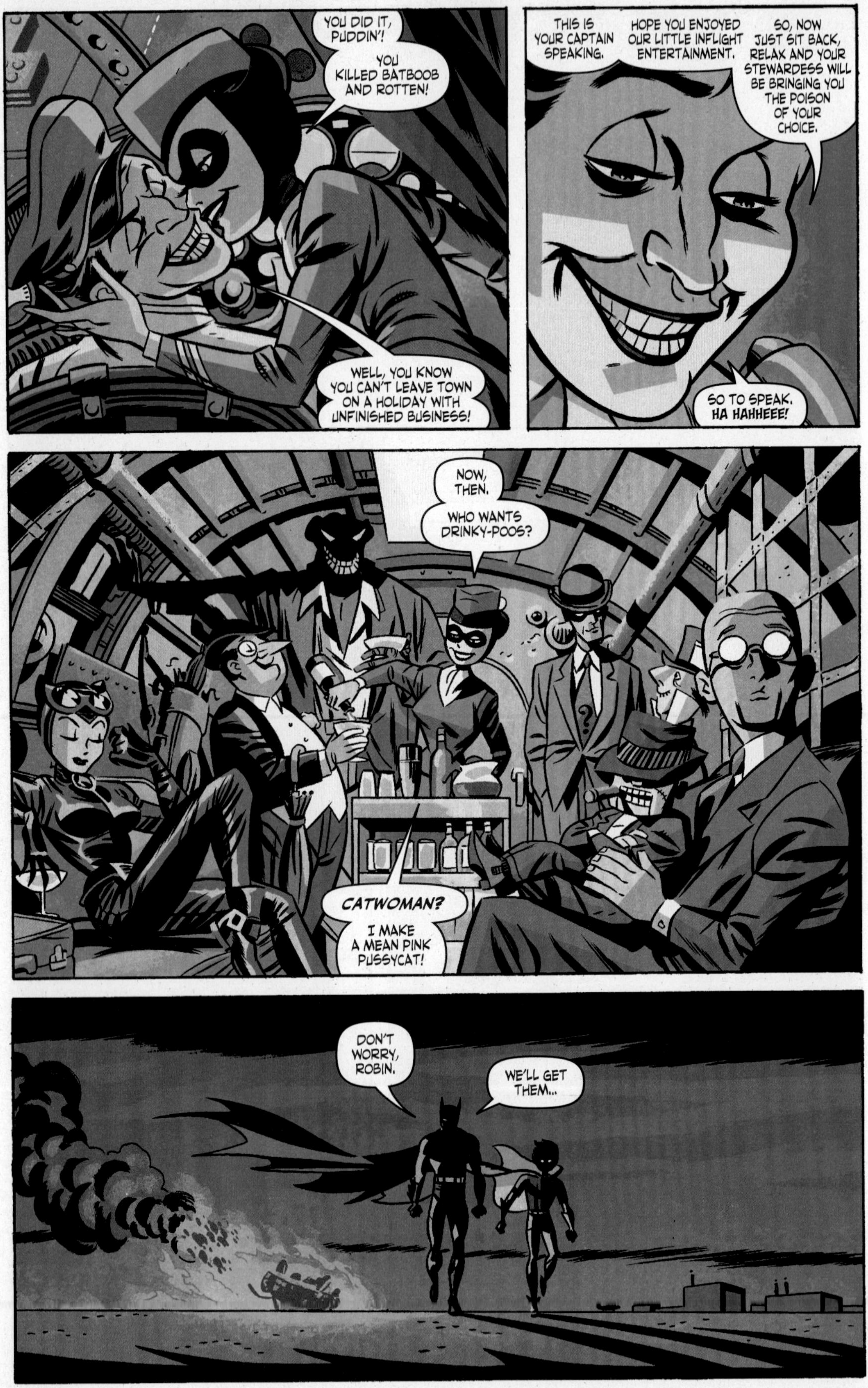
YOU DID IT, PUDDIN'!
YOU KILLED BATBOOB AND ROTTEN!
WELL, YOU KNOW YOU CAN'T LEAVE TOWN ON A HOLIDAY WITH UNFINISHED BUSINESS!
THIS IS YOUR CAPTAIN SPEAKING.
HOPE YOU ENJOYED OUR LITTLE INFLIGHT ENTERTAINMENT.
SO, NOW JUST SIT BACK, RELAX AND YOUR STEWARDESS WILL BE BRINGING YOU THE POISON OF YOUR CHOICE.
SO TO SPEAK. HA HAHHEEE!
NOW, THEN.
WHO WANTS DRINKY-POOS?
CATWOMAN?
I MAKE A MEAN PINK PUSSYCAT!
DON'T WORRY, ROBIN.
WE'LL GET THEM...

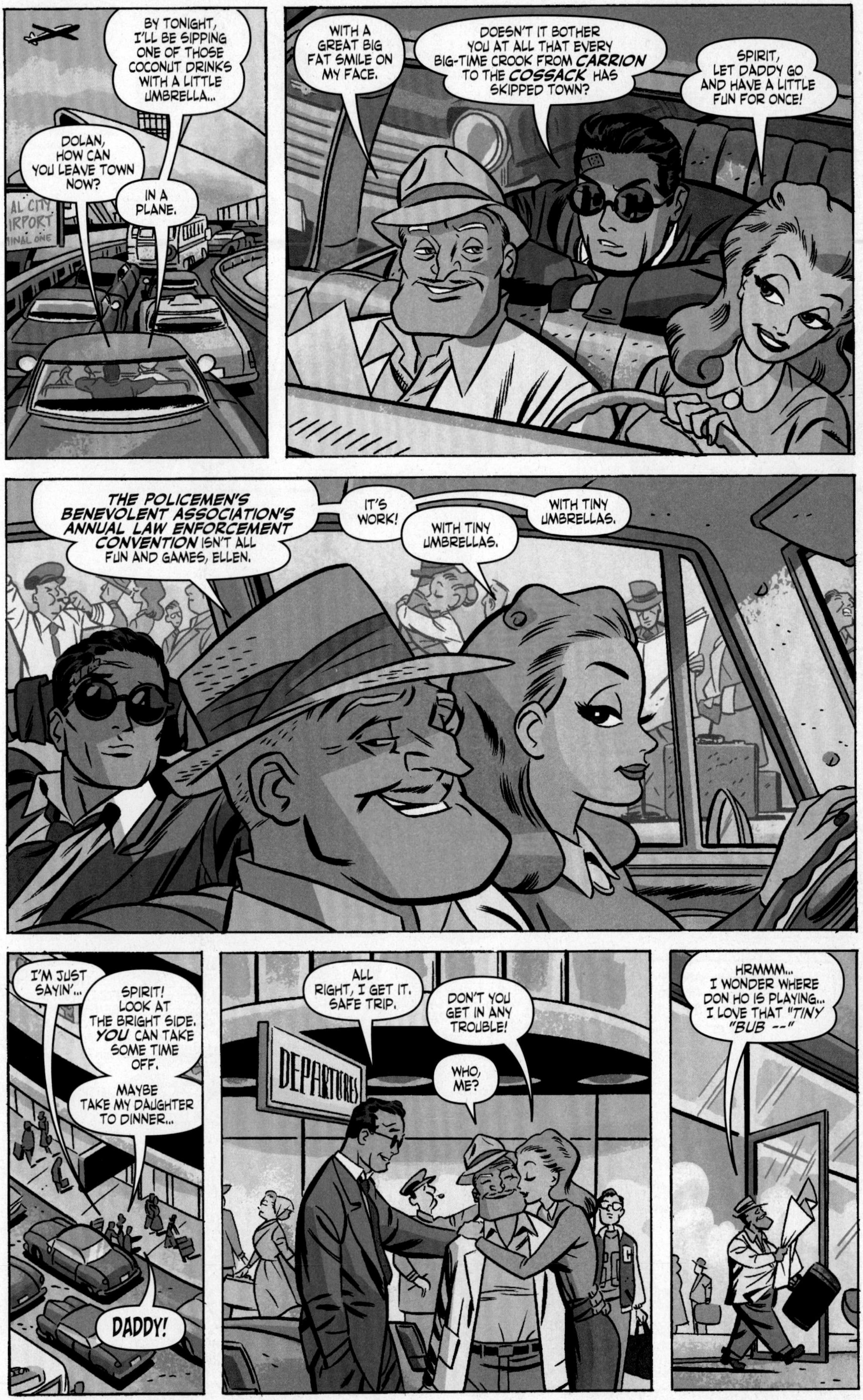

BY TONIGHT, I'LL BE SIPPING ONE OF THOSE COCONUT DRINKS WITH A LITTLE UMBRELLA...
DOLAN, HOW CAN YOU LEAVE TOWN NOW?
IN A PLANE.
AL CITY IRPORT INAL ONE
WITH A GREAT BIG FAT SMILE ON MY FACE.
DOESN'T IT BOTHER YOU AT ALL THAT EVERY BIG-TIME CROOK FROM CARRION TO THE COSSACK HAS SKIPPED TOWN?
SPIRIT, LET DADDY GO AND HAVE A LITTLE FUN FOR ONCE!
THE POLICEMEN'S BENEVOLENT ASSOCIATION'S ANNUAL LAW ENFORCEMENT CONVENTION ISN'T ALL FUN AND GAMES, ELLEN.
IT'S WORK!
WITH TINY UMBRELLAS.
WITH TINY UMBRELLAS.
I'M JUST SAYIN'...
SPIRIT! LOOK AT THE BRIGHT SIDE. YOU CAN TAKE SOME TIME OFF.
MAYBE TAKE MY DAUGHTER TO DINNER...
DADDY!
DEPARTURES
ALL RIGHT, I GET IT. SAFE TRIP.
DON'T YOU GET IN ANY TROUBLE!
WHO, ME?
HRMMM... I WONDER WHERE DON HO IS PLAYING... I LOVE THAT "TINY "BUB --"

-- UMMPPPH!

I -- I'M TERRIBLY SORRY. LET ME HELP YOU WITH THAT.

HOW NICE IT IS TO MEET A GENTLEMAN IN THIS DAY AND AGE.

AND SUCH A HANDSOME ONE AT THAT.

M-ME?

IN FACT, I SHOULD THANK YOU PROPERLY.

WITH A KISS.

I'M PAMELA ISLEY.

BUT MY FRIENDS CALL ME...

IVY.

WHAT A LOVELY NAME.

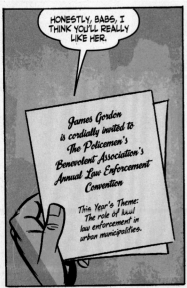

HONESTLY, BABS, I THINK YOU'LL REALLY LIKE HER.

James Gordon is cordially invited to The Policemen's Benevolent Association's Annual Law Enforcement Convention

This Year's Theme: The role of local law enforcement in urban municipalities.

ANYBODY WHO CAN GET YOU TO GO ON VACATION CAN'T BE ALL BAD, DADDY.

THERE'S THE OPEN-MINDED DAUGHTER I KNOW AND RAISED.

AND THIS LITTLE TRIP ISN'T A VACATION.

THE POLICEMEN'S BENEVOLENT ASSOCIATION'S ANNUAL LAW-ENFORCEMENT CONVENTION COUNTS AS WORK.

UH-HUH. AND YOU'LL JUST HAPPEN TO HAVE A MOMENT OR TWO TO WAVE "HELLO" TO YOUR NEW GIRLFRIEND BETWEEN SEMINARS...?

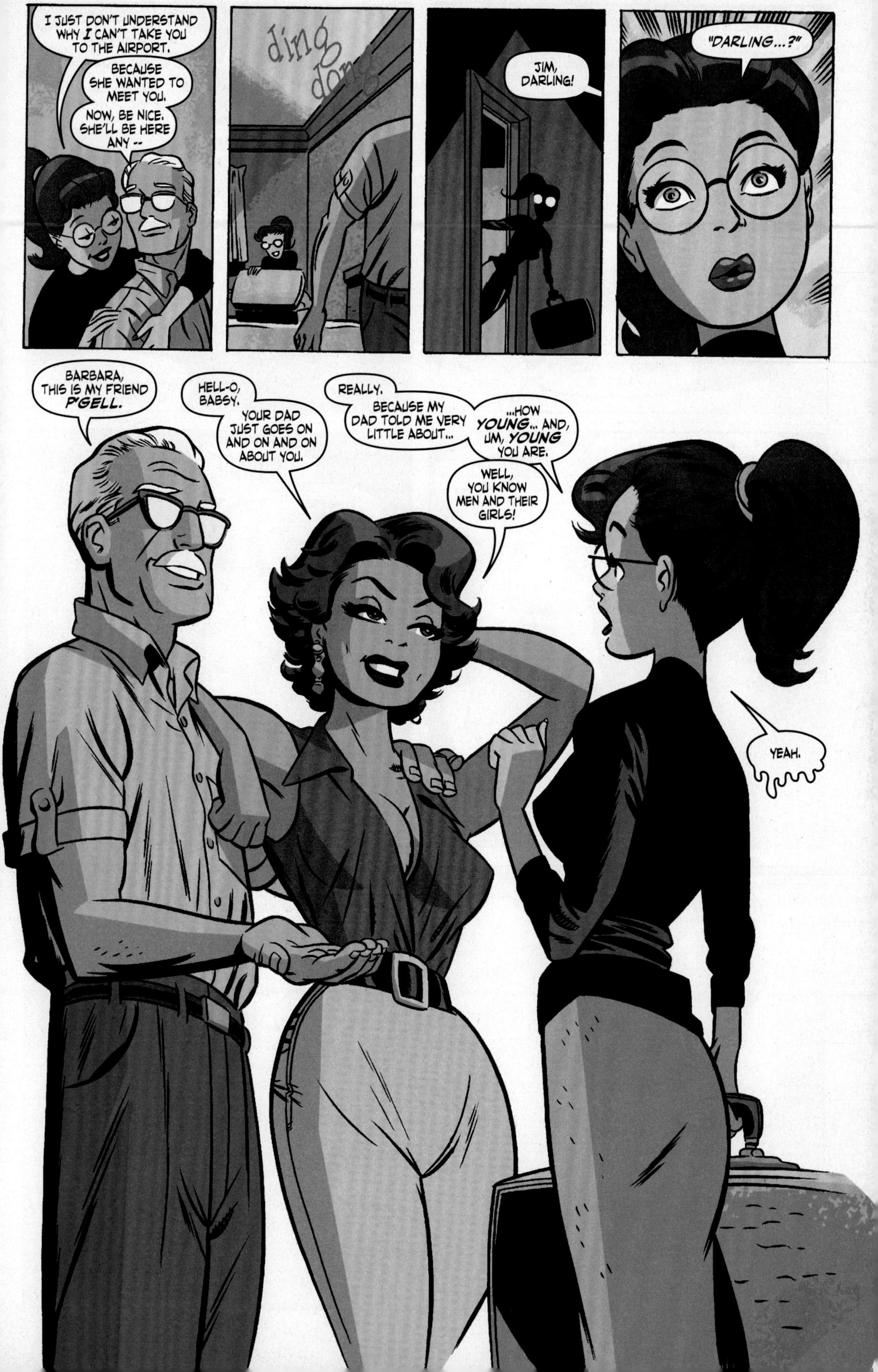
I JUST DON'T UNDERSTAND WHY *I* CAN'T TAKE YOU TO THE AIRPORT.
BECAUSE SHE WANTED TO MEET YOU.
NOW, BE NICE. SHE'LL BE HERE ANY --
ding dong
JIM, DARLING!
"DARLING...?"
BARBARA, THIS IS MY FRIEND *P'GELL.*
HELL-O, BABSY.
YOUR DAD JUST GOES ON AND ON AND ON ABOUT YOU.
REALLY.
BECAUSE MY DAD TOLD ME VERY LITTLE ABOUT...
...HOW *YOUNG*... AND, UM, *YOUNG* YOU ARE.
WELL, YOU KNOW MEN AND THEIR GIRLS!
YEAH.

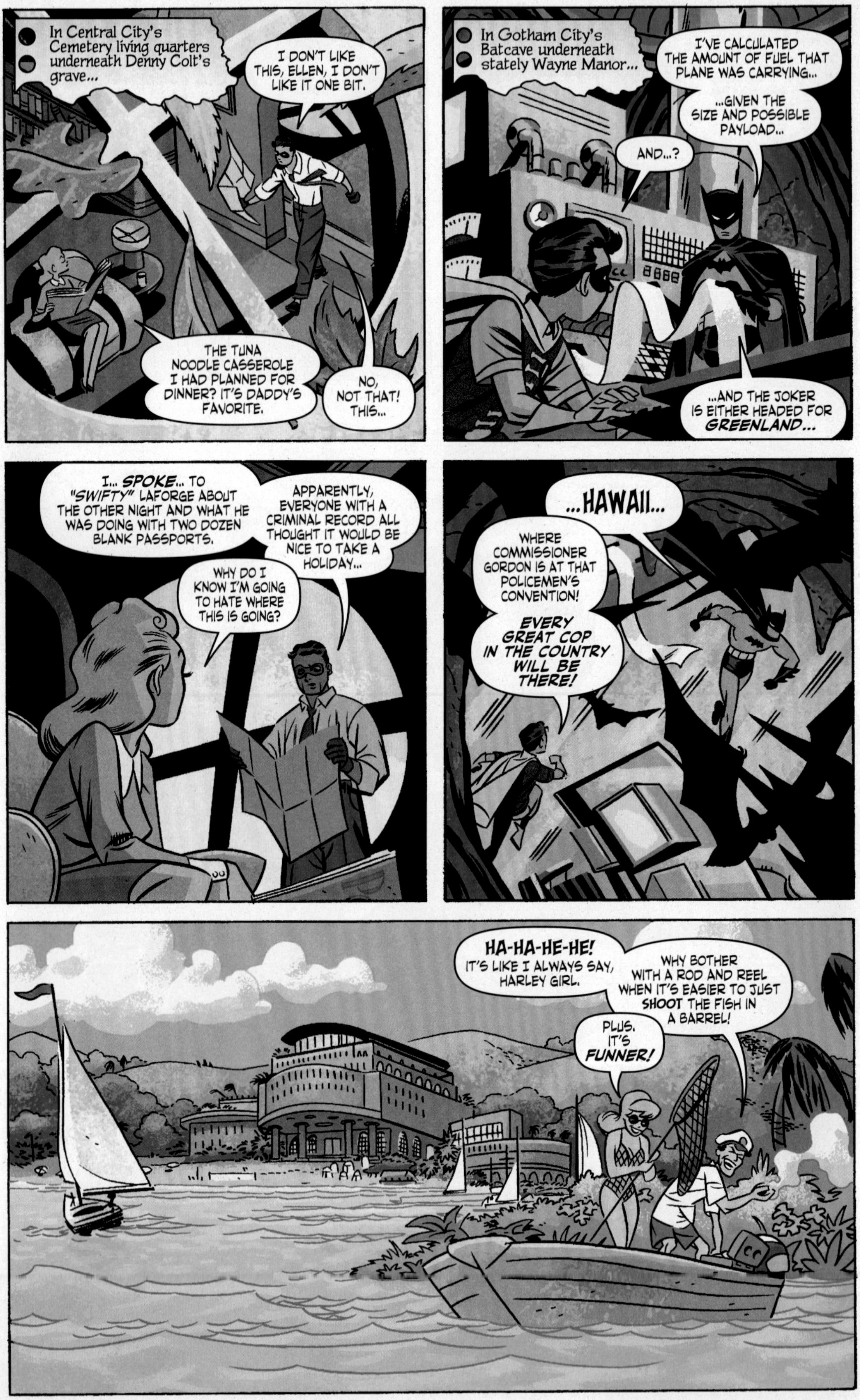
In Central City's Cemetery living quarters underneath Denny Colt's grave...
I DON'T LIKE THIS, ELLEN, I DON'T LIKE IT ONE BIT.
THE TUNA NOODLE CASSEROLE I HAD PLANNED FOR DINNER? IT'S DADDY'S FAVORITE.
NO, NOT THAT! THIS...
In Gotham City's Batcave underneath stately Wayne Manor...
I'VE CALCULATED THE AMOUNT OF FUEL THAT PLANE WAS CARRYING...
...GIVEN THE SIZE AND POSSIBLE PAYLOAD...
AND...?
...AND THE JOKER IS EITHER HEADED FOR GREENLAND...
I... SPOKE... TO "SWIFTY" LAFORGE ABOUT THE OTHER NIGHT AND WHAT HE WAS DOING WITH TWO DOZEN BLANK PASSPORTS.
APPARENTLY, EVERYONE WITH A CRIMINAL RECORD ALL THOUGHT IT WOULD BE NICE TO TAKE A HOLIDAY...
WHY DO I KNOW I'M GOING TO HATE WHERE THIS IS GOING?
...HAWAII...
WHERE COMMISSIONER GORDON IS AT THAT POLICEMEN'S CONVENTION!
EVERY GREAT COP IN THE COUNTRY WILL BE THERE!
HA-HA-HE-HE! IT'S LIKE I ALWAYS SAY, HARLEY GIRL.
WHY BOTHER WITH A ROD AND REEL WHEN IT'S EASIER TO JUST SHOOT THE FISH IN A BARREL!
PLUS, IT'S FUNNER!

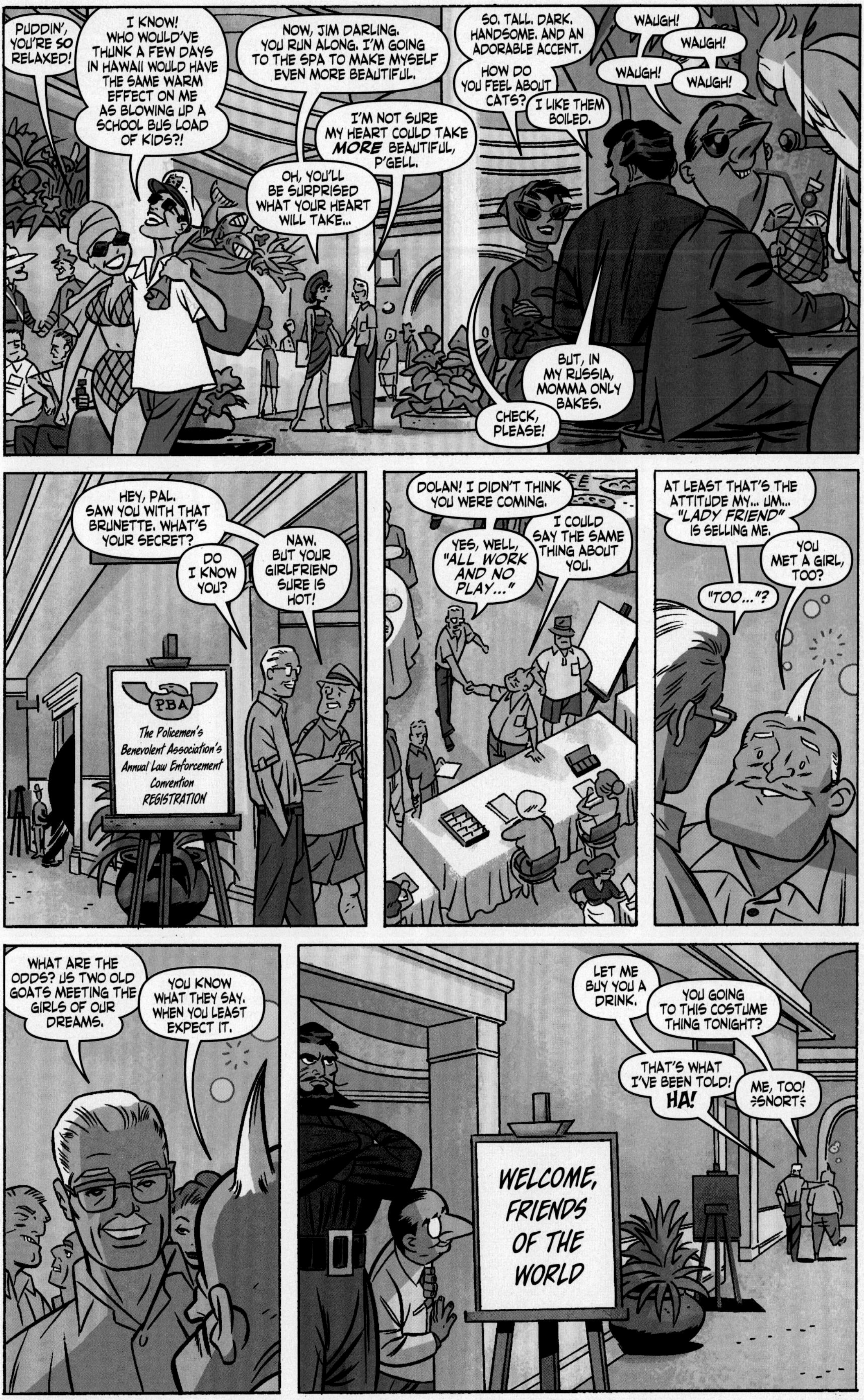
PUDDIN', YOU'RE SO RELAXED!
I KNOW! WHO WOULD'VE THUNK A FEW DAYS IN HAWAII WOULD HAVE THE SAME WARM EFFECT ON ME AS BLOWING UP A SCHOOL BUS LOAD OF KIDS?!
NOW, JIM DARLING. YOU RUN ALONG. I'M GOING TO THE SPA TO MAKE MYSELF EVEN MORE BEAUTIFUL.
I'M NOT SURE MY HEART COULD TAKE MORE BEAUTIFUL, P'GELL.
OH, YOU'LL BE SURPRISED WHAT YOUR HEART WILL TAKE...
SO. TALL. DARK. HANDSOME. AND AN ADORABLE ACCENT.
HOW DO YOU FEEL ABOUT CATS?
I LIKE THEM BOILED.
WAUGH!
WAUGH!
WAUGH!
WAUGH!
BUT, IN MY RUSSIA, MOMMA ONLY BAKES.
CHECK, PLEASE!
HEY, PAL. SAW YOU WITH THAT BRUNETTE. WHAT'S YOUR SECRET?
DO I KNOW YOU?
NAW. BUT YOUR GIRLFRIEND SURE IS HOT!
PBA
The Policemen's Benevolent Association's Annual Law Enforcement Convention REGISTRATION
DOLAN! I DIDN'T THINK YOU WERE COMING.
YES, WELL, "ALL WORK AND NO PLAY..."
I COULD SAY THE SAME THING ABOUT YOU.
AT LEAST THAT'S THE ATTITUDE MY... UM... "LADY FRIEND" IS SELLING ME.
YOU MET A GIRL, TOO?
"TOO..."?
WHAT ARE THE ODDS? US TWO OLD GOATS MEETING THE GIRLS OF OUR DREAMS.
YOU KNOW WHAT THEY SAY. WHEN YOU LEAST EXPECT IT.
WELCOME, FRIENDS OF THE WORLD
LET ME BUY YOU A DRINK.
YOU GOING TO THIS COSTUME THING TONIGHT?
THAT'S WHAT I'VE BEEN TOLD! HA!
ME, TOO! SNORT

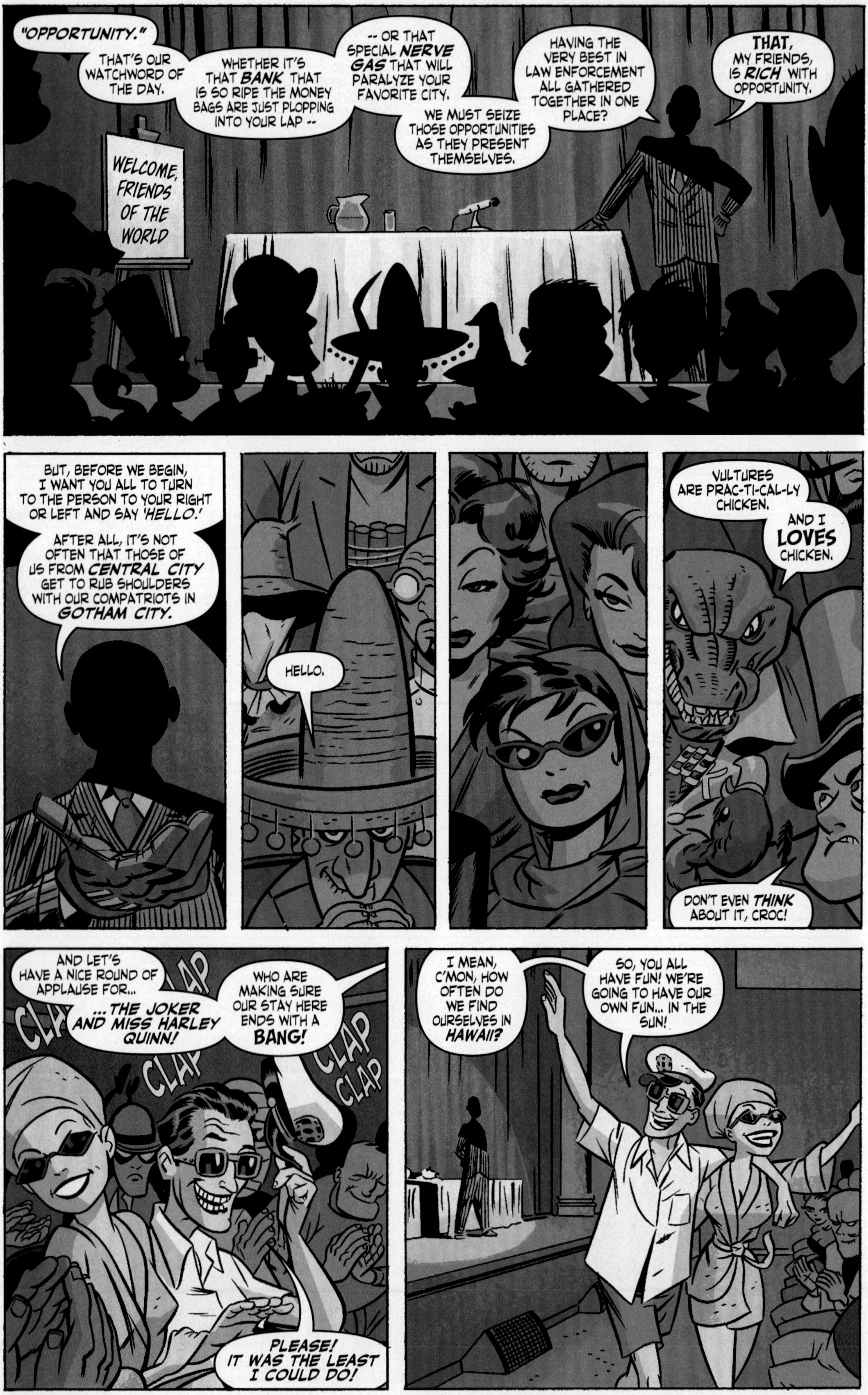
"OPPORTUNITY."
THAT'S OUR WATCHWORD OF THE DAY.
WHETHER IT'S THAT BANK THAT IS SO RIPE THE MONEY BAGS ARE JUST PLOPPING INTO YOUR LAP --
-- OR THAT SPECIAL NERVE GAS THAT WILL PARALYZE YOUR FAVORITE CITY.
WE MUST SEIZE THOSE OPPORTUNITIES AS THEY PRESENT THEMSELVES.
HAVING THE VERY BEST IN LAW ENFORCEMENT ALL GATHERED TOGETHER IN ONE PLACE?
THAT, MY FRIENDS, IS RICH WITH OPPORTUNITY.
WELCOME, FRIENDS OF THE WORLD
BUT, BEFORE WE BEGIN, I WANT YOU ALL TO TURN TO THE PERSON TO YOUR RIGHT OR LEFT AND SAY 'HELLO.'
AFTER ALL, IT'S NOT OFTEN THAT THOSE OF US FROM CENTRAL CITY GET TO RUB SHOULDERS WITH OUR COMPATRIOTS IN GOTHAM CITY.
HELLO.
VULTURES ARE PRAC-TI-CAL-LY CHICKEN.
AND I LOVES CHICKEN.
DON'T EVEN THINK ABOUT IT, CROC!
AND LET'S HAVE A NICE ROUND OF APPLAUSE FOR...
...THE JOKER AND MISS HARLEY QUINN!
WHO ARE MAKING SURE OUR STAY HERE ENDS WITH A BANG!
CLAP CLAP
CLAP
CLAP CLAP
PLEASE! IT WAS THE LEAST I COULD DO!
I MEAN, C'MON, HOW OFTEN DO WE FIND OURSELVES IN HAWAII?
SO, YOU ALL HAVE FUN! WE'RE GOING TO HAVE OUR OWN FUN... IN THE SUN!

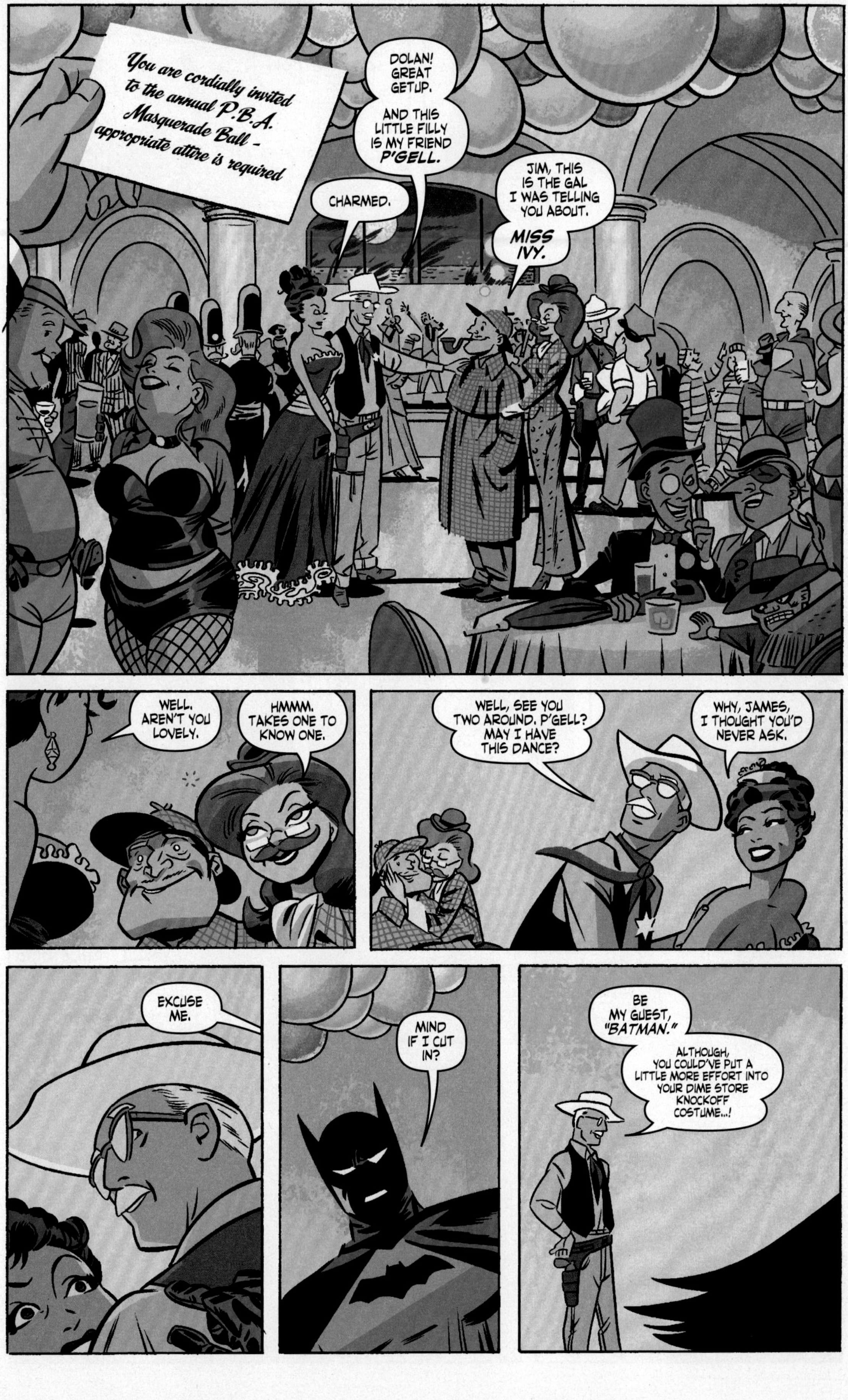
You are cordially invited to the annual P.B.A. Masquerade Ball - appropriate attire is required
DOLAN! GREAT GETUP.
AND THIS LITTLE FILLY IS MY FRIEND P'GELL.
CHARMED.
JIM, THIS IS THE GAL I WAS TELLING YOU ABOUT.
MISS IVY.
WELL. AREN'T YOU LOVELY.
HMMM. TAKES ONE TO KNOW ONE.
WELL, SEE YOU TWO AROUND. P'GELL? MAY I HAVE THIS DANCE?
WHY, JAMES, I THOUGHT YOU'D NEVER ASK.
EXCUSE ME.
MIND IF I CUT IN?
BE MY GUEST, "BATMAN."
ALTHOUGH, YOU COULD'VE PUT A LITTLE MORE EFFORT INTO YOUR DIME STORE KNOCKOFF COSTUME...!

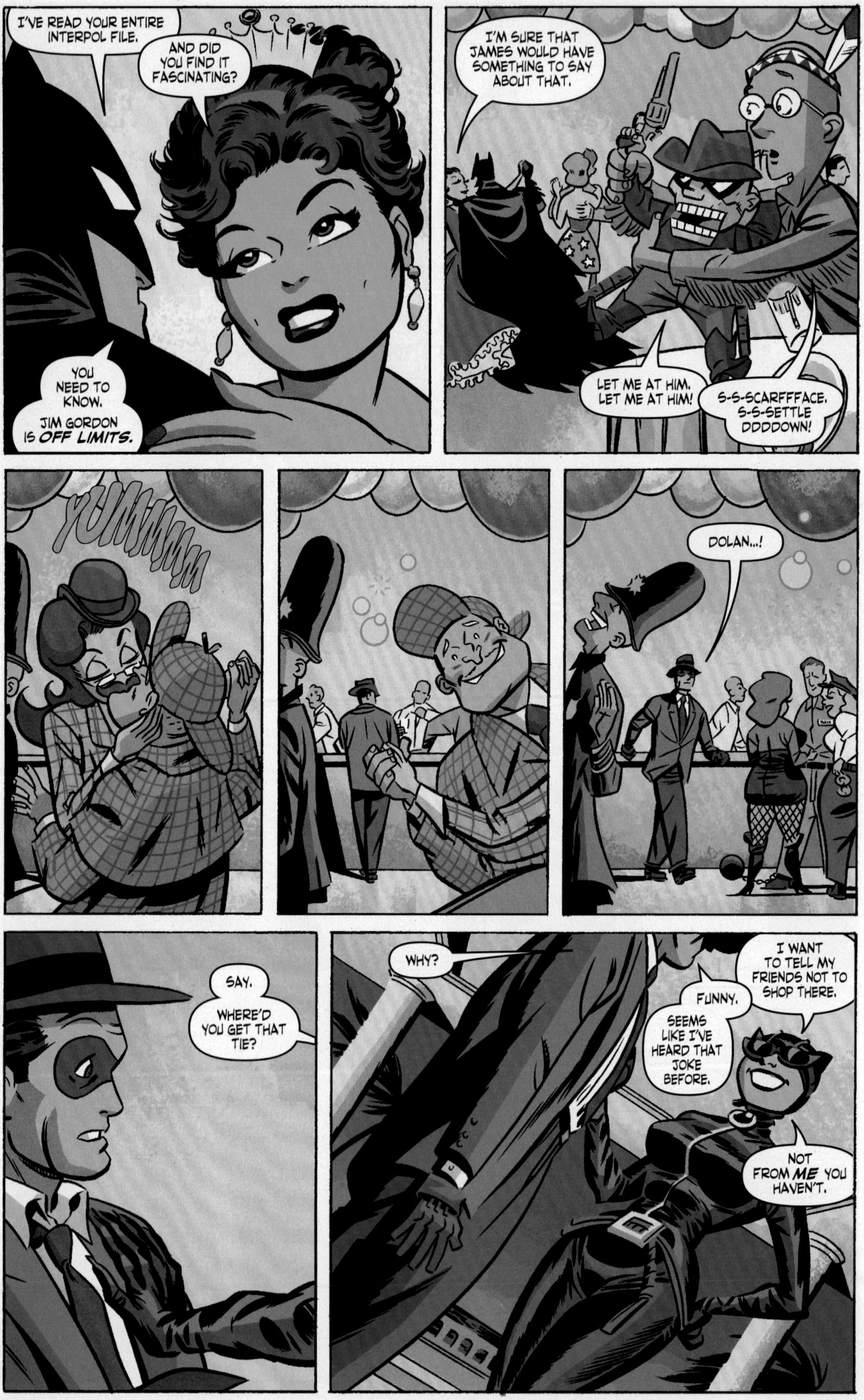
I'VE READ YOUR ENTIRE INTERPOL FILE.
AND DID YOU FIND IT FASCINATING?
YOU NEED TO KNOW. JIM GORDON IS OFF LIMITS.
I'M SURE THAT JAMES WOULD HAVE SOMETHING TO SAY ABOUT THAT.
LET ME AT HIM. LET ME AT HIM!
S-S-SCARFFFACE. S-S-SETTLE DDDDOWN!
YUMMMMM
DOLAN...!
SAY.
WHERE'D YOU GET THAT TIE?
WHY?
I WANT TO TELL MY FRIENDS NOT TO SHOP THERE.
FUNNY.
SEEMS LIKE I'VE HEARD THAT JOKE BEFORE.
NOT FROM ME YOU HAVEN'T.

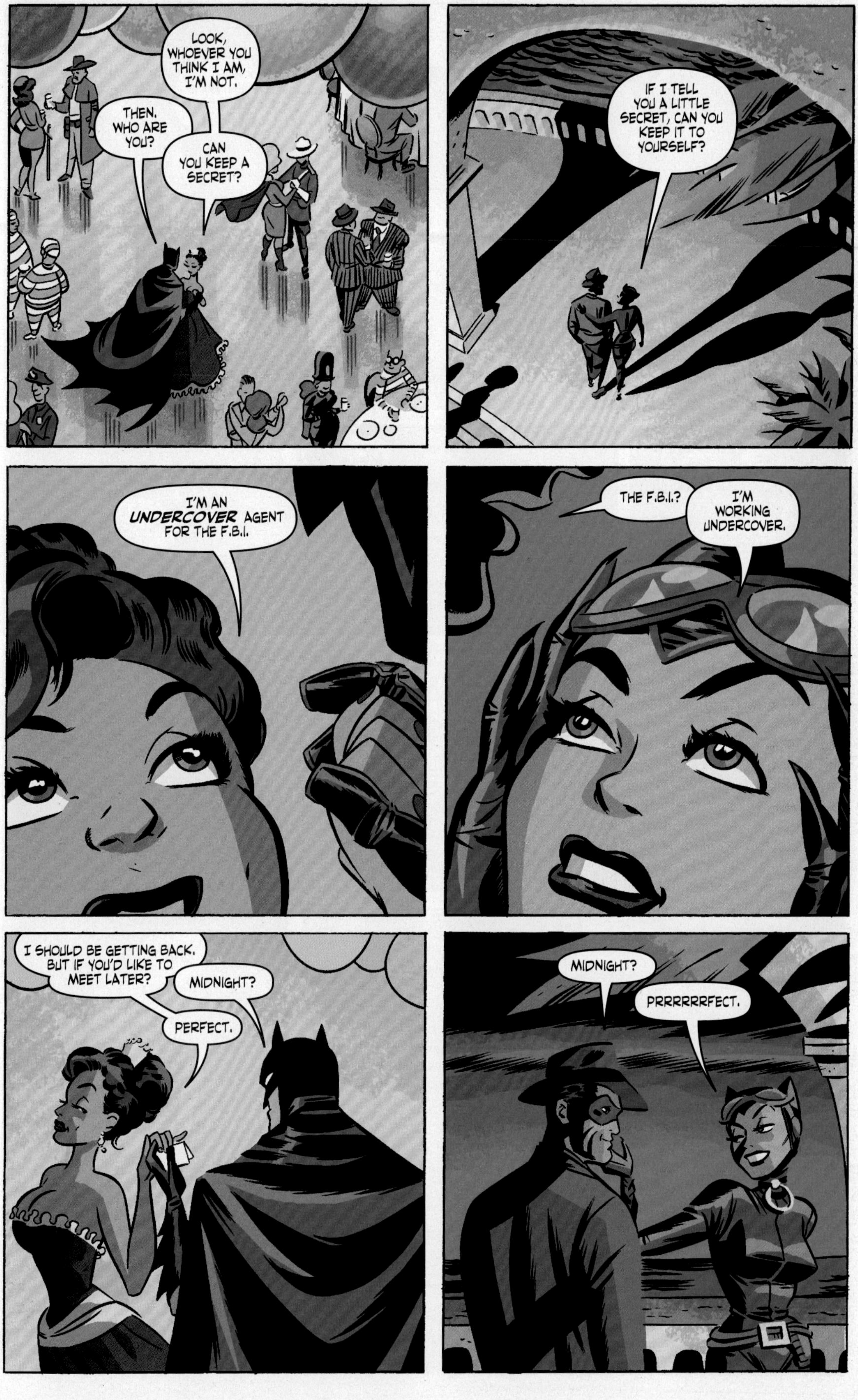
LOOK, WHOEVER YOU THINK I AM, I'M NOT.
THEN. WHO ARE YOU?
CAN YOU KEEP A SECRET?
IF I TELL YOU A LITTLE SECRET, CAN YOU KEEP IT TO YOURSELF?
I'M AN UNDERCOVER AGENT FOR THE F.B.I.
THE F.B.I.?
I'M WORKING UNDERCOVER.
I SHOULD BE GETTING BACK. BUT IF YOU'D LIKE TO MEET LATER?
MIDNIGHT?
PERFECT.
MIDNIGHT?
PRRRRRRFECT.

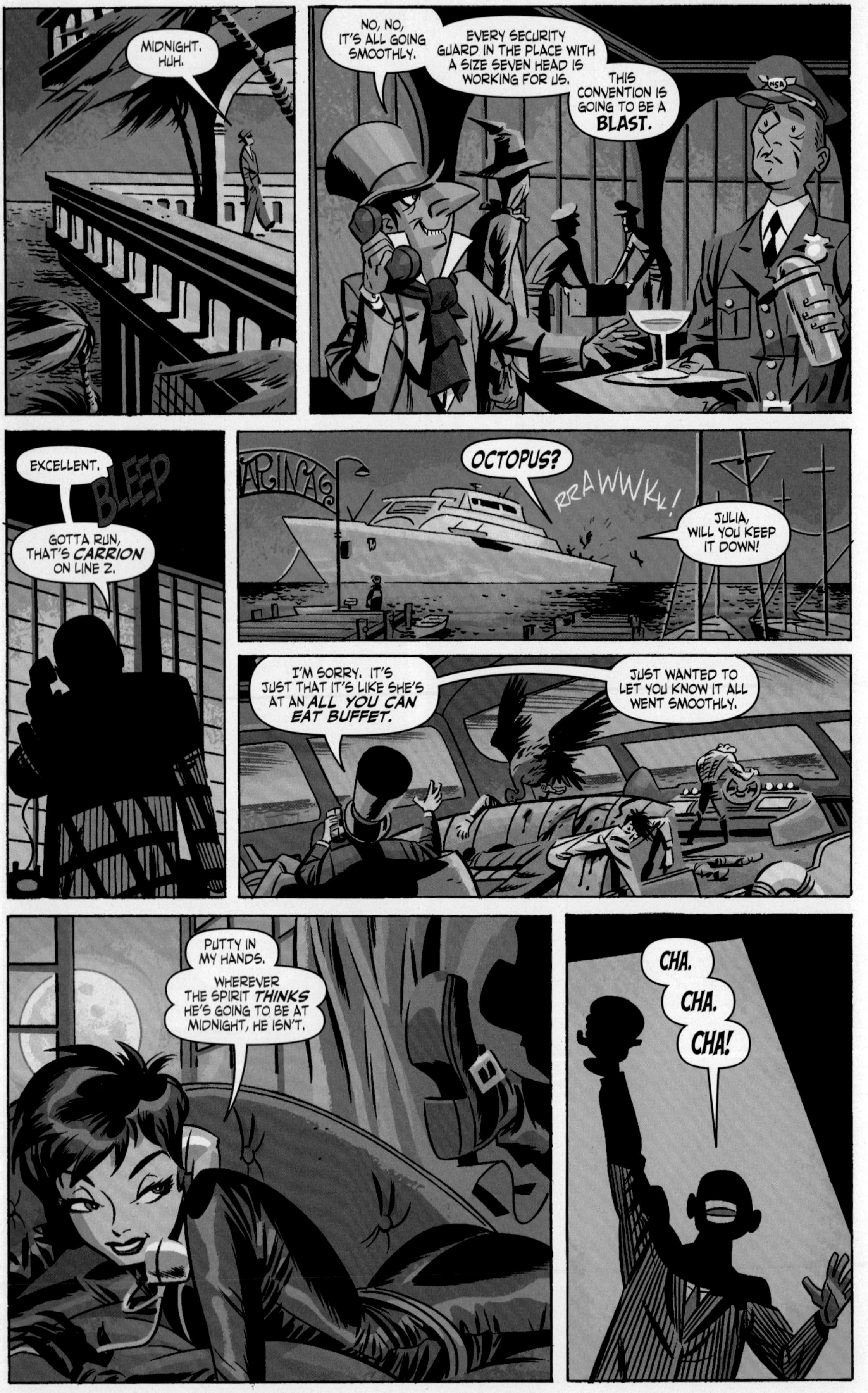
MIDNIGHT. HUH.
NO, NO, IT'S ALL GOING SMOOTHLY.
EVERY SECURITY GUARD IN THE PLACE WITH A SIZE SEVEN HEAD IS WORKING FOR US.
THIS CONVENTION IS GOING TO BE A BLAST.
EXCELLENT.
BLEEP
GOTTA RUN, THAT'S CARRION ON LINE 2.
OCTOPUS?
RRAWWKK!
JULIA, WILL YOU KEEP IT DOWN!
I'M SORRY. IT'S JUST THAT IT'S LIKE SHE'S AT AN ALL YOU CAN EAT BUFFET.
JUST WANTED TO LET YOU KNOW IT ALL WENT SMOOTHLY.
PUTTY IN MY HANDS.
WHEREVER THE SPIRIT THINKS HE'S GOING TO BE AT MIDNIGHT, HE ISN'T.
CHA.
CHA.
CHA!

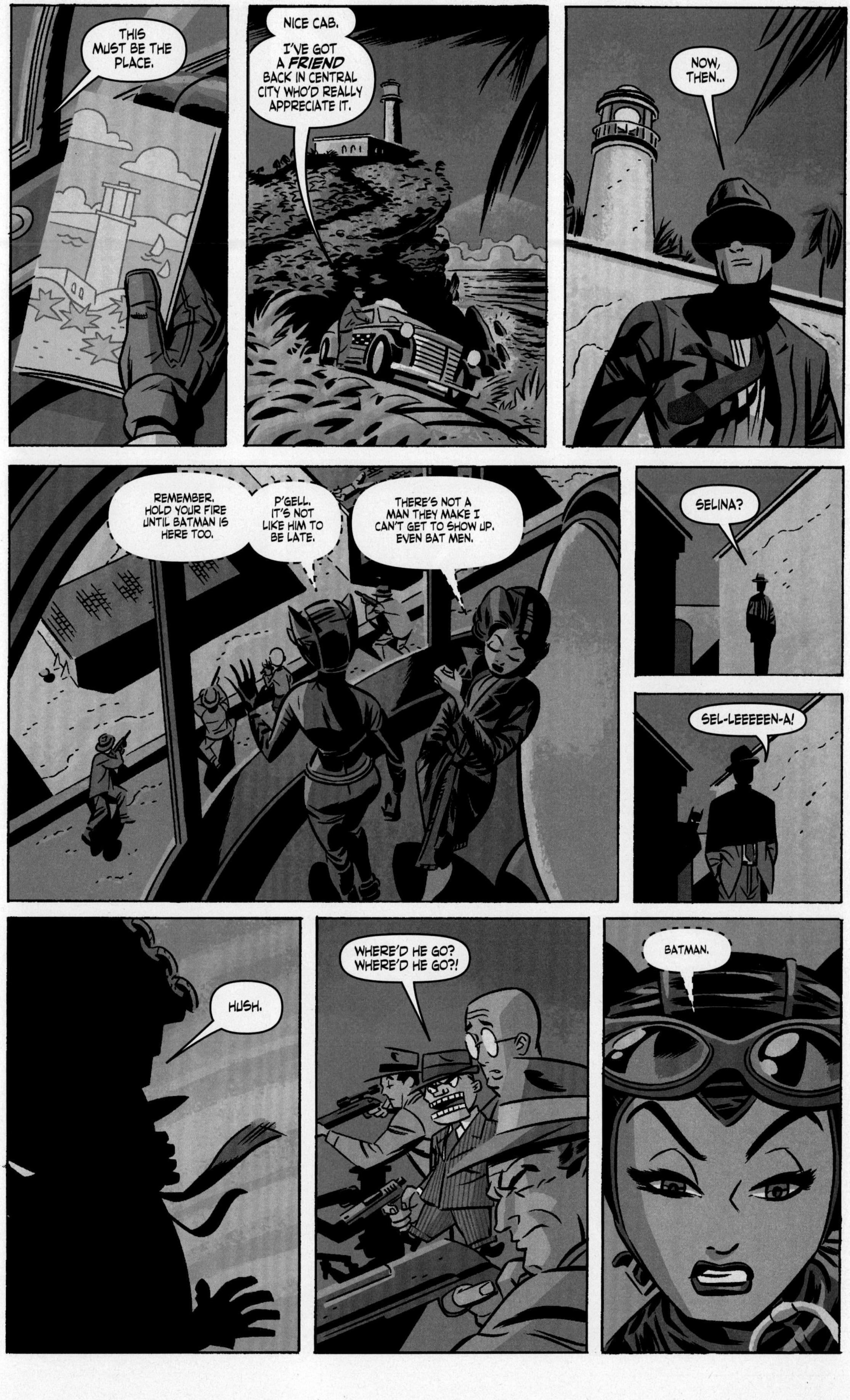
THIS MUST BE THE PLACE.
NICE CAB.
I'VE GOT A FRIEND BACK IN CENTRAL CITY WHO'D REALLY APPRECIATE IT.
NOW, THEN...
REMEMBER. HOLD YOUR FIRE UNTIL BATMAN IS HERE TOO.
P'GELL. IT'S NOT LIKE HIM TO BE LATE.
THERE'S NOT A MAN THEY MAKE I CAN'T GET TO SHOW UP. EVEN BAT MEN.
SELINA?
SEL-LEEEEEN-A!
HUSH.
WHERE'D HE GO? WHERE'D HE GO?!
BATMAN.

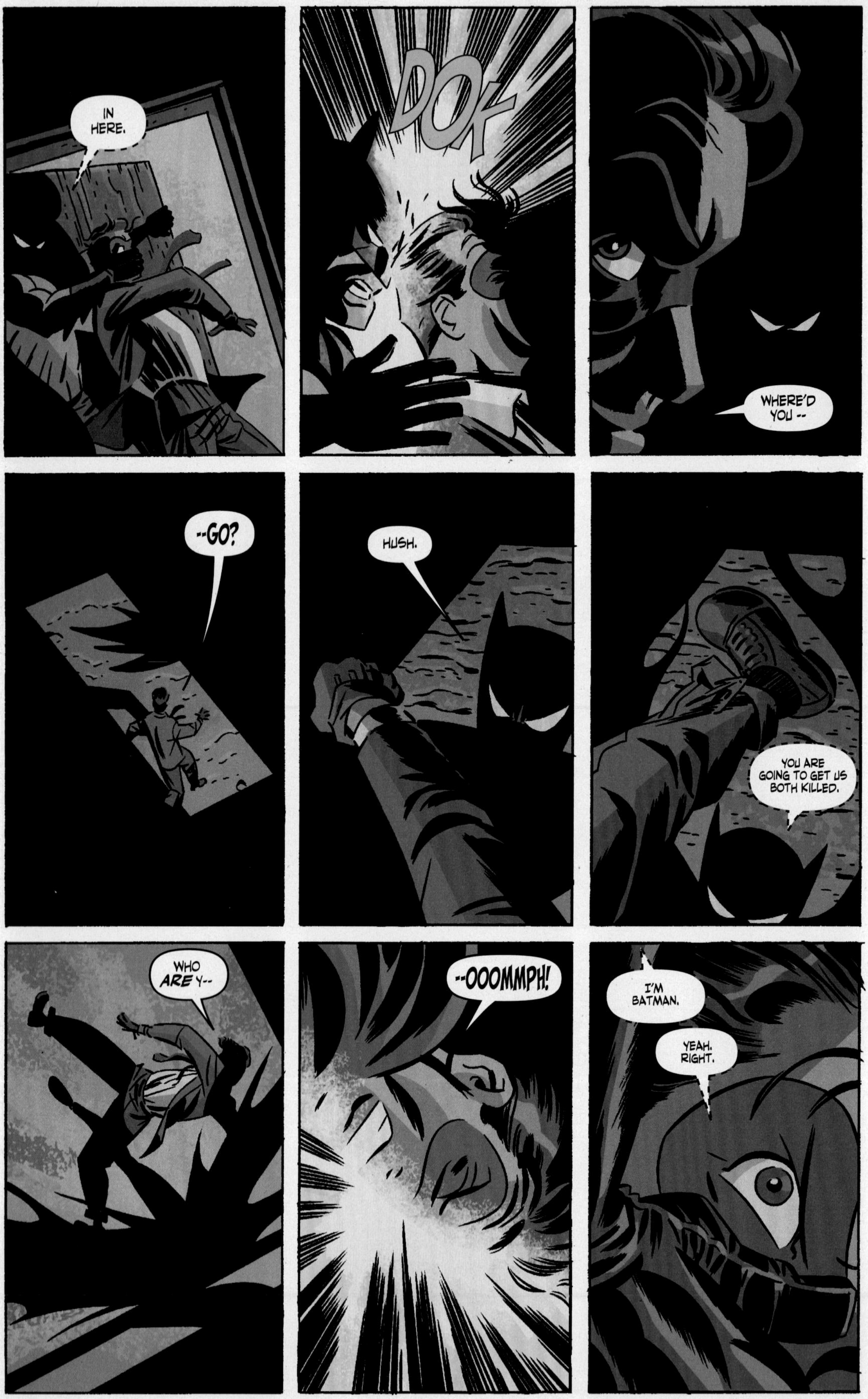
IN HERE.
DOK
WHERE'D YOU --
--GO?
HUSH.
YOU ARE GOING TO GET US BOTH KILLED.
WHO ARE Y--
--OOOMMPH!
I'M BATMAN.
YEAH. RIGHT.

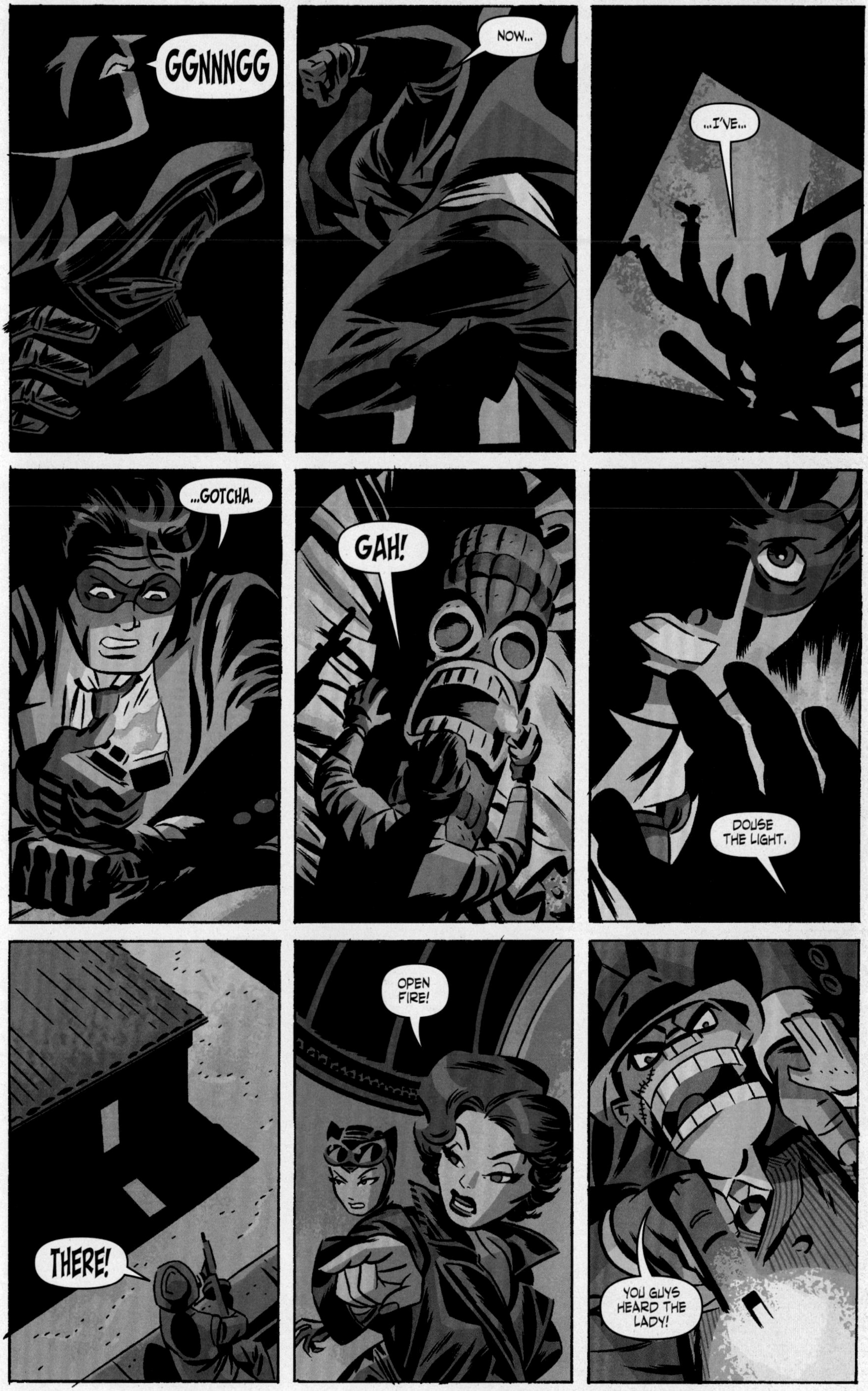
GGNNNGG
NOW...
...I'VE...
...GOTCHA.
GAH!
DOUSE THE LIGHT.
THERE!
OPEN FIRE!
YOU GUYS HEARD THE LADY!

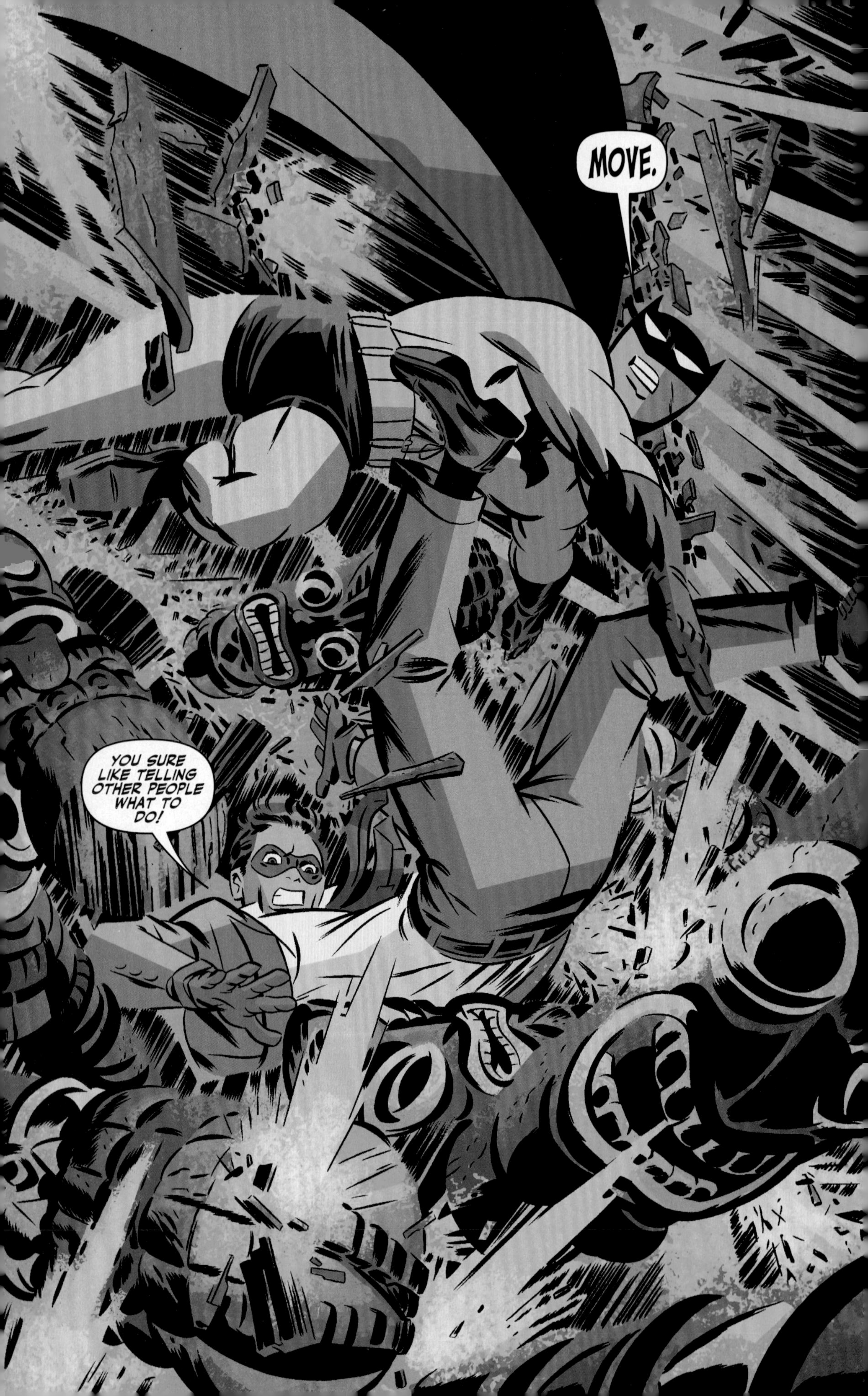
MOVE.
YOU SURE LIKE TELLING OTHER PEOPLE WHAT TO DO!

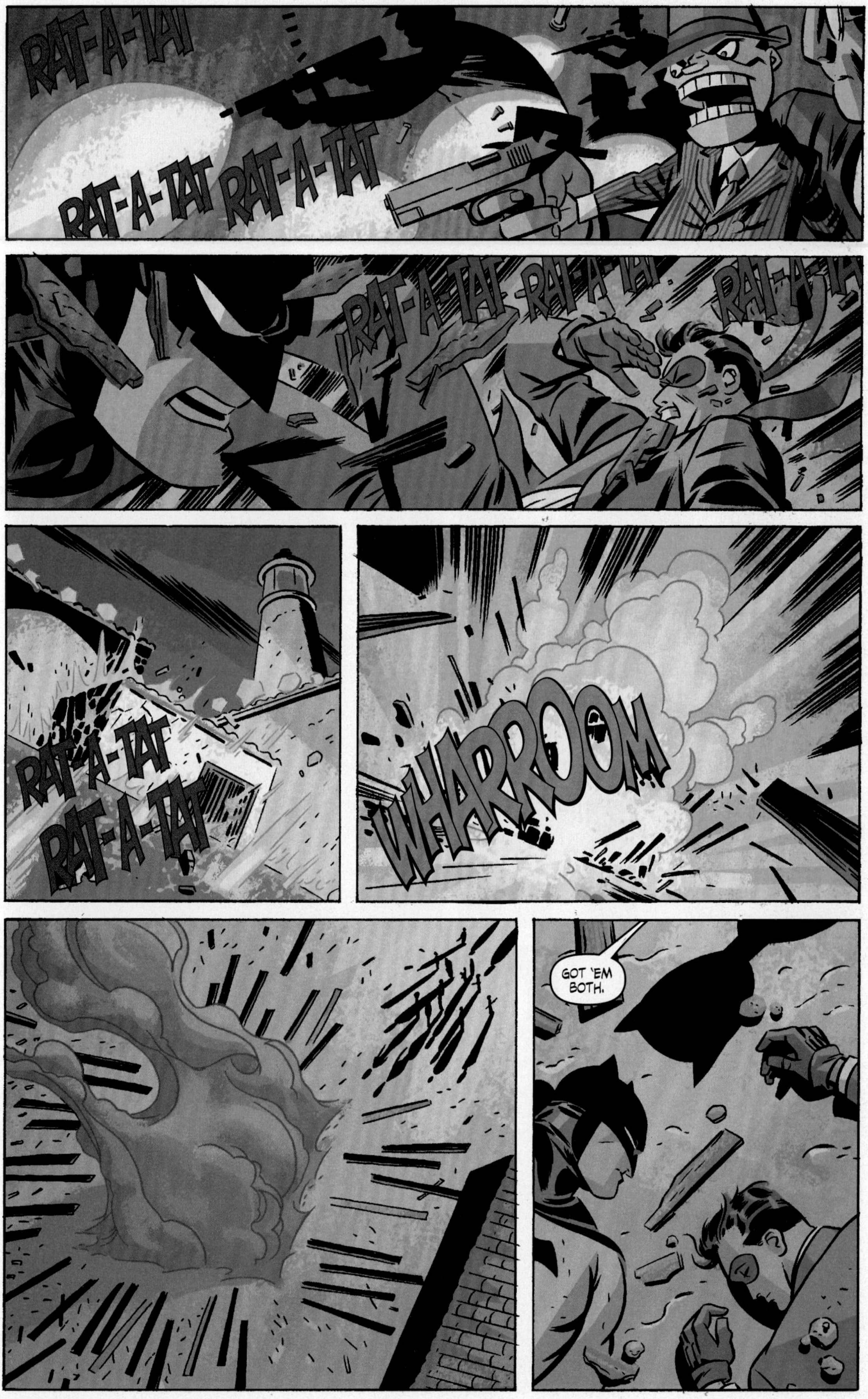
RAT-A-TAT
RAT-A-TAT
RAT-A-TAT
RAT-A-TAT
RAT-A-TAT
RAT-A-TAT
RAT-A-TAT
RAT-A-TAT
WHARROOM
GOT 'EM BOTH.

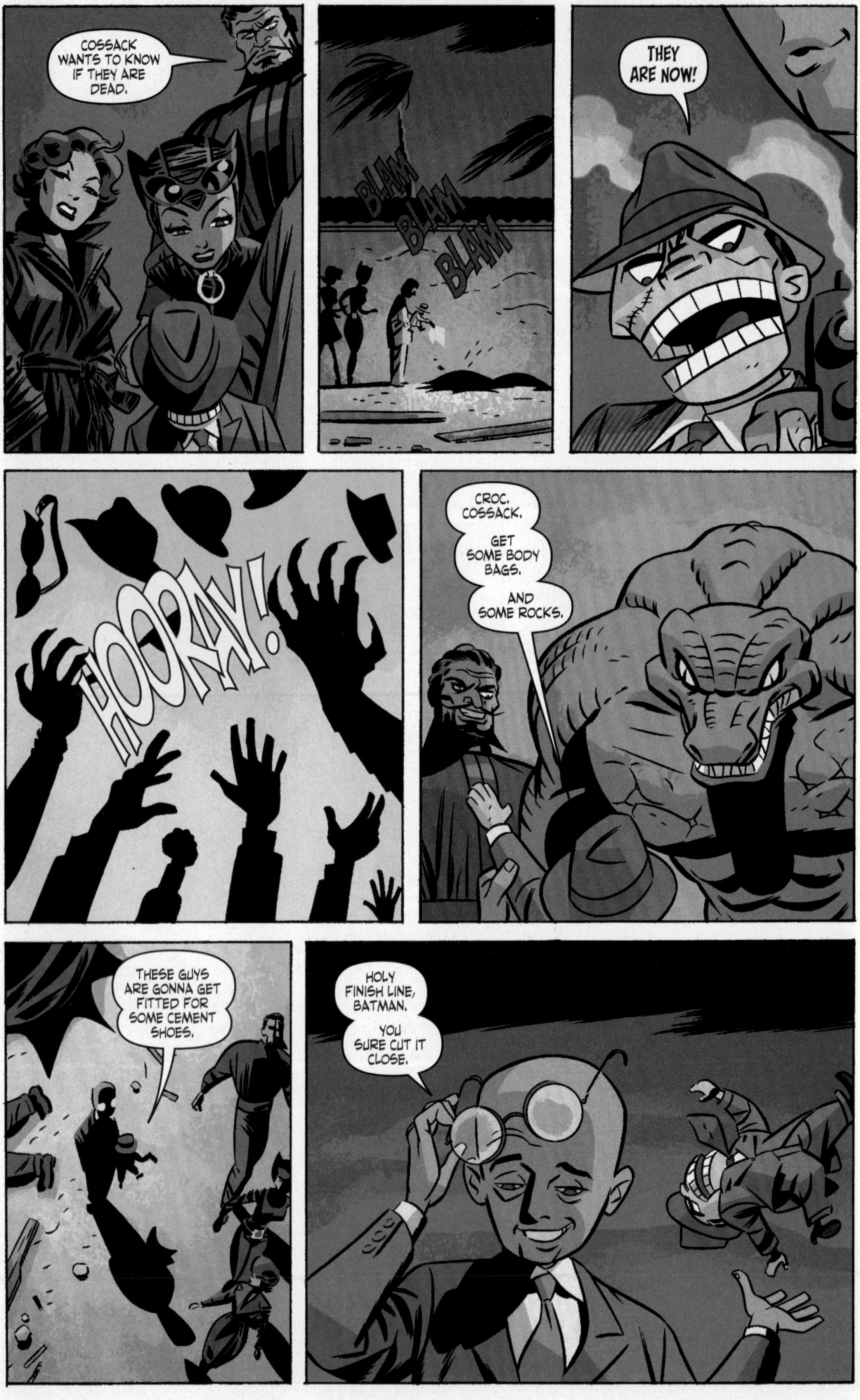
COSSACK WANTS TO KNOW IF THEY ARE DEAD.
BLAM BLAM BLAM
THEY ARE NOW!
HOORAY!
CROC. COSSACK.
GET SOME BODY BAGS.
AND SOME ROCKS.
THESE GUYS ARE GONNA GET FITTED FOR SOME CEMENT SHOES.
HOLY FINISH LINE, BATMAN.
YOU SURE CUT IT CLOSE.

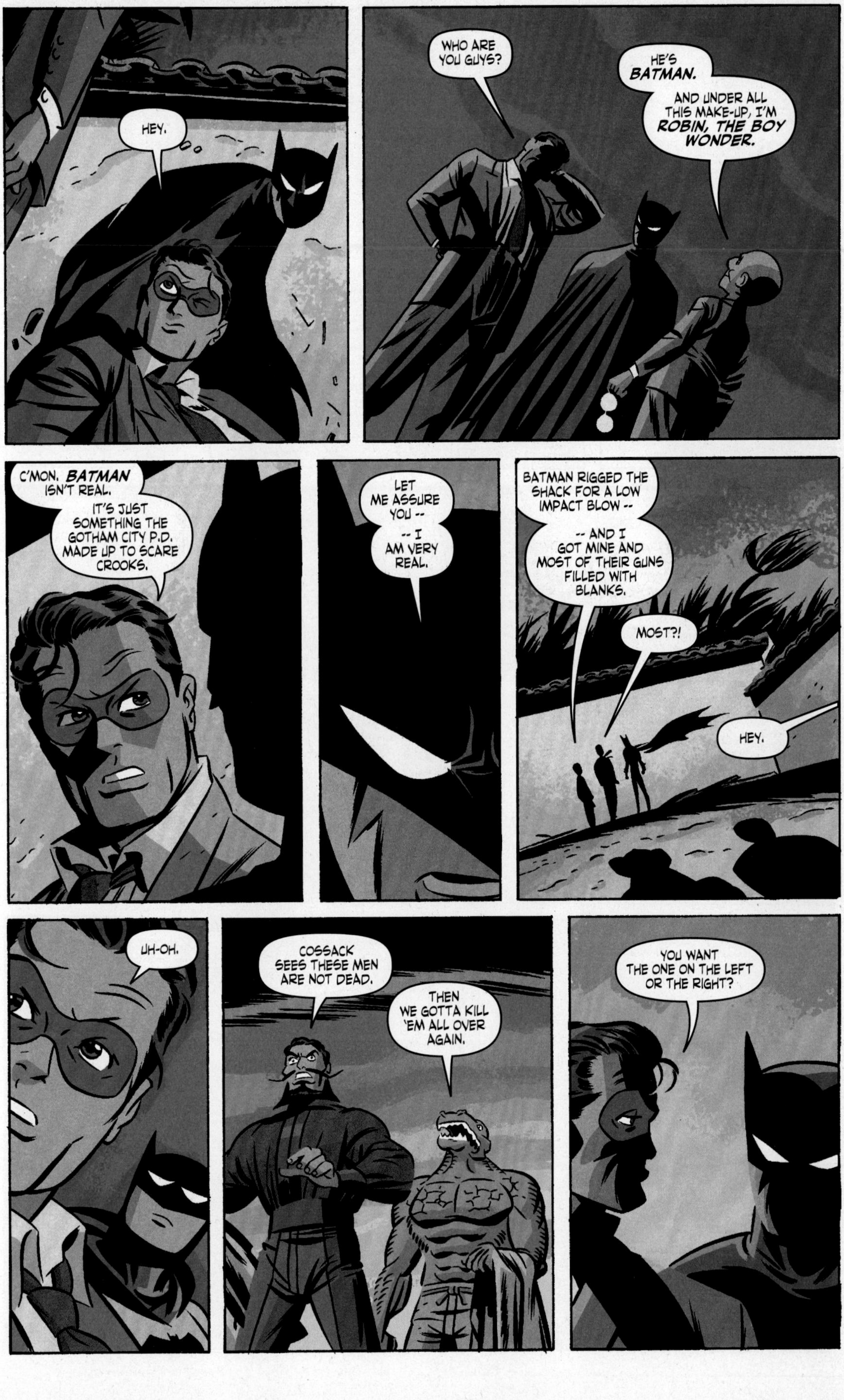
HEY.
WHO ARE YOU GUYS?
HE'S BATMAN.
AND UNDER ALL THIS MAKE-UP, I'M ROBIN, THE BOY WONDER.
C'MON. BATMAN ISN'T REAL.
IT'S JUST SOMETHING THE GOTHAM CITY P.D. MADE UP TO SCARE CROOKS.
LET ME ASSURE YOU --
-- I AM VERY REAL.
BATMAN RIGGED THE SHACK FOR A LOW IMPACT BLOW --
-- AND I GOT MINE AND MOST OF THEIR GUNS FILLED WITH BLANKS.
MOST?!
HEY.
UH-OH.
COSSACK SEES THESE MEN ARE NOT DEAD.
THEN WE GOTTA KILL 'EM ALL OVER AGAIN.
YOU WANT THE ONE ON THE LEFT OR THE RIGHT?

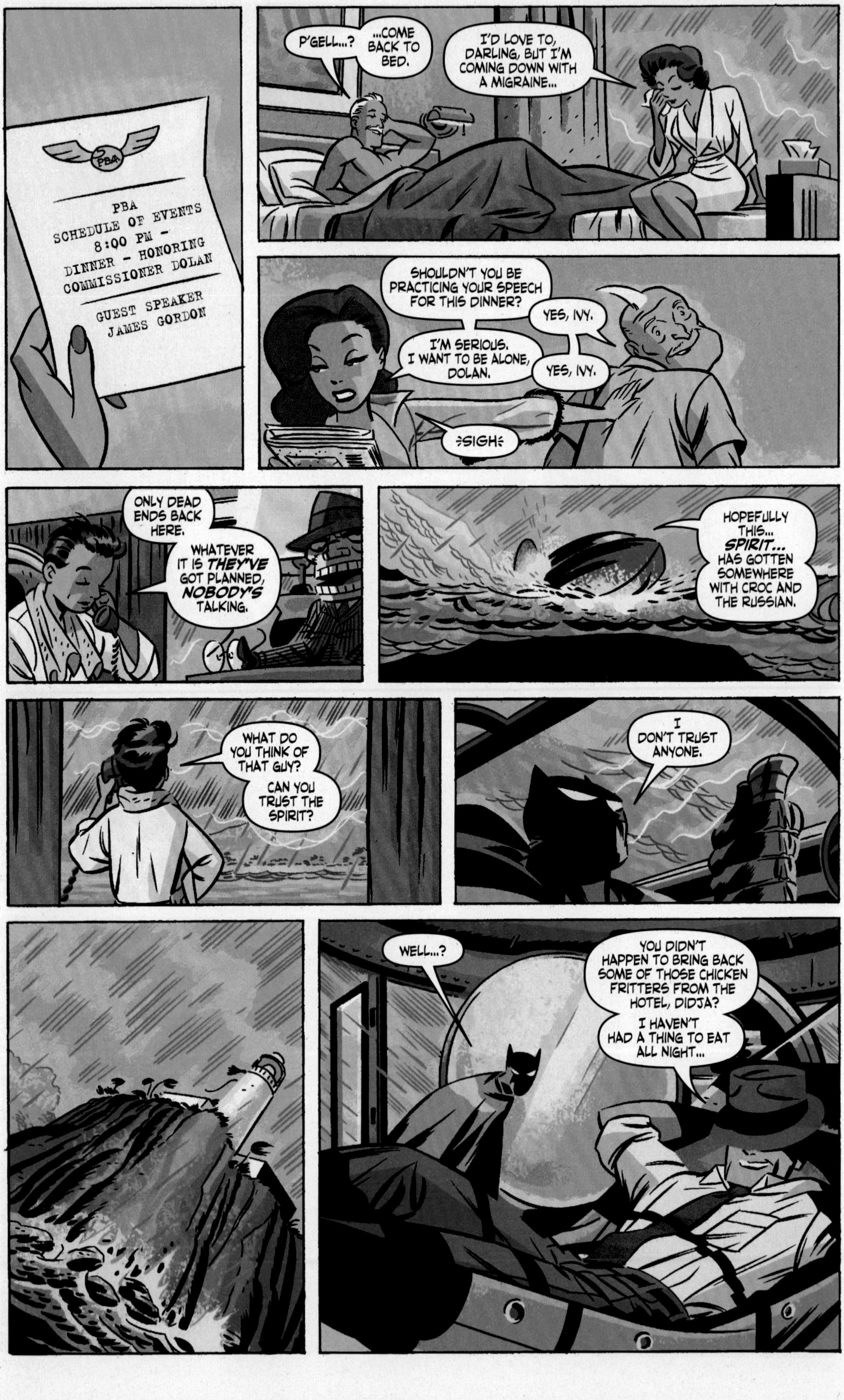
PBA
SCHEDULE OF EVENTS
8:00 PM -
DINNER - HONORING
COMMISSIONER DOLAN
GUEST SPEAKER
JAMES GORDON
P'GELL...?
...COME BACK TO BED.
I'D LOVE TO, DARLING, BUT I'M COMING DOWN WITH A MIGRAINE...
SHOULDN'T YOU BE PRACTICING YOUR SPEECH FOR THIS DINNER?
YES, IVY.
I'M SERIOUS. I WANT TO BE ALONE, DOLAN.
YES, IVY.
SIGH
ONLY DEAD ENDS BACK HERE.
WHATEVER IT IS THEY'VE GOT PLANNED, NOBODY'S TALKING.
HOPEFULLY THIS... SPIRIT... HAS GOTTEN SOMEWHERE WITH CROC AND THE RUSSIAN.
WHAT DO YOU THINK OF THAT GUY?
CAN YOU TRUST THE SPIRIT?
I DON'T TRUST ANYONE.
WELL...?
YOU DIDN'T HAPPEN TO BRING BACK SOME OF THOSE CHICKEN FRITTERS FROM THE HOTEL, DIDJA?
I HAVEN'T HAD A THING TO EAT ALL NIGHT...

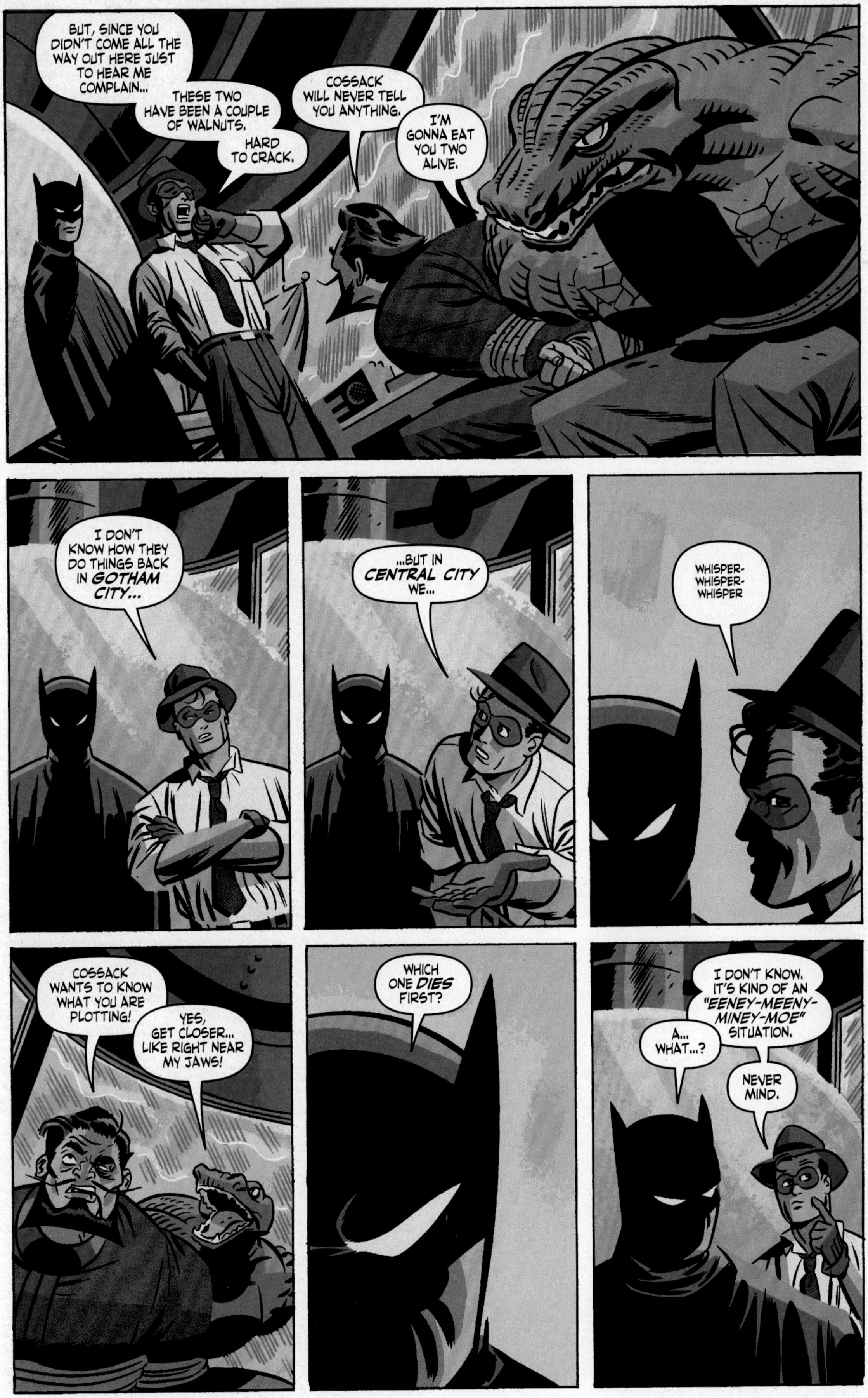
BUT, SINCE YOU DIDN'T COME ALL THE WAY OUT HERE JUST TO HEAR ME COMPLAIN...
THESE TWO HAVE BEEN A COUPLE OF WALNUTS.
HARD TO CRACK.
COSSACK WILL NEVER TELL YOU ANYTHING.
I'M GONNA EAT YOU TWO ALIVE.
I DON'T KNOW HOW THEY DO THINGS BACK IN *GOTHAM CITY...*
...BUT IN *CENTRAL CITY* WE...
WHISPER-WHISPER-WHISPER
COSSACK WANTS TO KNOW WHAT YOU ARE PLOTTING!
YES, GET CLOSER... LIKE RIGHT NEAR MY JAWS!
WHICH ONE *DIES* FIRST?
I DON'T KNOW. IT'S KIND OF AN *"EENEY-MEENY-MINEY-MOE"* SITUATION.
A... WHAT...?
NEVER MIND.

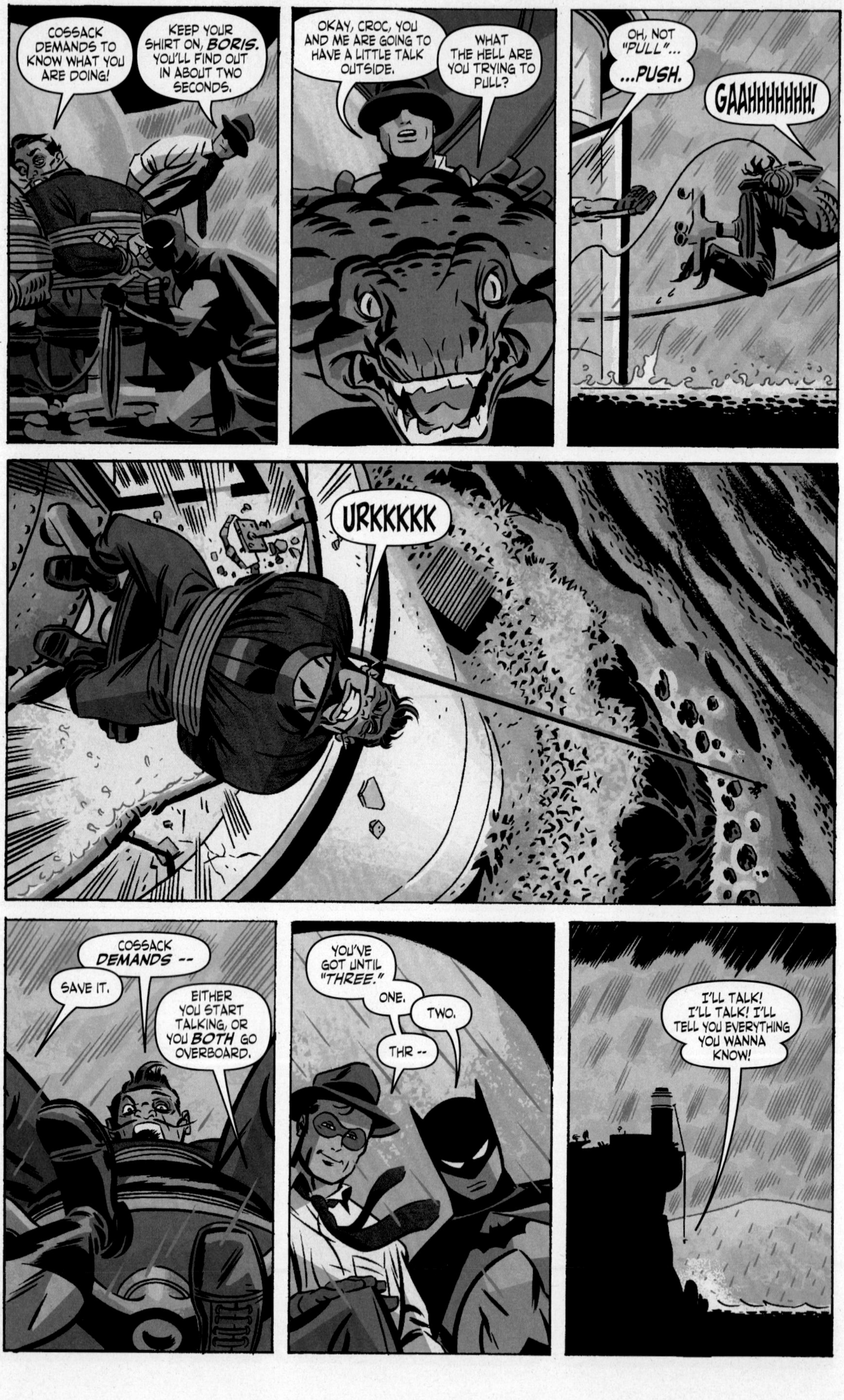
COSSACK DEMANDS TO KNOW WHAT YOU ARE DOING!
KEEP YOUR SHIRT ON, BORIS. YOU'LL FIND OUT IN ABOUT TWO SECONDS.
OKAY, CROC, YOU AND ME ARE GOING TO HAVE A LITTLE TALK OUTSIDE.
WHAT THE HELL ARE YOU TRYING TO PULL?
OH, NOT "PULL"...
...PUSH.
GAAHHHHHHH!
URKKKKK
COSSACK DEMANDS --
SAVE IT.
EITHER YOU START TALKING, OR YOU BOTH GO OVERBOARD.
YOU'VE GOT UNTIL "THREE."
ONE.
TWO.
THR --
I'LL TALK! I'LL TALK! I'LL TELL YOU EVERYTHING YOU WANNA KNOW!

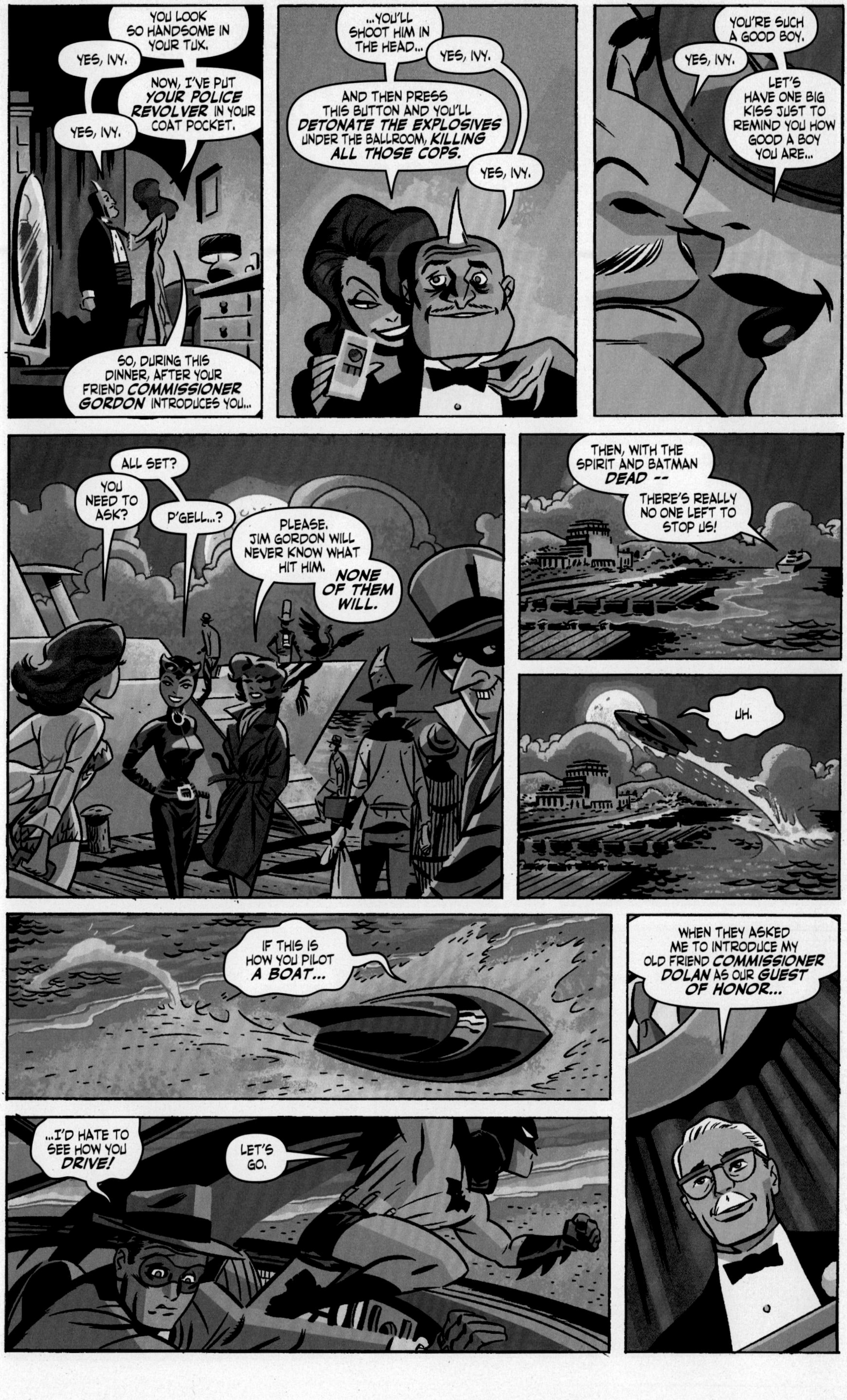
YOU LOOK SO HANDSOME IN YOUR TUX.
YES, IVY.
NOW, I'VE PUT YOUR POLICE REVOLVER IN YOUR COAT POCKET.
YES, IVY.
SO, DURING THIS DINNER, AFTER YOUR FRIEND COMMISSIONER GORDON INTRODUCES YOU...
...YOU'LL SHOOT HIM IN THE HEAD...
YES, IVY.
AND THEN PRESS THIS BUTTON AND YOU'LL DETONATE THE EXPLOSIVES UNDER THE BALLROOM, KILLING ALL THOSE COPS.
YES, IVY.
YOU'RE SUCH A GOOD BOY.
YES, IVY.
LET'S HAVE ONE BIG KISS JUST TO REMIND YOU HOW GOOD A BOY YOU ARE...
ALL SET?
YOU NEED TO ASK?
P'GELL...?
PLEASE. JIM GORDON WILL NEVER KNOW WHAT HIT HIM. NONE OF THEM WILL.
THEN, WITH THE SPIRIT AND BATMAN DEAD --
THERE'S REALLY NO ONE LEFT TO STOP US!
UH.
IF THIS IS HOW YOU PILOT A BOAT...
...I'D HATE TO SEE HOW YOU DRIVE!
LET'S GO.
WHEN THEY ASKED ME TO INTRODUCE MY OLD FRIEND COMMISSIONER DOLAN AS OUR GUEST OF HONOR...

...I GOT TO THINKING ABOUT HOW SIMILAR OUR JOBS ARE DESPITE THE DISTANCE BETWEEN OUR FAIR CITIES.

WE BOTH HAVE A COLORFUL GALLERY OF *ROGUES* WHO SEEM TO THINK THEY ARE ABOVE THE LAW...

...AND WE BOTH HAVE A COSTUMED *VIGILANTE* WHO...

The P.B.A. proudly congratulates our guest of honor Commissioner Dolan of Central City

...SHARES IN THE HARD WORK WHILE CREATING MORE THAN HIS FAIR SHARE OF HEADACHES...

CROC'S BEANS WERE SPILLED ACCURATELY.

LOOKS LIKE EVERY SECURITY GUARD IN THE HOTEL HAS BEEN TAKEN OUT BY THE MAD HATTER'S HATS...

...THAT MEANS THEY WERE DONE PRIMING THE EXPLOSIVES.

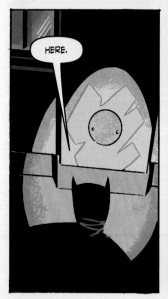

HERE.

IT'S RIGGED TO GO OFF IF WE TRY TO DISARM IT.

THERE'S NO TIMER.

THAT MEANS THERE'S GOT TO BE *A REMOTE TRIGGER.* C'MON!

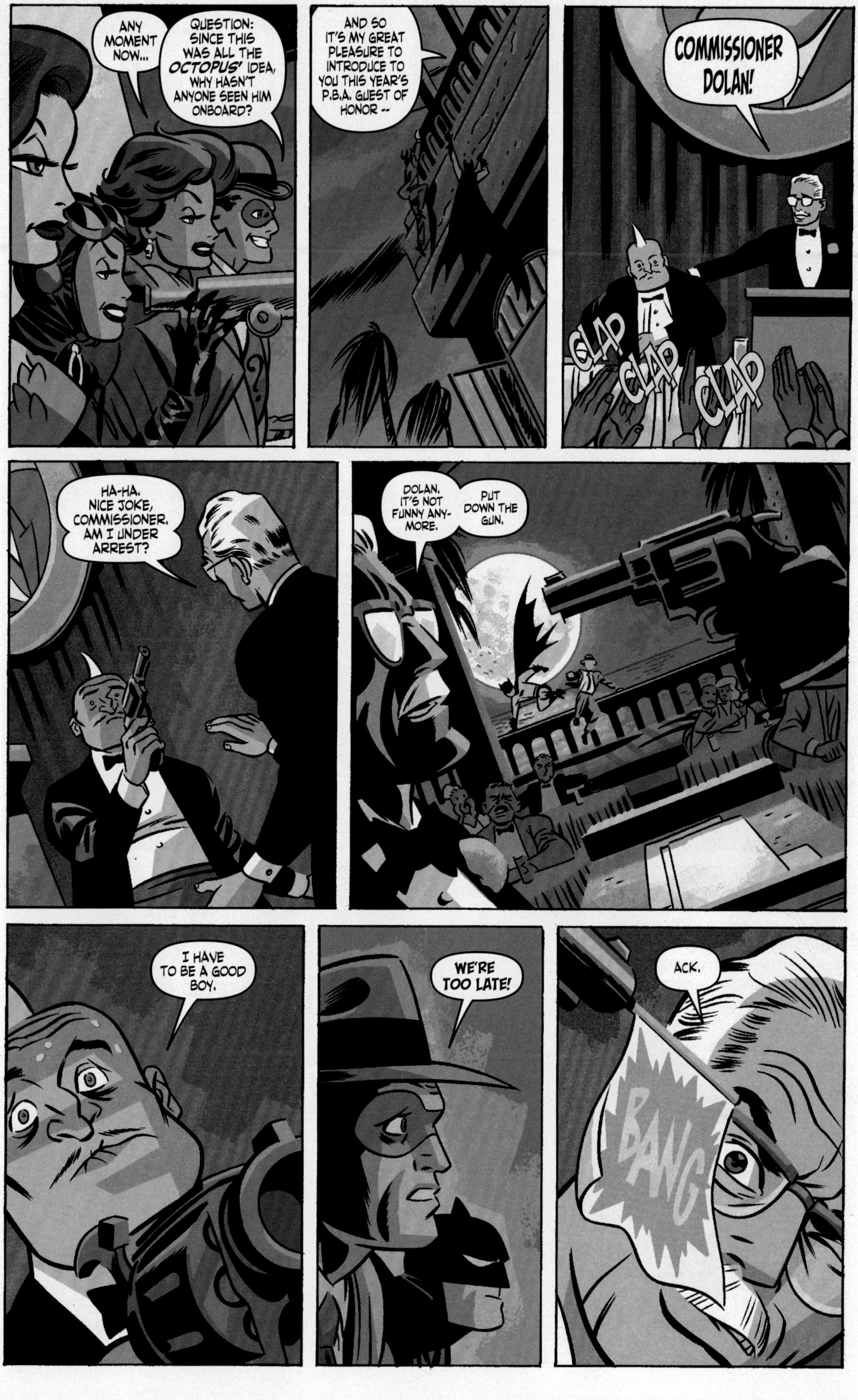
ANY MOMENT NOW...
QUESTION: SINCE THIS WAS ALL THE OCTOPUS' IDEA, WHY HASN'T ANYONE SEEN HIM ONBOARD?
AND SO IT'S MY GREAT PLEASURE TO INTRODUCE TO YOU THIS YEAR'S P.B.A. GUEST OF HONOR --
COMMISSIONER DOLAN!
CLAP
CLAP
CLAP
HA-HA. NICE JOKE, COMMISSIONER. AM I UNDER ARREST?
DOLAN. IT'S NOT FUNNY ANY-MORE.
PUT DOWN THE GUN.
I HAVE TO BE A GOOD BOY.
WE'RE TOO LATE!
ACK.
BANG

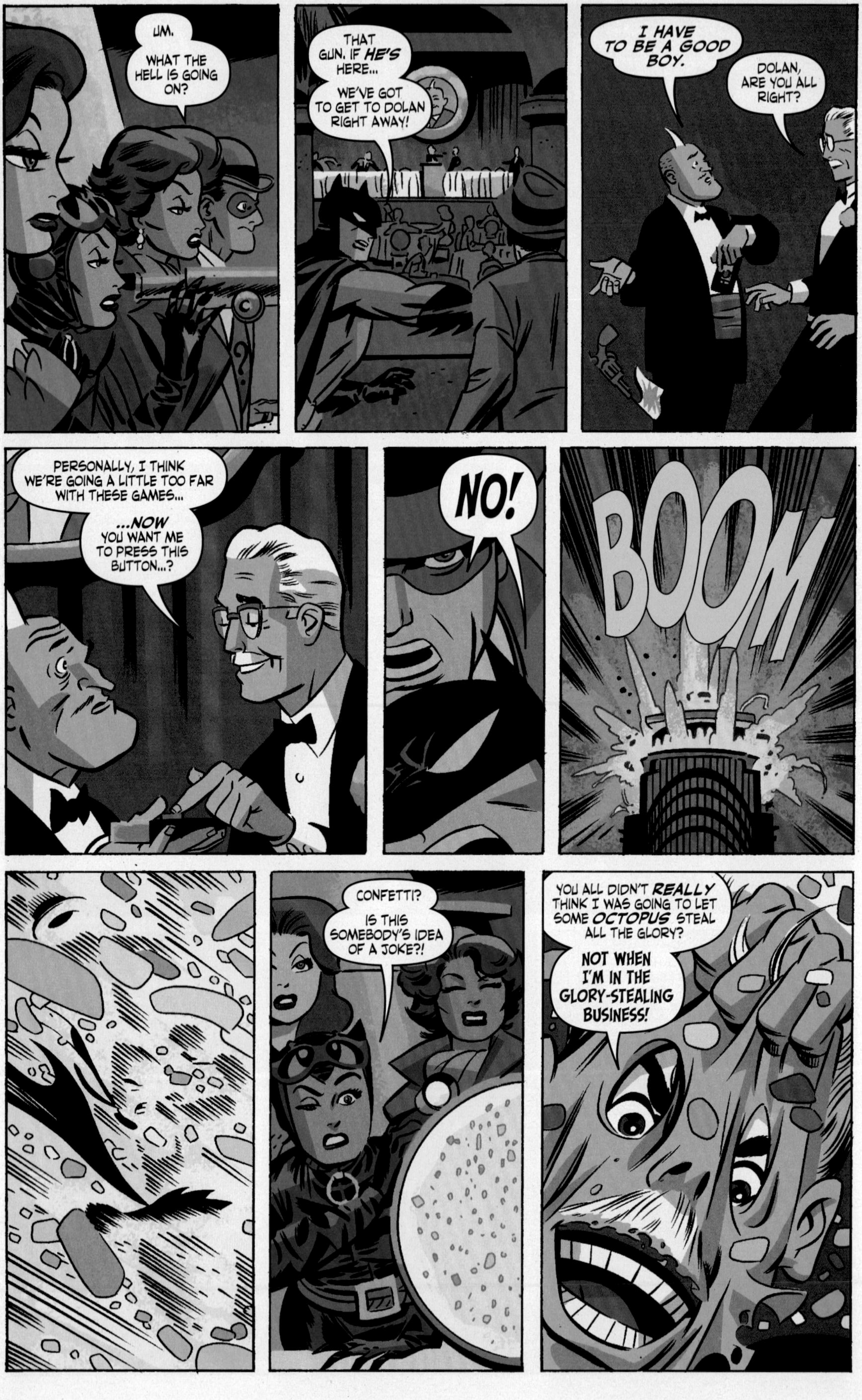
UM.
WHAT THE HELL IS GOING ON?
THAT GUN. IF HE'S HERE...
WE'VE GOT TO GET TO DOLAN RIGHT AWAY!
I HAVE TO BE A GOOD BOY.
DOLAN, ARE YOU ALL RIGHT?
PERSONALLY, I THINK WE'RE GOING A LITTLE TOO FAR WITH THESE GAMES...
...NOW YOU WANT ME TO PRESS THIS BUTTON...?
NO!
BOOM
CONFETTI?
IS THIS SOMEBODY'S IDEA OF A JOKE?!
YOU ALL DIDN'T REALLY THINK I WAS GOING TO LET SOME OCTOPUS STEAL ALL THE GLORY?
NOT WHEN I'M IN THE GLORY-STEALING BUSINESS!

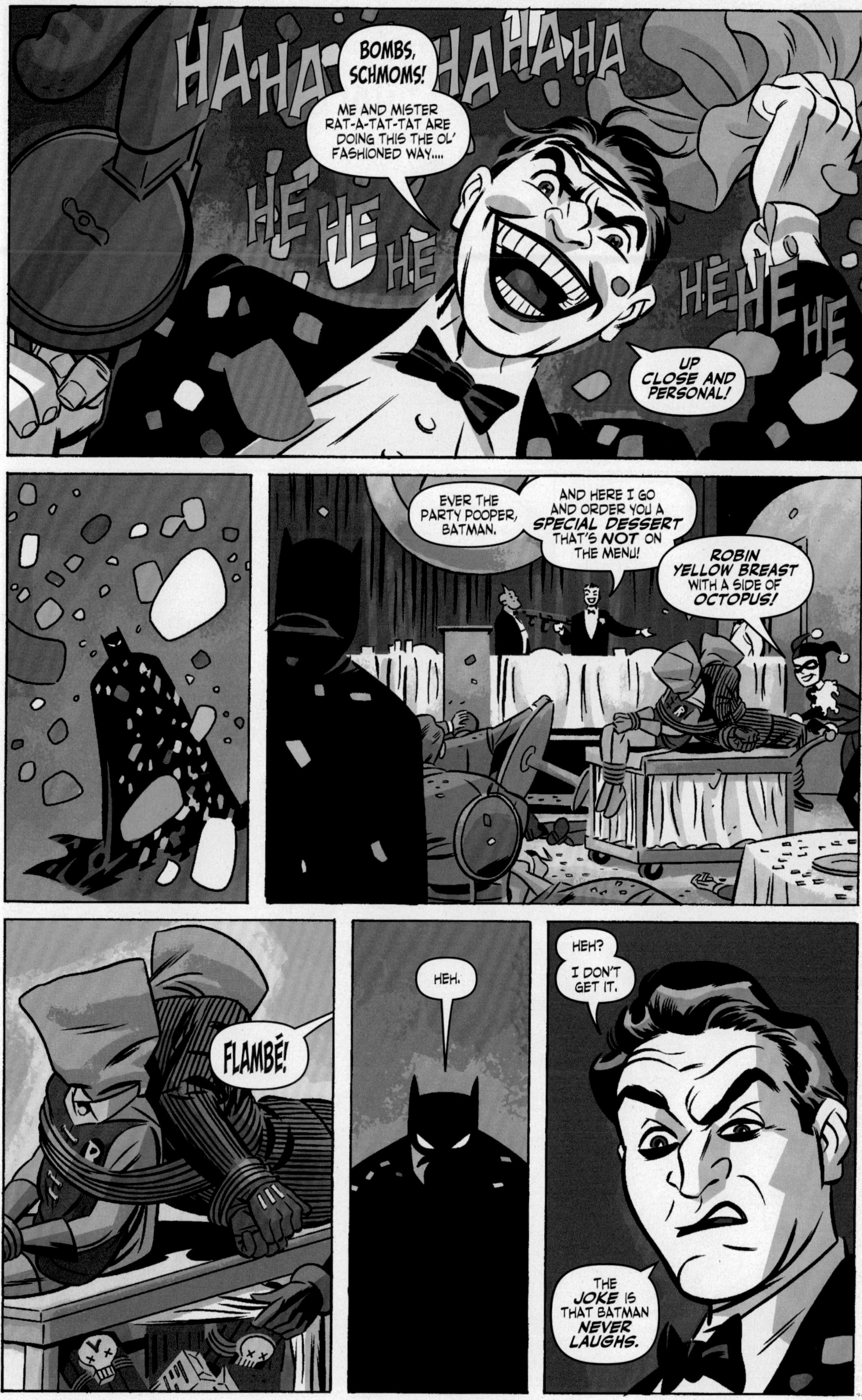

HAHAHA
BOMBS, SCHMOMS!
ME AND MISTER RAT-A-TAT-TAT ARE DOING THIS THE OL' FASHIONED WAY....
HAHAHAHA
HE HE HE HE
HE HE HE HE
UP CLOSE AND PERSONAL!
EVER THE PARTY POOPER, BATMAN.
AND HERE I GO AND ORDER YOU A SPECIAL DESSERT THAT'S NOT ON THE MENU!
ROBIN YELLOW BREAST WITH A SIDE OF OCTOPUS!
FLAMBÉ!
HEH.
HEH?
I DON'T GET IT.
THE JOKE IS THAT BATMAN NEVER LAUGHS.

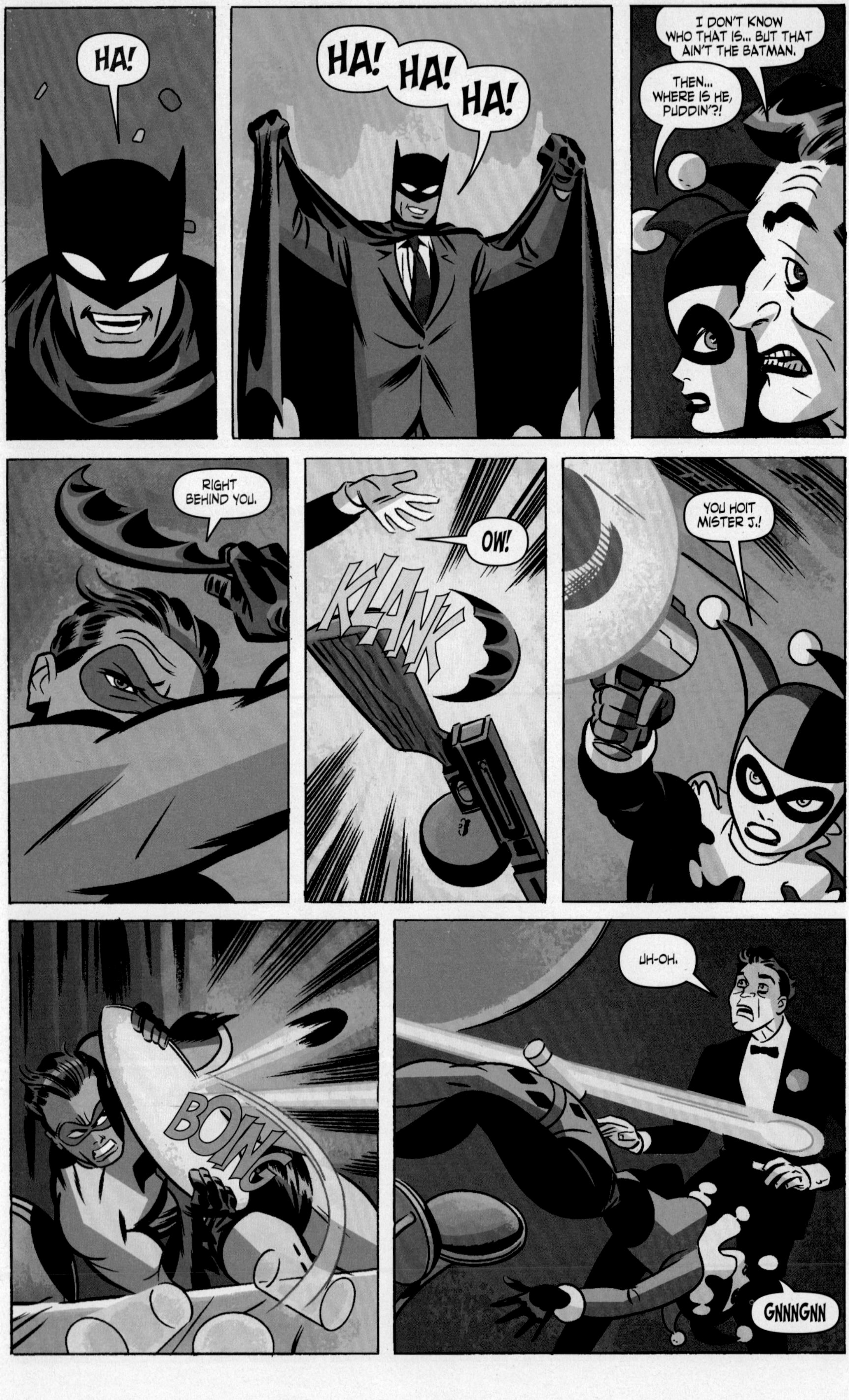
HA!
HA! HA! HA!
I DON'T KNOW WHO THAT IS... BUT THAT AIN'T THE BATMAN.
THEN... WHERE IS HE, PUDDIN'?!
RIGHT BEHIND YOU.
OW!
KLANK
YOU HOIT MISTER J.!
BOING
UH-OH.
GNNNGNN

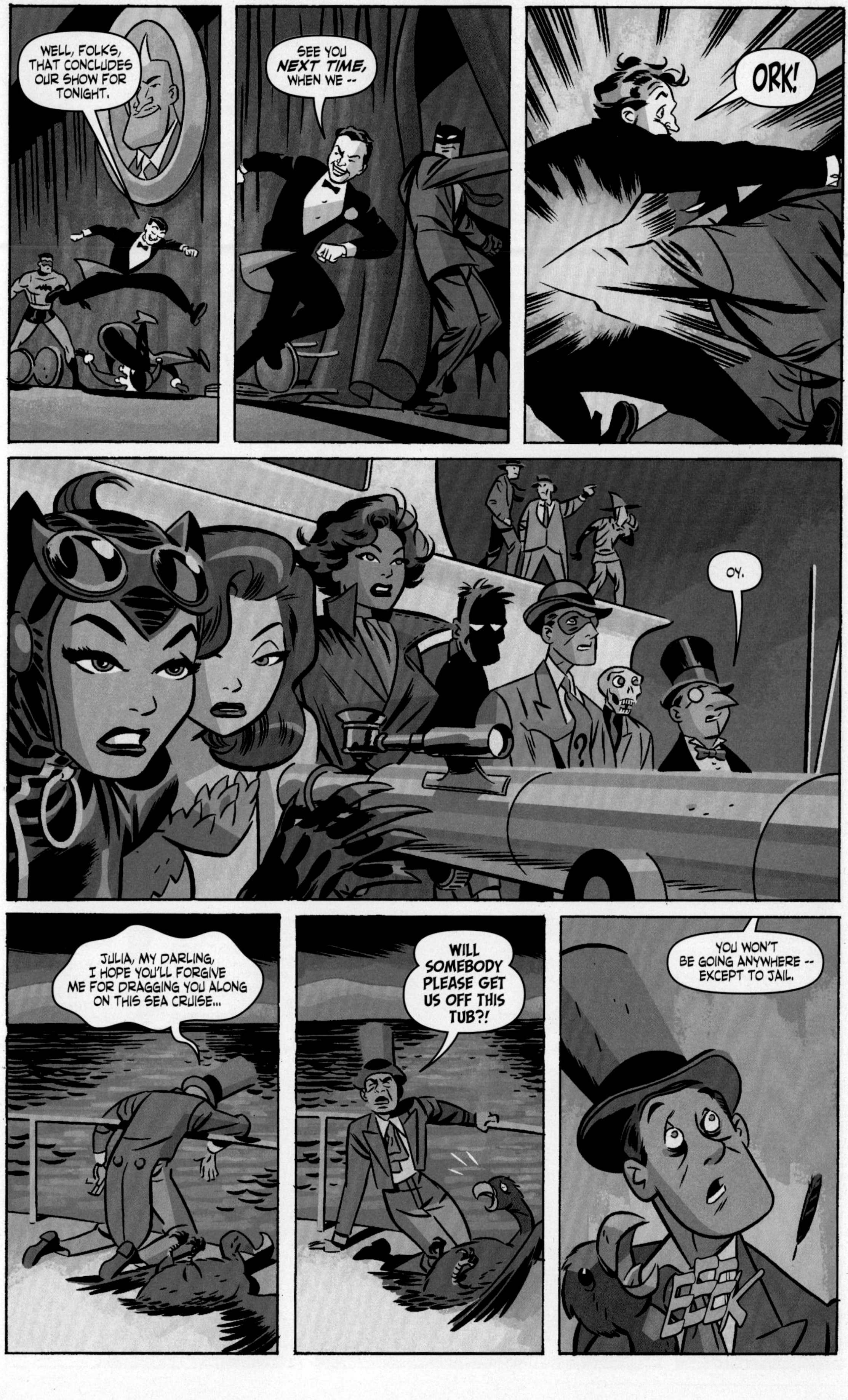
WELL, FOLKS, THAT CONCLUDES OUR SHOW FOR TONIGHT.
SEE YOU NEXT TIME, WHEN WE --
ORK!
OY.
JULIA, MY DARLING, I HOPE YOU'LL FORGIVE ME FOR DRAGGING YOU ALONG ON THIS SEA CRUISE...
WILL SOMEBODY PLEASE GET US OFF THIS TUB?!
YOU WON'T BE GOING ANYWHERE -- EXCEPT TO JAIL.
EEEK

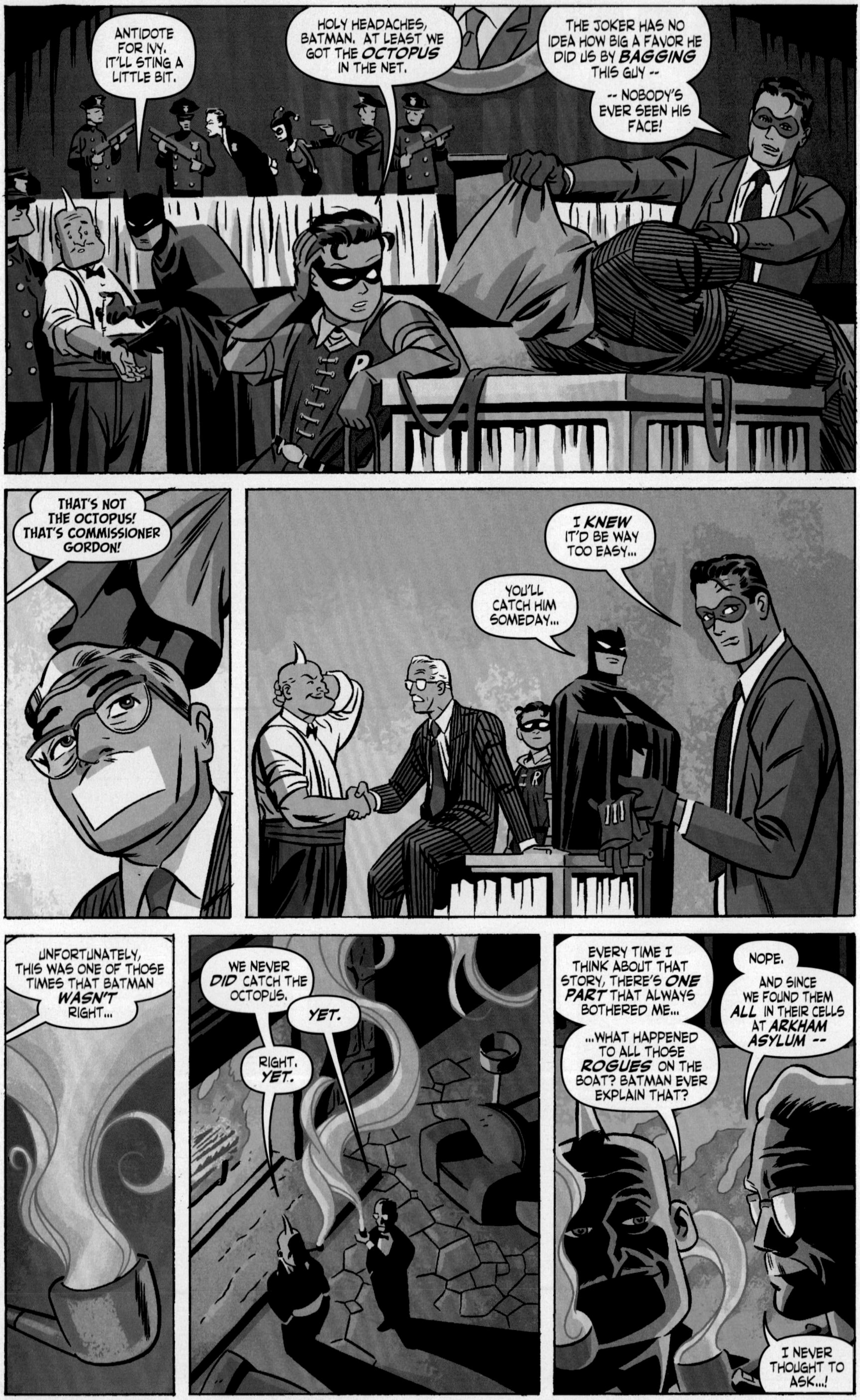
ANTIDOTE FOR IVY. IT'LL STING A LITTLE BIT.
HOLY HEADACHES, BATMAN. AT LEAST WE GOT THE OCTOPUS IN THE NET.
THE JOKER HAS NO IDEA HOW BIG A FAVOR HE DID US BY BAGGING THIS GUY --
-- NOBODY'S EVER SEEN HIS FACE!
THAT'S NOT THE OCTOPUS! THAT'S COMMISSIONER GORDON!
I KNEW IT'D BE WAY TOO EASY...
YOU'LL CATCH HIM SOMEDAY...
UNFORTUNATELY, THIS WAS ONE OF THOSE TIMES THAT BATMAN WASN'T RIGHT...
WE NEVER DID CATCH THE OCTOPUS.
YET.
RIGHT. YET.
EVERY TIME I THINK ABOUT THAT STORY, THERE'S ONE PART THAT ALWAYS BOTHERED ME...
...WHAT HAPPENED TO ALL THOSE ROGUES ON THE BOAT? BATMAN EVER EXPLAIN THAT?
NOPE.
AND SINCE WE FOUND THEM ALL IN THEIR CELLS AT ARKHAM ASYLUM --
I NEVER THOUGHT TO ASK...!

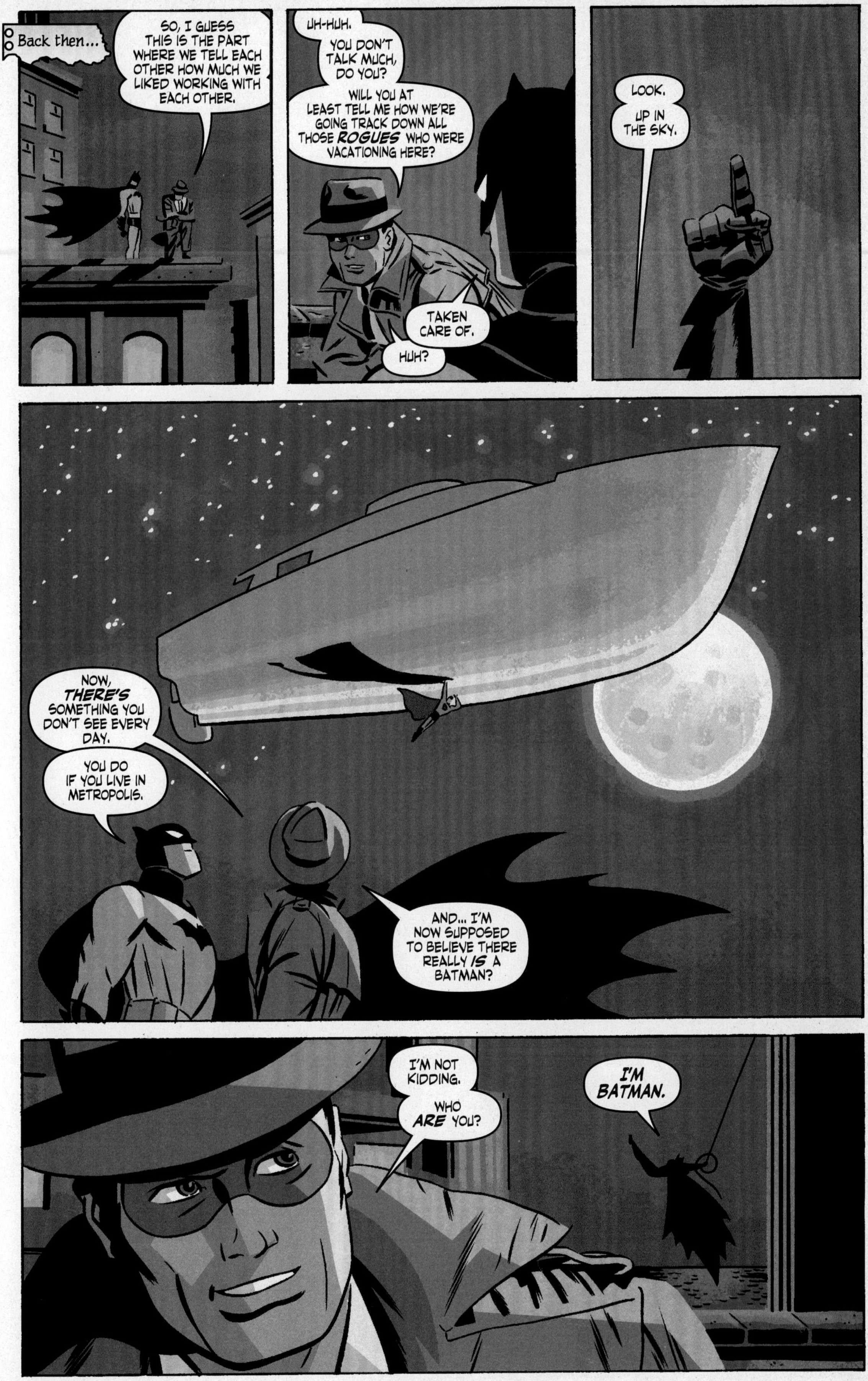
Back then...
SO, I GUESS THIS IS THE PART WHERE WE TELL EACH OTHER HOW MUCH WE LIKED WORKING WITH EACH OTHER.
UH-HUH.
YOU DON'T TALK MUCH, DO YOU?
WILL YOU AT LEAST TELL ME HOW WE'RE GOING TRACK DOWN ALL THOSE ROGUES WHO WERE VACATIONING HERE?
TAKEN CARE OF.
HUH?
LOOK.
UP IN THE SKY.
NOW, THERE'S SOMETHING YOU DON'T SEE EVERY DAY.
YOU DO IF YOU LIVE IN METROPOLIS.
AND... I'M NOW SUPPOSED TO BELIEVE THERE REALLY IS A BATMAN?
I'M NOT KIDDING.
WHO ARE YOU?
I'M BATMAN.

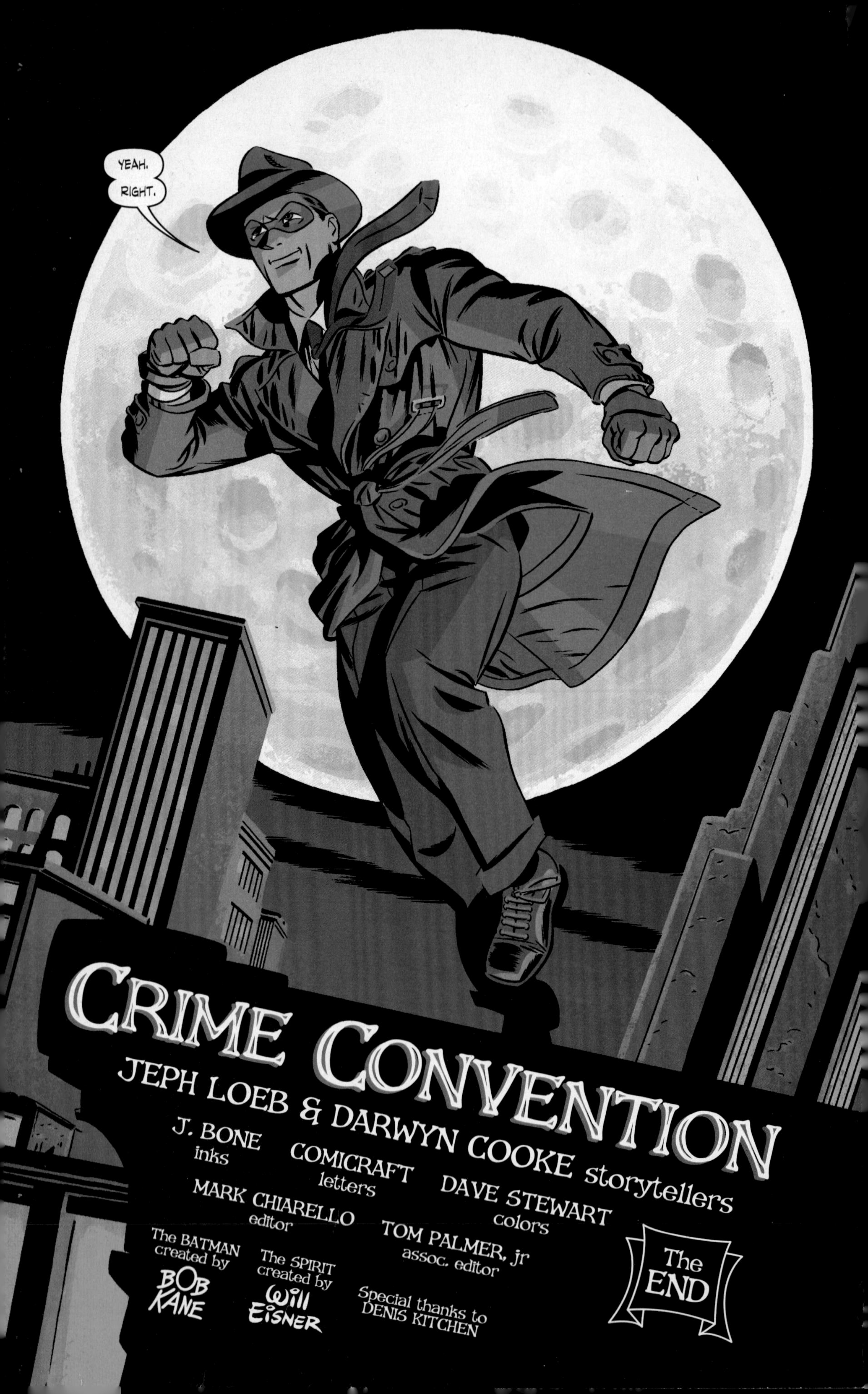
YEAH. RIGHT.
CRIME CONVENTION
JEPH LOEB & DARWYN COOKE storytellers
J. BONE inks
COMICRAFT letters
DAVE STEWART colors
MARK CHIARELLO editor
TOM PALMER, jr assoc. editor
The BATMAN created by BOB KANE
The SPIRIT created by Will Eisner
Special thanks to DENIS KITCHEN
The END

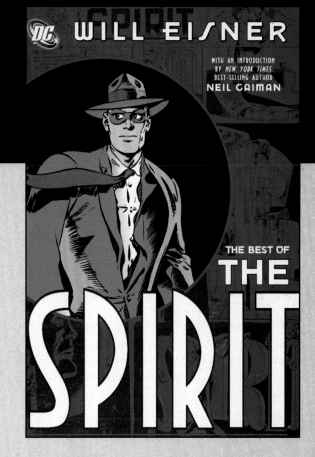